W9-DFK-563

UNDAUNTED

UNDAUNTED

MY FIGHT AGAINST
AMERICA'S ENEMIES,
AT HOME AND ABROAD

JOHN O. BRENNAN

CELADON
BOOKS
NEW YORK

UNDAUNTED. Copyright © 2020 by Insightful Books LLC. All rights reserved. Printed in the United States of America. For information, address Celadon Books, a Division of Macmillan Publishers, 120 Broadway, New York, NY 10271.

www.celadonbooks.com

Designed by Kelly S. Too

ISBN 978-1-250-24176-4 (trade paperback)

Our books may be purchased in bulk for promotional, educational, or business use. Please contact your local bookseller or the Macmillan Corporate and Premium Sales Department at 1-800-221-7945, extension 5442, or by email at MacmillanSpecialMarkets@macmillan.com.

First Celadon Books Paperback Edition: 2022

10 9 8 7 6 5 4 3 2 1

All statements of fact, opinion, or analysis expressed are those of the author and do not reflect the official positions or views of the Central Intelligence Agency (CIA) or any other U.S. Government agency. Nothing in the contents should be construed as asserting or implying U.S. Government authentication of information or CIA endorsement of the author's views. This material has been reviewed by the CIA to prevent the disclosure of classified information.

To my parents, Owen and Dorothy,
who taught me the importance of
hard work, honesty, and integrity.

To my wife, Kathy,
whose love, understanding, and
partnership have meant the world to me.

To my children, Kyle, Kelly, and Jaclyn,
who have given their father a lifetime of
great joy and deep pride.

And to my grandsons, Kaiden and John,
whose "Pop-Pop" wishes all their days to be
happy and all their dreams to be realized.

CONTENTS

AUTHOR'S NOTE

Undaunted is the story of my journey through life—focusing mostly on my time in the wilderness of mirrors that is the U.S. intelligence and national security community. Inevitably, the story contains many arcane acronyms and much government-speak. I have tried to spell out terms that are not generally known, but if you find yourself lost, please check the glossary on page 427.

There are many acceptable ways of transliterating Arabic words and names into English. For this book, I have chosen to use the formulations that I used in the Central Intelligence Agency. Neither "Usama" nor "Osama," neither "Hizballah" nor "Hezbollah" is more correct than the other—but for simplicity, at least for me, I have elected to use the spellings I have used throughout my life.

In a book like this one, the cast of characters is long. On page 435 there is a handy guide to who's who in case you need a reminder. There are a few people in this book, such as a former chief of staff of mine called Deb, whose last names I omit for their privacy and security reasons. For the vast majority of individuals I write about, however, I use their full (true) names.

You will also note that I include conversations I had with various people and place their remarks and mine within quotation marks. I have not been carrying a tape recorder around with me or taking copious personal notes for the past forty years—so I cannot assure you these are exact transcriptions. Other participants may remember some things differently, but I have written what are my best recollections.

UNDAUNTED

PREFACE

"This is a memoir that I never expected to write."

Those are not just my words. They are also the opening words of *A Look over My Shoulder,* the posthumously published memoir of Richard Helms, who served as director of central intelligence from 1966 until 1973. I wouldn't be surprised if, like Helms, the other former CIA directors and acting directors who have written memoirs—Bill Colby, Bob Gates, George Tenet, Michael Hayden, Leon Panetta, and Michael Morell—never thought they would write a memoir, until they did. I now join their ranks.

I had an extraordinarily rich thirty-three-year government career, working on a wide array of national security matters under the administrations of six presidents, from Jimmy Carter to Barack Obama. As a kid growing up in a blue-collar northern New Jersey neighborhood, I never dreamed that I would one day work in the White House as a senior adviser to the president of the United States or become the director of the Central Intelligence Agency, the world's greatest intelligence service. But, as fate would have it, I did both, witnessing history and maybe even helping shape a little bit of it along the way.

This memoir has two principal purposes. First, I want to share my experiences and perspectives on the fascinating and often mysterious world of national security. Over the course of my professional life, I have been queried by thousands of individuals—journalists, historians, academics, students, news junkies, family, friends, and neighbors—who craved insight into what it was like to work in a world of secrets and to interact with presidents, cabinet secretaries, members of Congress, kings, princes, and high-ranking foreign officials on issues of great consequence to America's security. By sharing my personal experiences, as well as some anecdotes of the missteps, joys, and heartbreaks that have marked my life's journey, I hope to convey the challenges, responsibilities, and opportunities that accompany what I consider a most noble profession. And if this memoir encourages even just a few more talented young Americans to pursue careers in public service, I will consider it a resounding success.

My second reason for writing this book pivots off the first, which is to correct some of the mischaracterizations and falsehoods that have been propagated over the years—some purposefully, others unintentionally—about the CIA, the national security community, and individual government officials, including me. Unfortunately, Mr. Trump and his supporters have been among the most recent and prolific purveyors of inaccurate information and disparaging commentary about the members and work of the intelligence community. I realize that I am unlikely to alter the views and public claims of those driven by ideological, political, or personal agendas and who are not interested in the truth, but I feel an obligation to present as accurate an account of the facts as I can. I have never been a member of any political party and am frequently a critic of both Democrats and Republicans. This memoir will likely burnish my well-deserved reputation of being an equal-opportunity offender.

When I made the decision in the fall of 2018 to write a memoir,

I requested the opportunity, as did all previous directors and acting directors who wrote memoirs before me, to review my official records. Specifically, I asked for access to classified and unclassified records that I "originated, reviewed, signed, or received while serving as Director of the Central Intelligence Agency from 8 March 2013 to 20 January 2017." The arrangements for such access are stipulated in an executive order, and all such requests by other former directors were promptly and routinely approved. Not so in my case, as I have been denied access to any classified information. After eleven months of haggling, the CIA in November 2019 provided only heavily redacted copies of my daily calendars and the tables of contents of my "daybooks," which held information relevant to my daily schedule. The material I was given was labeled FOR OFFICIAL USE ONLY, which means that it cannot be publicly disclosed but can be used for reference. All entries that referenced my foreign trips, calls with foreign officials, and other information that would have been useful were deemed classified by the CIA and were blacked out. Had I been given access to my actual records, no classified material would have been revealed to the public in this memoir because I am required, like all former CIA officers, to submit the manuscript to the CIA for a classification review before its publication.

The CIA's refusal to grant me the same access to Agency records afforded to all other former directors was not due to the alleged revocation of my security clearances as announced by the White House spokesperson Sarah Huckabee Sanders in August 2018. Despite her public comments, my security clearances have never been revoked because there is no legal basis to do so. I learned in November 2019, however, that Donald Trump had issued a directive in August 2018 that purportedly forbids anyone in the intelligence community from sharing classified information with me. I subsequently wrote a letter to CIA Director Gina Haspel in January 2020, telling her: "It is impossible to avoid the conclusion that the Agency's refusal to grant my request reflects the current administration's desire to punish and retaliate against me for speaking out as a private citizen—an abuse of power designed to chill the exercise of my First Amendment rights."

I have known Director Haspel for many years and worked very closely with her during my time as director of the CIA. It was therefore very disappointing that she did not respond to my letter or reach out in any way to discuss the situation with me.

So much for my fervent hope that interactions with my successors would be unencumbered by Washington's partisan waters.

Without the benefit of reviewing my records, and undaunted by Mr. Trump's attempts to intimidate me, I have had to rely on my memory, discussions with former colleagues no longer in government, and publicly available information when researching and writing this book. I tried to reconstruct events and conversations to the best of my ability and recollection. Any inaccuracies that might be in this book are the result of a faulty memory, for which I take full responsibility, and the result of an unprecedented denial of a former director's request to access his records, for which I do not.

Many thousands of Americans have served in the CIA since its founding in 1947, and I was privileged to be among them for nearly three decades. There was something very special about being part of an organization dedicated to protecting the security of my fellow citizens and defending the freedoms and liberties that define the country I love.

The privilege to serve America comes with the solemn obligation to honor the ideals and aspirations upon which it was founded. CIA officers are duty bound to "speak truth to power." I have lived my life in service of the American people, and this memoir is my effort to fulfill my obligation to them.

1

FRIDAY, JANUARY 6, 2017

The digital clock next to my bed showed 4:06 A.M. As usual, my body clock had stirred me awake before my bedside radio alarm was set to go off nine minutes later. I stared motionless at the pitch-black ceiling for a few minutes. With some effort and greater discomfort, I bent and stretched for a minute or two more before swinging my legs over the side of the bed. I shut off the alarm before it went off and then tiptoed awkwardly through the darkness to the bathroom, hoping not to stumble and wake my wife, Kathy, in the process. I had taken the same steps so many times over the preceding decades, I could have done it in my sleep. I probably did many times.

My eyes adjusted to the glare of the bathroom lights and I squinted at the reflection in the mirror. The Brennan genes had long coursed through my face, but I noticed something very different that morning. I could see my father's deep-set eyes, tired yet piercing, looking straight into mine. "You can do it, John," they seemed to be saying to me. "You can do it." The tears welled up in my eyes, as the memory of my father's life and the example he set filled me with deep pride and overwhelming sadness at the same time. The mere thought of briefing President-elect Donald Trump that afternoon and then gathering with my family a few short hours later at the wake of my father—the moral, ethical, and intellectual antithesis of Trump—jarred my very soul.

I splashed cold water on my face and tried to straighten my thinning yet hopelessly disheveled hair. I took one last glance at the mirror, looked into my father's eyes with newfound strength, and said aloud, "Don't worry, Dad. I can do it."

My security detail was waiting outside my Herndon, Virginia, house, as they unfailingly did every morning when I was CIA director. After I climbed into the back seat of the up-armored pitch-black SUV, a copy of the President's Daily Brief (PDB) and a collection of intelligence reports that had arrived at CIA headquarters overnight awaited me. I leafed through the material to see if there was anything especially alarming that would require my immediate action. Thankfully, there wasn't. By the end of the eight-minute ride to my local gym, I felt comfortable proceeding with my early-morning workout regimen. I spent fifty minutes sweating profusely as I lifted weights, rode a stationary bike, and moved back and forth on a rowing machine as strenuously as my sixty-one-year-old body would allow. I was on autopilot. As was the case with all previous mornings I spent at the gym, any physical fitness benefits that might accrue from my daily exertions were secondary to the opportunity to be alone with my thoughts and to prepare myself mentally for the rest of the day. This was my special personal time every morning, which I jealously guarded. I needed it more than ever on this Friday, one of the most unforgettable days in my life.

It was still dark at 6:30 A.M. when I arrived at CIA's Langley headquarters, a twenty-minute drive from my gym, when it's not rush hour. I showered, shaved, and dressed in the private bathroom that is part of the director's suite on the seventh floor. I loved being in my CIA office in the early morning. Spacious, with wood-paneled walls and floor-to-ceiling windows facing eastward, it is the same office that has witnessed the making of history and the life-and-death deliberations of every CIA director since the building was dedicated by President John F. Kennedy in March 1961. I was the nineteenth director to have the honor of using that office. Sipping hot coffee and consuming highly classified intelligence reports as the early-morning sun crept slowly skyward over the tall trees dominating the horizon between Langley and Washington, D.C., was the closest I ever came to a professional nirvana.

I had less than an hour to quickly review some binders and folders that my staff had pulled together before putting them into my lock bag and getting back into the SUV to head to Capitol Hill for the first of two briefings that were scheduled that day. I hadn't spent much time preparing for either, even though the briefings were for the most powerful members of Congress and for the president-elect. I had spent the previous five months intensely focused on Russian interference in the presidential election, and by that morning I could have virtually recited from memory the entire intelligence community assessment (ICA) titled "Russia's Influence Campaign in the 2016 US Presidential Election." Besides, my foxhole buddy and good friend Jim Clapper, the director of national intelligence, was going to take the lead in the briefings, as the formal assessment had been prepared under the auspices of his office.

Jim Clapper, FBI Director Jim Comey, National Security Agency (NSA) Director Admiral Mike Rogers, and I had already settled in the Capitol Hill conference room when the "Gang of Eight" started to trickle in. The Gang of Eight comprised the most powerful members of Congress from both sides of the aisle—the majority and minority leaders of the Senate, the Speaker and minority leader of the House, and Democratic and Republican leadership of the Senate and House intelligence committees. It was an elite group, and the most sensitive national security matters traditionally were reserved for them. Each member—Mitch McConnell, Chuck Schumer, Richard Burr, and Mark Warner from the Senate, and Paul Ryan, Nancy

Pelosi, Devin Nunes, and Adam Schiff from the House—brought along a senior member of their staff, each of whom dutifully sat behind their principal. Folding tables had been arranged to form a large hollow square in the middle of the room. Microphones and placards with the names of the intelligence community participants were lined up on one side of the square, with the other three sides left open for the congressional leaders to seat themselves as they wished.

Jim Clapper conducted the briefing consistent with the presentation we had given to President Obama and Vice President Biden in the Oval Office the day before. Jim presented from a coordinated script; Jim Comey, Mike Rogers, and I chimed in on Clapper's cues with details related to our respective agencies' authorities, capabilities, and insights. The fact that the Russians attempted to undermine the integrity of the presidential election was well known to all those gathered around the conference table that morning, even if most of the Republicans were following Donald Trump's lead in publicly downplaying, if not denying, the Russian role. The briefing was crisp and succinct. The strong confidence that we all expressed in the key judgments—that Vladimir Putin personally ordered the influence campaign to boost Donald Trump's election prospects while discrediting Hillary Clinton so that her anticipated presidency would be crippled from the start—seemed to make the greatest impression on them. Mike Rogers explained that the National Security Agency agreed with all of the judgments but had only "moderate" confidence that the Russian interference was specifically intended to help Trump win the election, which was only slightly less than the "high" confidence the rest of our organizations had in that specific conclusion.

When we finished our presentations, Pelosi and Schumer pressed us on what was being done to conduct follow-up investigations and to punish the Russians. "This can't happen again," Pelosi argued aggressively. Warner and Schiff made similar remonstrations about Russian interference. Among the Republican attendees, Ryan and

Burr concurred, highlighting the serious national security implications of Russian cyberattacks. I was not surprised that McConnell and Nunes, early and ardent partisan defenders of Mr. Trump, were silent in the face of what everyone else recognized was a clear national security threat.

As soon as the briefing concluded, I hustled back to my SUV, which had pulled up to a covered entrance on the House side of the Capitol to take me to Joint Base Andrews. I sunk into the soft black leather seat and leaned against the tinted and bullet-resistant window, oblivious to the world outside. My security agents rode up front in stoic silence. In all my years riding in such protective cocoons, I had never felt more comforted by the SUV's seclusion and solitude than I did on that cold January morning. I closed my eyes and thought about my father's death the week before, his heart finally giving out after nearly ninety-seven years. Thinking about my father brought back wonderful memories of growing up in New Jersey. Behind closed eyes, I could see my family gathered in our small, modestly appointed kitchen in North Bergen. My mother dishing out the standard dinner fare of a blue-collar family—potatoes, green beans, and meat loaf. My father sitting with his sleeveless T-shirt, his arms resting on the dinner table, his powerful biceps bouncing rhythmically while he buttered his bread. My older sister, Kathleen, younger brother, Tommy, and I competing for our parents' attention as we told stories about our days.

Tears began to fill my eyes for the second time that morning. Closing them, I wanted so badly to be a carefree teenager once again, enjoying life with my family in North Bergen, rather than being the CIA director.

"We're here, sir."

I must have dozed off briefly, as the words of the lead security agent sitting in the front passenger seat startled me. I opened my eyes and could see that we had pulled alongside an air force C-40, the military version of a Boeing 737. The C-40 was on the tarmac of

Andrews, ready to take me, along with Jim Clapper, Mike Rogers, and our respective security teams, to Newark International Airport. Jim Comey was traveling separately on a Bureau plane so that he could stay longer in the New York area to see his FBI agents, analysts, and support officers who worked in the Big Apple. I must have flown on several hundred U.S. military aircraft during my career, and whenever I boarded one, I could feel the enormous strength and might of the greatest superpower the world has ever known. On this sunny and brisk morning, however, the glistening blue and white aircraft had an especially majestic yet solemn quality to it. If its powerful engines were revving, I don't think I heard them. My attention was drawn to an air force airman wearing a crisply pressed blue uniform who was standing at attention with perfect posture at the base of the carpeted mobile stairs. The cabin door, twenty feet above ground, was open and beckoned me to board my last flight as a government official on a U.S. military aircraft.

"Welcome aboard, Director Brennan."

The professionalism, sense of duty, and pride that were evident on that young man's face really struck me. Despite the deep concerns I felt that morning about Donald Trump's lack of experience on national security issues, my confidence in the strength and resilience of our country was renewed simply by looking at a single American serviceman less than half my age.

"Thank you. Thank you very much."

Feeling a surge of patriotism, I attempted to bound up the stairs but had to settle for an unsteady and less-than-speedy hobble on my two prosthetic hips and one prosthetic knee. I made my way without stumbling, which I considered an unqualified success.

Jim Clapper was already on board when I entered the plane, and Mike Rogers joined us a few minutes later. We sat together and discussed the briefing we had just completed for the Gang of Eight. Clapper and I took some delight in telling Mike that it would be up to him and Jim Comey to carry on the fight with the Russians and

American politicians after Inauguration Day, since we were about to leave government. We told him that we weren't sure which fight would be toughest. Both Jim Clapper and I had retired from government previously—Jim had done it several times, while I had done so only once—and we were both looking forward to catching up on the sleep, books, cultural events, and, most important, family time that had eluded us over the past eight years. Nevertheless, we also knew that we would deeply miss being part of the national security mission and witnessing firsthand the camaraderie and the selfless sacrifice that defined the women and men of the intelligence community. For much of the flight, I sat silently and then gazed out the window as we entered the airspace of the state of my birth. As we approached Newark, I tried to pick out the surrounding northern New Jersey landmarks that had borne witness to my youthful exploits many years before. Once on the ground, we waited for Jim Comey's aircraft to arrive so that we could deplane and caravan together, heralded by police sirens and lights, through the Lincoln Tunnel under the Hudson River to our appointed meeting in midtown Manhattan.

Our respective SUVs, security details, and NYPD escorts converged on Trump Tower in near flawless traffic-paralyzing synchronization, much to the dismay of nearby New York commuters, taxi drivers, and even pedestrians who were forced to come to a dead stop. Quickly exiting our vehicles, we made our way to the Trump Tower service entrance elevator bank, each of us flanked by our own earpiece-wearing, gun-toting, grim-faced security agents. We piled into several elevators and ascended to an intermediate floor before transferring to another bank of elevators that would bring us to the floor where the briefing was slated to take place. The two Jims, Mike, and I were directed by our security details to a windowless conference room with ten chairs surrounding a rectangular conference table in the middle of the room.

The lock bag containing my briefing notes was not the only thing I brought with me to the Trump Tower conference room that day. I also carried a mental catalog of the many unfavorable impressions of Mr. Trump I had accumulated over the previous decades. Since I was a product of a northern New Jersey upbringing and a university education at Fordham University's Bronx campus, I had long been familiar with the antics of the New York City–based Mr. Trump. Over the years, I had heard and read many stories of Trump's reliance on intimidation, untruths, ruthless litigation, and bankruptcy laws—augmented by his routine defaults on contractor payments—to fuel his eponymous business ventures and to achieve some measure of financial wealth. His renown for playing fast, loose, and without principles gave him a well-deserved reputation for being a self-promoting and publicity-seeking blowhard, even by generous New York City standards.

My jaded view of Trump was reinforced by his performance in the run-up to the November election and his disparagement of the intelligence community after he won. While I had witnessed many politicians over the years make hollow campaign promises and specious claims about their own accomplishments and the failings of their opponents and previous administrations, no individual came close to Trump's dishonesty, unabashed self-aggrandizement, and demagogic rhetoric. When Trump officially announced at Trump Tower, on June 16, 2015, that he was running for president, I had dismissed it as yet another one of his many clever public relations gambits designed to raise his public profile and name brand, which would bring him financial benefit afterward. But when he proceeded to trounce his Republican opponents in the primaries in scorched-earth fashion, it was undeniable that he possessed a charisma that allowed him to repackage his political snake oil as a magical national elixir.

But like most Americans, including Donald Trump, I was shocked at his subsequent electoral college victory. I could not understand how so many voters thought he was qualified—intellectually, morally, ethically, temperamentally, or experientially—to be president of the United States. I had badly underestimated the appeal he had to a large segment of the American electorate that clearly was fed up with Washington politics as usual. But were American voters so gullible as to believe that Donald Trump could assume and carry out the responsibilities attached to the presidency of the United States of America—the most powerful position the world has ever known? Was the number of Hillary Clinton haters far larger than anyone had realized, and much greater than I could fathom, such that Trump won in what amounted to a protest vote? Or did the Russian interference that the intelligence community had warned about tilt the election in key swing states so that Trump came out on top? Those questions haunted me that day as I prepared to meet Donald J. Trump. They haunt me still.

We had been seated around the table in the conference room for about ten minutes when the door opened, and Trump and his retinue entered. Trump led the procession, followed closely by Vice President–elect Mike Pence and national security adviser designate Mike Flynn. Others in the group included CIA director nominee Mike Pompeo, chief of staff designate Reince Priebus, deputy national security adviser designate K. T. McFarland, and homeland security adviser designate Tom Bossert. Press spokesperson Sean Spicer joined mid-briefing. A senior intelligence community officer I will not name, who was responsible for giving Trump his daily intelligence briefing whenever he decided to take it, also was present.

It was the first time I had ever seen Trump in person. He was larger than I had anticipated, both in height and width, even when he removed his expensive black overcoat. He made his way around the table and proceeded to shake our hands, making good eye contact each time. He thanked us for coming to New York and said he was interested in hearing what we had to tell him. He sat at the head of the conference room table, folded his hands, and asked us to begin. Vice President–elect Pence sat at the other end of the table and was flanked by Flynn and Priebus; the rest of Trump's team sat in chairs along the wall to his right.

Jim Clapper took out the same scripted briefing he had used on Capitol Hill a few hours before and began his presentation. I studiously watched Trump during the approximately seventy-five-minute briefing. He was attentive and focused throughout and only rarely adjusted his body posture. He took no notes. The briefing was interrupted several times by the Trump team members in the room, mostly to ask for clarification or for something to be repeated. Pence, Flynn, Priebus, and Bossert showed the most curiosity about the nature and scope of Russian meddling. At predetermined points of the briefing, Jim Clapper turned to Jim Comey, Mike Rogers, and me to provide our agency-specific offerings. I had decided beforehand that I would share the full substance of CIA intelligence and analysis on Russian interference in the election without providing any specific details on the provenance of our knowledge. The sensitive sources and methods related to counterintelligence and Russia are among the nation's most prized jewels, and I lacked confidence that all the individuals in that conference room had the requisite understanding of classification procedures and controls—not to mention the personal discipline and integrity—to avoid devastating disclosures, either inadvertent or willful. Moreover, given his public praise of WikiLeaks, strange obsequiousness toward Vladimir Putin, and disdain toward the U.S. intelligence community, I had serious doubts that Donald Trump would protect our nation's most vital secrets.

Trump's alertness never faded during the briefing, but his demeanor as well as his questions strongly revealed that he was uninterested in finding out what the Russians had done or in holding them to account. Rather, he seemed most focused on challenging the intelligence and analysis underlying the judgment among the CIA, FBI, NSA, and the Office of the Director of National Intelligence that Russia interfered in the election and that the interference was intended to enhance his election prospects. It also was my clear impression—based on thousands of such briefings I have conducted over more than three decades—that he was seeking most to learn what we knew and how we knew it. This deeply troubled me, as I worried about what he might do with the information he was being given. Foreign intelligence services take much the same approach when they are briefed by the U.S. intelligence community on wrongdoing by their governments. They look for perceived weaknesses in the intelligence and analysis that could be exploited as well as for clues that could help them uncover and then seek to eliminate the human or technical sources providing sensitive and damning information.

During the briefing, Trump posited his own theories about election interference and his skepticism that the culprit was Russia, articulating what would become a well-honed attack strategy of seeking to discredit any suggestion that his election was fraudulent or in any way influenced by Russian interference. "It could have been the Chinese," he interjected several times during the briefing, seeking to deflect focus away from the unanimous assessment that the Russians were responsible. We each took turns debunking his counterclaims, as there was not a scintilla of doubt in any of our minds that what we witnessed in the run-up to the election was an intense, determined, and broad-based effort by the Russians to interfere in the election.

As the briefing was beginning to wrap up, Trump looked at me and made unsolicited disparaging remarks about human sources. "Anyone will say anything if you pay them enough. I know that and you know that," he said. At that moment, my thoughts went to the many foreign nationals who had worked with the CIA throughout its history and had courageously risked and even given their lives because they believed in America and what it stands for. I also thought of how every president I had briefed during my career was deeply appreciative of the CIA's human sources, even if not all of the intelligence they provided was accurate. I stared at Trump, shook my head in disgusted disagreement, and bit my tongue nearly hard enough to draw blood. I knew that he saw me at that time not as

John Brennan the person but as the director of the CIA, and I did not want to spoil irredeemably the CIA's relationship with the incoming president before it even got started. It was one of the few times in my professional career that I successfully suppressed my Irish temper when dealing with a politician. I wish I hadn't.

In the preparatory session Jim Clapper had convened the day before, it was agreed that Jim Comey would talk to Trump separately about the now-infamous Steele dossier, which alleged misconduct and conspiracy between the Trump campaign and the Russian government, at the end of the formal briefing. While the dossier was fast becoming the worst-kept secret in Washington at the time, Jim Comey believed it was important that Trump understand that such information was circulating in media and political circles inside and outside Washington. Although Trump and his team most likely already had a copy of the dossier or at the very least were cognizant of its salacious and unverified contents, we agreed with Comey that it would be best to ensure that at least the president-elect was aware of it. Comey told Trump that he had some information to share with him privately but allowed that he could have someone from his team join him. Trump opted not to have anyone else participate. Given the nature of the allegations, it was understandably best handled one-on-one.

As soon as I left the conference room, I immediately went to the elevators and descended Trump Tower accompanied only by my security detail. While the briefing was uneventful and the president-elect was relatively well behaved, I had become even more convinced that my long-held assessment of Trump's narcissism, lack of principles, and unfitness for the country's highest office was accurate. He showed no intellectual curiosity about what Russia had done and how it had carried out its campaign to interfere in the election, which suggested to me that he wasn't interested in learning the truth or in taking action to prevent a recurrence. More ominously, I left with a dark feeling that our country was entering what would be a very painful and dangerous chapter of its history.

It was a relief to leave Trump Tower and to have the day's briefings finally over. I just wanted to get to New Jersey, so I could be with my family to grieve for my father and to console my mother. As I emerged from the building, the New York sunlight never felt so refreshing. I climbed into my SUV and swung closed its heavy doors, once again melting into the comfortable leather back seat. The members of my protective security detail rode in silence up front. Usually, I would engage them in friendly banter during such rides, but not that day. I just couldn't bring myself to talk. Very faintly, I occasionally would hear them whisper into the microphones that were attached to the cuffs of their shirtsleeves, as they communicated with their colleagues in the accompanying vehicle. Several of the agents had been with me during my increasingly frequent travel from Virginia to New Jersey in the previous weeks to be with my dying father. While my siblings, Kathleen and Tommy, and I kept a twenty-four-hour bedside vigil during the last days of my father's life, my security detail would remain in the SUV outside the Mountainside, New Jersey, assisted-living facility that my parents called home. I would return to the SUV periodically to participate in secure conference calls with Clapper, Comey, and Rogers to discuss the assessment on Russian interference in the election and to read classified reports that continued to stream in. My security detail had been like family ever since my first day as director nearly four years before, so it was fitting that they were going with me to the final farewell to my father.

A few minutes after we arrived at the Higgins and Bonner Echo Lake Funeral Home in Westfield, New Jersey, Kathy and our children, Kyle, Kelly, and Jaclyn, pulled into the parking lot after their four-hour drive from Herndon. Steadily, other family members, friends, and former neighbors poured into the funeral home to say goodbye to Owen Brennan and to tell his children and grandchildren how lucky we were to have had such a good and decent man as father, grandfather, and role model. That evening, Kathleen, Tommy, and I, accompanied by our spouses and children, went to see my mother, Dottie, who, in her ninety-sixth year, was too feeble to venture out to the funeral home to be with her life's partner one last time. "How is Daddy?" she said to us, as we gathered round her.

"He's fine, Mom," we said. "He's now with God." She then blessed herself, as tears rolled down her face.

The ground was already covered in a blanket of snow when our family gathered at the funeral home early on Saturday morning to pay final tribute to my father's legacy. A brewing snowstorm was forecast to hit the northeast coast later that day, so some family members had already started the trip back to their homes in New England early that morning to get ahead of snowfalls that promised to make roads treacherous. As Kathleen, Tommy, and I once again greeted family and friends as they arrived at the funeral home, I was taken aback when I saw two familiar faces arriving within minutes of each other. Jim Clapper and Denis McDonough, President Obama's chief of staff, were two of my closest colleagues and friends in the Obama administration. Unbeknownst to me or to each other, they had traveled separately early that morning from their homes outside Washington, D.C., to pay their respects to my father. Over the years that we worked together, Jim, Denis, and I frequently shared stories about our families, and I had always taken great delight in bragging about my New Jersey roots and my wonderful parents. As my father's medical condition steadily deteriorated during December, Jim and Denis regularly asked about him and extended their heartfelt personal condolences when he passed.

The gently falling snow and the handsomely attired Irish bagpiper made for a fittingly picturesque scene when my father's casket, flanked by his six grandchildren, was slowly guided through the front doors of the Catholic Church of Our Lady of Lourdes in

Mountainside. The priest showed a bit of excitement and nervousness when he realized that the director of national intelligence, the chief of staff of the president of the United States, and the director of the CIA were all in attendance. "Owen," he said during the homily of the Mass, "was a man of humble beginnings who made his way from Ireland to America, found happiness and love in his family and friends, and lived a good life." With those few words, my father's life was captured in a way that I know would have made him both happy and proud.

The snowfall became more intense as the funeral procession made its way along Route 22 to bring my father to his final resting place in Holy Name Cemetery in Jersey City. When we arrived, our family gathered around the casket one last time. Despite being surrounded by my family and so many friends, I felt alone for the first time in my life. It was at that moment that the reality sunk in that I would no longer be able to talk to my father and be comforted by his innate wisdom. I would not be able to ask him questions that ranged from how to repair a leaky bathroom faucet to the meaning of life itself. And I would no longer hear his soft Irish brogue when he recited the poetry he learned in his youth, as he did with the nineteenth-century Irish poem "The Croppy Boy" the day before he died.

My father's death and my mother's infirmity also made me more aware than ever before of my own mortality. I bowed my head and pledged I would never forget the lessons of goodness, integrity, and honesty of my parents' lives. It was an honor to be their son.

2

JERSEY BOY

Hudson County, New Jersey, was a great place to grow up. At least it was for me. I was a proud Hudson County resident from the time of my birth, in 1955, until Kathy and I married in 1978 and headed off to Austin, Texas, to begin our life together. Due west across the Hudson River from New York City, Hudson County has long been one of the most densely populated counties in the United States. With a population hovering between half and three-quarters of a million over the last century, Hudson County's relatively small size never seemed to inhibit the ambitions or the egos of those who cut their teeth, often literally, on the county's numerous urban playgrounds, hardscrabble city streets, and sidewalks pockmarked with maple, elm, and oak trees. I always considered Hudson County's ethnic heterogeneity one of its greatest features and strengths. Over the past two hundred years, the county benefited from successive immigration waves; initially it was Germans, Irish, and Italians, then came Cubans and Central Americans, who were followed more recently by Middle Easterners and South and East Asians.

I entered the world at Christ Hospital in Jersey City in the early morning hours of September 22, 1955, weighing in at a respectable eight pounds, two ounces. My mother was always amazed that her five-foot-one-inch, 105-pound frame could give birth to such a big baby, especially one with a rather large head. At the time, my parents were living in a small third-floor one-bedroom apartment in West New York, which, despite its name, is a small municipality in northeastern New Jersey. My sister Kathleen was almost two years old when I was born, so my arrival put some serious pressure on the already limited floor space in the modest Brennan household. When my brother Thomas joined our clan in early 1959, we moved eight blocks away to a two-bedroom apartment. Tommy slept in a crib in my parents' bedroom, while Kathleen and I shared a bunk bed. I got the top bunk.

WHILE MY BIRTH ROOTS ARE in the urban jungle of Hudson County, I come from 100 percent rural Irish stock. I was always exceptionally proud of being a first-generation Irish American, and that pride was reinforced by the stories about family history and life in "the old country" that were the conversational centerpieces of the gatherings of aunts, uncles, cousins, and Irish immigrant friends that took place practically every weekend of my youth. The accounts of life in Ireland and the experiences and antics of my ancestors when they arrived in America took on a magical quality for me. I nagged my parents incessantly to tell me about their childhoods.

My father's life held particular fascination for me. Owen was born in a small four-room family farmhouse, a stone's throw from the Shannon River, in Clooneskert, County Roscommon, Ireland. He was the seventh child and fifth son among seven boys and three girls raised by Owen Brennan—known as "Odie"—and Ann Kelly. The family farm consisted of several dozen rock-strewn acres, which most years produced enough potatoes and other vegetables to keep the family fed, with enough left over to sell or barter at the nearby local markets in Roscommon town and Athlone. In addition to the dozen Brennans crammed into the thatched cottage, a few cows, pigs, sheep, and chickens as well as a horse or two rounded out the farm's constituency.

My grandfather Odie was considered the best plowman in Roscommon and could survey and measure a field within inches of accuracy, as our father would tell us, "with the walk of his boots." Odie was known for speaking candidly about the perceived failings of some of his neighbors, oftentimes wryly noting outside his parish church, "If I were Jesus Christ, I wouldn't have died for half these people." He was even less kind to the British, having lived through Ireland's occupation and bloody fight for freedom. A courier for the Irish Republican Army before Ireland's independence, he was once stopped by British soldiers at a checkpoint along one of Roscommon's many winding and hedge-lined roads. The soldiers took time to admire the fine horse he was riding, and, distracted by Odie's ability, as my father would say, "to talk a starving dog off a meat wagon," they never found the secret IRA maps and documents hidden under his saddle. I guess spy work ran in the Brennan family long before I was born.

Like his older siblings, my father Owen left the family farm in Clooneskert when he finished his local schooling to look for work. Barely sixteen, he was able to find blacksmith and farrier apprenticeship opportunities at several small forges in Roscommon. But times were tough and jobs hard to come by in western Ireland in the late 1930s, so Owen sought out World War II–driven employment opportunities in Northern Ireland, which was engaged in supporting the United Kingdom's war effort. He eventually found a job at the main blacksmith forge in Castledergh, County Tyrone. Two years later, he landed a much-coveted job back in the Republic of Ireland, as a master farrier at the Mount Juliet estate in County Kilkenny, where he lived above the horse stables.

Owen had long wanted to emigrate to the United States and join his older siblings Pat and Sarah, who had left Ireland many years before. But the sharp reduction in immigrant visas to the United States during World War II delayed the pursuit of his dream. In late 1947, however, Owen and his younger brothers Dan and Hugh received notice that their immigrant visa applications had made it through the bureaucratic backlog and been approved. As soon as he could, Owen bought a ticket to cross the Atlantic by ship and, after packing up the few possessions he owned, set off on his bike for Roscommon to say goodbye to his parents. It would be the last time he would ever see Odie.

Owen's ship was the *Marine Jumper,* a World War II troop transport ship that had been converted into a low-fare transatlantic commercial vessel that found new life ferrying European emigrants, including Jewish refugees, to America. The *Marine Jumper* set sail in late May 1948 from Ireland's southeastern seaport of Cobh, County Cork, formerly known as Queenstown, which also happened to be the last port of call in 1912 of the ill-fated RMS *Titanic*.

Owen had no qualms about embarking from Cobh despite its tragic nautical history, but he grew increasingly leery as well as queasy when the *Marine Jumper* hit stormy seas as soon as it set out on its ocean journey. Several days of bobbing off the coast of western Ireland left most passengers, including Owen, hopelessly seasick within the incommodious and increasingly malodorous quarters. "The most awful sickness you could ever imagine," Owen would say with a tinge of green in his face whenever the topic of seasickness would come up years after.

The waters calmed and the sun shone brightly during the last two days of the ocean voyage, which were marked by large schools of leaping sailfish that seemed to guide Owen and his fellow émigrés into New York Harbor on June 13. His eldest brother, Pat, who had sailed to America twenty years before, and his recently arrived youngest brother, Hugh, were at the dock when the *Marine Jumper* pulled in. They quickly whisked Owen off to the obligatory

"Welcome to America" party at their sister Sarah's apartment, just off St. Nicholas Avenue on 191st Street, in Washington Heights, upper Manhattan. That same afternoon, Babe Ruth was bidding a final farewell to his adoring fans at Yankee Stadium, less than three miles away.

Owen met his future wife, Dottie, at an Irish dance in New York City on a Saturday night in the summer of 1950. Dottie was born and raised in Hoboken, a two-square-mile city in Hudson County that hugs the shoreline directly across the Hudson River from midtown Manhattan. She was a secretary at Moore-McCormack shipping lines, which had its main office near Battery Park in lower Manhattan. When a girlfriend decided at the last minute not to accompany her to the dance, Dottie decided to go alone, an unusual decision for a single woman at the time ("What was I," she would laughingly say when she was well into her nineties, "a floozy?"). For some reason, she felt compelled to make the trek solo into Manhattan from Hoboken that night. My siblings and I are eternally grateful that she did, as it was there that she met the Irishman with the muscular arms, graceful dance steps, lilting brogue, and the most beautiful brown eyes she had ever seen.

Dottie had her own Irish story. She was born Dorothy Helen Dunn, the only child of Jersey City–born natives Thomas John Dunn and Mary Agnes Hingston and the granddaughter of émigrés from Ireland. Tom had been barely eighteen when both his parents died of influenza within two months of each other in the winter of 1906. He took whatever odd jobs he could find in order to take care of three younger brothers and a sister. When his brothers and sister were able to finally fend for themselves, Tom joined the army at the age of thirty. He trained at Fort Dix, New Jersey, and was promoted to corporal before being shipped out to France in early 1918. As far as I know, he saw no battlefield action.

When Tom returned from France and was given an honorable discharge from the army, he found work with his brothers as a longshoreman on Hoboken's notorious waterfront docks. A haven for corruption and thievery during the Prohibition-era 1920s, the docks presented the Dunn brothers with ample opportunity to line their pockets with ill-gotten gains. The youngest, Frankie, became the wealthiest and the most notorious, gaining the newspaper moniker "Beer Baron of New Jersey." Not satisfied with the proceeds that accompanied his rum-running and other bootlegging endeavors, Beer Baron Frankie also hijacked the delivery trucks of the clients to whom he had just sold liquor. It was therefore unsurprising when Frankie was tommy-gunned to death when he exited an elevator in the hallway of his downtown Hoboken office building on March 7, 1930.

IN JANUARY 1963, WE MOVED a mile and a half to North Bergen, Hudson County's northernmost town. Owen and Dottie had saved enough money from my father's earnings as a union steamfitter working construction in New York City for the down payment needed to purchase a seventeen-thousand-dollar two-family house that was built in 1916. Staying local made sense. Dottie's aging parents were living in nearby Hoboken, and Owen could easily grab a bus that would get him to work in Manhattan in less than thirty minutes. The real estate agent who sold my parents their North Bergen house was Bill Freeh, another parishioner of St. Joseph of the Palisades, our local church. Freeh also lived on the same street and extolled the neighborhood's virtues for children, including his own. His oldest, Louie, was six years older than me and was making his way through the St. Joseph's school system at the time. Louie always seemed to be the studious type. Many years later, I envied the sharp-looking briefcase he carried as he passed our house on his way to take a bus that would bring him to Rutgers Law School in Newark. His daily attire of a jacket and tie together with a close-cropped haircut, much in contrast to prevailing fashion norms, made him look like an aspiring

FBI agent. Little did I imagine at the time that Louie would join the FBI and ultimately rise within its ranks to become its fifth director in 1993.

My years growing up in North Bergen provided wonderful memories of what life was like in "simpler times." In the converted-storefront classrooms of Immaculate Heart of Mary, the North Bergen satellite school of St. Joseph's parish, I was a good student, mainly because I did not think I had the option not to be. Kathleen was always at the top of her class, so my parents and teachers held her grades up as the standard I was expected to meet. Math came easily to me, probably because my father would incessantly drill me on addition, subtraction, multiplication, and division problems whenever I would help him with house repairs, which mainly consisted of my holding a drop light for him at night until my arm ached. "Figure out the answer in your head," he would say to teach me numeric relationships, a skill he apparently mastered in his youth. Dottie had the lead on vocabulary and grammar, reinforcing in the evenings the lessons taught at school by the nuns during the day. An avid reader herself, she would prohibit her children from watching television in the evenings unless reading was done first.

But it was history and geography that held the most fascination for me. A&P and ShopRite, our two local food stores, sold children's serial encyclopedias and books on American history that our family would buy during our weekly grocery shopping runs. The books were replete with drawings, photos, and pictures of famous paintings that made the accounts of the Revolutionary, Civil, and World Wars and the accomplishments of presidents, generals, and other notables come alive for little John Brennan. When I found out that Nathan Hale, America's first spy, was hanged at twenty-one years of age on September 22, 1776—my birthday, 179 years before I was born—I would fantasize about being a modern-day spy who was captured but who heroically escaped before being subjected to the same fate.

My friends tell me that I was considered a Goody-Two-shoes during those early years. I guess I just wanted to avoid getting into trouble lest I tempt the nuns to belie their saintly appearance and repeat on me what I had witnessed many times being meted out to my classmates—the smashing and even breaking of wooden rulers over trembling and soon-to-be-red knuckles. In addition to escaping the pain of worldly corporal punishment, I am certain that the fear of eternal damnation was a powerful motivating force as well. At home and in school, there was a consistent emphasis on doing what was "right" rather than what might be personally advantageous or expedient.

My deep religiosity as a young boy convinced me that I would eventually enter the seminary to join the priesthood, with the goal of ultimately becoming the first American pope. It was my very strong childhood impression that priests had the inside track to heaven. And if I was going to become a priest, I thought, why not aim high and become the first American to wear the papal miter? By my youthful calculation, there would be no way Saint Peter could deny entry through the pearly gates to anyone who had "Pope" on their earthly résumé. To further improve my chances of a heavenly reward, I became an altar boy and served countless weekday and weekend Masses in my black and white, and sometimes black and red, altar garb. My timing wasn't great, though, as the reforms of the Second Vatican Council had not yet kicked in, so I had to learn the liturgical prayers in Latin when I was barely ten years old. While a bit rusty, I can still recite the confiteor in the language of ancient Rome.

When I wasn't doing schoolwork or practicing my faith, sports dominated my life during elementary school. My schoolmates and I would play tackle football, basketball, and baseball in seasonal sequence at nearby Hudson County Park, since renamed James J. Braddock Park, after the world heavyweight boxing champion of the mid-1930s who called North Bergen home. I was a good athlete, not a great one. I usually tried to compensate for any deficit in natural ability with extra hustle, which included diving recklessly on the fields of Hudson County Park, which were rockier than they were grassy, and on asphalt basketball courts. I consider my many orthopedic operations and joint replacement surgeries in later years as penance for the carefree and rather reckless athletic play of my youth.

In the Brennan household, faith, school, and sports had to be accompanied by some type of part-time job if movies, baseball cards, ice cream, and other childhood delights were to be had. Beginning in fifth grade, I became a wage earner as a paper boy for the *Hudson Dispatch,* rising by 6:00 A.M. six days a week so that I could fold more than one hundred papers and toss them with pinpoint accuracy onto the front stoops of homes in my North Bergen neighborhood. Delivering prescriptions for Virgona's Pharmacy on weekends, stocking shelves at Raessler and Pathmark grocery stores, and launching a house painting company with my best friend Gerry Boyle—getting top billing when we decided to call it "BrenBoy"—augmented my paper route earnings and gave me enough money to buy birthday and Christmas presents for my family and to join my friends in social activities.

I played varsity baseball and basketball at St. Joseph's. Basketball was my first love, which is why I was so devasted when I was cut during tryouts in my freshman, sophomore, and junior years. Setting my mind to making the team in my senior year, I practiced daily for months before tryouts on the aluminum-backboard courts of Hudson County Park until my entire body ached. With an all-out effort to earn a St. Joseph's varsity basketball uniform in my senior year, I defied the odds and somehow survived the final cut. "It was your hustle that got you on the team," Coach Frank Grasso told me a few years later when I ran into him on the Jersey Shore. The experience was a very good and early lesson for me on how hard work, determination, and persistence can make a real difference in achieving results. Except for one late-season game, when I both scored and rebounded in double digits in an upset win, my varsity basketball career was eminently forgettable, for me as well as for the team as a whole.

While a family car trip to Canada and a two-week visit to Ireland to meet Grandma Brennan were my only travels abroad during my high school years, I gained greater appreciation of the diversity of our planet through the letters and audio recordings that my cousin Tom, my uncle Pat's son, would send home during his service as a Peace Corps volunteer in Malaysia and as a U.S. Agency for International Development officer in Vietnam. Tom's detailed descriptions of the challenges of everyday life for children and adults in impoverished rural villages and hamlets on the other side of the world brought into stark relief for me just how special it was to live in America. It also helped me understand why my father and mother would tell Kathleen, Tommy, and me that, despite our modest upbringing and social status, we should never take our exceptional good fortune of being Americans for granted. "This is the greatest country in the world," our immigrant father would tell us, "which is why so many people want to come to America. Too often, it's those born here who don't understand just how fortunate they are."

It also was during my high school years that I started to think more deeply about life and what I wanted to do with mine. I was no longer subjected to the heavily dogmatic and doctrinaire religious teaching of my elementary school nuns, and the Christian Brothers and lay teachers I had in high school stimulated a much greater intellectual curiosity than I had experienced previously. English literature classes introduced me to books and plays—such as *Who's Afraid of Virginia Woolf?* and *Inherit the Wind*—that explored human relationships and the origins of life in ways that I had never seriously considered before. My heavily sheltered Catholic upbringing was forever ruptured at sixteen years of age, when Brother Richard took our English literature class on a school excursion to New York City to see the now-classic dystopian film *A Clockwork Orange*. It was an act of brotherly defiance of the Catholic Church, which had condemned the movie and forbade Catholics to see it because of its raw sex and violence. Even some of my religion teachers had a rebellious side. I remember vividly Mr. Callahan, a former Christian Brother who taught at the high school after he left the religious order, quizzing me and fellow students on the foundations of our faith, asking us pointedly why we believed in God and whether we did good rather than bad simply because we were selfishly pursuing a heavenly hereafter. When I finally admitted to Mr. Callahan and myself that I didn't know why I accepted the reality of a God or if I did good things simply because of a fear of hellish damnation, I felt as though I had transformed virtually overnight into a doubting Thomas. From that point on, I routinely would seek out empirical proof before accepting as immutable truth something I had read or had been told that I considered dubious or unfounded. Although my heretofore strong Catholic faith was the first casualty of my newfound agnosticism, little did I realize at the time that my high school teachers had prepared me well for my future intelligence profession, where assumptions and untested acceptance of purported "facts" can produce national security disasters.

3

COMING OF AGE

When my plans to enter the seminary and ultimately become pope evaporated during my high school years, I needed to find a new academic path and professional calling. I still strongly identified as a cultural Catholic, so I researched mainly Catholic colleges and universities, believing they might help strengthen my lagging faith. I applied to three schools: Georgetown University, in Washington, D.C.; Siena College, near Albany, New York; and Fordham University, in the Bronx. My cousin Tom encouraged me to apply to Georgetown, as its Edmund A. Walsh School of Foreign Service was, and remains, the premier feeder school for the Department of State's diplomatic corps. I applied to Siena because one of its recruiters came to St. Joseph's and gave me inflated hope that I could actually play on Siena's basketball team. Fordham was my safety school. A Jesuit institution with a prominent reputation in the New York metropolitan area, especially among the Irish diaspora, Fordham had the family imprimatur, as my cousin Jim McGuire had played baseball at Fordham while pursuing an accounting degree. Fordham and

Georgetown had law schools, which also piqued my interest, as be-coming a lawyer seemed to be a reasonable career option.

I was accepted to Georgetown but decided to go to Fordham as a commuter student. The decision was a financial one. Since I had to finance my own college education, the thought of going into thou-sands of dollars of debt in order to study and live at Georgetown was less than appealing to my practical self. Fordham offered me a much more attractive combination of grants and student loans, leaving me to cover about five hundred dollars a year in tuition and another couple hundred dollars for books.

I decided to be a political science major at Fordham, for no other reason than that it sounded like the most appropriate course of study that would allow me either to attend law school or to pursue my dream of traveling the world. I was most interested in courses in international relations and comparative politics; political theory was simply too abstract for my taste. It was my philosophy and theology courses at Fordham, however, that had the deepest and most lasting influence on me. Fresh off the mind-expanding experiences of my high school years, I was eager to hear what the much-vaunted Jesuit scholars thought about life, God, and the reason for "being." My interest in Greek philosophy sparked my subsequent study of the world's other great philosophers, especially those who explored "just war theory," such as Saint Augustine of Hippo and Saint Thomas Aquinas. The philosophy textbooks and articles I read and the papers I wrote during my days at Fordham have traveled with me across country and continents and remain with me to this day. Little did I realize during my Fordham years that I would search out those books and papers on many a late night at home when I had to make life-and-death recommendations and decisions during my years at the White House and at the helm of the CIA.

In the spring of my freshman year, my cousin Tom invited me to spend the summer with him in Indonesia, where he was then serving as a Food for Peace officer for USAID at the U.S. embassy in the archipelago's capital, Jakarta. Tom said he would pay for my round-trip plane ticket. The offer to get away from the tedium of a hot New Jersey summer was too good to pass up. The day after I received Tom's letter of invitation, I spoke to one of my political science professors, John Entelis, who agreed that it would be a great opportunity for me to travel and to do field research early in my college career, and he recommended that I do a research paper focused on oil and politics in Indonesia. After a quick trip to the registrar's office to explain my hope to travel to Indonesia, I had official Fordham approval for a tutorial research project.

My family brought me to New York's JFK Airport in the late afternoon of June 29, 1974. The trip to Jakarta took two days. I flew Air France to Paris, befriending an American GI and self-described "farm boy from Iowa" who sat next to me on the flight. He was only nineteen years old and was going back to Germany after a short visit home. We wandered through Paris-Orly Airport together for the next couple of hours before heading to our respective flights, his to Frankfurt and mine to Amsterdam. In the span of ninety minutes, I learned about his unit in Germany, his large family, and his dream of saving enough money during his military duty—augmented by "poker winnings," he said—to buy a small farm back in Iowa and then to marry the "prettiest girl" he could find. I guess getting to know him for even a short amount of time made real for me the willingness of young Americans to leave the comforts of home to serve their country. I always wondered whether that Iowa farm boy eventually realized his American dream.

I flew from Paris to Amsterdam, where I spent the night. The twenty-hour flight from Amsterdam to Jakarta seemed never-ending. It was a small plane by today's standards, and there were intermediate stops in Vienna, Bahrain, Karachi, Colombo, Bangkok, and Kuala Lumpur. The only stop where my fellow passengers and I were able to get off the plane was in Karachi where we streched our legs in a transit passenger lounge. It proved to be a very hot and generally unpleasant interlude.

When I eventually descended the unsteady mobile aluminum stairs that were walked up to the side of the plane at Jakarta's airport, I was immediately struck by the scent in the air. It was very different from anything I had ever experienced previously. There was something very warm, humid, gritty, and distinctly intense about it. It was as though I had opened a door to a new world, with my olfactory nerves sending a signal to my brain that I had embarked on a new and exciting chapter of my life. That scent was powerful and long lasting, and I would always detect some semblance of it whenever I would visit East and Southeast Asia in subsequent years, prompting fond memories of my first visit to the region in the summer of 1974.

My time in Jakarta was my first exposure to an American diplomatic community, and I was struck by the camaraderie as well as the evident pride of U.S. officials, spouses, and children who had the privilege of representing the government and people of the United States while posted abroad. The Fourth of July celebration that took place at the U.S. embassy pool a few days after my arrival evoked strong feelings of patriotism in me, especially when the marine security guard detachment stood at attention during the presentation of the flag and the singing of the national anthem. Almost overnight, I felt that I had become a part of a family that was dedicated to bringing America's ideals, values, resources, and capabilities to the rest of the world. It was a really good feeling.

While in Jakarta, I learned a lot about the national oil company, Pertamina, and the central role its oil production and exports played in Indonesia's economy as well as in its politics. Tom set up a series of meetings and interviews for me with American officials, most notably Ambassador David Newsom and AID Director Richard Cashin—two exceptionally able career U.S. diplomats. It seemed

remarkable then, and it still does now, that an eighteen-year-old
college student was able to gain that kind of access. But I interviewed them as well as some local oil company representatives. Several weeks of additional interviews and research followed by a couple
of weeks of writing produced a research paper that Professor Entelis
ultimately would deem acceptable. It was the politics, history, and
culture of Indonesia, however, that most captured my attention. Less
than a decade before I arrived, a bloody slaughter had taken place of
more than one million card-carrying as well as suspected members
of the Communist Party of Indonesia (PKI), ethnic Chinese, and
other presumed opponents of the army-backed regime of President
Sukarno. Political tensions still simmered under the increasingly
corrupt rule of Sukarno's successor, President Suharto, whose image
I regularly spotted on billboards and on the front pages of daily
newspapers. During my discussions in Jakarta, I heard stories from
Indonesians and Americans alleging CIA support for the Indonesian
army's roundup and summary execution of Communist Party leaders as part of a general U.S. effort to stop Communist momentum
in Southeast Asia. Although a thousand miles of water separated
Jakarta from the conflict that was still raging between North and
South Vietnam, I realized that I had parachuted into a region of the
world that was distinctly different from the one I had left behind.

Tom was determined to make sure that my visit to Indonesia was
not limited to the diplomatic, government, and business circles of
Jakarta, so he regularly took me to see the poverty that existed in
and around the city. Wherever we went, our light skin and obvious
foreignness generated keen interest among the locals. While some
took to begging, more wanted to use the few English words they
knew to inquire about our nationality and why we were in Jakarta.
Unfailingly, our acknowledgment that we were Americans and not,
as most presumed, from the Netherlands—Indonesia's former occupying colonial power—brought thumbs-up gestures from smiling
albeit gaunt faces.

The most exciting part of my summer in Indonesia was my solo weeklong round trip to Bali. Tom wanted to make sure that I saw the Javanese countryside up close and personal, so he sent me on a seven-hundred-mile journey across the island. He deposited me, along with a handful of Hermann Hesse novels, at the Jakarta train station, and, over the course of twenty-four hours and despite a severe bout of dysentery, I boarded multiple trains and buses until I finally arrived in the eastern Java seacoast town of Banyuwangi, where I caught an overcrowded ferry to Denpasar, Bali. Once safely across the Bali Strait, a quick taxi ride took me to what was then a very undeveloped Kuta Beach, where I stayed in a modest thatched beach cabana that cost me six dollars per night. After a few days, I met and toured with some teenage dependents of Jakarta-based American diplomats and spent the rest of the time motorcycling around the predominantly Hindu island and surfing and lounging on Kuta's topless beaches.

One of the most memorable and welcome aspects of my summer in Indonesia was the social, religious, and cultural tolerance I witnessed in a country with the world's largest Muslim population. Islam certainly was dominant, but Christianity, Buddhism, and Hinduism all seem to have a respected social place—and their adherents had economic opportunity—in the heterogenous island nation. And wherever I went, I never felt in danger or was looked upon menacingly because of my foreignness. Indeed, once acknowledged, my American nationality was applauded.

By the time my sojourn to Indonesia had ended in late August, I felt as though I had been through an intense eight-week introductory course on life. I couldn't wait to experience what additional offerings lay ahead.

4

DISCOVERING THE MIDDLE EAST

When I returned to the States and began my sophomore year at Fordham, the commute from North Bergen to the Bronx got old real fast. There were more than a few days when I decided the trip to Fordham was not worth the effort and stayed home. But I apparently decided that I should make the trek on Tuesday, March 25, 1975, a day that changed the trajectory of my life. I was taking a class that semester on politics in the Middle East, which was taught by Professor Entelis. His specialty was the Middle East, and he taught with such extensive knowledge and passion that it instilled in me a strong interest in the region. It was on that March day when Professor Entelis distributed to the class a brochure on the American University in Cairo (AUC).

On the way home from Fordham that day, I heard on the radio that King Faisal of Saudi Arabia had been shot to death by his nephew, Prince Faisal Bin Musaid. The evening news was consumed with commentary on the assassination and on the uncertain implications for Saudi Arabia, the Middle East, and the United States. The extensive media focus on Faisal's death immediately deepened my interest in visiting and learning more about this conflict-ridden region. I went to the library at Fordham the next day and read everything I could find about AUC and life in Cairo. I scoured copies of *National Geographic,* looking for articles that had photos of Cairo and the Egyptian countryside. It all looked exotic and very appealing, and I told my parents that I wanted to go to school in Egypt. "Why?" was my mother's response; "Why not?" was my father's. I filled out the AUC application that evening and by mid-June was accepted to AUC's year-abroad program.

I departed JFK Airport for Cairo on TWA Flight 840 on September 15, 1975. As the plane approached Cairo International Airport shortly before dusk the following day, I could see the pyramids and the Sphinx through the sandy haze out my window, a most appropriate first glimpse of the Middle East. It didn't take long before I fell in love with the streets, sounds, and people of Cairo. In 1975, AUC was located entirely in the heart of Cairo, a literal stone's throw from Tahrir Square, the focal point of Egypt's 2011 uprising against President Hosni Mubarak. I arrived a few days before classes started, so I had the opportunity to roam around the city, looking for the landmarks I had read about in history books and novels. During the day, I would wander around the yet-to-be renovated Egyptian Museum, where dusty ancient artifacts and mummified remains were piled on top of one another, stacked on even dustier shelves. Seeing the exceptionally well-preserved mummy of Ramses II, with his arms crossed above his chest, was breathtaking.

What charmed me most about Cairo were its people. Very early one morning, when I was on one of my strolls through the mostly empty backstreets there, I noticed a middle-aged Egyptian dressed in a traditional full-body galabeya garment, which is typical of a rural villager. He had an intense look on his face, and he was walking straight toward me. Before I could walk around him, he put up his hand and motioned me to stop. "Inta Amriki ow Sovieti?" he said in a firm voice. While I had just started my Arabic classes

and didn't have much familiarity with the language, I knew immediately what he was asking—was I an American or a Soviet? I immediately grasped my dilemma, as America had been Israel's main
political, economic, and military benefactor while the Soviet Union
was Egypt's.

"Uh-oh," I said to myself. For a moment, I wondered whether I
should claim to be a Canadian or a citizen of Ireland, Switzerland,
or some other traditionally neutral European country. As I looked at
the Egyptian, he appeared more curious than threatening. Muster-
ing a surge of youthful patriotism, and remembering my positive
experiences in Indonesia, I said, "Ana Amriki."

As soon as the words came out of my mouth, the Egyptian broke
into a huge smile, thrust a crooked thumb into the air, and announced, "Mumtaz!" (excellent). He patted my arm, dipped his head
in respect, and then continued his morning jaunt.

Curious about the Egyptian's positive reaction to the admission
of my American nationality, I recounted the story to my Egyptian
and Arab classmates when I returned to the dormitory. It was true,
they said, that Egyptians resented U.S. support to Israel, believing
it responsible for Israeli occupation of Arab and Palestinian lands
seized in 1967. Nevertheless, they argued, Americans were greatly
admired by Egyptians as well as by other Arabs, the majority of
whom viewed the God-fearing United States as a vital bulwark
against the expansionist designs of an atheistic Soviet Union. For
the rest of my time in Cairo, I never hesitated to say proudly "Ana
Amriki" whenever I had the chance, even when unsolicited.

Cairo was marked by many firsts for me. It was the first time I
learned to read, write, and speak Arabic, a most beautiful language
that I ultimately would learn, forget, and relearn several times in
subsequent decades. It also was the first and only time I had the
opportunity to play basketball at the college level and according to
international rules, as I was one of two Americans who played on
AUC's basketball team along with French, Egyptian, and Palestinian

teammates. Games were played on a hard sand basketball court located in the center of campus. I can still hear the cheers of the AUC students who lined the court and filled the stands to rally our team over visiting colleges and police academies.

Another of my "firsts" during my days in Cairo was smoking hashish, which I did inhale, with my American, Egyptian, and Palestinian friends. We would buy a pack of Marlboro cigarettes and then carefully open several in order to remove a small amount of tobacco before sprinkling small bits of hashish in them. Using gummed rolling paper, we would close up the hashish-laced cigarettes and then enjoy them as we sipped Scotch whiskey and listened to Elton John songs. While I broke the hashish-smoking and Scotch-sipping habits as soon as I left Cairo, I unfortunately became addicted to the tobacco and struggled for many years with occasionally smoking cigarettes to relieve stress.

I decided to travel to Israel and the West Bank during AUC's holiday break, in the second half of December. On December 20, I flew to Amman, Jordan, where I spent a night nearly freezing while staying at an unheated youth hostel. The next day, I walked miles to multiple Jordanian government offices to obtain documented permission to travel across the Jordan River on the Allenby Bridge to the Israeli-occupied West Bank.

Once on the western side of the bridge, I dutifully got in the line for "non-Arabs" and watched the dozens of Palestinians who were herded into a holding area that already seemed overcrowded. When I got to the front of my line, an Israeli soldier had his hand out and asked for my passport.

"I don't want my passport stamped, please," I said, just as I had been instructed many times by AUC staff as well as by U.S. embassy officials before I left Cairo. Any Israeli marking in my passport, they said, would prevent me from being allowed back into Egypt, which was still technically in a state of war with Israel at the time. The grim-faced Israeli soldier looked at me and said, "Don't tell me what to do." My heart sank, believing that he would ignore my entreaties, which would force me to discard my passport and apply for another one at the U.S. embassy in Tel Aviv. He then stamped a separate piece of paper and stapled it into my passport. Handing it back to me, he said with a smile, "Welcome to Israel."

The week I spent traveling in Israel and the West Bank was thrilling. I explored the ancient narrow streets of Jerusalem and visited the Jewish, Muslim, and Christian holy sites. I slowly walked along the Via Dolorosa, trying to imagine what it was like for Jesus to have carried his cross along the same stone-paved street nearly two thousand years before. Jerusalem—"al-Quds" in Arabic—will always, always be my favorite city.

On Christmas Eve I took a taxi to Bethlehem. The midnight Mass at the Church of the Nativity was oversubscribed, so I contented myself by watching a scratchy televised projection of the Mass on an exterior wall of the church. In Nazareth, I visited the taxi-owning family of a Palestinian classmate and was given free guided tours and history lessons of the towns and villages that dotted the rock-strewn West Bank landscape. And when I stopped for lunch in Ramallah, I had no idea that two and a half decades later I would break bread and attend many meetings in that same town with Yasir Arafat and many other Palestinian leaders.

I also spent two days touring and visiting the beautiful sites of Israel with a fellow American classmate from AUC. I felt very much at home in the modern and cosmopolitan city of Tel Aviv, with its seaside cafés and vibrant nightlife. We were warmly greeted by shopkeepers and merchants who applauded our study in Cairo and had endless questions about their Egyptian neighbors. We spent the better part of a day visiting and learning about life in Kiryat Brenner, a kibbutz located about twenty miles south of Tel Aviv. We also visited Hebrew University in Jerusalem and were struck by the contrast between the new and impressive facilities there and the dated and forlorn buildings and equipment at its Egyptian equivalents.

When I returned to Cairo, I realized that I was growing short of funds, which, combined with an unappealing list of spring classes at AUC, convinced me to pull up my Egyptian stakes and head home in late January. It was with a heavy heart that I said goodbye to my many Arab and American friends. On the way to Cairo Airport to catch my flight home, I remember promising myself that I would return to the region one day, if only to rekindle memories of my youth. Little did I know then that I would wind up spending the bulk of my professional career working on, traveling to, living in, and agonizing over the Middle East.

5

"SO, YOU ARE INTERESTED
IN JOINING THE CIA?"

My return to Fordham was anticlimactic. By the time of my senior year at Fordham, my plans to enter law school, like my earlier plans to enter the seminary, had completely fallen by the wayside.

I briefly explored going into the military, mainly because there was a U.S. Navy recruitment office around the block from my parents' house in North Bergen. I did a bit of research on careers in the navy and became intrigued with its Officer Candidate School, which required a college degree. Getting off the bus on the way home from Fordham one fall day in 1976, I decided to find out what nautical adventures might await me and visited the navy recruiting office. I told a recruiter that I would be graduating from Fordham in May and was interested in career options they might have for me.

After a few pleasantries, the lead recruiter got right down to business. "What is your major? And what about your GPA?"

Gulp.

"My major is political science, and my GPA is about 3.0." I could tell immediately that a political science degree from Fordham with a very mediocre GPA was not impressing him. He plied me for more information. "Have you taken many science or engineering courses at Fordham?" Heck. I didn't even know if Fordham offered engineering courses, and the last time I took a science course was in high school.

"Not really," was the best response I could come up with. Without much more discussion, I was told that I was not a good candidate for Officer Candidate School and was not even a shoo-in to be accepted as an enlisted man.

With the seminary, law school, and the navy scratched off my what-to-do-after-college list and my graduation date looming, I decided to investigate the possibility of going to graduate school. Professor Entelis pointed me toward the University of Texas, which had received a hefty monetary grant from oil-rich Libya in the mid-1970s that it used to establish a much-respected Middle East Studies program at its flagship Austin campus. The more I investigated the University of Texas and life in Austin, the more excited I became about the prospect of once again taking off for a new destination. I signed up to take the GRE and, when I received notification that I did well on it, submitted a late application for the doctoral program in the government department of UT-Austin.

While awaiting word from Texas, traveling on a bus to Fordham one morning, I noticed a CIA advertisement in the employment section of *The New York Times*. Rather vague in its description of the types of jobs available, the ad nevertheless sparked my interest. It didn't take long for me to pull together a résumé on my short life and even shorter list of relevant experiences, which I sent to the address in the ad. Surprisingly, I received a written response within three weeks, inviting me to a personal interview at a CIA recruitment office located in Federal Plaza in lower Manhattan.

It was on a sunny February day in 1977 when James T. Fitzgerald greeted me with a big smile and a warm handshake as I entered his Federal Plaza office. "So, you are interested in joining the CIA?"

"Absolutely," I said, although a more accurate response would have been, "I'm really just looking for something to do when I graduate from Fordham." We had a nice conversation about my studies at Fordham and my travels to Indonesia and Egypt, and he described very generally the different types of work done at CIA headquarters in Langley, Virginia, and at posts overseas. Putting my cards on the table, I told Fitzgerald that I had applied to graduate school at the University of Texas and was waiting to hear whether I would be accepted.

"Graduate school would be a good thing for you to do, and it certainly would improve your chances of getting hired by the Agency," he said, as he handed me a CIA application. "You can fill out this application now or, if you go to Texas, send it to us about six or nine months before you graduate. I think we could find a spot for you."

Nearly forty years later, I would greet Fitzgerald warmly during his visit to CIA headquarters as a retiree when I was director of the CIA. "Well, Jim," I said as he sat down in my office. "You need to know that there are a lot of people in Washington who desperately want to find the person to blame for allowing me to join the Agency many years ago. But your secret is safe with me."

An even more significant life-changing event took place during my last year in college. The end-of-year holiday season was the time when former St. Joseph's High School classmates and friends would gather to catch up on old times. It was on a snowy Monday night in December that I joined a dozen or so of my friends at Xandar's, an Edgewater, New Jersey, bar/restaurant/lounge that offered live music and stiff drinks. It was there that I noticed, and couldn't take my eyes off, Kathy Pokluda, who I found out was a North Bergen High School graduate a year younger than me. After I was able to convince a mutual friend to introduce us, I learned that Kathy was the sister of a Little League baseball teammate of mine and that she was then a junior majoring in physical education at William Paterson College in Wayne, New Jersey.

I am not sure if I knew that Kathy and I would eventually get married when I first met her, but I sensed that there was something very special about her. The physical spark was exhilarating, and there was even a deeper emotional attachment that propelled me to pursue Kathy aggressively in the weeks and months that followed. By spring, either I had succeeded in my efforts or she had relented from fatigue, because we were going steady and sharing our deepest thoughts as well as our hopes and dreams with one another. And when I surprised Kathy by getting my left ear pierced in Greenwich Village one night, I knew we were destined to be together. I appeared suddenly with a gold earring and she readily accepted my rebelliousness, saying, "It looks great!" Owen and Dottie were much less impressed.

When I received word in late spring that I was accepted into the graduate program at UT's government department, I quickly said yes. The opportunity to do in-depth research on the Middle East and to study Arabic again was simply too attractive to pass up. My initial move to Austin, however, was short-lived. Within six weeks of my arrival, I was admitted to the university health center with a 104-degree fever, swollen lymph nodes, and severe headaches. Ten days of tests finally revealed that I had developed mononucleosis, necessitating my withdrawal from school and return to New Jersey in early November. After regaining my strength over the holidays, I received assurance that I could return to Austin the next fall to resume my studies.

Kathy and I were still going steady when we started to discuss my planned return to UT in August. I knew that I didn't want to go to Austin without her, so in early March I took Kathy to dinner at Xandar's, where we had first met. At the conclusion of the entrée, I got down on one knee, took a diamond engagement ring out of my pocket, and proposed to her, saying, "Although I don't know what I will do with my life, I know for sure that I will always love you and want to spend the rest of my life with you." When Kathy said that she would marry me, I felt more joy than I had ever experienced before. We were married on Sunday, August 13, 1978, at St. Joseph's of the Palisades Church in West New York.

Three days later, we packed up our car and headed to Texas. Soon after we arrived, Kathy found a job teaching and coaching volleyball in the Austin Independent School District. I was given a teaching assistantship at UT, which allowed me to pay in-state tuition. But I also had to quickly learn about Texas government and politics— about which I knew nothing—as it was the undergraduate course I was required to teach. Life in Austin in the late 1970s was terrific, especially for two transplanted and just-wedded New Jerseyites who enjoyed the beautiful lakes, hills, and carefree lifestyle that was in full display at Barton Springs Pool, on the grounds of Zilker Park.

I concentrated on international politics, national security issues, and Middle East studies during graduate school, working closely with my professors for my research on human rights in Egypt, which I had decided early on would be the focus of my eventual doctoral dissertation. I also took Arabic classes. By the beginning of my second year of graduate study at UT, however, my enthusiasm for extended academic study started to wane. I was becoming more and more intrigued by what was happening in the Middle East during that time—the Camp David Accords and the signing of a peace treaty between Israel and Egypt; the Iranian Revolution and U.S. diplomats being held hostage in Tehran; the takeover of the Grand Mosque in Mecca, Saudi Arabia, by violent extremists, and their bloody expulsion; and regional reaction to the Soviet invasion of Afghanistan. As a result, I became impatient to get on with a professional career that would allow me to once again travel outside the United States and become involved in world events.

I also detected that Kathy longed to live closer to her New Jersey family and was less than enthused about my generally lax graduate school routine, which was in stark contrast to her rather full teaching and coaching schedule. "Do you still have that CIA application?" she asked me one evening.

"Uh, yeah, I do."

There was an extended pause, and then I folded before she did. "Why?" I asked, despite knowing what she was thinking.

"Well, it might be worthwhile to see if you could get hired by the CIA."

It didn't take much convincing to get me to fill out the application and to send it in the next day. Within two weeks, I got a call from a CIA recruiter, who said he would be in Austin in a couple of weeks conducting interviews and asked if I would meet with him.

The interview took place in a hotel room on the outskirts of town. The interviewer was a pleasant fellow, who was all business after the exchange of greetings. He asked and I answered a series of questions about my past foreign travel, drug use, and non-U.S.-citizen friends and acquaintances. Once that portion of the interview was over, he asked if I would mind taking a short Arabic test over the phone. While a bit unprepared, I agreed and stumbled through a conversation with a native Arabic speaker, who could quickly tell that I was still a novice in speaking her native language. "That's it," the interviewer said. "You should hear from us in about two weeks."

The Agency was true to the recruiter's word. I received a letter from the CIA within ten days, inviting me to Washington for two days of interviews as well as medical and psychological evaluations, Arabic testing, and a polygraph test.

My medical tests went relatively smoothly. I then took a written test that was designed to provide insight into my psychological makeup. I met with a staff psychologist afterward who discussed the results with me. "You're applying to be an operations officer, Mr. Brennan, but your test results show that you are a pretty strong introvert," she said, as she stared intently at me in what I believed was an effort to observe my reaction. "Your responses also indicate that you do not seem to have the personal traits that lend themselves to meeting, developing, recruiting, and handling foreign assets."

She had me dead to rights. I had always been socially shy and introverted, and I knew it would be a stretch for me to glad-hand strangers and comfortably strike up a conversation with them, which was an absolute requirement for operations officers, the CIA employees who conduct spy work in the field. But I figured the CIA would teach me how to gain greater self-confidence in social situations and become an extrovert. I wasn't sure what she meant by my lack of operationally useful personal traits, but I desperately wanted to be hired and quickly became a bit creative.

"Yes, I agree that my natural disposition is to be an introvert," I said with a smile, trying to remain calm and not send any signals that I wasn't cut out for a career in espionage. "But I find that I can pretend to be an extrovert whenever I want. As an operations officer, my introversion will be very useful overall cover that will conceal the extroversion and the personal traits I need to employ when I want to engage in operational activity." I had no idea what I was saying. The psychologist looked at me curiously, tilting her head to one side as if that was going to make my argument any more cogent. I kept talking in hopes that I would be able to prove to her that I could shed my introversion at a moment's notice. When I finished, she simply nodded her head and said something like, "We'll see." She then wished me well in the rest of the application process.

My Arabic test and polygraph were scheduled for the following morning. Language testing involved speaking and listening comprehension as well as reading and writing ability. My Arabic was far from strong, but my pronunciation was rather good, and I had a sufficient vocabulary and understanding of verb tenses from my study at AUC and UT to get by.

I was exceptionally nervous as I entered the small room where I would take the polygraph exam. One of my UT professors who had been through a polygraph with the government had advised me to be completely honest when responding to questions. "They will know if you are holding anything back," he admonished. With a strong sense of Catholic guilt still deeply engrained in me, I knew that I would have virtually no chance of deceiving my questioner, especially after being hooked up to the machine. I had already told the CIA recruiters about my hashish-smoking in Cairo, and I made it clear that I had not done any drugs at all since then. "About a dozen times and nothing at all in the last four years," I responded to the polygrapher when he asked me about the totality and recency of my drug use.

The polygraph session turned out to be relatively uneventful except for two memorable exchanges. The first was when the polygrapher asked me if I had recently lied to anyone about something important. As soon as he finished asking the question, I had my answer. I told him that I had spoken to my parents in New Jersey the day before and, when my mother asked if I had attended Mass on Sunday, I said "yes," although I hadn't. I explained to the polygrapher that my mother was a very devout Catholic, and I did not want her to get upset and worry about my soul's salvation. With deadpan seriousness, the polygrapher listened to my explanation and then, in seeming moral disbelief, said very slowly and with emphasis, "You lie to your mother about going to church?????"

That was not the reaction I was expecting.

The second exchange was much more unnerving. And I did not know at the time that its retelling many years later would garner national media and lasting public attention. "Have you ever worked for a foreign government or for an organization dedicated to the subversion or the overthrow of the U.S. government?" I thought for a moment. Nothing came to mind, and I was about to respond in the negative when it hit me like a ton of bricks.

"Oh my God," I said to myself, as I remembered my vote in the 1976 presidential election. It was my first time voting in a presidential election, and, while only twenty-one years old, I was already disenchanted with the state of partisan politics in America. Entering the voting booth, I had no idea for whom I was going to cast my vote, but I was thrilled at the opportunity to exercise my newfound citizenship privilege. I scanned the seven names listed and stopped at the Communist Party candidate, Gus Hall. I was vaguely familiar with the name but knew nothing about him. Without giving it a second thought, I pulled the lever on my protest vote and became one of the 58,709 Americans who voted for Gus Hall that year.

I strongly suspected that the CIA polygrapher sitting across from me was going to view my vote for a Communist even more dyspeptically than he did the deception of my mother about my churchgoing record. Steeling myself for his reaction, I took a deep breath and said, "Well, I voted for the Communist Party candidate for president in 1976, but only because I was fed up with the partisan politics of both the Democrats and the Republicans. I guess I was being a bit rebellious at the time." I held my breath and looked closely at his face to see if I could detect a reaction. Nothing. He then asked if I had any other experience or interactions with the Communist Party. "None. Just that one vote," I said plaintively, fully expecting him to show disapproval if not outright disdain over my vote for Gus Hall.

He must have seen the look of fear on my face and caught me off guard by smiling just a bit and saying, "As an American, it is your absolute right to vote for whomever you choose. It will not affect your application to CIA."

I was flabbergasted at his reaction. With those two simple sentences—affirming my rights as a citizen and the CIA's respect for them—the polygrapher dispelled any concerns I had about joining an organization that had been routinely accused over the years of flouting American values and liberties. I finished the polygraph without being told whether I had passed, but I felt good about my chances.

It was more than thirty-six years later when I publicly acknowledged my vote for Gus Hall. I was on a panel on diversity in the intelligence community at the Congressional Black Caucus's annual conference in Washington, D.C., and a young African American woman asked whether her political activism on campus would hurt her chances of getting a security clearance. In response, I recounted my first polygraph experience and said that my vote for the Communist candidate for president didn't prevent me from getting hired or even becoming director of the CIA. I added that she needed to engage in appropriate political activism on campus and not bomb the administration building or participate in other such foolish actions. Despite my full-throated appeal for diversity and for young Americans to consider a career in national security, it was my vote for a Communist that was highlighted in the media and has kept my critics literally a-Twitter ever since.

I returned to Austin the day after my polygraph, and the waiting game started. Within two weeks, several of my UT professors told me they had been called by security officials in Washington who asked about my work and involvement in campus activities. My North Bergen neighbors also received visits from official-looking individuals who flashed badges and said they were conducting a background investigation on me related to a job application. "What was he like growing up in the neighborhood? Did he have any run-ins with the police? Was he involved with drugs?" This was exciting stuff for the residents of Seventy-fourth Street. They went straight to their phones to call my parents with the news.

"We were just visited by someone asking personal questions about John. Is he in trouble? Is he really looking for a job in the government? What should we say if they come back?"

I had told my parents that if anyone asked about my job pursuits, they should say that I was applying to be a foreign service officer with the Department of State. My mother, concerned that she might undermine my chances of being hired or get in trouble with the feds if she bollixed the directions, wrote herself a script and kept it next to the phone. Kathy's father, ill with cancer at the time, found the directions a bit confusing and did not want to deal with follow-up questions. Whenever an inquisitive family member or friend asked about my employment pursuits, he would simply say, "John has applied to the

Post Office." He figured that pointing to the federal government, albeit an entirely different agency, was the safest course.

Every day that passed that spring following my battery of tests, I felt that I was on a razor's edge of realizing my dream, or not, of working in a field that would allow me to continue to experience the world. I knew that a final decision was going to take time, as I had been told by my recruiters that, depending on one's previous travels and activities, background investigations could take months, sometimes even years. With my hopes of becoming a CIA officer raised, I made plans to curtail my graduate study at UT at the end of the academic year, departing with a master of arts degree in government.

Kathy and I flew to New Jersey in late May in advance of my sister Kathleen's wedding at the end of the month. While in New Jersey, we alternated between staying at my parents' house and at Kathy's father's house. To pick up a few extra dollars during the summer break, I sought out odd jobs for neighbors, who charitably obliged by finding some work for me. I was near the top of a twenty-foot ladder painting the trim of a neighbor's house when my mother appeared below with a dish towel in one hand and the just-delivered mail in the other. "You received a letter from the government, and it looks official," she said as she waved it at me. I quickly descended the ladder and took the letter from my mother, opening it in front of her. Scanning it, I saw the word "Congratulations!" and reference to "GS-9," and a salary of "$17,340."

"I made it!" I yelled, as I hugged and kissed my mom. I ran across the street and up the steps of my parents' house to call Kathy, who was visiting with her father. "We did it! We did it!" I said breathlessly. "We're going to Washington!"

6

OUT OF OPERATIONS

From the moment I received the firm offer of CIA employment, Kathy and I talked constantly about how best to make the transition to living in the Washington, D.C., area. After canvassing available living accommodations, Kathy and I decided to rent a one-bedroom apartment near the heavily trafficked and frequently congested Seven Corners intersection in Falls Church, Virginia. While a bit expensive for our budget, the Oakwood Apartments were a favorite for newly arriving professionals in the area, especially those going to work for "the government," because the apartment complex offered month-to-month leases.

"I start work with the U.S. government in Washington, D.C., on Monday," I said to family and friends at my grandmother's eighty-fifth birthday party in New Jersey, adhering to the Agency's admonition not to reveal my soon-to-be CIA affiliation.

In my employment letter, I had been directed to report to the Arlington Chamber of Commerce building at 8:30 A.M. and, if driving, to park several blocks away, ostensibly to avoid aggravating residents living in the area. The directive to park a distance from the Chamber, I quickly found out, was designed to prevent my cover and the cover of my fellow classmates—and therefore our clandestine careers—from being blown during our first days as CIA officers. While the fact that the CIA was using the building for administrative and training purposes was not openly acknowledged at the time, Soviet intelligence services had long surveilled buildings they knew or suspected of being used by the CIA or FBI. The Soviets were inveterate collectors and hoarders. Intelligence files at the Soviet embassy in Washington were full of photos of people and license plates observed near such buildings and even discarded restaurant receipts found nearby.

Ever since my days as a *Hudson Dispatch* paper boy in North Bergen, I have had an obsessive compulsiveness about punctuality when it comes to meetings, appointments, dinner reservations, and especially fresh starts. Monday, August 5, 1980, was no different. I left our Oakwood apartment nearly two hours before my designated arrival time, even though the Chamber building was just twenty minutes away. There was no way I was going to arrive late on the first day of my CIA career.

I took a rather circuitous route to the Chamber, just in case the Soviets were already onto me. "This clandestine stuff is cool," I thought. Dutifully, I parked on a tree-lined residential street several blocks away. Unlike current-day Arlington, the neighborhood surrounding the Chamber in 1980 was relatively sedate, with only a few eateries or coffee shops within walking distance, none of which opened before 7:00 A.M. After meandering aimlessly for almost an hour, I was finally able to buy a coffee from the first sleepy-eyed merchant to open. Forty minutes later I entered the ground floor of the Chamber.

I was directed to a room set up with tables and chairs that could accommodate the forty career trainees, commonly referred to as CTs, who would be administered the oath of office that day. I knew only one other individual in the class, a UT-Austin colleague who also had just finished his master's program in government. White males made up about 90 percent of the class, several of whom were already Agency employees and were transferring into the yearlong career training program. A small number of CTs in the class had been hired to be analysts, scientists, or technical experts. Like me, everyone else was slated to become a case officer in the Directorate of Operations.

Our class was formally welcomed by the same CIA recruitment officer I had met in Austin several months earlier, although he introduced himself this time using a different name, which I presumed was his real one. I tried to catch his eye, thinking that he would recognize me from our discussion in the spring. He didn't.

The oath of office was administered midmorning by a senior executive from the Directorate of Administration (since renamed the Directorate of Support), the Agency component responsible for ensuring that the CIA has the resources, personnel, and support system needed to carry out its statutory authorities. It was the first time I was ever asked to raise my right hand and affirm an oath of allegiance to the United States of America. There was something very solemn, almost sacred, about the occasion. Many years later, when I would administer the same oath of office to an incoming class of CIA employees every month in front of the CIA's Memorial Wall, I would recall my own oath of office and the strong sense of duty and professional obligation I felt:

> I, John Brennan, do solemnly swear
> that I will support and defend the Constitution of the
>   United States
> against all enemies, foreign and domestic;
> that I will bear true faith and allegiance to the same;
> that I take this obligation freely,
> without any mental reservation or purpose of evasion;
> and that I will well and faithfully discharge
> the duties of the office on which I am about to enter:
> So help me God.

For the next nine and a half days, my fellow CTs and I were given briefings on how to handle payroll options, banking issues, health and life insurance plans, and other routine matters affecting our daily lives, and those of our spouses, in a manner that would not reveal our CIA employment. Although the cover requirements were a bit complicated, the yet-to-emerge Internet was not a factor at the time, so we mainly needed guidance on how to fill out application forms and how to respond to queries about our employment status. In addition to this important administrivia, we received briefings on major intelligence successes and failures as well as historic counterintelligence cases. It also was a time to get to know and develop friendships with classmates who had to deal with many of the same challenges associated with moving to the Washington, D.C., area for the first time.

At the end of the chamber of commerce orientation program, I began the first of two "interim" assignments, with each lasting about twelve to fourteen weeks. For the initial interim, each CT was assigned to the CIA component that most closely matched their previous academic or professional experience or language expertise. On account of my study of the Middle East and my Arabic language training, I was sent to the prestigious Near East Division of the Directorate of Operations. "NE," as it was known, was the organizational home of some of the CIA's most colorful characters as well as its most adventurous and courageous operatives. In the several decades since the CIA's founding in 1947, the Middle East had been beset by four wars between Israel and its Arab neighbors, civil strife, political coups, terrorism, and Cold War intrigue between Washington and Moscow. In each chapter of the region's history during that time, the CIA played an important role. Moreover, when I entered the CIA, NE had been heavily involved for more than a year in trying to help free the fifty-two American diplomats and citizens who were still being held hostage at the U.S. embassy in Tehran. When I joined the CIA, it was an honor for me to become part of an agency that was integral to keeping America safe and secure.

I served my NE interim working on North Africa, which covered the Arab countries of Morocco, Tunisia, Algeria, and Libya. I was exposed to sensitive CIA human and technical collection capabilities abroad as well as the nature and extent of the Agency's liaison relationships with intelligence and security services worldwide. I became familiar with CIA terminology and phrases as well as the major elements of the organization. The CIA's two largest directorates, then and now, are Operations and Analysis. Operations officers are involved in the clandestine collection of human intelligence and have primary responsibility for liaising with foreign intelligence services and conducting covert action. Analysts sift through mountains of information collected by a variety of means and produce assessments for senior officials. Within the Directorate of Operations (DO), there were two major professional categories: "case officers," trained to spot, assess, develop, recruit, and handle foreign nationals who spy for the CIA, and "reports officers," since renamed "collection management officers," focused on the processing, refining, and distribution of clandestinely acquired intelligence obtained by case officers from foreign spies. Reports officers also played a key role evaluating the reliability of a source and the quality and accuracy of a source's information.

At the end of my first interim, I was scheduled to go to "the Farm," the CIA's premier training facility, located in the woodlands of Virginia, for extended operational training along with the rest of my CT classmates. The Farm is where many generations of CIA officers have learned the tradecraft of espionage and intelligence, earned their weapons qualifications, and mastered the art and skills of defensive and countersurveillance driving techniques. I was very much looking forward to heading off to the Farm and was disappointed when I learned that my training would be delayed by several months due to a shortage of instructors. As one of the youngest CTs in my class, I drew the short straw and was told that I would go to training as soon as I finished my second interim assignment. Having enjoyed my NE Division experience on North Africa, I asked to serve my second interim assignment in the Directorate of Operations' analytic counterpart, which at the time was called the National Foreign Assessments Center. I had interacted frequently with the analysts working on North Africa in the previous months and very much respected their in-depth understanding of the history, politics, and culture of the region. I was given an interim in the Office of Political Analysis (OPA), which was headed by a very talented senior officer, Helene Boatner, who served as one of the original trailblazers for women in the Agency.

My interim assignment in the analytic ranks exposed me to a distinctly different mission and culture from what I had experienced in my few short months on the operational side of the house. No longer working in an environment that was replete with pseudonyms, cryptonyms, false personas, and an overriding "need to know," I was encouraged and expected to consume as much as I could about the political institutions, players, and developments in the region and their relevance to U.S. interests in the broader Middle East. I was given the responsibility to write several items for the CIA's daily publication—the National Intelligence Digest, called the "NID"—as well as longer assessments on Libyan tribes and Muammar Qadhafi's relationship with terrorist organizations.

By the middle of my second interim assignment, I started to wonder whether I was better suited for a career in analysis than one in operations. As a fledgling analyst, I enjoyed the intellectual challenges associated with piecing together and sorting out the wheat from the chaff found in clandestinely acquired intelligence from human and technical sources, in diplomatic reporting, and in open-source information, which often were inconsistent in their representations of reality. Unlike in graduate school, when I would write papers that would be read only by professors and, on occasion, fellow students, I was excited by the opportunity to author analytic products, even pieces consisting of only a few sentences, that would be read by individuals—up to and including the president—who actually were involved in shaping and implementing U.S. foreign policy

It was during this period of career introspection that I seized an opportunity to attend a weeklong course at the Farm, where I had an exchange with a longtime and very seasoned case officer. "Jack" had served multiple tours overseas, mostly in Southeast Asia, including in Vietnam during the height of the war, when the CIA had hundreds of officers working hand in glove with the U.S. military and South Vietnamese intelligence and security services. Jack was in his late forties but looked much older. The story going around the Farm was that Jack had a serious drinking problem and had come back to the States to dry out. One look at Jack's face gave credence to the story. For my training course, Jack led a small classroom discussion on the challenges associated with handling recruited assets who, for whatever reason, decide that they want to extricate themselves from their CIA relationship. Jack related a few stories from his own experiences and how he was able to keep his assets on board. We were all listening intently when one of my classmates posed a probing question. "Let's say that the asset is providing important information to us, but he is genuinely concerned about his security and afraid of getting caught by the local intelligence service. He tells us he wants to end his relationship with us. What do we do?"

To Jack's credit, he gave a thoughtful initial response. "You do what you can to put the asset's mind at ease, including taking additional precautions to prevent his work with us from coming to the attention of the locals." But then he went on. "And that is why it is important early in the relationship to get your asset to sign a receipt for his pay or even just for the reimbursement of his expenses. If he gets cold feet later on, you can remind him that you have that signed receipt and that it would be very unfortunate for him and his family if that receipt were to fall into the wrong hands—the hands of those who could give him a hard time."

What!?! Did I hear that correctly? Did Jack just recommend that a case officer should coerce an asset into continuing a relationship with the Agency by implying that the Agency might expose him? I couldn't restrain myself. "That sounds like blackmail," I blurted out. Jack turned toward me and just glared for a moment. My use of the word "blackmail" had clearly hit a nerve, and his anger showed.

"We're talking about doing what is necessary to keep our country safe," he said sternly. "You need to be tough if you want to be a case officer." He then used disparaging terms to refer to Department of State employees as well as Agency analysts, comparing them unfavorably to case officers who must deal with the "hard stuff."

I was taken aback by the vehemence of Jack's response. I didn't say anything more and left the classroom shaking my head in disbelief. I knew that the CIA's work was critically important to our country's security, but I did not believe that we should coerce individuals to cooperate with us. Intimidation, bullying, and threats of physical violence were tactics I had associated with Soviet, Chinese, and other intelligence services, not the CIA. Was Jack telling me that my impression was wrong?

As I walked back to my room, I remembered what the CIA staff psychologist had said to me during my application process less than a year earlier about not having the "personal traits" needed for operational activities. "Is this what she meant?" I thought to myself. That night, I tossed in my bunk, agonizing over whether I had what it took to be a successful CIA case officer, or even whether I wanted to be. Literally overnight, my view of the Agency grew very dark. If I slept, I did so only briefly. By morning, I had made my decision. I wanted out of operations and would submit a formal request to transfer to the analytic side of the agency.

My decision to leave operations had been building for some time. I had two earlier memorable experiences during my CT program that raised suspicions in my own mind as to whether I was cut out for the life of a sleuth. The first occurred early on, during my Near East Division interim. My boss approached me one morning and said that the

division was looking for someone who could escort a visiting senior
Arab military officer and his family for a few days while they went
shopping and sightseeing in northern Virginia. I was told nothing
about the military officer other than he was an important CIA source
and was accompanied by his wife and two young children. "Are you
interested, John?" my branch chief asked.

"You bet!" I said, eager to participate, if even marginally, in an
operational activity. I was delighted when my boss told me that I
would need to wear a light disguise during the escort activity to
conceal my identity.

I was directed to report to the CIA's disguise unit, which was in
another building in the Washington, D.C., area. As soon as I entered
the unit's interior office, I felt like I had walked into a makeup artist's studio in Hollywood. The room was full of all sorts of disguise
"stuff"—wigs, false mustaches and beards, full-face masks, eyeglasses,
hats, and counters covered with makeup, mascara, and powder. "Take
a seat, young man," said the CIA officer who would be responsible
for making me look like someone else, or at least not like myself.
He observed me from different angles before he started to pull out
a few items from his collection. A dark brown wig with sideburns,
tortoiseshell-rimmed tinted eyeglasses, and a lift to place in the heel
of one of my shoes to give me a different gait as I walked. When
he finished darkening my eyebrows and reddish-blond mustache to
match my newfound hair color, he took a step back and said "Voilà!"
to the apparent satisfaction of his colleague standing nearby. I had
to admit, I looked quite different—older and more sophisticated.
Well, at least older.

As I was leaving, the makeup artist advised me to wear the disguise a few times in public. He also said I should practice putting
it on and taking it off in my car so that I would get comfortable
transitioning to my new physical appearance and persona. The first
few times I put the disguise on at home, Kathy couldn't control her
laughter, which convinced me that I probably should do my initial

practice sessions without her. After a few dry runs, I felt increasingly comfortable as well as adept in donning and removing the wig, the glasses, and even the makeup.

On the appointed day, I accompanied a senior NE case officer to Dulles Airport to pick up the source and his family and drive them to their hotel. They were eager to visit an American shopping mall, so I drove them to the nearby Tysons Corner Center. The source thanked me profusely for the assistance in shepherding his family around town. He spoke passable English, and I didn't reveal that I knew some Arabic, so I was able to listen in a bit on the family's conversation. The source told his family that I was their bodyguard, evoking an "Alhamdulillah!" (Praise be to God) from his shy and somewhat nervous wife.

All went well until the final day of their visit. I drove the family once again to Tysons Corner Center and pointed out a specific store that they wanted to visit. I then left them alone, promising to pick them up a few hours later after they had time to shop and have lunch, which also gave me time to go back to Langley, remove my disguise, and get some work done. On my return to the mall, an accident on Route 123 slowed me down. Arriving with only a few minutes to spare, I drove to an empty corner of the parking lot and hurriedly put on my disguise again. I then bolted out of the car and made it inside the mall just in time to see the family arrive at the appointed meeting spot. I waved and motioned them to follow me. As I walked through the mall, I noticed that several shoppers seemed to be taking extra notice of me, as did the children when we got to the car. At the end of the short drive to their hotel, I bid them goodbye, as it was the last day of my escort/bodyguard duty. The source expressed his gratitude but appeared nervous as he hurried his children out of the car and into their hotel.

Once the hotel was out of sight, I pulled into a nearby empty parking lot to remove my disguise. Before doing so, I took a quick look at myself in the rearview mirror.

"Oh, shit! Oh, shit!" I said aloud to myself.

In my earlier haste to put on my disguise, I apparently put the stems of my eyeglasses under rather than over the stays that were inside the sideburns of my wig. As a result, I had been wearing the wig with its sideburns sticking almost straight out from the sides of my face. A wave of deep embarrassment immediately consumed me. I'm on my first operational mission, and I wind up looking like Sally Field in *The Flying Nun,* the TV show of my youth.

At least it wasn't a windy day.

A second experience was only slightly less embarrassing. Later in my CT program, I participated in a training exercise in Washington, D.C. An experienced case officer was about to travel to a post overseas that had an especially challenging operating environment. American diplomats and CIA officers had recently been subjected to increasingly aggressive surveillance from the local intelligence and security services. All outgoing CIA officers, therefore, needed extensive additional countersurveillance training before arriving in that country. I was asked to be part of a four-person team that would conduct discreet surveillance of the soon-to-be-assigned case officer, who would try to identify the surveillants while he spent several hours shopping and sightseeing in Washington. Despite my lack of surveillance training, I jumped at the opportunity.

The exercise took place on a brisk but sunny morning in late February. I never lost track of the surveillance target yet kept what I thought was a safe distance from him. I never detected his eyes on me, as I tried to blend into the crowd of shoppers, government workers, and school groups that were milling about. When the exercise concluded, I felt pretty good about my fledgling surveillance skills, believing that the case officer never spotted me.

The case officer met first with his countersurveillance instructor to give a readout of what and whom he had observed. Then we all gathered, and the instructor told us that the case officer had spotted every one of his surveillants. The case officer explained how he had done so. Embarrassingly, he started with me, as he said I was the first he detected.

"I noticed you as soon as I left the bookstore," he said. "You were the only person I saw not wearing an overcoat, and your light tan suit on a cold February day was noticeable. For the rest of the morning, it wasn't difficult to find you, or should I say, find your light tan suit, with my peripheral vision when you showed up in subsequent locations."

Seasonally appropriate attire obviously was not my forte, nor was my ability to surveil clandestinely.

With my ego tarnished, I then listened to the case officer recount how he had identified the other three members of the surveillance team. I didn't feel great about my performance that day, but I developed a very healthy appreciation and respect for the importance of countersurveillance training and for the quality of the tradecraft skills acquired by Agency officers. Numerous times during my CIA career, especially when I was director, I was awestruck when I was briefed on the exceptionally ingenious, courageous, and remarkably successful instances of CIA officers defeating the surveillance efforts of foreign intelligence and security services so that they could meet surreptitiously and, most importantly, safely with foreign contacts.

My internal Agency transfer from the Directorate of Operations to the Directorate of Intelligence (the new name for the National Foreign Assessment Center) went smoothly at the end of my one-year CT program. My Directorate of Operations bosses recognized that I was a better match for the analytic side of the house, and the Directorate of Intelligence was eager to hire a fully cleared new employee with a year of organizational and relevant regional experience already under his belt. I was especially pleased to learn that my new home office would be the Office of Near Eastern and South Asian Analysis—known by its acronym NESA—in the Directorate of Intelligence and that Bob Ames, a legendary DO/NE officer with deep expertise on Palestinian, Yemeni, and broader Middle Eastern issues, had been appointed as its first director. It was very unusual for a DO officer to head up a major analytic component, but Bob previously had served as the national intelligence officer for the Middle East on the National Intelligence Council and had gained broad respect inside and outside the CIA for his knowledge and creativity. Bob's appointment brought immediate gravitas and credibility to the new office, and the enthusiasm among NESA troops for his selection was palpable. NESA seemed to be the perfect organizational fit for me. It was, and I would spend the bulk of the next fifteen years of my Agency career learning the craft of intelligence analysis from my NESA colleagues.

7

JOHN OF ARABIA

It was during my first year as an Agency employee that I realized that my personal and professional lives would be forever intertwined. I had been warned by some former Agency employees I had met while in Austin that the insular and secretive lives of CIA officers can take a toll even on the best of relationships. This is exactly what happened to Kathy and me soon after I started working at the Agency. I was spending long hours at work and went off to attend multiday training courses outside the D.C. area, which cut down significantly on the time I could spend with Kathy, who had a full-time job at a fitness club and taught aerobics classes. Even when we were together, I did not tell Kathy what I was doing at the CIA in fear of violating some security regulation prohibiting discussion of classified information with uncleared individuals, even a spouse. Kathy and I started to drift apart, and by early 1981, we had separated. I moved into an apartment near Bailey's Crossroads in Falls Church, and Kathy shared a house in McLean with two other women. It was during this time that I thought a lot about how individuals involved in intelligence work, especially Agency officers serving abroad who, by necessity, spend so much time engaged in clandestine activities, need to tend to their family responsibilities as well as their professional duties.

Kathy and I worked hard over the next year to reconcile, discussing how we could make our marriage a success despite the challenges of my profession. We both knew that the long hours would continue, but I needed to make a better effort to talk about my work, without getting into classified information, so that she felt more a part of my life. It was a lesson that I had learned and that I shared with new employees years later when I was director. "You will have enormous professional responsibilities in the years ahead," I would tell them. "But make sure you don't neglect your responsibilities on the home front, as your loved ones will be the greatest source of support and inspiration for what will be a demanding profession."

Kathy and I talked about ending the separation, but her decision was far harder than mine because of the path my Agency career had already started to take. In early spring 1982, I had been selected to serve a two-year rotation with the Department of State as a political officer at the U.S. embassy in Saudi Arabia. I was eager to live in the Middle East once again, especially if I could do so as a bona fide American diplomat. Realizing that I was asking Kathy to join me for a two-year assignment in the most socially conservative country in the Middle East, I tried to sweeten the pot by promising that we would find time to travel and save money while living abroad, which would allow us to buy a house in the expensive D.C. market when we returned home. Kathy understood I was presenting a glass-more-than-half-full picture of a posting in the Saudi kingdom. After giving it careful consideration, Kathy agreed that we would make another go of our marriage, even if it meant doing so in an extremely hot and far-off land. Each day since then, I have been eternally grateful and fortunate that she decided to give us a second chance.

To prepare for my tour in Saudi Arabia, I took full-time Arabic language training for five months at the same building in Arlington where I had spent my first two weeks as an Agency employee. Each day, I would ride to class on my brand-new Yamaha XS 400 Maxim motorcycle, a very unexpected and much treasured gift from Kathy. Most days, I would put in my diamond earring only for the ride home, as I apparently was not brave enough at the time to expose my Easy Rider inner self to my Agency colleagues.

During the months I was in full-time Arabic training, I would go into NESA on weekends to read intelligence assessments and to catch up on dynamic developments in the Middle East. There was so much to digest, as a flurry of events, including the assassination of Egypt's president, Anwar Sadat, in October 1981 and Israel's invasion of Lebanon in June 1982, had major repercussions and implications for U.S. national security interests in the region. One week after Israel's move into Lebanon, King Khalid of Saudi Arabia died of a heart attack, and his half brother Crown Prince Fahd ascended to the throne. The sudden change of leadership in Saudi Arabia prompted me to spend most of the following weekend in NESA so that I could understand how Fahd's elevation was likely to affect Saudi domestic and foreign policies. As I was concentrating on opening the combination lock on one of NESA's doors on the sixth floor of CIA headquarters early on Saturday morning, I heard the determined cadence of footsteps behind me.

"Brennan."

Turning around, I saw that it was a broadly grinning Bob Ames, in his signature tinted glasses.

"We decide to send you to Saudi Arabia, and you change kings before you even arrive. What gives?" he joked. Bob then switched to Arabic, attempting to find out how proficient I had become as a result of my language training. A few sentences were exchanged, and then he quickly opened the combination lock on his door while I continued to fumble with mine. As I watched him walk into his office, I wondered whether he knew just how impressive he was and how much his NESA troops respected him. I would never get the chance to tell him.

When it became time to head out on the new assignment, Kathy and I flew out of JFK Airport after visiting with our New Jersey families and, after an overnight stay in Germany, boarded another flight bound for Saudi Arabia. It was midnight when our flight touched down in Jeddah, the port city on the Red Sea where the U.S. embassy and all other embassies in Saudi Arabia had been located since the founding of the kingdom in 1932. Jeddah had been selected by the Al Sa'ud ruling family to serve as the kingdom's initial diplomatic capital, as the city had long been the region's commercial hub and had a history of hosting non-Saudis. Consequently, the social environment of Jeddah was more tolerant of foreign influences, including diplomats, than Riyadh, the national capital—the usual location for embassies in other countries. Despite Jeddah's unbearable humidity, which made Saudi Arabia's daily heat even more onerous, Kathy and I were pleased to be living in what came closest to a cosmopolitan city in Saudi Arabia and near the beautiful beaches along the Red Sea. We arrived in 1982, several years after the Saudi government issued a directive that all foreign embassies were required to move by October 1, 1984, to the newly established diplomatic quarter in Riyadh, which culturally sequestered embassy officials and their families while facilitating diplomatic interaction with Saudi government ministries located in the capital. When Kathy and I departed Jeddah in early October of 1984, we were among the very last embassy personnel to be resident there. The embassy building and compound in Jeddah transitioned to a U.S. consulate when the new embassy in Riyadh opened for business.

Serving as a political officer at the U.S. embassy in Jeddah was an invaluable opportunity at such an early stage of my career to learn how embassies function and how the different embassy components interact with one another and with host government officials.

Considering my background in intelligence and analysis, I was given the responsibility of briefing U.S. Ambassador Richard Murphy each morning on the latest intelligence on regional and global events that the embassy received via cables from Washington. Ambassador Murphy was widely recognized as one of State's most respected and polished Arabists—he was appointed assistant secretary of state for Near Eastern and South Asian affairs midway during my Jeddah tour—and it was rather humbling for me, as a national security novice, to provide him my own analysis about what was happening in the very complicated world of the Middle East. Murphy detected my reticence early on and would ask me questions every morning simply to get me to feel more comfortable sharing my views. He was a wonderful mentor.

It was during my time in Jeddah that I first met Alan Fiers, the CIA's senior intelligence liaison official to the Saudi government. Alan was one of the most talented, creative, and hard-charging intelligence officers with whom I had the opportunity to work. Since I got to know Alan fairly well while I was in Jeddah, I followed his CIA career closely afterward, especially when he became embroiled in the Iran-Contra affair several years later. Alan eventually pleaded guilty to two misdemeanor counts of withholding information from Congress, for which—in consideration of his cooperation with the investigation—a judge suspended the imposition of any sentence beyond a fifty-dollar fine and one hundred hours of community service. Alan also gave a very public accounting of his actions as well as his regrets during his open testimony, which was related to the confirmation hearing that same year for Bob Gates as director of the CIA. He was ultimately pardoned by George H. W. Bush. I've watched Alan's 1990 testimony in front of that committee several times over the years and consider it to be one of the most honest, forthright, and compelling accounts of the challenges associated with being a CIA operations officer. Alan acknowledged that he let his interest in "winning" contests against American adversaries color his judgment and his actions. Such honesty in CIA officers should be the norm, not the exception.

My political officer portfolio at the embassy was intentionally very broad, and I was regularly encouraged to get "out and about" so that I could learn as much as possible about the kingdom, its people, and its politics during my tour. Many days I would visit the campus of King Abd al-Aziz University. I later learned that not-yet-a-terrorist Usama Bin Ladin had been a student there a few years before. I befriended several Saudi and Palestinian professors and would talk to them fairly regularly about a range of topics such as the political views of Saudi students, tensions in the kingdom between the forces of tradition and modernity, and prevailing attitudes toward Saudi Arabia's relationship with the United States. Many of the professors had studied in the United States and enjoyed the free-flowing banter. My discussions at the university were complemented by meetings with Jeddah-based publishers and journalists from Saudi and Arab newspapers. In those sessions, I competed with my interlocutors to ask the most questions, as they all seemed eager to pick the brain of a young American diplomat from the U.S. embassy. Only occasionally would I call upon the Saudi Foreign Ministry's office in Jeddah, usually at a level befitting my status as a third secretary, the lowest rung on the diplomatic ladder.

I was careful during my discussions with Saudis to tread lightly on matters dealing with the royal family or the intelligence and security services, as I didn't want to stir up concerns or conspiracy theories about my intentions and affiliation. Nevertheless, I read extensively about the Al Sa'ud and kept a large handwritten spreadsheet in my embassy office that allowed me to keep track of the government positions, business activities, and marriage ties of hundreds of princes who were direct descendants of the kingdom's founder, King Abd al-Aziz, as well as of prominent members of the collateral branches of the royal family. The genealogy of the Al Sa'ud became a lifelong hobby of mine, which served me well throughout my national security career.

One of the most fascinating experiences of my tour in Jeddah was a weeklong camping trip that Kathy and I, along with my visiting brother Tommy and several friends, took to remote sections of the Hijaz and the Asir, the western and southwestern regions of Saudi Arabia. The Hijaz and the Asir are notable for their breathtaking escarpments as well as their wandering Red Sea coastlines with beautiful coral reefs, which were ideal for scuba diving and snorkeling. We made the trip during the Islamic month of Dhul al-hijrah, which is when the annual hajj gets under way. As non-Muslims, we were not permitted to enter Mecca, but we took some back roads that skirted the city's perimeter, which allowed us to see the steady stream of vehicles pouring into the center of gravity of the Islamic faith.

More than a million and a half pilgrims, mostly from abroad, had come to Mecca that year to fulfill their religious obligation to visit the birthplace of the Prophet Muhammad at least once in their lifetime. National Guard personnel in machine-gun-mounted jeeps were visible at all checkpoints; the Saudi government wanted no recurrence of the violent takeover of the Great Mosque by Saudi extremists, which had left many hundreds dead and many more injured only four years before. As we drove away, we could see the huge sand cloud in the sky over the city, as pilgrims performed *tawaf,* walking seven times around the cubic structure of the Kaaba—the holiest site in all Islam.

Wherever we camped, we would inevitably invite the interest of local tribesmen, who also were camping under the stars. With their camels tethered to their Toyota pickup trucks and their gas generators cranking away to support their portable TVs and tape cassette players, they would first observe us from a distance before approaching with words of welcome and offers of assistance. Much like my encounter eight years before in Cairo, the tribesmen were pleased to hear that we were Americans who were interested in experiencing life in Saudi Arabia. At no time did we ever feel in danger. Indeed, it was during this trip and my subsequent visits to tribes throughout Saudi Arabia that I experienced renowned Bedouin hospitality, born out of the custom that nomadic life depends on the kindness of others. Many years later, I would think back on these times and the Bedouin tradition of welcoming strangers, and how stark a contrast it was to the murderous actions of the more than a dozen 9/11 hijackers who hailed from these same tribes.

My tour in Jeddah also gave me deep appreciation for the dedication and importance of the work of the locally hired foreign service nationals (FSNs) who serve at U.S. embassies and consulates worldwide. FSNs work in a variety of capacities—motor pool, security, logistics, mail rooms, facilities maintenance, food service, and telephone operators, to name just a few. Many FSNs work for decades at our diplomatic facilities in the hopes of one day obtaining immigrant visas that would allow them to emigrate to the United States with their families. In some countries, FSNs are subjected to significant pressure from local intelligence and security services, which seek inside information about the work and activities of U.S. diplomatic personnel. Honoring their obligations to the U.S. government while staying on the good side of local officials often can be challenging.

While in Jeddah, I developed a close personal friendship with Ali al-Babkri, a senior FSN who worked directly for the embassy's regional security officer (RSO). Among other duties, Ali oversaw the unarmed Bangladeshi security personnel who controlled access to the embassy compound and inspected all vehicles that were allowed through the gates. Ali was born in the mid-1920s in the Hadhramaut region of southern Yemen, where the Bin Ladin family has its origins. By 1940, Ali had made his way to Singapore—at the time, a British protectorate, like Yemen—where he joined his Hadhrami relatives who had prospered from their work on the seafaring trade routes of South and Southeast Asia. But when the Japanese invaded and ousted the British from Singapore in early 1942, Ali became a prisoner of the Japanese army and was sent off to the jungles of Burma to join the ranks of other Asian laborers. At one point, Ali was assigned to the detail working on a bridge being built over the Kwai River. Most days, his work consisted mainly of carrying the bodies of dead and nearly dead laborers and Allied POWs to mass graves. For three years, a steady diet of turbid water and spoiled rice, which produced regular bouts of cholera and dysentery, turned Ali into a near skeleton. By the time of Japan's surrender in 1945, Ali's flesh and eyesight were nearly gone, as was his spirit.

Ali eventually made his way home to Yemen and was nursed back to a semblance of health by his family. He owed his life to America, he said, because it was American forces that brought Imperial Japan to its knees and gave Ali his freedom. So, he set off for Saudi Arabia and he found work at the U.S. embassy in Jeddah by the late 1960s. "The best decision I ever made," Ali would tell me years later. "I love my work, and I love America."

There are many, many other FSNs around the globe who, like Ali, have their own unique stories to tell about how they came to work at a U.S. embassy or consulate and what it means to them to work in support of America's role in the world. And whenever I bow my head in commemoration of American personnel who have perished in terrorist attacks against U.S. diplomatic facilities abroad, I also think about the thousands of FSNs who have died in the service of a nation not their own but for which they gave their lives.

I was heartbroken when I learned on a visit to Jeddah in the early 1990s that Ali had been struck and killed by a car while crossing a street near the American compound. Ali's poor eyesight finally caught up to him. May he rest in eternal peace.

On April 18, 1983, I had just returned to my office after having lunch with Kathy at the embassy snack bar when word started to trickle in through official channels about a bombing that had occurred at the U.S. embassy in Beirut. Whenever an attack takes place against U.S. diplomatic facilities or personnel, all U.S. embassies and consulates are directed to step up their security to guard against potential follow-on attacks. I stayed at the embassy late that evening, waiting without success for word about American casualties before deciding to head home for dinner with Kathy.

I arrived early the following morning and immediately retrieved the cables from Washington that had been slotted for me. They detailed the extent of the devastation and the dozens of casualties, including American personnel. As I perused a list of those killed, I recognized the names of a few CIA officers from my time at headquarters. And then I read the name "Robert Ames."

"Robert Ames?" I said to myself. "It can't be Bob. He should be at Langley."

But it was Bob. He was on a short official visit to Beirut when the explosives-laden van detonated, collapsing much of the embassy building. Bob was in the stairwell and was killed by the concussion of the blast. When his body was identified, no wound was visible. It was the first time (but sadly not the last) I personally knew someone killed in a terrorist attack, making the violence of the Middle East that I had read about for so many years much too real. Bob was six months short of retirement when he was killed. His star is one of many on the CIA's Memorial Wall that has special meaning to me. I would see Bob's widow, Yvonne, and some of Bob and Yvonne's children and grandchildren at the annual memorial ceremony at CIA headquarters honoring the fallen when I became director thirty years later. And when I did, it would bring back bittersweet memories of Bob's last words to me in the NESA corridor and my regret at never having the opportunity to tell him just how much I respected him.

Our two years in Jeddah went by much too quickly. I thoroughly enjoyed my embassy responsibilities, and I felt that I had been well schooled in the politics, culture, and people of the enigmatic desert kingdom as well as in the underpinnings of the U.S.-Saudi relationship. But Kathy and I were ready to get back to the States. Like all women in Saudi Arabia at the time, Kathy had not been allowed to drive—at least not legally—during our tour, and while Jeddah was less austere than Riyadh, it was still rather restrictive in its cultural mores. Moreover, we were looking forward to buying that house I had talked about when I made the hard sell about Jeddah to Kathy a couple of years before. We even talked about it being time to start thinking about having children.

8

ANALYZE THIS

Kathy and I were excited to be back in the States. With our housing expenses in Jeddah paid by the U.S. government, except for our very costly international telephone bills, we had been able to save enough money for the down payment on a town house in Annandale, Virginia. Kathy went back to work full-time as the athletic director of the McLean Racquet and Health Club, and I returned to the Office of Near East and South Asian Analysis at CIA headquarters to serve as an analyst on Saudi Arabia and North and South Yemen. NESA's new director was Bob Layton, a very capable manager who had served as Bob Ames's deputy, and his excellent interpersonal skills and encouragement of young analysts eased my transition back to a desk job. While I wrote some items for the CIA's daily publications, my NESA managers were most interested in having me draft longer analytic assessments on social and political dynamics in Saudi Arabia that were distributed to policy makers and Saudi watchers throughout the government. As a result of my two years living and working in Saudi Arabia, I frequently was trotted out by my supervisors to brief senior U.S. officials and military officers who were scheduled to travel to Jeddah, Riyadh, or both. I was encouraged to tell them what daily life was like in the kingdom, for Saudis and for Americans. I began to feel more like a travel agent and tour guide than an analyst.

As I was becoming more familiar with the life of a CIA headquarters analyst, Kathy and I were settling into our northern Virginia home. We decided it was time to start a family, and our son Kyle was born in April 1986. I had always wondered what it would be like to be someone's father, but I never imagined just how exciting and humbling it would be to bring another life into this world. And when Kyle's twin sisters, Kelly and Jaclyn, were born prematurely, at twenty-eight weeks, less than two years later, I realized just how precious and fragile human life can be. After two months in the hospital, the girls were finally able to come home. When they did, they each were connected to blinking heart monitors that fascinated Kyle but terrorized Kathy and me whenever the alarms went off, which usually was in the middle of the night. I later looked back at this experience as good practice for those numerous occasions when I would be awakened by a phone call about some national security crisis that needed my immediate attention. No subsequent phone call, however, raised my blood pressure as high, made my adrenaline flow as rapidly, or made me move as quickly as I did when I heard those dreaded "beeps" on the second floor of our town house in Annandale.

I was fortunate to be asked a few months after Kyle was born to serve as principal drafter of an intelligence community "special national intelligence estimate" that would be titled: "Implications of an Iranian Victory." An "estimate" represents the intelligence community's most authoritative and coordinated judgments on a specific national security issue, usually one of significant concern to policy makers. In this case, the war between Iran and Iraq had been raging for six years, and Iran had been steadily reversing many of Iraq's earlier territorial gains, raising concerns in Washington, as well as in the region, that Tehran might emerge victorious. To gauge the potential impact of such an outcome, I traveled to Iraq, Jordan, Israel, Egypt, Saudi Arabia, and Kuwait in late August to talk to U.S. and foreign government officials. It was my first time in Baghdad, and I have two recollections of my stay. First, it was the hottest place I had ever visited in my life. There was a stiff wind coming off the desert at the time, and it felt like I had a hair dryer turned to "high" blowing on my face. Second, I was struck by how many billboards, photos, statues, and other depictions of Saddam Hussein I encountered as I wound my way on foot through the streets of the Iraqi capital. While the Iraqi people I met were very pleasant and seemed to be enjoying themselves as they strolled and shopped in the city, the omnipresent and heavily armed security and military forces left no doubt in anyone's mind that an oppressive authoritarian regime was fully in control.

Upon my return to Washington, I drafted the estimate. Unsurprisingly, its main analytic judgments were that an Iranian victory would strengthen the forces of Islamic fundamentalism, increase prospects for unrest in several Arab states, shift regional attention to the Arab-Israeli conflict, possibly affect the reliable flow of Persian Gulf oil, and spur U.S. and Soviet competition for influence in Tehran. I was invited to attend the senior-level meeting in late October, at an intelligence community annex located a block away from the White House, that was held to discuss and approve the estimate. The director of central intelligence, Bill Casey, chaired the meeting. It was only the third or fourth meeting with Casey that I had ever attended. He was seated at the head of the conference room table, hunched over his copy of the paper, with the shoulders of his suit jacket covered with his trademark dandruff. He looked very old and tired. I had difficulty understanding him as he spoke, as his tendency to mumble had increased over time. His comments that I was able to discern indicated that his mind was still agile and that he had absorbed the estimate's analytic bottom lines. I was thrilled when he referred to the estimate as "well written" and "realistic" in its conclusions. At least that's what I think he said.

It was the last time I ever saw Casey. Mired in the Iran-Contra scandal, he collapsed about six weeks later and had emergency surgery for a cancerous brain tumor. Casey resigned in late January and died in May.

Drafting the estimate whetted my thirst to work on the entire Middle East and South Asia. NESA had recently set up an "Issues Branch" to cover regional topics such as extremism, interstate rivalries, nuclear proliferation, and Arab-Israeli tensions. Staffing the Issues Branch was challenging for NESA managers, as most analysts considered it a bit of a backwater. Analysts with country-specific accounts had primacy on judgments involving the plans and intentions of foreign governments, and they also had more opportunities to write for the daily publications and to brief policy makers. Despite what others considered downsides, I decided to seize the opportunity to work on topics across such a wide expanse of geography— from Morocco to Nepal—especially since the Issues Branch chief, Jack Duggan, had a strong reputation as a manager, mentor, and all-around nice guy.

The move was a good one, as it allowed me to undertake yet another important research effort that significantly increased my knowledge and understanding of the history and politics of the Middle East. The project was on the Arab-Israeli conflict. It had been twenty years since the 1967 war and Israel's occupation of the West Bank, East Jerusalem, Gaza Strip, and Golan Heights. Accordingly, I wanted to explore whether there might be some combination of political and economic inducements that could offer a glimmer of hope for a durable peace. I did field research in Egypt, Israel, the West Bank, Jordan, and Syria and had the opportunity to share my preliminary findings with numerous former U.S. officials with Middle East expertise. I met individually with Henry Kissinger, Zbigniew Brzezinski, George Ball, Joseph Sisco, Sol Linowitz, and Phil Habib, all of whom offered their wise counsel on the practicality and sequencing of potential ingredients of a peace deal. Brzezinski provided

the most thoughtful feedback, including the recommendation that
territorial exchanges between Israel and its Arab neighbors be implemented over the course of twenty years. It was the consensus of
all my interlocutors that the religious holy sites of Jerusalem ultimately have some patina of international status given the depth
of emotions attached to the city. My research and findings, which
included a discussion of the advantages of an independent Palestinian state in a confederation with Jordan, were not presented in a
policy-prescriptive manner, which would have been inappropriate
for an intelligence product. Rather, the study was designed to help
policy makers identify a range of approaches and options that might
pave the way to an eventual peace agreement between Israel and its
Arab neighbors.

With several major analytic projects completed, I was made chief
of the Issues Branch in late 1988, much to the surprise of my fellow branch members, many of whom were older and had worked
on the region far longer than I had. I also was rather shocked by
my elevation, as I had no management experience or training beforehand. And it showed. Regrettably, I had difficulty filling Jack
Duggan's shoes, and I made a series of mistakes early on. Not only
was I an exceptionally heavy editor, believing I needed to turn the
prose of analysts into my own, I also was rather officious at times in
how I conveyed my changes. I was particularly harsh in the written
evaluations I gave subordinates, making an assignment in the Issues
Branch even less attractive than it already was.

It didn't take long before I started to receive negative feedback
from analysts as well as supervisors about my unwelcome and counterproductive proclivity to be a micromanager. The most helpful
"advice" I received at the time was from Jim O'Brien, an experienced
analyst in the branch who was nearly twenty-five years my senior.
Jim and I were friends and had worked closely together on several
papers when I was an analyst in the branch, but that didn't prevent
him from speaking his mind to me one day. "Stop being a jerk," Jim

said, as he practically pinned me against the wall in one of NESA's corridors. "Just because we have different writing styles than you, it doesn't mean we're not good analysts." I looked at him, stunned. He wasn't finished. "So, give your editing pencil a break and talk to us about the changes you want to make on our drafts; don't just make 'em." Jim was one of the better writers and analysts in the branch, so I had the distinct impression that he was selected to carry the water for others. I had to give the analysts high marks for their analytic judgment that sending a stern-looking Irishman to hit me upside the head had the best chance of success. It worked, and I am eternally grateful that Jim spoke to me.

Once I worked my way through the initial bumps of being a first-time supervisor, I grew to enjoy and relish the substantive latitude and learning opportunities offered by the Issues Branch. Much of my time was spent trying to negotiate arrangements for the analysts in the branch to be able to work on issues that, by definition, touched upon the substantive portfolios of other analysts in NESA and throughout the directorate.

With the end of the Iran-Iraq war in 1988, intra-Arab squabbles came into starker relief, especially between financially strapped Iraq and its wealthier Gulf Arab neighbors. NESA analysts, including in the Issues Branch, were carefully watching the growing war of words between Saddam Hussein and the Kuwaiti leadership. When Iraq began to move military forces closer to the Kuwaiti border, NESA's analytic consensus was that Saddam Hussein was seeking to intimidate the Kuwaitis into relenting on a demand for repayment of fourteen billion dollars in loans but that an Iraqi invasion of Kuwait was unlikely. The analytic consensus was wrong. Dead wrong.

9

COUNTERING TERROR

Saddam Hussein's army invaded Kuwait in a blitzkrieg-like attack on Thursday, August 2, 1990, occupying the country within forty-eight hours while Kuwait's al-Sabah leadership hightailed it to safer yet still luxurious living quarters in Ta'if, Saudi Arabia. On Monday afternoon, Bob Layton called me into his office to tell me that I was being assigned to the CIA's Counterterrorism Center, known as CTC, to be chief of its relatively small analytic team—the "Terrorism Assessments Branch." The center was barely four years old at the time, having been established as an organizational experiment in 1986, during Bill Casey's tenure. The rationale for its creation was the anticipated benefits of integrating the CIA's operational, analytical, technical, and covert-action capabilities into one component in order to deal more effectively and forcefully with what was a growing scourge of international terrorism. A flurry of terrorist attacks in the 1980s carried out by state sponsors and a variety of sectarian and secular groups in Europe, Asia, and South America were not only taking more and more American lives but also were undermining U.S. national security and foreign policy interests around the globe. The establishment of CTC was designed to reverse that trend.

It was the looming prospect of a U.S. military response to Iraq's takeover of Kuwait that led CIA leadership to decide that my Middle East experience was needed in CTC. I was told that my immediate objective was to ensure that CTC could meet the increased demand for analytic assessments on Saddam's capabilities and plans to use terrorism to intimidate the United States and its allies and partners. The concern that Iraq might use terrorist attacks was well founded. By 1990, Iraqi intelligence services were well known for their long-standing support for several of the most notorious Palestinian terrorist groups, including the infamous Abu Nidal Organization and the Palestinian Liberation Front, which were responsible for scores of innocent deaths in international terrorist incidents. The Iraqis themselves also were quite proficient in tracking down and killing Iraqi dissidents living abroad. State-sponsored terrorism had always presented a special challenge for counterterrorism professionals, as intelligence and security services of state sponsors use the prerogatives of sovereignty to move and conceal operatives, money, technical equipment, explosives, and other terrorism-related material via diplomatic pouches and in diplomatic facilities, which are beyond the monitoring of other countries.

As soon as I arrived in CTC, it became immediately apparent to me that the urgency, gravity, and amount of work in CTC would far exceed what had been my daily routine in the research-heavy and slower-paced Issues Branch of NESA. My workdays promptly began to stretch late into the evenings, and my weekends were frequently spent catching up on the previous week's work before having to deal with another week's onslaught.

I was barely three weeks into my tenure at CTC when Bob Layton called late one day with a request. "John, are you free tomorrow afternoon to go to the White House to brief the president?" Dumbfounded, I asked whether he was talking about the president of the

United States. "That's the only one I know who lives at the White House," he said. "Do you know another?" Bob's sense of humor was one of the many reasons I liked him. I was glad that Bob gave me less than twenty-four hours to prepare and worry about briefing a U.S. president for the first time. And it was no ordinary U.S. president. It was George H. W. Bush, one of the most experienced individuals in international affairs ever to become president. He also happened to be a former director of the CIA who knew the intelligence profession exceptionally well.

The meeting in the Oval Office the following day was attended by a veritable who's who of national security and Middle East experts at the time, including Secretary of State James Baker, Deputy National Security Adviser Bob Gates, National Security Council staffers Richard Haass and David Welch, and U.S. Ambassador to Iraq April Glaspie. I was seated between Gates and Bruce Riedel (another senior NESA analyst at the time) on the sofa to the president's left. I was quite nervous for the first few minutes but eventually settled down as a result of President Bush's affability as well as his genuine interest in hearing what we had to say. By the time the meeting concluded, forty-five minutes later, I was deeply impressed by President Bush's intellectual curiosity and his intense interest in finding the best policy course to protect and promote U.S. interests.

As the inevitable march toward military confrontation with Iraq became more apparent, I was spending less and less time at home. Kathy understood the importance of the work I was doing in CTC—my Oval Office meeting helped my case—but the children found it hard to understand why they didn't see me until right before they went to bed, if then. On the night that the United States began the first phase of Operation Desert Storm, launching a torrid aerial bombing campaign against Baghdad that would continue for forty-two days and nights, I sat on the side of Kyle's bed and explained to him what was going on. When I finished, I wrote down what we had talked about and read it back to him.

On the evening of 16 January 1991 Kyle and I discussed the bombing of Iraq, which is currently under way. I explained that the man in charge of Iraq is a bad man, who has hurt a lot of people and has taken over another country. I explained that war is very serious and very sad, because a lot of people get hurt and some die. Kyle said he understands.

Kyle and I then signed it. Kyle signed it twice, because he wanted to. I am not quite sure why I felt compelled to tell Kyle, who was three months shy of his fifth birthday, what was happening in Iraq that night, but sleep deprivation can make you do and say some odd things. Good thing Kelly and Jaclyn, not yet three years old, were already asleep. Otherwise, I would have read it to them and tried to get their signatures as well.

My time in CTC was one of the most formative, rewarding, and enlightening experiences I had as a young CIA officer. I was thrust into a role that forced me to navigate the shoals of an even larger bureaucratic environment. Although I had substantial authority, I often faced active opposition by other Agency components claiming analytic primacy.

I had never served in an integrated office before. CTC was an anomaly, nested within an Agency comprised of mostly stovepiped offices organized geographically and according to operational, analytical, technical, and support functions. But CTC was an amalgam of those functions, bringing together officers from throughout the Agency to work collaboratively under a unified leadership on shared objectives. The integrated model of CTC was similar to what had already taken root in the U.S. military with the passage of the 1986 Goldwater-Nichols Act, which brought together the army, navy, air force, and marine corps in unified combat commands organized both geographically and functionally. I quickly came to appreciate how the colocation and organizational integration of the CIA's diverse capabilities, authorities, disciplines, and expertise combined to score many successes on the terrorism front. During my time in CTC, CIA officers, working with assignees from other government agencies, were able to identify undercover Iraqi intelligence officers, forcing Baghdad to shelve terrorist plans. CTC officers also pieced together fragmentary evidence from the 1988 bombing of Pan Am Flight 103 over Scotland that determined conclusively that Libya was the perpetrator. Frequently, I was tapped to travel overseas to brief foreign government leaders on Iraq's terrorist plans and U.S. efforts to thwart them.

My time at CTC also gave me deep insight into the CIA's growing capabilities in the counterterrorism arena, the importance of having close liaison relationships with allies and partners abroad, and the interdependence between the CIA's operational mission and its analytic capabilities. Most important, I began to understand the imperfect balance and difficult trade-offs between, on the one hand, acting decisively against terrorists based on incomplete data in the interest of saving innocent lives and, on the other hand, waiting for greater confidence and clarity before acting and, by waiting, risking losing the opportunity to act. I would struggle with this balancing act for the rest of my government service.

I also learned the importance of maintaining analytic independence and integrity while I was in CTC, which was administratively housed within the Directorate of Operations and led by a DO officer. The center's first director was the legendary and swashbuckling Dewey Clarridge, a colorful character who enjoyed strutting through the corridors of Langley in a striking white suit. By the time I had arrived in the center, Dewey had already departed and was dealing with the legal fallout from his previous role in the Iran-Contra affair. Like Alan Fiers, Dewey was indicted but subsequently pardoned by President George H. W. Bush. Dewey's successor in CTC was Fred Turco, an accomplished DO officer who was unrelenting in his push to find and stop terrorists from carrying out their deadly agendas.

Fred usually was very complimentary of the analysis coming out of my unit. He took special delight whenever we ran analytic pieces in the President's Daily Brief (PDB), as they helped keep the most senior policy makers focused on the terrorist threat and highlighted the work being done by the CIA to counter it.

But Fred and I did not always see eye to eye on substance, and we locked horns at times. On one very memorable occasion, my analysts were closely tracking the immediate aftermath of a February 1992 helicopter strike in southern Lebanon that killed Hizballah leader Abbas al-Musawi, along with Musawi's wife and son, that appeared to be the work of the Israelis. This was the type of event that would be written up in our daily publications, wherein we would recount the details of the strike and address the likely implications. When I reviewed a draft analytic item, I saw that the analysts appropriately focused on the likelihood of Hizballah retaliation against the Israelis, either inside or outside Israel, consistent with the "eye-for-an-eye" mentality that prevails in the Middle East. I edited the piece and told the analyst to drop off copies for Fred and Karl Ruyle, Fred's deputy in CTC's front office. It took less than five minutes before I heard Fred walking with purpose toward my cubicle. Turning around in my chair, I saw Fred towering over me with the draft clutched tightly in his hand. "You need to say that Hizballah is also likely to retaliate by hitting U.S. targets," Fred said in a raised voice.

"No, Fred," I said, as I watched his jaw muscles tightening. "We believe that Hizballah will lash out against the Israelis and will not want to bring the United States into this dustup. The United States did not play a role in the strike."

"It doesn't matter," Fred said in a voice loud enough to attract attention from analysts as well as other CTC officers in nearby bullpen cubicles. "Hizballah sees America as its sworn enemy because we give the Israelis their military weapons!" By now Fred was getting agitated, and I could feel my own blood pressure starting to elevate.

"I know that, Fred!" I yelled back at him. "But that doesn't mean that they will carry out a terrorist attack against the United States in retaliation for the assassination of Musawi."

We volleyed back and forth like this for another minute or two, with neither one of us giving an inch. After working with me for eighteen months, Fred knew that I had a stubborn streak, especially when defending the judgments of analysts in my branch. I could see that Fred was getting increasingly exasperated with me, and the feeling was mutual. In a final dramatic flair before stomping back to his office, Fred tossed the draft onto my desk and roared, "You're going to get Americans killed!"

This last comment left me speechless. I knew that the analysis—with or without reference to the potential for retaliatory strikes against U.S. targets—was not going to alter Hizballah's targeting calculus. Nor would it lead to an adjustment in the force-protection status of U.S. government and business interests in the region, which was already high. Karl came to see me a few minutes after Fred left. With a smirk on his face, he said, "I understand that you and Fred might have a slight difference of view on Hizballah's reaction to Musawi's death." I laughed and told Karl what happened. Karl said that he concurred with the analysis in the piece. Since I considered Karl the best analyst in the CIA at the time, I was reassured by his comment. But Karl also helped me put Fred's reaction to the piece into perspective. "Look at it this way, John. We're lucky to have someone like Fred in the CIA who worries day and night about what we can do to save American lives, even if he gets a bit overwrought on occasion."

Karl was right. I met a lot of people like Fred during my time in the Agency. Whenever I did, Karl's words came back to me. Despite the occasional heated argument with Fred, I had tremendous respect for his dedication, work ethic, and readiness to give junior officers the opportunity to participate in important meetings. Fred was sub-stantively strong on terrorism matters, but, at the end of the day, he knew that it was the responsibility of the analysts to provide the official CIA assessment of terrorist plans and intentions. Whenever he would head out to a meeting that involved a senior-level policy maker or foreign official, he would invariably swing by the branch and ask that someone accompany him. Which is exactly what he did barely a month after the killing of Musawi, when Hizballah bombed the Israeli embassy in Buenos Aires, Argentina, tragically killing twenty-nine and injuring more than 240 others. Hizballah had retaliated against the Israelis, not Americans. The analysts had it right.

10

BRIEFING THE "FIRST CUSTOMERS"

I returned to NESA by the summer of 1992 to become the deputy division chief of the Arab-Israeli Division, working for the very talented Martha Kessler, another early trailblazer for women analysts and managers in the CIA. Martha had strong Middle East credentials, having served as Bob Ames's assistant when he was national intelligence officer for the Middle East. She was also my branch chief when I was an analyst in NESA working on Saudi Arabia and the Yemens in the mid-1980s. A gifted writer and editor, Martha was widely respected in the directorate and had excellent relations with her operational counterparts in the Near East Division, so I was eager to have the opportunity to work with her again. The Arab-Israeli division consisted of four branches: North Africa; Egypt-Sudan; Israel, Palestine, and Jordan; and Syria and Lebanon. As deputy division chief, I was now on the second rung of the management ladder in the Agency and started to attend more leadership training courses, which I sorely needed. I also learned to delegate more responsibility to branch chiefs, as I quickly realized that attempting to micromanage the work of dozens of analysts was not only impossible but also foolishly counterproductive.

My two years in the Arab-Israeli Division were busy ones, as we were consumed with providing analysis on Israeli-Palestinian negotiations in Norway that culminated in the signing of the Oslo I Accord. Israel's decision to recognize the PLO as the representative of the Palestinian people and the PLO's recognition of the state of Israel were breakthroughs that were captured poignantly in the historic handshake between Israeli prime minister Yitzhak Rabin and PLO chairman Yasir Arafat on the South Lawn of the White House following the signing of the accord on September 13, 1993. Oslo I established interim arrangements for Palestinian self-government and for Israeli military withdrawal from the Gaza Strip. I remember wondering at the time whether my research and analysis a half dozen years earlier in the Issues Branch might serve as the basis for eventual territorial compromise and a durable peace. Unfortunately, hard-liners and obstinacy among Israeli and PLO leaders as well as lackluster U.S. diplomacy in the following decades prevented the realization of Oslo I's vision.

It was during this time that I was given the opportunity to lead a team of experienced analysts in a comprehensive review of analytic tradecraft in the Directorate of Intelligence. Over the course of several months, our "process action team" conducted dozens of interviews with CIA analysts, managers, and instructional staff; reviewed outside literature on effective training, process reengineering, and quality control; and benchmarked against private industry, media, and other government agencies. Our final report to the senior management of the Directorate of Intelligence identified analytic thinking, productive behavior, presentational skills, knowledge of customer, and data gathering and handling as the key analytic tradecraft skills. Our team also made several major recommendations that called for an overhaul of the directorate's training, evaluation, assignments, accountability, and reward systems. Feeling our oats, we pointedly called for senior management to take training courses on analytic thinking and productive behavior so that they could be better role models for directorate analysts. In addition to relishing the ability to shape the Agency's analytic culture, I was fortunate to become close friends with another member of the process action team, Michael Morell. Little did I know then that Michael and I would be the CIA's leadership team nearly twenty years later when I became director and he was deputy director.

By the spring of 1994, Karl Ruyle, my former boss in CTC, was overseeing the production and delivery of the PDB. Although Karl and I were no longer working together in the same office, we stayed in close contact with each other, playing basketball and golf whenever we could arrange to be out of the office at the same time. It was no surprise, therefore, when I received a call from him one day in April. "John, I have an idea that I would like to discuss with you. Can you come up to my office for a moment?"

When I got to his office, I noticed that Karl had his serious face on.

"We're going to make some personnel changes on the PDB staff, and I would like you to be one of the new briefers for President Clinton and Vice President Gore. We need to shake things up a bit," he said. "It's important that we hold the attention of our 'first customers.' If we don't get them to want and to use our intelligence, it's our fault, not theirs."

Wow! I was in shock. While I had written and edited dozens if not hundreds of items for the PDB during my career up to that point, I had always been in awe of the CIA briefers who had the opportunity—indeed, the honor—of delivering the CIA's daily intelligence offering to the most important consumers of the Agency's clandestinely acquired intelligence and analysis. For many years, that privilege went to Chuck Peters, a tall and stately CIA officer who not only edited the PDB every evening but also conducted the morning briefings in the Oval Office throughout the Reagan and George H. W. Bush administrations. Pipe-smoking Chuck was a rather intimidating legend at the Agency. After a dozen years conducting the PDB sessions in the Oval Office, Chuck had an encyclopedic knowledge of U.S. national security matters and the CIA's ability to report on them. He had a very heavy editing pencil, and PDB drafts that were submitted to him were barely recognizable by the time he got through with them. When I was a young analyst, I had the temerity to challenge Chuck several times after I had arrived in his office and saw that he had essentially shredded and rewritten my drafts. It was only rarely, and usually after a very lengthy debate, that Chuck agreed to revert to some of my original language. He probably did so just to get me out of his office.

I knew that being a PDB briefer would require a significant change in my daily schedule, as I would need to get to Langley in the middle of the night in order to prepare sufficiently for the early-morning briefing routine. After checking with Kathy that evening, I told Karl the following day that I would love to be a White House briefer. "Great, you'll start in six weeks," he said. And then with a big smile, he added, "That should give you enough time to learn everything about what's going on in the world so that you will be ready for your daily briefings for the president." Karl's words turned my enthusiasm into a deep wave of panic and trepidation. What did I just get myself into? How am I going to get prepared in six weeks' time to brief the president and vice president of the United States on worldwide developments and know what the heck I am talking about? The Middle East and terrorism were complicated enough, but Russia, China, the Balkans? There was simply too much to learn in the course of six weeks.

I soon took up full-time residence with the PDB staff, and Karl told me that I would be part of a two-person briefing team responsible for taking care of all PDB recipients at the White House— President Clinton, Vice President Gore, National Security Adviser

Tony Lake, Principal Deputy National Security Adviser Sandy
Berger, Deputy National Security Adviser Nancy Soderberg, Na-
tional Security Adviser to the Vice President Leon Fuerth, and
Senior Director for Intelligence Programs George Tenet. A CIA an-
alyst who had specialized in Soviet and Russian affairs was the other
White House briefer. We were told that we would alternate briefing
assignments every two weeks, with one of us briefing Clinton, Lake,
Berger, and Tenet while the other would brief Gore, Fuerth, and
Soderberg.

My daily routine was turned upside down during my PDB briefing days. I would try to go to bed no later than 8:30 P.M. Sunday
through Thursday nights—the same time as six-year-old Kyle and
four-year-old Kelly and Jaclyn—so that I could get to headquarters
by 2:30 A.M. I needed a good four hours in the office to read each
item in the PDB several times as well as to absorb the underlying
source material, which frequently was dense and lengthy. When I
was a White House briefer, the PDB was produced only as a hard-
copy document of six to eight pages, with each PDB document individually numbered; it was during the Obama administration that
the PDB was disseminated on a highly secure computer tablet, which
allowed source documents and other relevant material to be readily
available to the reader. The PDB comprised a range of items, from
short intelligence updates consisting of only a few lines—referred to
as "snowflakes"—to articles of three to eight paragraphs with bulleted
subtext. The contents, covering dynamic issues of immediate concern
as well as longer-term strategic topics, would incorporate clandestinely
acquired human and technical intelligence, diplomatic reporting, and
open-source information. Analysis was identified by italics.

The PDB was strictly controlled, including inside the CIA. Until
I became a PDB briefer, I had never seen an entire PDB, only individual articles that pertained to my area of responsibility. For distribution outside the CIA, it is up to each President to decide who should
receive the PDB. For the two dozen or so senior U.S. officials who

had been approved by President Clinton to receive the PDB, such as the secretaries and deputy secretaries of state, defense, and treasury and the chairman and vice chairman of the Joint Chiefs of Staff, CIA briefers would carry the PDB, along with related classified intelligence documents and their briefing notes, in locked briefcases and travel in chauffeured CIA vehicles. Once they arrived at their respective destinations, the PDB was handed directly to the authorized official and was read in the presence of the CIA briefer, who would follow along with his or her own copy. During the session, the briefer would supplement items in the PDB with additional background, context, and updates on overnight developments. The briefer also would respond to questions raised by the reader. Depending on the question, the answer would be provided immediately, by a follow-up memo delivered later that day, or during a subsequent session.

I do not recall what substance was covered in my first PDB briefing, but I vividly remember how proud and humbled I felt when I was introduced to President Clinton as his new daily intelligence briefer in July 1994. Although I had voted for George H. W. Bush in 1992—I found it hard to vote against a former CIA director—I had grown to admire Clinton for his obvious intellect as well as for his professed interest in working across the political aisle to advance U.S. domestic and foreign policies. I had never met Clinton previously, and I was exceptionally nervous as I was escorted by National Security Adviser Tony Lake for my first visit to the Oval Office in nearly four years. Clinton warmly welcomed me as I entered and invited me to take a seat on the sofa. He asked about my CIA background and then expressed admiration for the Agency's work, which he said he had come to rely upon over the previous eighteen months. Ever the politician, he then complimented me on my choice of necktie—a pattern of Greek Parthenons set against a royal blue background—which immediately made Clinton one of my all-time favorite presidents.

Clinton was a very careful reader. After the first half-dozen sessions with him, I realized that he had an amazing ability to ingest, process, analyze, and retain voluminous amounts of information on virtually any topic. During my ten-month stint as his PDB briefer, there were numerous dynamic issues covered in the PDB, and his ability to recall obscure information he had read weeks and months before was in constant evidence.

Most briefings for President Clinton took place in the Oval Office; only rarely would I meet with him in another location in the White House complex or while he was on domestic travel, such as when he attended the United Nations General Assembly in New York City. Vice President Al Gore, Tony Lake, and Deputy National Security Adviser Sandy Berger were almost always in attendance for an Oval Office briefing; Chief of Staff Leon Panetta would frequently dart in and out while he was busily working on other matters.

On days I was slated to brief the president, I would arrive at the White House at least an hour before my first briefing was scheduled to take place. I didn't want to take the chance of getting caught in rush-hour traffic or delayed by an accident on the heavily congested roads leading into the District. It also was a real thrill for me, a relatively junior thirty-nine-year-old CIA officer, to be able to wander around inside the gates of the White House complex. The grounds were always beautiful and awe inspiring, but never more so, I found, than when snow fell at dawn on a winter's morning. With deep and, at times, emotional patriotic pride, I would walk back and forth in the snowfall on West Executive Avenue, seeing the power and majesty of the U.S. government revealed with each office light that came alive in the West Wing and in the adjacent Old Executive Office Building. I will never forget that feeling.

President Clinton's travel and appointment schedule—as well as his frequent late arrivals to the Oval Office that would lead to the cancellation of a PDB session—would determine the frequency of his PDB sessions. Generally, the briefings would occur one to three times a week. Clinton would read the PDB as I sat on the sofa, usually to his left, from where I would add a few analytic points or additional bits of intelligence to supplement the written prose. Clinton generally read in studied silence, occasionally asking Tony Lake or Sandy Berger to follow up on an issue mentioned in the PDB. Whenever he asked me a question, I would provide a substantive response only if I was sure I knew the answer; the last thing I wanted to do was misinform the president of the United States about a national security issue. Frequently, I would take the question and relay a response either later that day through White House channels or in a subsequent briefing session. This approach was commonly referred to as "going dumb early"—a term used by intelligence professionals to describe wisely avoiding giving faulty information or getting drawn into a subject about which they have limited personal knowledge.

I remember going dumb early one time when President Clinton was reading a PDB article on the Balkans. When the article made brief mention of a Serbian official with an especially difficult-to-pronounce last name, Clinton turned to me and said, "Didn't the PDB have an article a few months ago saying this person was accused of human rights atrocities?" Concealing my much more modest powers of recall, I said, "I think so," promising to get back to him with a definitive answer. As soon as the briefing was over, I made a secure call to headquarters and asked whether President Clinton was right. Sure enough, he had remembered correctly.

"Damn," I said over the phone. "Why couldn't I remember that?"

"Well," came the smartass reply from one of my PDB colleagues, "that probably explains why he's president and you're not."

The briefings for Vice President Gore were much less formal, more frequent, and much more interactive. When I had "Gore duty," I would arrive at his residence at the Naval Observatory about twenty minutes before his scheduled departure for the White House. Upon my arrival, I would transfer from my Agency vehicle to the back seat of the vice president's limousine and wait for the vice president to enter for the subsequent ten-to-fifteen-minute ride to the White House or for the longer ride to Andrews Air Force Base on days he was scheduled to travel. When the vice president entered the limousine, I would hand him the PDB and would share additional intelligence nuggets or take his questions while he read through the articles during the ride. Despite routinely participating in the PDB session with the president in the Oval Office, the vice president always took an earlier briefing so he could be well prepared for the Oval Office discussion.

Vice President Gore was, and remains, a very intellectually curious person about how the world and mankind are evolving. When I was his briefer, he regularly showed keen interest in learning whatever he could about technical, scientific, and commercial innovations taking place in the United States and abroad. He encouraged me to bring him intelligence reports and open-source material related to breakthrough technologies that could have a disruptive impact on our economy, politics, climate, and culture. As vice president, he retained strong interest in a program he had spearheaded in the Senate called the Measurements of Earth Data for Environmental Analysis (MEDEA), which used the intelligence community's aerial surveillance records and expertise to monitor and assess the rate and impact of global climate change. And while jokes are made about Gore inventing the Internet, his understanding of and emphasis on the transformative nature of the digital domain far surpassed anything I had heard from any other senior U.S. official at the time.

During my PDB stint, I served for a couple of months as the "holder" of Vice President Gore's breakfast tray of scrambled eggs, fruit, toast, and juice inside the limousine. The vice president had torn his Achilles tendon while playing basketball in August 1994, and it was logistically difficult for him to juggle his PDB, foot boot, and breakfast tray all at the same time. The vice president was always gracious, apologizing for any inconvenience caused as we maneuvered to find a comfortable position during the ride. I told him it was always a privilege to support him, whether my job was to provide his daily intelligence briefing or to help keep his eggs and juice from spilling onto his lap.

I remember well the morning following the Democrats' disastrous showing in the 1994 midterm election, when the Republicans picked up eight seats in the Senate and fifty-four in the House, giving them control of both congressional chambers for the first time since the 1954 elections. A drubbing was too generous a term for the beating the Democrats took from the Republicans. A subdued vice president entered the limousine on schedule and said "good morning" without looking at me. No breakfast joined us. I handed him the PDB, which he opened to the first page. For the rest of the ride, he stared at the page. He did not say a single word; he just stared. I do not think his eyes blinked even once. He was in a total state of shock. When we arrived at the White House, the Secret Service agents stood at the ready outside his door, waiting for him to exit. The vice president remained motionless, oblivious to the fact that we had arrived. With the Secret Service agents standing outside the car, I decided to break the silence after about thirty very long seconds and said, "Have a good day, sir." Startled out of his trance, he softly said, "Okay," exited the limousine, and went into the West Wing. Mercifully, the Oval Office session scheduled for that day was canceled.

Leon Fuerth, Vice President Gore's national security adviser, had the most ravenous appetite for intelligence and analysis among all my PDB briefees. There was no national security issue too trivial or too mundane for Leon's intellectual curiosity—he was much like his boss in that regard—and he would regularly request in-depth analytic pieces from the CIA on a broad range of subjects. Leon never hesitated to challenge the analysis in the PDB if he believed it missed the mark or was weak in its tradecraft. "I don't agree" was a not-infrequent refrain from Leon as he stared at me after reading a PDB item. If my explanation on the reasons for the analytic judgments did not suffice, a meeting would be set up for Leon and the analysts who had drafted the PDB article. Such engagements with senior U.S. officials were much appreciated by CIA analysts, who welcomed being challenged by senior policy makers because it demonstrated to them that their analysis not only was being read but also mattered.

My stint as a PDB briefer lasted less than ten months. It was the most exciting and enjoyable assignment of my CIA career up to that point. I didn't realize at the time that its most lasting impact would be the professional and personal relationship forged with one of my PDB recipients—George J. Tenet.

I had met Tenet only once before I started briefing him.

"We call him the space invader."

That was how one of my CIA colleagues referred to George, after he saw George standing immediately in front of me with less than ten inches separating our noses. It was in early 1994, a few months before I became his PDB briefer, and George was on one of his frequent visits to Langley. A former staff director for the Senate Select Committee on Intelligence (SSCI), George was the senior director for intelligence programs at the National Security Council. CIA Associate Deputy Director of Intelligence David Cohen—a good friend as well as an unrelated namesake of my future deputy years later—introduced me to George as I passed them chatting together in the hall.

With a big smile on his face, George invaded my space and said, "So, what do you do here?"

For a moment, I wondered whether nearsightedness prompted George's up-close-and-personal stance. But that was George just being George. Personable, gregarious, wicked smart, and exceptionally hardworking, George had a far deeper understanding and appreciation of the CIA's work than any other outsider by dint of his portfolios on the Hill and at the NSC. His positions gave him virtually unfettered access to the CIA's most sensitive programs, including on the covert action front, and he was very comfortable interacting with

CIA officers of all backgrounds and disciplines. When I became his PDB briefer, we would discuss a wide range of intelligence topics during our one-on-one sessions, and he frequently shared more insights about the CIA with me than I did with him.

Given George's deep intelligence experience, it was not surprising that in May 1995, John Deutch, the newly confirmed director of central intelligence, asked him to be his deputy. The day after the announcement, I showed up in George's office for our scheduled PDB session and extended my congratulations. "You'll love being in the Agency," I said to George, as he chomped on what had become his signature unlit cigar.

"Thanks. But I have some news for you," he said, as he pulled bits of wet tobacco out of his mouth and flicked them across the room. "You're coming with me."

"Huh?"

"You heard me," he said with his infectious laugh. "I need someone to help me during the confirmation process. You will have to give up your PDB job, of course, but that means that you won't have to wake up at two A.M. anymore. Feel free to sleep in until at least three," he added with a loud cackle. I didn't know if I was being given a choice. It didn't matter, though, as I genuinely liked and respected George and saw the opportunity to work with him as an exciting new adventure. It certainly was.

George was sworn in as deputy director of central intelligence on July 11, 1995, and I spent the next twelve months working as his executive assistant. It was my first staff job on the CIA's seventh floor, where the director, deputy director, and the rest of the leadership team reside. For the first fifteen years of my Agency career, I had very limited interaction with the Agency's senior ranks. Occasionally, I attended a meeting in the director's wood-paneled conference room, usually to provide an analytic briefing on terrorism or on some breaking development in the Middle East. Even when I was President Clinton's daily briefer, I was never asked to meet with then-director James Woolsey to discuss my PDB sessions, which was odd, since Woolsey had virtually no other opportunity to gain insight into Oval Office discussions. Woolsey and Clinton did not have a close relationship, and it was widely known that the two rarely met. When a stolen Cessna aircraft crashed onto the White House lawn on September 11, 1994, the prevailing joke in Washington was that Woolsey was trying to get in to see Clinton.

George introduced me to the dizzying world of executive leadership in the national security realm. From 1947 until 2005, the director and deputy director of central intelligence had responsibility for leading the CIA as well as the broader intelligence community, an increasingly difficult challenge as the size, capabilities, and demands on the intelligence agencies steadily grew. Fresh off his deputy secretary of defense role, John Deutch focused heavily on strategic intelligence community initiatives and programs and left oversight of day-to-day CIA activities to George and other senior CIA officials. This division of responsibilities was well received by the Agency, as George's knowledge and support for the CIA's mission gave him instant credibility with the workforce.

My time as George's executive assistant was a learning experience like none other I ever had. What struck me most was the sheer range of intelligence community activities and capabilities and the importance of aligning resources—dollars and personnel—against an array of dynamic national security challenges. The curtains that shrouded the most sensitive CIA programs were opened to me, as I accompanied George on his visits throughout the Agency and participated in most of his headquarters meetings with U.S. and foreign officials. I also traveled with him frequently on his foreign trips, when he would meet not only with the heads of intelligence and security services but also with foreign government leaders. George relied heavily on his staff, although I have come to realize that his approach was designed as much to mentor others as it was to help himself.

More than anything else, George's decision to make me his executive assistant when he was deputy director of central intelligence altered the trajectory of my national security career.

I will be forever thankful for the opportunity he gave me and for the guidance he has provided ever since.

11

SAUDI ARABIA REDUX

By late spring 1996, I was beginning to tire of my seventh-floor duties. I had been working directly for George for more than a year and very much enjoyed watching him in action and learning about the Agency and the intelligence community at the strategic level. But I missed having substantive and supervisory responsibility for the CIA's intelligence mission. Moreover, I was getting more and more frustrated and short-tempered when dealing with some of the petty internal squabbles—typical of any large organization—that were taking place inside the CIA. George knew I was beginning to drag, and he called me on it one evening when he pulled me into his office.

"What's up?" he asked. "You seem like you're no longer having fun." I avoided the question, which he sensed right away. "You've been here long enough," he said without hesitation, "so we need to find you another job that will give you the additional experience you need to eventually run this place."

George was always prone to resorting to hyperbole when talking about individuals who worked directly for him. I rolled my eyes and dismissed out of hand his illusion about my becoming director one day, but I did allow that it might be good for the both of us if I found another position. I told George that the NESA deputy director position had recently come open and that I would like to throw my hat in the ring for it. "It's the region I know best, and I really would like to get back to doing analysis." I told George that I didn't want him to weigh in on my behalf, noting, "I want to get the job or be rejected for it based on my own record." He agreed, or at least said he did.

The NESA director at the time was Tom Wolfe, with whom I had worked when I returned from my posting in Jeddah many years before. Tom had remained a close friend and mentor over the years, and he encouraged my application despite the fact that the NESA deputy director job was at the Senior Intelligence Service (SIS) level, equivalent to a flag officer (general or admiral) in the armed forces, and I was only a GS-15.

I was selected for the NESA position the week before promotions to and within the SIS ranks were announced. As with military flag officers, there were tiers within the SIS cadre, ranging from SIS-1 to SIS-6. New members of the SIS were given the rank of SIS-1 and promoted to higher SIS grades as they assumed positions of increasing responsibility within the organization. As a GS-15, I was hoping to be promoted to SIS-1, which was the traditional practice for all promotions into the SIS ranks. In a rather astounding break with precedent, I was informed that I was being promoted directly from GS-15 to SIS-3. I objected strenuously to George, who told me to raise my objections with Nora Slatkin, a John Deutch protégée who was serving as executive director, the number-three position in the Agency. "It will smack of favoritism," I told her, "and I don't want any favors done for me."

"Too late," Nora said with a smile. "Director Deutch has already signed off on it." She tried to convince me that I deserved the SIS-3 because of my hard work with George, but I disagreed, believing that it was directly related to my working for George. "Most people work hard at the Agency," I told her, "and I know of no one else who has been promoted three grades in one fell swoop."

I knew there would be legitimate grumblings about the leap-frog nature of my promotion, which took some of the luster off the prize that I had long sought. Nevertheless, when I walked across the stage of the CIA auditorium to accept the SIS-3 certificate from John Deutch with Kathy, Kyle, Kelly, and Jaclyn in the audience, I felt a deep sense of satisfaction that my work over the previous sixteen years had been worth the effort.

After a couple of weeks in my new job in NESA, I became aware that the senior intelligence liaison position in Saudi Arabia needed to be filled immediately. The individual slated to go had to bow out for medical reasons. During one of my visits to the Near East Division in the Directorate of Operations, I said, half tongue in cheek, that I wished I were going to Saudi Arabia. Steve, the chief of NE Division, looked at me and said, "Are you serious?"

"Yup," was my knee-jerk response.

Intrigued, he asked if my Arabic was still good.

"It's rusty, but I could brush it up."

Senior liaison positions overseas usually were reserved for operations officers, and I did not think I had much of a chance getting the job. However, in addition to my Arabic and my previous tour in Saudi Arabia, my counterterrorism experience was viewed as a plus following two terrorist attacks that had occurred in Saudi Arabia over the previous year. The first attack was a car bomb in downtown Riyadh against the Office of Program Management–Saudi Arabia National Guard that killed several American military advisers and injured dozens of Saudis and other nationals. It was the first attack against Americans anywhere by individuals affiliated with al-Qa'ida. A second attack occurred in late June 1996 in Saudi Arabia's Eastern Province. A huge truck bomb destroyed the Khobar Towers housing complex, which had been used as the living quarters for U.S. and coalition forces assigned to Operation Southern Watch, which patrolled no-fly zones over Iraq. The attack was carried out by Hizballah al-Hijaz (Saudi Hizballah) at the direction of Iran and killed nineteen U.S. Air Force personnel and dozens of others as well as injuring several hundred.

As I thought about the increased terrorist threat in Saudi Arabia, I quickly realized that I was getting a bit ahead of myself and needed to slow things down. "I have to talk to Kathy about it first, Steve," I said. "This would be a pretty major family decision."

"No shit," was his response.

"What am I doing?" I thought to myself as I walked back to my office. "Do I really want to go back to Saudi Arabia? Do I want to bring Kathy and the children there, especially in light of the increased terrorist threat?" I wasn't sure of the answers to those questions, and I knew that I would not know the answer until a family discussion was had. As I dwelled upon the issue the rest of the day, I remembered the many conversations I'd had over the years with CIA officers who were torn between their family responsibilities and the obligations they felt to the CIA and to the country they had sworn an oath to protect and defend. Striking the proper balance between family and work is a lot easier said than done, especially when facing a choice between one and the other. Unfortunately, too many women and men in the Agency have had to make that choice many times in their career, including when they are asked to serve in dangerous war zones.

I made sure that I arrived home at a reasonable hour that night so that I could broach the idea of an overseas assignment with the family. Kathy and I had considered other overseas assignments since our return from Jeddah a dozen years before but were not successful finding the right one. I raised the topic gingerly as the five of us sat around the dinner table. "I heard about a job overseas that I could apply for and might have a shot at getting. It would give us the chance to travel and even go to Ireland for a visit!" Since I had already indoctrinated our children with stories about our Irish heritage and the leprechauns that roamed the Irish countryside, I thought I would start off by making the opportunity sound as attractive as possible. Kathy looked at me quizzically. "Really?" she said with interest. From a family perspective, the timing was right. Kyle was in the fifth grade and Kelly and Jaclyn were in the third grade, and we had agreed that an overseas posting should take place when the children were in elementary school, not high school. "Well, as long as it's not Jeddah, I'm interested," Kathy said.

I knew that Kathy had always entertained the notion that we would one day have the opportunity to live and work in a European capital. And while a tour in Europe certainly would have been nice from a quality-of-life perspective, such posts did not hold much professional attraction—or even opportunity—for me. "Oh, it's not Jeddah," I reassured her. I then swallowed hard and said, "But it is in Saudi Arabia." I am sure I winced as I said those words. I had visited the city where the position was located several times when we lived in Jeddah, but Kathy never had, probably because of its reputation for being inhospitable to foreigners, especially Western women. (Absurdly, the CIA has prohibited me from identifying the city where my family and I would live for three years.)

"You have got to be kidding. Another tour in Saudi Arabia!?!" she said with a disbelieving look on her face. I knew I had my work cut out for me; I spent the rest of the night talking up whatever upsides of going to Saudi Arabia I could present. "I've already checked, and there is an excellent international school that the children can attend . . . the housing looks very good, and we'll be able to hire some domestic help . . . we'll be living in an area where Western attire is permitted . . . we'll travel out of Saudi Arabia as often as possible . . . we'll save money, and we can buy a bigger house when we get back . . . I promise that we'll stay for only two years." I am sure that my soliloquy was very similar to the words that thousands of other CIA, U.S. military, Department of State, and other U.S. government officials with professional opportunities to serve overseas have used with their families prior to accepting a less-than-ideal foreign assignment.

And like countless other spouses over the years, Kathy selflessly said okay, not for the personal benefits associated with an overseas tour but because she knew that it was important to me and that we would be contributing, as a family, to our nation's security. As happened numerous times during my government career, Kathy was the one who made it possible for me not to have to choose between my family and my profession.

We arrived in Saudi Arabia in mid-November 1996. Contrary to my initial pledge that we would return to the States in two years, we opted to stay in Saudi Arabia for a third year. I convinced the children to vote to remain for a third year while we were vacationing at a beach resort in Bahrain. I was especially fortunate to serve once again in a country where U.S. government officials thrived on teamwork and that had strong leadership in Ambassador Wyche Fowler, a former U.S. senator from Georgia, and Deputy Chief of Mission Ted Kattouf, both of whom put great value on U.S. intelligence. Unlike my tour as a junior diplomat in Jeddah in the early 1980s, which gave me a good feel for the people and culture of Saudi Arabia, my second tour in the kingdom gave me the opportunity to interact regularly with senior Saudi officials and to gain personal insight into the complexities of the multidimensional relationship between the United States and Saudi Arabia. It was an experience that would serve me well in my subsequent national security roles.

My principal counterpart in Saudi Arabia was Prince Turki al-Faisal, the head of Saudi Arabia's General Intelligence Directorate (GID). By the time I had taken up my duties, Prince Turki had been in position for seventeen years and was extremely well versed in regional and international affairs. The son of former king Faisal and full brother of Foreign Minister Saud, Turki had impeccable English, political sophistication, and an urbane demeanor that made him a natural interlocutor for visiting U.S. officials keen to win Saudi support for policy initiatives or intelligence activities. While unfailingly polite and seemingly sympathetic to U.S. interests, Turki was generally loath to cause waves within the rather byzantine Saudi political and security environment. (Turki would become more outspoken in royal family councils when he served as ambassador to the United States nearly a decade later, which led to his ostensible resignation after only fifteen months). Trying to get Saudi intelligence to cooperate more fully in counterterrorism investigations was frequently an exercise in futility, although I strongly suspect that it was due more to professional incompetence of the rank and file within his organization than to Prince Turki's political caution.

There were a few times when Prince Turki showed a willingness to follow through on issues of importance to the United States. In early 1998, U.S. intelligence learned that the Saudis had intercepted an al-Qa'ida shipment of Sagger antitank missiles coming across the border from Yemen. At the time of the interdiction, Saudi intelligence did not inform U.S. officials, despite it having taken place only weeks before a scheduled visit by Vice President Gore. I confronted Turki with the Saudi failure to notify the United States, highlighting the concern that the missiles might have been part of a broader security threat related to the vice president's trip. Turki looked puzzled by my comments and said he knew nothing about the missiles. While I had been on the receiving end of previous Saudi denials of known facts, Turki's reaction seemed genuine. Indeed, I believe it was. Saudi Arabia's Ministry of Interior, led by Turki's uncle Prince Nayif Bin Abd al-Aziz, apparently had kept the information secret not only from the United States but also from the GID. Angered and embarrassed by the slight, Turki confronted his politically more powerful uncle and was able to obtain information on the missiles that he passed to me. A subsequent visit by George Tenet, who had become director of central intelligence following the resignation of John Deutch in December 1996, prompted Crown Prince Abdullah to accede to a CIA request that it be granted direct access to the missiles for intelligence exploitation. The al-Qa'ida plot to smuggle the missiles into Saudi Arabia was planned by Abd al-Rahim al-Nashiri, who later was the mastermind of the bombing of the USS *Cole* off Yemen's coast in 2000 that killed seventeen U.S. sailors and injured several dozen more. Nashiri is currently detained at Guantánamo Bay.

The al-Qa'ida threat to U.S. interests intensified significantly in 1998. In February of that year, Bin Ladin and four others signed a public statement calling for the indiscriminate killing of Americans and Jews everywhere, which triggered increased U.S. pressure on Saudi Arabia for additional counterterrorism cooperation. During his visit to Saudi Arabia that spring, George pressed the Saudis to get the Taliban, which was in control of the government in Afghanistan, to cease providing safe haven to Bin Ladin and his al-Qa'ida followers. Crown Prince Abdullah directed Prince Turki to go to Afghanistan a few months later to meet with Taliban leader Mullah Omar. I do not know exactly what was discussed in that meeting, although I am skeptical that Turki explicitly asked the Taliban to turn Bin Ladin over to Saudi Arabia. The Saudis would not have wanted to deal with the Bin Ladin problem themselves, as his presence in the kingdom, whether in detention or not, likely would have stirred up popular support for the al-Qa'ida leader. More likely, Turki encouraged Mullah Omar to restrict Bin Ladin's terrorist activities or to turn Bin Ladin over to a third country. When Turki gave me a partial readout of the visit, he said that Mullah Omar received him courteously and did not reject outright whatever Saudi request was made. "He said he would think about it," Turki said.

After al-Qa'ida carried out devasting attacks in August against U.S. embassies in Dar es Salaam, Tanzania, and Nairobi, Kenya—killing more than two hundred, including twelve Americans, and injuring several thousand—we asked Turki to meet Mullah Omar a second time and press for Bin Ladin's extradition to Saudi Arabia or to the United States. Once again, at Crown Prince Abdullah's direction, Turki traveled to Afghanistan in September, only weeks after the United States had launched retaliatory cruise missile strikes against al-Qa'ida targets in Afghanistan and Sudan. The reception Turki received in the second meeting was hostile. "Mullah Omar was a different person this time," Turki told me. "He was angry and anxious, and he did not want to talk at all about deporting Bin Ladin. He was furious at America's missile strikes, which he said killed Afghans and their guests." Sensing little ability to affect Mullah Omar's attitude toward Bin Ladin and his al-Qa'ida organization, the Saudi leadership contented itself, and tried to placate the United States, with freezing its diplomatic ties to the Taliban. Saudi Arabia did not officially break diplomatic relations with the Taliban until after al-Qa'ida's 9/11 attacks against the United States.

Although GID was the CIA's principal organizational counterpart, I worked hard to strengthen ties to Saudi Arabia's main internal security service, the Mabahith, which falls within the Ministry of Interior. With extensive investigative, arrest, detention, and interrogation authorities, the Mabahith was and remains the main Saudi agency responsible for domestic counterterrorism programs as well as for uncovering subversive activities considered a threat to the monarchy. Despite Mabahith's reputation for using harsh and coercive methods for extracting information from detainees, I felt that it was imperative to establish a better relationship with the organization that had the best insight into al-Qa'ida's presence and influence in the kingdom. Besides, closer ties to Mabahith would enable a better understanding of its counterterrorism capabilities and provide an opportunity to help it professionalize its ranks.

Since the FBI has responsibility for investigating and bringing criminal indictments against the perpetrators of terrorist attacks against Americans abroad, the Bureau was working principally with Mabahith on the Khobar Towers bombing. As a result, I coordinated CIA counterterrorism collection efforts closely with FBI Director—and fellow St. Joseph's High School alumnus—Louie Freeh during his many visits to Saudi Arabia. Although the FBI and CIA had different priorities when meeting with Mabahith—the FBI was keen to learn details about the bombing that would help determine culpability, while the CIA sought information to prevent future attacks—I found that maximum transparency and information sharing between the two organizations was the best way to advance the mission of both organizations. While the FBI legal attaché in Riyadh, Bassem Youssef, shared that view, there were many individuals in our respective organizations who did not. It was an object lesson for me in future years.

I learned another valuable lesson about information sharing during my second posting in Saudi Arabia, which was that the CIA should always demonstrate the attributes of a professional intelligence service when dealing with its foreign counterparts. CIA officers at Langley were understandably frustrated at the limited counterterrorism cooperation shown by both GID and Mabahith. Repeated CIA requests for information about Saudi citizens and expatriates living in Saudi Arabia who were known or suspected to be affiliated with al-Qa'ida were met with denials or silence. Frequently, I received direction from CIA headquarters to ask Mabahith to detain and question individuals without the benefit of sharing with the Saudis information on which the request was based. While I understood Langley's frustration over Saudi foot-dragging, I felt that the CIA could release some incriminating information about the individuals to the Saudis without compromising sources and methods. Unfortunately, the chief of the CIA's al-Qa'ida unit, Michael Scheuer, was strongly derisive of the Saudis and refused to release any relevant information until they became more cooperative. Scheuer's obstinacy led me to lose my cool, and I profanely, and unprofessionally, denounced his position in my correspondence with headquarters, arguing that the CIA was the world's premier intelligence agency and needed to lead by example. I found the views expressed by Scheuer before and after his retirement, when he regularly and publicly spewed anti-Israel and anti-Arab vitriol, a discredit to the Agency.

While there, I played host to a series of congressional delegations traveling to the kingdom to consult with Saudi leaders and embassy staff. One visit that stands out was by Senator Arlen Specter, who was then serving as the powerful Republican chairman of the Senate Select Committee on Intelligence (SSCI). The visit was scheduled during the Islamic month of Ramadan, when all Muslims are required to abstain from eating and drinking between sunrise and sunset. Prior to his visit, Specter had been advised that U.S. diplomats and visiting U.S. officials show respect for the Islamic custom by not eating or drinking in public or in the company of Muslims during Ramadan. On the first full day of his visit, Specter and I spent the morning with Ambassador Fowler and embassy officers discussing the state of U.S.-Saudi relations and the challenge of getting the Saudis to share terrorism-related information with us. "I'll do whatever I can to help," Specter said as we prepared to depart the embassy for a meeting with GID Director Prince Turki.

When we climbed into our armored vehicle, I noticed that Specter had a can of Diet Pepsi with him, so I felt compelled to remind him about the Ramadan restrictions. "No problem, John," the senator assured me. "I've traveled the world many times and have been accustomed to dealing with different cultures and religious practices."

When we arrived at the entrance of GID headquarters, I was surprised but pleased to see about two dozen GID officers standing at attention in the midday sun in a show of respect for the visiting intelligence committee chairman. "They're giving you the royal treatment," I said to Specter, as we pulled up to the front door and came to a stop. Specter smiled but said nothing as he began to exit. Then, shockingly, Specter stood next to the vehicle and proceeded to take repeated gulps from his Diet Pepsi in full sight of the Saudis nearby. Placing the can of Diet Pepsi on the roof of the car, he slowly put on his jacket before taking one last gulp. I felt like throttling him right there and might have if Prince Turki had not suddenly appeared at the entrance to personally greet the senator. I had to satisfy myself by giving Specter a brusque "goodbye" at the conclusion of our meeting with Prince Turki and by not spending any more time with him for the rest of the visit.

Specter's appalling performance outside GID headquarters epitomized the Senate version of the the Ugly American who is insensitive to social and cultural practices of foreign lands, as portrayed in the 1958 novel by Eugene Burdick and William Lederer. Tragically, I have found in recent years that increasing nationalism, nativism, isolationism, and xenophobia within too many segments of American society have made insensitivity such as Senator Specter's all too prevalent, including at the highest levels of our government.

12

BACK AT LANGLEY
DURING STORMY TIMES

By the summer of 1999, Kathy and I were more than ready to return home. We enjoyed our second adventure in Saudi Arabia and were glad that the children had the opportunity to experience life in a foreign culture and to travel with us on several occasions outside the kingdom. But after nearly five years combined during our two tours in Saudi Arabia, we both found living in the kingdom to be increasingly stifling. Moreover, my Saudi portfolio, while important, was limited in scope, and I yearned to be involved in broader national security matters. A few days before we departed, George called on the secure line to follow up on an earlier conversation about my next assignment. "So, I've been giving some thought to what you should do when you return to headquarters," he said.

"That's great, George. As long as you think it will be interesting, I'm happy to do it." I knew George had much more important things to do than serve as my personal career development officer, but if he had found a job for me, I was prepared to say yes to whatever it was.

"Oh, it definitely will be interesting," George said, and then added with a laugh, "but you'll be working for a real pain in the ass." George needed to say no more, as his familiar cackle told me that he would be the "pain in the ass" I would be working for. He didn't reveal the specific job he had in mind during the phone call, and it wasn't until I showed up in his office in late August that I learned I would become his chief of staff. I remember feeling very nervous about assuming chief-of-staff responsibilities, despite having served a similar function when he was deputy director. But George was now in charge of the entire intelligence community as well as the CIA, and I didn't know if I was ready to handle the pace and volume of the workload, which I knew would be crushing. Being chief of staff to the head of any U.S. government department or agency is simultaneously one of the very best as well as one of the most challenging jobs in public service. A chief of staff has enormous influence on the daily schedule, priorities, and even decision-making of the principal. At the same time, a chief of staff frequently serves as negotiator, arbiter, counselor, complaint department, and "bad cop" on behalf of their boss when dealing with bureaucratic battles and disputes among senior officials. While I would be exposed to a broad range of very interesting substantive issues, I also would be enmeshed in a lot of less-than-titillating administrative and organizational "stuff."

I didn't know it then, but serving as George's chief of staff was the best preparation I could have had for my eventual tenure as CIA director. I had unfettered access as chief of staff to all CIA and intelligence community programs, activities, and problems. Along with other members of George's staff, I helped oversee the flow of people and paper into his office, and I was shocked at how much information he had to absorb daily. Even after full days of back-to-back meetings, I would hand him a large folder of homework as he was heading out the door every night—things to read, sign, and comment on—which made me an unpopular person in the Tenet household. When I became director, I always felt that my chiefs of staff took a little bit too much delight in handing me my homework folder as I headed out the door. It always brought back memories of when I served in their role.

My chief-of-staff perch also gave me unique insight into the CIA's dependence on the strong relationships it had developed over the years with foreign intelligence and security services and how the CIA director sustains them. I traveled extensively with George on his overseas trips, and I watched the way he nurtured close ties with heads of services and of governments, who often saw the CIA as an honest broker without partisan agendas. George's work in the Middle East was especially noteworthy. I accompanied him many times when he shuttled back and forth between Tel Aviv, Jerusalem, Ramallah, and Gaza to negotiate cease-fires between Israelis and Palestinians, with both sides looking to George to bridge differences between them. In George's many meetings with Yasir Arafat, I would be the scribe and not-infrequent whisperer in George's ear, which led the PLO chairman to refer to me as a lawyer. "Have the lawyer write it up," Arafat would say in his heavily accented English as he pointed to me after he described the steps—never the concessions—he was willing to take to end violence. George's carefully cultivated personal relationship with his foreign counterparts made a lasting imprint on me, and I tried to emulate his example when I became CIA director.

I also had a front-row seat as chief of staff during the 2000 presidential election, when the outcome remained in doubt until a Supreme Court ruling effectively gave George W. Bush the electoral college victory five weeks after the last popular vote was cast. The CIA provided daily support to two "presidents-in-waiting" during that time. After Bush was declared the winner, George met with him in Washington in mid-January to brief him on CIA covert-action programs. George also began to participate in Bush's daily PDB sessions and, within a few weeks, developed a good relationship with the new president. When the Republican Bush asked the Democratic-appointed Tenet to remain as director, it sent a strong signal to the intelligence community that its work was above partisan politics and that its director was viewed as a strong asset to America's national security.

After serving as chief of staff for eighteen months, I moved to a new position on the CIA's seventh floor in March 2001, when George shuffled his executive leadership team. George had decided to select Buzzy Krongard, the former CEO and chairman of the investment bank Alex Brown, to serve as the CIA's executive director, a position akin to a chief operating officer in the private sector (the position title was changed to chief operating officer in 2017). George had brought Buzzy into the Agency two years earlier to serve as his senior adviser, and Buzzy impressed George with his no-nonsense and decisive business approach to dealing with nettlesome Agency matters. Since Buzzy was still learning the full range of CIA programs and activities, George asked me to be his deputy, serving as "Mr. Inside" to Buzzy's "Mr. Outside."

Buzzy was an excellent mentor. While he and I sometimes had philosophical differences regarding certain CIA programs—Buzzy was a very strong advocate of aggressive CIA activities and covert action abroad—I learned a lot from his straightforward management style and his intolerance of bureaucratic inertia and dishonesty. On the day we both learned that I would serve as his deputy, he gave me a piece of advice that I regularly shared with those who subsequently worked for me. "John, I want you to know that you are authorized to make mistakes," he said to me with a serious look on his face. I was taken aback by what I heard and looked at him with a blank stare. I had never received such guidance from anyone I had worked for previously. He went on. "Let me explain. I want you to feel empowered to make decisions in a timely fashion and not to agonize over them." I was nodding my head as he spoke. "But let me qualify that a bit. I don't want you to make the same mistake twice, because that would indicate you are not a learning individual. And second, make sure you understand the difference between decisions that are 'above the waterline' and those that are 'below the waterline.'" Buzzy, who had served in the marine corps, used the nautical metaphor to explain that the Agency can take a lot of hits as long as they do not compromise the seaworthiness of the CIA ship. "Hits near or below the waterline can be devastating," he said, "so before making any decision that could result in a hit that might result in the CIA taking on water, raise it up the chain of command."

It was very sound advice, and I have since used that same metaphor many times. It has been my experience that the best leaders and managers—at the CIA, in other government agencies, and in the private sector—are those who have a good sense of what they are empowered and need to do on their own volition and what they need to push up the organizational ladder. After listening to Buzzy's approach to leadership and management, I was eager to join him in the executive director's suite as deputy executive director. Buzzy, as executive director, was referred to as "EXDIR," and I was given the moniker "DEXDIR," a name that my children still occasionally roll out to this day when they believe I am plying my management traits at home.

Soon after I started working for Buzzy, I witnessed his leadership style in action, including his determination to never let a problem fester, even small ones, lest they get worse over time. Buzzy and I received regular briefings from the office of security, and one day we were told that an Agency officer was suspected of pilfering lunch items from the Agency cafeteria. I could see Buzzy's eyes grow wider as he listened to the account. "If he's stealing food," he said, "who knows what else he might be doing that we don't see." Buzzy gave direction that he wanted to be notified the next time the employee was headed to the cafeteria so that he could catch him in the act. Sure enough, Buzzy surveilled and then detained the employee as he bypassed the cashier. Buzzy was right. The theft of even a few dollars' worth of food reflected a lack of integrity on the part of the employee, a character flaw with no place in the Agency. Years later, when I was director, there were more than a few days when I wished that Buzzy was still roaming the halls of Langley so that he could have found any employees who might have been falling short on the integrity scale.

On the morning of September 11, 2001, I was in George's seventh-floor conference room attending the morning meeting of CIA senior executive staff. Deputy Director of Central Intelligence John McLaughlin was chairing the meeting, as George was having breakfast with former SSCI chairman Senator David Boren in Washington, D.C. At the very end of the meeting, the head of CIA's Operations Center opened the conference room door and announced that a plane had just crashed into the World Trade Center. He had no further details on whether the aircraft was large or small, and it was unclear at that moment whether it was a tragic accident or the intentional targeting of the iconic twin towers. The staff meeting ended abruptly, and we all headed back to our offices with an uneasy feeling about what we had just heard and what we might soon find out. Returning to my office directly across the hall from the conference room, I stopped to watch the television in the outer office of the executive director's suite, which was tuned to CNN's coverage of the smoldering North Tower. As I watched along with several of my colleagues, a large passenger plane hit the South Tower, sending a billowing cloud of smoke and debris into the air. "Oh my God!" we said in virtual unison. "We're under attack," someone behind me added in a solemn voice.

As soon as the second plane hit, I suspect that virtually everyone at the CIA immediately concluded that al-Qa'ida was responsible. In the months leading up to the attack, there had been a steadily increasing drumbeat of reporting about al-Qa'ida's plans to carry out a major terrorist attack against the United States, but the crucial details about where and when the attack would take place were lacking. No longer. Over the next hour, and as George returned to the building, we learned that the Pentagon had been attacked and that a plane had crashed in Shanksville, Pennsylvania, after being commandeered by terrorists who were subsequently overpowered by heroic passengers. George called his senior staff back into the conference room to coordinate actions that the CIA would need to take as the attack against our homeland was unfolding. According to earlier intelligence reports, CIA headquarters was on a list of potential al-Qa'ida targets, so one of the first decisions was to evacuate the building. George and other senior staff along with essential personnel relocated to the CIA's printing plant, which was in a separate building on the Langley compound. Most other CIA employees would be directed to go home.

As the building emptied over the next several hours—gridlock on local roads prevented a faster evacuation—I walked through the halls, knocking on doors to make sure everyone was getting out of harm's way. From the director's suite on the seventh floor, I scanned the brilliant blue skies in search of any commercial aircraft that might still be airborne in the capital region. It was an eerie feeling, as the building never sounded so silent or seemed as vulnerable as it did that afternoon. There was a notable exception to the emptying of offices. The hundreds of women and men of the Counterterrorism Center stayed at their posts and worked furiously to understand what was happening and what might yet occur on that September day. Their offices were humming with activity, as they carried out their responsibilities to channel intelligence and analysis to George and other senior government officials without regard to the danger they faced.

The days, weeks, and months that followed were among the busiest I had ever experienced at the CIA. As the U.S. government organized itself to recover and respond to the worst foreign attack ever on U.S. soil, the CIA demonstrated its agility and foreign area and language expertise by deploying a handful of officers to Afghanistan just two weeks after the 9/11 attacks. Those officers and others who followed would be the vanguard of the massive U.S. military forces that would flow into Afghanistan. And when Mike Spann, one of the CIA's own, was the first American killed in combat during an uprising by Taliban prisoners on November 25, it was a tragic portent of the many years of fighting and the many deaths that would follow. While George and John McLaughlin were involved in what seemed like nonstop meetings at the White House, Buzzy and I did our best to ensure that CIA components had the money, personnel, and logistics support they needed to carry out their missions. The toughest part of my job was ensuring that CIA components not working on counterterrorism were still able to carry out their missions. Money wasn't the problem, as the Agency's budget was significantly increased after 9/11. The real challenge was finding enough people to surge on counterterrorism and to fill slots in other components. There were some painful trade-offs, and CIA coverage of other issues had to be trimmed.

The CIA determined early on that al-Qa'ida had second and third rounds of attacks against the homeland planned, including what would have been a deadly wave of attacks using aircraft against the West Coast. Thankfully, those plans were thwarted by effective intelligence work carried out by the CIA and its American and foreign intelligence and law enforcement partners. But large-scale terrorist attacks were not the only serious threat to emerge at that time. Beginning one week after 9/11, letters containing anthrax were mailed to U.S. news media outlets and to the offices of Senators Tom Daschle and Patrick Leahy, ultimately killing five individuals and injuring seventeen. With physical security measures at CIA facilities already heightened, we added new procedures and technical capabilities to irradiate all mail sent to CIA buildings. In the months following 9/11, the CIA had the attributes of an organization at war, which we were.

In October 2002, the Washington capital region was again the target of violent attacks, when ten people were killed and three critically injured in what became known as the D.C. sniper attacks.

As al-Qa'ida's plans to carry out strategic attacks were being disrupted, there was concern that it might be opting for what became known as "lone wolf" or "lone actor" terrorist attacks. Following several shootings in northern Virginia, local police departments noticeably stepped up patrols and nervous neighbors were regularly asking whether it was safe for their families to venture outdoors. It was quite evident that the series of terrorist, anthrax, and sniper attacks in the span of thirteen months had profoundly shaken the psyches of people living in the Washington, D.C., area.

Free time was an especially rare commodity in the year following 9/11, with long days and nights the norm for most CIA officers. I certainly did not have the most difficult job at the CIA, as many case officers, analysts, support specialists, and technical experts—women and men—were working around the clock and routinely deploying at a moment's notice to far corners of the world to track down al-Qa'ida operatives and their support networks. Nevertheless, the long days were starting to catch up with me, and I was beginning to drag by the fall of 2002. Kathy insisted I see the doctor, and during a physical exam and subsequent sonogram, I was told that I had testicular cancer. The medical recommendation was straightforward: more sleep, a better diet, surgery, and radiation therapy four times a week for five weeks. I scheduled my radiation sessions for late in the afternoon so that I could continue to carry out my deputy executive director responsibilities during the day. By the time I finished my radiation treatments, in mid-December, I was physically exhausted and looking forward to a bit of a holiday break.

In early January 2003, George came into my office and said that he and his wife, Stephanie, wanted to go to dinner that weekend with Kathy and me. The pace of events over the past sixteen months had left little time or energy for the four of us to socialize except for the occasional CIA event. "We can celebrate the end of your radiation treatments as well as my birthday!" George said with a smile. It was a wonderful idea.

George picked the restaurant, and given his Greek American heritage, it was fitting that we dined at the Greek Taverna in Mc-Lean, Virginia. As we made our way through the meal, I could tell that George wanted to talk about work. He had been on a grueling schedule for much of his tenure as director and before that as deputy director. All told, he had been at the Agency for seven and a half very busy years, and he was tired. "I had planned to stay as director for a year or two at the most after Bush was elected so there would be continuity between the two administrations," he said, "but 9/11 changed all that. I had to stay longer."

"You've done more than your part, George," I responded. "You can leave now before you run yourself into the ground. You owe it to yourself as well as to Stephanie and John Michael [their son]."

"I can't," he said. "The folks downtown want to start a war with Iraq, and I need to make sure that the Agency does not get sidelined or, even worse, used in the process. If I leave, it will." George didn't say who was itching for war, but I knew that he was referring to Vice President Dick Cheney, Secretary of Defense Donald Rumsfeld, Deputy Secretary of Defense Paul Wolfowitz, and Undersecretary of Defense for Policy Doug Feith, all well-known advocates of toppling Saddam Hussein by military force. Feith had even set up a shop at the Pentagon to produce his own "intelligence reports" that falsely alleged a close connection between the Baghdad government and al-Qa'ida. Jami Miscik, a close colleague and friend in charge of all CIA analysis at the time, was engaged in an all-out battle with Cheney's chief of staff, Scooter Libby, who was circulating a misleading paper that included all reported contacts, no matter how specious, between Iraq and al-Qa'ida. I could see by the look in George's eyes that no matter how much he wanted to take off his increasingly heavy director's pack, he wouldn't. He simply cared too much for the men and women of the Agency and wanted to do what he could to protect them.

George wound up staying for another eighteen months. He was

never an advocate for war with Iraq. In George's memoir, *At the Center of the Storm,* he explained that his use of the term "slam dunk" with President Bush in December 2002 was in reference to his certainty that additional intelligence on the judgments in the estimate—that Iraq had chemical weapons, had the ability to make biological weapons, was in the process of reconstituting a nuclear weapons program, and was building missile systems to deliver biological, chemical, and nuclear warheads to target—could be declassified for a public presentation. He did not say that the judgments were a slam dunk, as many pundits have alleged. Nevertheless, George was director of central intelligence when President Bush and his national security team were given what turned out to be an intelligence community assessment that was seriously flawed as a result of numerous analytic missteps. One of the most noteworthy was that intelligence community experts had relied heavily on information provided by a source of German intelligence—the now infamous "Curveball"—who turned out to be a fabricator. Readers of the estimate believed that its analytic conclusions were correct.

They were not.

13

FALLING SHORT

Based on the intelligence I saw at the time as well as in the years that followed, I am absolutely certain that al-Qa'ida would have succeeded in carrying out additional devastating attacks against the United States after 9/11, including in the homeland, had it not been for the outstanding work of CIA officers around the world. George, John McLaughlin, and virtually everyone else at the CIA worked feverishly in the days, weeks, months, and years that followed 9/11 to do everything possible to disrupt al-Qa'ida's follow-up plans. As deputy executive director from March 2001 until March 2003, my job was to work with Buzzy to ensure that sufficient funding, matériel, people, and logistical support were available to CIA components. Others were responsible for the actual conduct of CIA's foreign intelligence missions—clandestine collection, all source analysis, covert action, counterintelligence, and liaison relationships.

The CIA has been involved in many controversial programs during its long history but none more so than the Rendition, Detention, and Interrogation covert-action program, known by its initials, RDI. Initiated in response to al-Qa'ida's 9/11 attacks, the RDI program has been the focus of extensive debate and criticism for its use of interrogation tactics that involved physically abusing detainees in the belief that it would elicit intelligence on al-Qa'ida's terrorist plans and organizational structure. Contrary to an unfortunate widespread misimpression, the CIA does not decide on its own to conduct covert actions abroad or to determine the contours of any such program. Rather, all CIA covert-action programs, including the RDI program, are authorized by a formal written document called a "finding" signed by the president. Findings can be modified by a document called a memorandum of notification (MON), which also is signed by the president. Following the 9/11 attacks, the Agency's existing covert-action authorities to go after terrorists were modified in a MON signed by President Bush on September 17, 2001. That document authorized the CIA to "undertake operations designed to capture and detain persons who pose a continuing, serious threat of violence or death to U.S. persons and interests or who are planning terrorist activities." Typically, presidential findings and MONs authorizing CIA covert-action programs are the result of a rigorous interagency process taking place over a matter of months involving extensive discussions among policy makers, intelligence officials, subject matter experts, and lawyers. In the case of the RDI program, the gravity and exigencies of the terrorist threat following 9/11 prompted a MON to be drafted by the CIA, reviewed by the National Security Council, and signed by the president within a matter of days. Over the next year, a series of memos authored by the Office of Legal Counsel in the Department of Justice, considered the highest legal advisory component in the executive branch, described the legal rationale and authorization for the CIA to use enhanced interrogation techniques, including waterboarding, during its interrogation of detainees. It was the first time in CIA history that it was authorized to capture, detain, and interrogate individuals.

All CIA covert action is conducted under the authority of the director of the CIA and the auspices of the CIA's deputy director for operations, who is colloquially known as the DDO. The DDO assigns primary responsibility for the covert-action program to a specific component in the CIA. For the RDI program, the Counterterrorism Center was given the lead.

As deputy executive director, I had broad access to virtually all Agency programs and activities. My executive assistants would put a variety of cables, memos, action items, intelligence reports, and other items they deemed important for me to see in both my hardcopy and computer inboxes throughout the day. I am not sure how many cables from the field detailing the application of enhanced interrogation techniques, including waterboarding, on CIA detainees made it into my inboxes. But I vividly remember learning the sordid details for the first time in August 2002, when I read about the interrogation and waterboarding of Abu Zubaydah, an al-Qa'ida member who was mistakenly believed at the time to have had greater influence within the organization than was the case. The description of the interrogation session was graphic and stomach turning. It recounted the repeated waterboarding applications and how Abu Zubaydah frequently gagged and threw up. During the interrogation, CIA officers and medical personnel in attendance made sure that Abu Zubaydah did not drown, bringing him back from the brink of unconsciousness and reviving him before once again pouring water onto a cloth covering his nose and mouth from a height of twelve to twenty-four inches. The account also made clear that the entire interrogation was carried out in strict conformance with CIA authorities as articulated in the presidential finding, MON, and Department of Justice memos that authorized the program and the techniques employed.

As soon as I read the cable, I told my staff that I needed to take a walk. I first grabbed an opened pack of stale cigarettes that I kept stashed in my bottom desk drawer for emergencies and headed out to the parking lot. I found an area at the far end of the lot with no one around and lit up. "My God," I thought, "what are we doing?"

I was aware that the CIA was detaining al-Qa'ida members, and I knew that Abu Zubaydah was severely injured when captured in Pakistan in March and had recovered sufficiently to undergo interrogation. I did not attend meetings of the Covert Action Review Group (CARG), where details of the RDI program were discussed. Nevertheless, I was aware that harsh interrogation techniques had been approved for use by CIA interrogators.

I guess it was reading an actual account of the application of the enhanced interrogation techniques that made me question the appropriateness and ethics of the program. I had been in the CIA for more than twenty years, but I felt that I was confronting for the first time an ongoing CIA activity that I found morally repugnant. I knew that al-Qa'ida was working overtime to carry out more devastating terrorist attacks, and the CIA needed to do what it could to thwart Bin Ladin's plans. But I also had a strong sense that the practices were brutal and inhuman and should not be carried out by the U.S. government, especially by my fellow CIA officers.

I had another couple of cigarettes and, feeling light-headed, started my walk back to the building. To burn off some pent-up frustration, I walked up the stairwell to the seventh floor. On the sixth floor, I ran into Rob Richer, a very talented and conscientious operations officer who I had come to know and respect when we had overlapping tours in neighboring Middle East countries in the late 1990s. When I ran into Rob in the stairwell, he was serving as the head of the DO's human resources component. While the position was eschewed by virtually every other senior case officer, Rob saw it as an opportunity to reform the rather antiquated culture and human resource practices of the DO. The fact that he agreed to take the position was another reason why I liked and respected Rob, and I tried to support him as best I could from my perch as the Agency's deputy executive director.

"Rob, have you received any readouts of the interrogation sessions?" I asked him. "I just did," I said, "and I feel sick." The cables from the field providing details of the interrogation sessions were very closely held within the CIA, and I did not know whether Rob was privy to them. But he was aware of the contours of the RDI program and said that he shared my concerns about what the CIA was doing.

"This will become public one day, and, when it does, the Agency will pay a heavy price for years to come," he said presciently. He then added, "I'm certainly glad that I'm not involved in that program."

When I got back to my office, I went to see Buzzy and told him that I had just read the cable about Abu Zubaydah's waterboarding and found the details horrifying. As always, Buzzy heard me out but was his usual tough self. He acknowledged that the interrogation program was nasty business, and then he quickly pivoted to talking about what al-Qa'ida had done to innocent men, women, and children on 9/11 and what they were still plotting to do. "We're not killing them, and we need to find out what they know. This is the only way we're going to get it from them."

I couldn't shake the mental images of Abu Zubaydah's waterboarding session and decided to wander the halls for a bit before tackling my inbox again. In those days, it seemed like everyone on the seventh floor, and on the floors below, was staying late at work. There was simply too much to do and not enough time to get it done. CIA officers of all grades and of all professions were involved in something of importance around the clock and around the globe. Most evenings, I would wander across the hall and into the DCI's suite to check in with George or John Moseman, who was my very able replacement as George's chief of staff. On this night, I asked George's special assistant, Dottie Hanson, to give me a call when George had a minute to see me before he headed home. It was nearly 8:00 P.M. when Dottie got back to me.

"He just got back to his office, but he's beat," she said. "He's heading home in a few minutes, so if you want to see him, you better come over right now."

"I'll be right there, Dottie," I said, as I jumped from behind my desk.

George's stamina was legendary, but I knew from our years working together that once fatigue descended upon him, it did so quickly and with a firm hold.

"Hi, George," I said, as I peered into his office from behind his half-open heavy wooden door. "Do you have a minute?"

George was sitting in his chair, looking totally exhausted, as Dottie had forecast. "Sure," he said as he leaned back with his eyes half closed, "what's up?"

"I just read the report of the Abu Zubaydah interrogation. It was awful." I told George what I had read and provided some of the graphic details. His eyes remained closed for a few more moments and then he opened them, saying forcefully, "You need to talk to Buzzy and Pavitt [referring to Jim Pavitt, the deputy director for operations at the time]. We sure as hell better not be doing anything that has not been explicitly authorized by DOJ."

"That's the problem, George," I said. "We're not."

As CIA director, George had the legal authority and the professional obligation to carry out a covert-action program that had been duly authorized by the president of the United States and deemed lawful by the Department of Justice. Moreover, the RDI program was designed to prevent al-Qa'ida from ever again murdering in cold blood thousands of innocent men, women, and children, and the CIA was integral to the realization of that goal. But the program was far different from anything else the CIA had undertaken since its founding, and we had no experience in managing such difficult, controversial, and politically fraught activities. Maybe it was the images of the iconic World Trade Center towers burning and collapsing in a hail of dust, ashes, and human detritus in the streets of lower Manhattan; or of the dozens of individuals who jumped to their deaths from far above concrete sidewalks and asphalt streets in a vain effort to escape the deadly embrace of flames; or of the more than four hundred first responders—New York City's bravest and finest—who rushed to save the lives of their fellow citizens only to sacrifice their own. Whatever it was, it stimulated an unwavering surge of adrenaline in CIA officers who wanted to do their part in the war against al-Qa'ida, even if it involved the use of brutal interrogation methods. George and I were alone in his office that evening, except for that ever-present adrenaline.

"Okay, George. I'll follow up with Buzzy and Pavitt."

George was right to press the CIA's senior leaders to monitor carefully the implementation of the interrogation program to make sure that there were no excesses that went beyond the authorities that the CIA had been granted. As I headed toward the door, George barked one last order.

"And make sure we get DOJ to review and approve everything we do once again. I sure as hell do not want CIA officers hauled in front of a judge some day for what they are doing."

I returned to the executive director's suite and gave Buzzy a readout of my conversation with George. Like George, Buzzy had always been a stickler for ensuring that everything the CIA did was consistent with its legal authorities, so I knew he would act upon George's admonition to have the DOJ again review and approve the program. True to form, Buzzy immediately went to see the CIA's general counsel, Scott Muller, and told him to make sure there was no daylight between what the CIA was doing and what the DOJ was approving. Indeed, in addition to getting DOJ approval before the interrogation program started, George suspended the program several times (as did John McLaughlin when he served as acting director) to make sure the Department of Justice reaffirmed its view that the interrogation techniques were all lawful.

In the weeks and months that followed, I had a deep sense that I had failed George and the Agency. George was serving as the CIA's wartime commander, and he was doing his level best to deploy and wield the Agency's formidable intelligence and covert-action capabilities, consistent with its legal authorities, to achieve the goals that had been set out by President Bush, the commander in chief. In my view, George's senior CIA leadership team, of which I was a part, had a moral responsibility to raise questions and concerns with George about the ethics of what the CIA was being asked to do. But I do not remember many questions being raised at the time, probably because the program was so compartmented inside the Agency and because many CIA officers involved were strong advocates of the harsh interrogation techniques being employed.

For my part, I pulled my punches in my conversations with George once I was exposed to the grim reality of the interrogation sessions. I never said to him, "George, this program is unethical. It is wrong. No CIA officer—no American for that matter—should be carrying out these practices. They are un-American." I also did not consider resigning from the CIA in protest. With another three years to go before being eligible to retire, I simply decided to never read another interrogation cable or have another conversation about the enhanced interrogation techniques with George, deciding instead to focus only on my job. The seriousness of the threat posed by al-Qa'ida provided an all-too-convenient excuse for why I suppressed my strong misgivings about the program. I am sure other CIA officers did the same.

I have committed many sins of omission during my lifetime, but I consider my failure at the time to convey my concerns about the program in clear and unequivocal terms to George and to other senior officials at the CIA my most egregious. Over time, I would realize the mistake I made, and I would vow never to remain silent again.

During my subsequent tenure as CIA director and while writing this memoir, I have thought long and hard about the interrogation program. Too often and for too many, myself included, the context of the post-9/11 environment is lost when commenting on the "morality" of the program (a much different calculus applies when evaluating the efficacy of the interrogation techniques and whether they produced reliable threat information). With the embers of the World Trade Center still smoldering, the United States government was in a desperate race against time to avert further and potentially far greater loss of life. There was no doubt that al-Qa'ida made plans for follow-up waves of attacks, and intelligence reporting indicated that crudely designed nuclear weapons might be used (George traveled to Pakistan six weeks after the 9/11 attacks to highlight to President Pervez Musharraf the gravity of U.S. concerns about the potential for Pakistani nuclear bomb designs to be obtained by al-Qa'ida). The threat was considered so real that the Department of Energy's Nuclear Emergency Support Team, which is trained to respond to nuclear events anywhere on the globe, was deployed to New York City.

It was against this backdrop of an existential threat that the CIA was authorized to use harsh interrogation techniques in an effort to extract information from cold-blooded killers. Was the obligation of the U.S. government to protect its citizens from such a fate a sufficient ethical basis to use enhanced interrogation techniques, including waterboarding? Was the program proportional to the seriousness of the threat? Did it take greater moral courage to refuse to implement the program or to allow it to take place?

Like other critics of the program, I did not have to make that very difficult decision in real time and without the benefit of hindsight. But I am sure the prospect that tens if not hundreds of thousands of innocent people might die at the hands of al-Qa'ida weighed heavily on those who did.

14

THE CHALLENGE OF A GOVERNMENT "START-UP"

In late 2002 George asked me to serve as the CIA's representative on an interagency working group that was set up by the Bush White House to look at ways to address government deficiencies that might have contributed to the failure to stop the 9/11 attacks. The group, comprising senior officials from the Departments of Defense and State, the FBI, the CIA, and the White House, was asked to come up with recommendations that would break down the organizational, cultural, and legal obstacles that stood in the way of connecting the proverbial and frequently illusive terrorism "dots" collected by the intelligence and law enforcement communities. There is little doubt in my mind that if terrorism-related threat information had been shared more broadly among U.S. government agencies prior to 9/11, we would have had a far better chance of uncovering the plot before the hijackers boarded those planes on the fateful day.

I suspect George picked me for the job because over the years that I had worked for him I had vented about the need to integrate the capabilities of the increasingly large and diverse intelligence community. More integration was clearly needed, and I had worked closely over the previous year with Larry Kindsvater, executive director for intelligence community affairs, on ways to reorganize the intelligence community in order to deal more effectively with the ever-increasing number and sophistication of intelligence challenges. Larry and I shared similar views about the need to deconstruct bureaucratic stovepipes within the national security realm, and we conducted a series of briefings to a variety of groups, inside and outside government, in hopes of kick-starting some changes that we believed were long overdue. It was well known at the time that congressional committees were sharpening their pencils on a plan to redesign the intelligence community, and many of us believed that intelligence professionals were better positioned to make recommendations on how to make more effective and efficient use of intelligence resources and capabilities than were congressional staffers.

By the middle of January 2003, the White House sent out word that it wanted to use President Bush's State of the Union address later that month to advance key national security objectives, and our working group was asked to come up with a proposal the president could highlight during his address. The group had already reached agreement that terrorism-related information obtained by individual government agencies needed to be more widely shared, so we submitted a proposal to the White House that called for the establishment of a new multiagency organization that would have access to all terrorism-related threat information. The proposal was given to President Bush's speechwriters, who liked its fresh approach. While the January 28, 2003, State of the Union address is best remembered for President Bush's listing real and purported Iraqi misdeeds that would be used to justify the U.S. invasion of Iraq less than two months later, his remarks also included the following passage:

Tonight, I am instructing the leaders of the FBI, the CIA, Homeland Security, and the Department of Defense to develop a Terrorist
Threat Integration Center, to merge and analyze all threat information in a single location.

When a president makes such an announcement, especially in a
State of the Union address, things happen. George called me into his
office the following morning and told me that the CIA was given the
responsibility of creating this new entity, and he asked me to take
the lead on designing the new center, which immediately became
known by its acronym "TTIC" (pronounced "tee-tick"). Neither
George nor I had a clear sense of how TTIC would function, but I
felt honored to be entrusted with the responsibility of taking the
lead for the CIA. Having no experience in designing and building
new organizations, I consumed as many books and scholarly articles
as I could find on how to do so. Straying from my liberal arts background, I talked to experts in systems engineering and convened
countless meetings with information technology specialists, database
managers, and lawyers to understand what was technically feasible,
legally permissible, and institutionally palatable. Large poster-paper
flip charts adorned my office, and George would drop by at least once
a day to look at TTIC's emerging organizational model. "We need to
make counterterrorism organizations more interoperable and more
interdependent," I told George, "which means we're likely to get
pushback. These organizations are notoriously insular, especially the
CIA, and they are bound to resist giving TTIC their most sensitive
intelligence." It turned out I was right.

On March 11, the White House announced that I had been appointed director of TTIC "by the Director of Central Intelligence
George Tenet, in consultation with the Director of the F.B.I., the
Attorney General, and the Secretaries of Homeland Security and Defense." The announcement also said that TTIC would begin operations on May 1. Almost overnight, I realized that I had to make good

on my years of lobbying for a more integrated approach to national security. Start-ups are rare within the government. They usually occur only after extended deliberation, debate, and compromise within and between the executive and legislative branches, with the process culminating in an act of Congress that identifies the responsibilities, appropriates sufficient funding, and authorizes the hiring of personnel for the new department or agency. TTIC had no such gestation. It had gone from concept to reality within the span of a few months and at the initiation of a very small circle of executive branch officials. Most CIA, FBI, and other government officials first learned of TTIC when the president announced its creation at the State of the Union speech. While I desperately wanted to find out for myself whether my integration imperative could work as well in practice as it functioned in theory, I began to see myself as a crash test dummy.

I had all of six weeks to get TTIC ready by the White House–imposed deadline of May 1 to reach "IOC"—initial operating capability—which would require staff, office space, computers, access to classified networks, an implementation plan, and, most important, a clear articulation of mission that would be understood and respected inside and outside TTIC. Fortunately, I was still serving as the CIA's deputy executive director, and, as such, oversaw decisions regarding the allocation of office space in CIA facilities. Donning my CIA hat, I told George and Buzzy that I had found some office space on the fourth floor of the CIA's original headquarters building in Langley that could serve as temporary quarters for TTIC's start-up. It had existing classified-network connectivity and enough space for the planned initial staffing complement of sixty. Some construction would need to be done to build a few offices and conference rooms, but I knew that the CIA's support officers were more than up to the task, if I had support from Buzzy and George. "Do it," they said.

Given the scope and importance of the presidentially authorized mission of TTIC, I knew that we would quickly outgrow our temporary quarters at CIA headquarters, so I set my sights on a larger prize. As deputy executive director, one of my responsibilities was to find additional locations for the CIA in the northern Virginia area, as the Agency's post-9/11 mission was steadily expanding well beyond the capacity of Langley. The Agency group responsible for identifying new office space had decided the previous year that a large compound in McLean, about four miles from CIA headquarters, would be an ideal second campus. A vacant six-story office building that had been used by Litton Industries, a major defense contractor acquired by Northrop Grumman in 2001, stood on the compound and would need to be razed to its girders, but it would be less costly than starting anew. I made the pitch to Buzzy and George, highlighting the importance of realizing the president's vision for TTIC. They agreed to allow TTIC to lay claim to the building if enough funds could be found to acquire and renovate it. "Don't worry," I told them, "we'll get the funds." We were able to tap into intelligence community funds for the new building, which was ready for occupancy in early 2004. As TTIC was designed to be the institutional intersection of intelligence that would help keep America safe, we gave the new facility a most appropriate name: Liberty Crossing.

My other immediate task was to recruit the smartest and hardest-working folks I could find to help me get TTIC up and running. Knowing how bureaucracies work, I was concerned that TTIC would get "castoffs" from departments and agencies rather than their strongest performers. The best way to offset the inevitable arrival of below-average contributors (some of whom did show up) was to hand-select the members of my leadership team. I first asked Deb, my chief of staff as deputy executive director, to join me. I had first encountered Deb in 1990, when she was a young and very promising analyst working for me in CTC. I had always been impressed by her intellect and tenacity. She had a well-deserved reputation for not suffering fools gladly, and I was pretty sure that we would be confronting our fair share of bureaucratic fools as we tried to get TTIC operational.

With less than sixty days remaining before TTIC was expected to be up and running, recruitment of talented people became my obsession. To my surprise, I started to get calls from individuals wanting to sign up, many of them women. One of the most welcome calls came from Cindy Bower, an accomplished senior CIA officer who was serving as the Agency's deputy chief financial officer. Cindy had always been a no-nonsense individual who had an exceptionally strong understanding of complex budget matters and related topics. Cindy and I had known each other for many years. We had numerous tussles during that time, and I was usually on the losing end whenever I made the mistake of tangling with her. She was exactly the type of person I wanted to do battle on the budget and administrative fronts, so I offered her the position of deputy director of TTIC for management.

Perhaps the male-dominated environment that had existed in the CIA since its founding caused other CIA women to see this new enterprise as a way to make their mark. Over my CIA career, I came to work closely with and admire women who were able to power through adverse gender headwinds and succeed in the Agency. Cindy and Deb certainly fit that mold, as did Vicki Jo McBee, Darlene Connelly, and Heidi Avery. Vicki Jo was a jack-of-all-trades with whom I had worked on several complicated matters in the previous two years. Although not a technical engineer, Vicki Jo had a knack for designing and implementing complex information-technology systems to support intelligence programs. Since TTIC was slated to be an unprecedented multiagency entity that would need to access, leverage, correlate, and ultimately integrate different sources of terrorism-related intelligence, I could think of no better person than Vicki Jo to tackle a very challenging systems-engineering task. Darlene Connelly was a crackerjack lawyer who worked with Buzzy and me in the executive director's suite. A former navy lawyer—officially a judge advocate general, more commonly known by the acronym JAG—Darlene was a workaholic with a brilliant legal mind. She had an effervescent personality that could soften even her toughest legal adversaries. And Heidi Avery, a recent arrival at the Agency from MITRE—a not-for-profit federally funded research and development center—had heard about TTIC's intriguing multiagency mission and wanted to support what she saw as an overdue initiative. I was especially glad that the key CIA officers joining TTIC were women, as I soon learned that the senior people being assigned to TTIC from other government departments and agencies were all men.

Getting competent professionals from outside the CIA to serve as part of TTIC's leadership team was a priority, and I was fortunate to have had good working relationships with agency heads whose support to TTIC was crucial. In consultation with George, I decided that TTIC's principal deputy should be from the FBI, and FBI Director Bob Mueller tapped senior FBI Special Agent Jim Bernazzani for the position. Jim was a twenty-year veteran of the Bureau, and he most recently had been assigned to the CIA as deputy director for law enforcement in CTC. I viewed Jim's counterterrorism experience and vast network of contacts in the Bureau and in CTC as a real plus. Admiral Lowell "Jake" Jacoby, the director of the Defense Intelligence Agency (DIA), assigned Russ Travers, an exceptionally talented senior civilian intelligence professional who had been advocating for reform within the intelligence community, including in DIA, for several years. Jake was a good friend and a strong supporter of TTIC, but I suspected he nominated Russ because he preferred that Russ implement his reform ideas at TTIC rather than in DIA. Russ soon became one of my closest confidants, a leading visionary of TTIC's full potential, and an eventual acting director of the National Counterterrorism Center who was summarily and unfortunately dismissed in March 2020 by Richard Grenell, an unqualified and inexperienced acting director of national intelligence appointed by Donald Trump.

The National Security Agency (NSA) was the other major element of the intelligence community that needed to play a large role in TTIC, as the value and volume of terrorism-related SIGINT—intercepted signals intelligence—skyrocketed following the 9/11 attacks. I had a very good relationship with NSA Director Mike Hayden when I was George Tenet's chief of staff and afterward when I was deputy executive director. A three-star air force general, Mike grew up in the intelligence business, and he knew the profession inside and out. As director of the NSA, he didn't shy away from confronting the CIA when he felt that Agency officers were not playing straight with their NSA colleagues. Frequently, I would be on the receiving end of a phone call from Mike or his deputy Bill Black and, more often than not, I would learn that Mike and Bill had a legitimate gripe with CIA actions. When TTIC was announced, Mike jumped at the opportunity to lend support, seeing the new organization as a worthwhile initiative to break down bureaucratic stovepipes between agencies that had long hamstrung collaboration on the counterterrorism front.

During one of his visits to Langley, Mike stopped by my office to chat about TTIC. "I'm going to send you one of my most experienced CT experts. He's not a trained analyst, but he is a long-ball hitter who will help you get the job done." Whenever Mike used a sports analogy, I knew that his word was as good as gold, and it proved to be the case when Bill Gaches joined the TTIC band in early April. Bill was a blunt-talking NSA civilian who had made his way to the senior ranks by taking on difficult assignments at Fort Meade, the NSA's headquarters in Maryland, as well as overseas and doing well in them. One of the first things I noticed about Bill was his diamond stud earring, which was a rarity among intelligence professionals and usually prompted double takes if not smirks from passing colleagues. I saw Bill's earring as a sign of his independence and self-confidence, two traits I very much wanted to have in TTIC. I also was jealous of the earring, having taken mine off many years before out of concern that I would be ostracized by my more conventional colleagues. That night, much to my dismay,

I conclusively determined—after repeated painful attempts to put on my earring—that the hole in my left earlobe was forever closed.

Rounding out the senior leadership team was a scholarly yet tough former marine colonel, Bill Parrish, who was assigned to TTIC by Secretary of Homeland Security Tom Ridge. Bill had served as Ridge's special assistant as well as acting assistant secretary of homeland security for information analysis, so he had the right experience and connections to be the principal liaison channel between TTIC and the fledgling Department of Homeland Security. In addition, Bill had commanded the Marine Corps Security Forces, giving him a practitioner's insight into the challenges of securing facilities and installations that could be targeted by terrorists.

With office space and staff falling into place, the most pressing challenge became getting access to the classified and unclassified networks that were owned and operated by the individual departments and agencies. After all, TTIC's main purpose was to access bits and pieces of terrorism-related information that were collected and stored by individual agencies and departments. By bringing together and then correlating relevant data that previously had been kept in separate databases, new knowledge could be attained about terrorist connections, activities, and threats. If TTIC was unable to get full and unfettered access to those networks and databases, it would fail in its mission.

While there were significant technical, legal, and logistical challenges associated with putting together a TTIC information-technology architecture to handle different types of intelligence—I wound up with more than a half dozen computer servers under my desk that I would toggle back and forth to access—those challenges paled in comparison to the political antibodies that developed inside agencies that felt threatened when they were told TTIC wanted access to their databases and computer networks. The CIA and FBI were the hardest nuts to crack. While senior officials at both agencies were eager to obtain intelligence that had been denied to them by other organizations, they were not interested in allowing employees of other agencies to access their internal files and sensitive intelligence and law enforcement data. As I tried to work through the access issue, I was accused by my CIA colleagues of abandoning the "need to know" principle essential to protecting the CIA's secrets and, most importantly, its human sources. The FBI, on the other hand, saw the TTIC experiment as a cleverly disguised effort by the CIA to purloin the FBI's sensitive law enforcement information, including information on U.S. persons. The fact that TTIC was led by a CIA officer, was housed in a CIA facility, was administratively supported by the CIA, and reported to the director of central intelligence, who also happened to be the director of the CIA, lent credence to FBI conspiracy theories about a CIA bureaucratic plot.

I had a rather loud and animated telephone conversation with FBI Director Bob Mueller, in which I pushed back forcefully on his contention that TTIC was a CIA entity and that I was carrying out clandestine CIA organizational objectives. "You are badly mistaken, Bob," I practically shouted over the phone. "The CIA is on the warpath against me for the very same reason your organization is now rebelling against the TTIC model—you guys don't want to share your data. Well, the president says you must, so I am going to continue this fight until TTIC gets access to FBI networks, CIA networks, and any other network critical to the counterterrorism mission." Eventually, both the FBI and CIA gave TTIC access to their classified systems, with some narrow legitimate exceptions, but only after I told George and Bob that otherwise I might have to inform President Bush that the CIA and FBI were actively thwarting TTIC's presidentially appointed mission.

I knew that TTIC's small size would inhibit its ability to establish itself early on as a central player in the large and diverse counterterrorism community, and I worried that some in the CIA, the intelligence community's premier all-source analytic organization, might try to stifle the work of TTIC analysts. Relying on the

CIA-dominated PDB process to deliver TTIC analysis to senior U.S. officials was not an attractive option, so we decided to develop our own daily report that would go to the president and other PDB recipients. Leveraging the presidential imprimatur of TTIC's creation, we called it the "President's Terrorist Threat Report," affectionately known by its acronym "PTTR," pronounced the same as its golf club homonym—"putter." It was a short document of only two or three pages, providing information at the top-secret code-word level on key terrorist threats and what the U.S. counterterrorism and homeland security communities were doing to thwart them.

My time at TTIC allowed me to participate in numerous meetings at the White House with President Bush and the senior members of his national security team. Usually, I would be George Tenet's "plus-one," and it was my job to brief participants on the latest available intelligence and analysis on terrorist threats to U.S. interests. As the head of a multiagency organization, I was expected to provide a coordinated community assessment as well as to identify any differences of view among intelligence agencies. Those briefings served as preludes to the ensuing policy discussion among national security principals on how to mitigate the threat. The candid discussions that took place among the U.S. government's top officials at those meetings gave me a much better impression than I had previously of the various attendees.

George W. Bush was an especially strong consumer of intelligence. He was an avid reader of the PDB and other intelligence products and seemed to thrive and learn most from free-flowing discussions with substantive experts—analysts, operations officers, and individuals returning from overseas assignments. He had far more intellectual curiosity than many outsiders presumed, and his stamina and focus remained undiminished even during marathon meetings. The nature of his questions revealed an effort to fully understand a situation so that he could identify what he believed would be the best course of action to protect the national security of the United States.

Despite my strong disagreement with some of his policy choices, such as the ill-fated 2003 U.S. invasion of Iraq, I never had the sense that President Bush used a political or partisan prism when making crucial national security decisions.

President Bush also was unfailingly courteous, which stood in stark contrast to some in his cabinet. I was George Tenet's plus-one at a National Security Council meeting on al-Qa'ida chaired by President Bush in the Situation Room in late 2004. As I was describing to the attendees an especially worrisome al-Qa'ida terrorist plot, I added some emphasis to my prepared remarks by saying something like, "To be honest, this is the most serious and well-sourced threat information we have received in several months."

Defense Secretary Don Rumsfeld interrupted before the final words were out of my mouth. "What did you say?"

I repeated my point about the seriousness of the threat and the very strong sourcing.

"No, no. Before that," he said. I had no idea what he was referring to. He continued with even stronger conviction. "Did you say, 'to be honest'? So, are you telling us that you will be honest with some things and not with others?"

I didn't even realize that I had said, "to be honest." I am sure that the blood drained from my face as Rumsfeld stared at me in what seemed like utter disbelief. Looking around the table, I could see Vice President Cheney try to stifle a grin while others rolled their eyes. Before I could say anything in response, President Bush spoke up, "Don, enough. Please go ahead, John."

I guess I was naïve to think that every cabinet member would focus only on the terrorist threat at hand rather than seek an opportunity to make rhetorical points by embarrassing a much more junior official. Still, it was an object lesson taught by a master of literal precision of the vernacular.

Rumsfeld was the major antagonist in many of the Situation Room meetings I attended. I had the impression that he often had coordinated his actions in advance with Vice President Cheney, who would sit stoically while Rumsfeld engaged in his disruptive antics. "I don't understand any of this, and it's not even paginated," Rumsfeld said in one meeting after he quickly perused a PowerPoint slide deck on the situation in Iraq that National Security Adviser Condoleezza Rice had distributed to guide the discussion. Tossing Condi's presentation aside, Rumsfeld then passed out a set of his own slides and began to brief. I could tell that Condi was angry, but she was always a model of decorum and professionalism and relied on President Bush and Secretary of State Colin Powell to help steer the discussion back on track.

Secretary Powell was an early and enthusiastic supporter of TTIC, and I especially appreciated how he handled TTIC's most notable public debacle. When TTIC was established, the CIA gave it the less-than-glamorous responsibility of counting and compiling statistics on the number of international terrorist attacks and resultant deaths, to be published in the Department of State's annual report "Patterns of Global Terrorism." In TTIC's first year handling the resource-intensive effort, a database error resulted in a significant undercounting of the statistics for 2003 that were published in the report released in April 2004. The mistake was first noticed by California congressman Henry Waxman. The report said that in 2003 there were 190 attacks with 307 killed. In fact, the correct count was 208 attacks and 625 deaths. As expected, there were extensive allegations in the media as well in Congress that the undercounting was an intentional effort by the Bush administration to overstate the success of its War on Terror. Unlike many cabinet secretaries I have known over the years, Secretary Powell could not have been more magnanimous in his understanding of the TTIC mistake, which was published in a Department of State report bearing his signature. He certainly was not happy it occurred and wanted to know what had happened and why. But, once given the facts, he told me, "Okay, mistakes happen. Now, let's get this thing cleaned up and get on with our work." Unlike the knee-jerk response of too many in Washington when problems arise, Powell never pushed to have someone fired for the mistake. I joined Secretary Powell at a Department of State press conference the following week to explain how the error occurred and to dispel the impression that the administration was deliberately trying to mislead the public about its success in the war on terrorism.

The mistake was an early blemish on TTIC's reputation, but Secretary Powell's attitude and support for TTIC's retaining the responsibility for tallying the number of terrorist attacks and deaths worldwide in the next annual report—especially in light of the flawed intelligence assessment on weapons of mass destruction in Iraq that Powell presented at the United Nations the year before—was greatly appreciated by the TTIC workforce. In my subsequent conversations with Secretary Powell over the years, the subject of the TTIC glitch frequently would come up. "Remember when we had to eat some crow on that statistics issue on terrorist attacks," he said with a hearty laugh when he called in early 2013 to congratulate me on my Senate confirmation as CIA director. "You can look back on it now as good preparation for your upcoming congressional hearings."

Some members of Congress, including Congressman Pete Hoekstra, a member of the House intelligence committee, were miffed that the Bush administration decided to establish TTIC without first seeking congressional approval, and I was hauled in front of numerous Senate and House committees that claimed some jurisdiction over TTIC's mission. Over time, I was very pleased that some key members of Congress became strong advocates of the TTIC experiment, with several visiting Liberty Crossing to encourage the multiagency workforce to persevere despite the bureaucratic challenges. I especially appreciated the bipartisan support, very thoughtful input, and tough questioning from the leadership of Senate and House homeland security committees—Senators Joe Lieberman (D) of Connecticut and Susan Collins (R) of Maine and Representatives

Chris Cox (R) of California and Jim Turner (D) of Texas. One of the most memorable congressional visits to TTIC was from Senator Ted Kennedy, who spent an entire afternoon at Liberty Crossing receiving briefings and meeting folks. I was most struck by Kennedy's kindness and politeness toward everyone, including to his own staff, the latter quality being a bit of a rarity among many members of Congress.

In addition to having a few strong advocates in Congress and the Bush administration, TTIC benefited from the creation of similar organizational models that were taking shape at the same time in the United Kingdom, Canada, and Australia. I had an especially close relationship with my British counterpart, Alan Lovell, a senior MI5 official, who raised the flag at the UK's Joint Terrorism Analysis Centre (JTAC) less than a month after TTIC's birth. Like TTIC, JTAC brought together representatives of British security and intelligence services and of government agencies with a counterterrorism mission. The ability of TTIC and JTAC to share and to coordinate terrorism threat assessments on behalf of their respective governments strengthened the already close counterterrorism cooperation between American and British intelligence and counterterrorism professionals that had been forged in the aftermath of the 9/11 attacks.

Despite several TTIC organizational and analytic missteps in its first year, for which I take full responsibility, I was confident that President Bush as well as other key administration officials and congressional leaders would consider TTIC an organizational model worthy of further development. More than anything else, TTIC's future was assured when the congressionally established 9/11 Commission released its final report in July 2004 and called for the establishment of a "civilian-led unified joint command for counterterrorism" patterned after TTIC. The following month, President Bush issued Executive Order 13354, which transformed TTIC into the National Counterterrorism Center (NCTC). I was appointed the NCTC's first director, albeit with the title "Interim Director" in deference to pending legislation that called for the center to be led by a Senate-confirmed presidential appointee. In December 2004, the president signed the Intelligence Reform and Terrorism Prevention Act of 2004, which anchored NCTC in law and placed it organizationally within the newly created Office of the Director of National Intelligence. And it was with great pride that I joined the rest of the NCTC workforce in June 2005 in welcoming President Bush for his first visit to Liberty Crossing, where we demonstrated the benefits of bringing together the knowledge and expertise of the U.S. counterterrorism community.

I was not nominated to be the first Senate-confirmed NCTC director, despite my role in establishing the center. I was never given a reason by the Bush administration as to why I wasn't selected, but I think my stubbornness and streak of independence probably had something to do with it. George Tenet had stepped down as director of central intelligence in July 2004, so I no longer had a senior-level advocate within the administration, which is usually required for presidential appointments. Retired navy vice admiral Scott Redd was subsequently nominated and confirmed as NCTC director.

Playing a role in the creation of TTIC and NCTC was one of the most professionally rewarding and personally satisfying chapters of my career. It gave me tremendous insight into the vast collection, processing, and analytic capabilities of the U.S. intelligence community, an experience that served me well throughout the rest of my government service. More profoundly, it allowed me to appreciate the importance of bringing together, despite ingrained bureaucratic opposition, all available data, knowledge, expertise, and authorities to accomplish national security missions. Too often, members of Congress and executive branch officials opt to increase the size of individual departmental budgets and bureaucracies they favor without looking at how to streamline and integrate capabilities across the government to be more effective, less unwieldy, and more efficient.

TTIC and NCTC proved the maxim that bigger government is not always better.

Smarter and more integrated government is.

15

A NEW TAC(K)

My disappointment at not being nominated to be NCTC director sapped my interest in taking on another assignment back at the CIA, especially since George had left the Agency the year before. Fortuitously, it also coincided with my eligibility to retire, which allowed me to enter the CIA's career transition program in August 2005 after twenty-five years of service. The transition program offers retiring CIA officers an opportunity to craft unclassified résumés that try to do justice to their professional experience without compromising any classified aspects of their past. As an overt employee who had held senior and publicly acknowledged positions during my career, I could list several of my specific assignments, which provided a sense of my institutional and supervisory responsibilities. It is much more challenging for Agency officers who have lived their lives in the clandestine shadows to capture the true essence of their work. Their résumés consist mainly of bland references to seemingly unexceptionable thirty-year government careers, belying the depth and breadth of their experience as well as their significant contributions to U.S. national security.

The last official day of my twenty-five-year CIA career was on Friday, November 4, 2005. I chose not to have a CIA retirement ceremony, although I had a nice farewell event at NCTC that George, Buzzy, and other close colleagues from the CIA attended. After two and a half years at TTIC and NCTC, I felt disconnected from the Agency and its senior leadership. George, John McLaughlin, Buzzy, Jami Miscik, and many others with whom I had worked closely over the previous half-dozen years were gone. I had a cordial relationship with the new CIA director, Porter Goss, who had impressed me as genuinely interested in the well-being of the CIA during our interactions when he was the chairman of the House Permanent Select Committee on Intelligence (HPSCI). A former CIA case officer whose intelligence career was unfortunately cut short due to health issues, Porter was one of the few members of the intelligence committees in either chamber who had an intimate understanding of intelligence work. He also had been personally supportive of NCTC's mission and workforce.

I continued to have a good relationship with Porter after he became director. I had little regard and even less respect for a number of the individuals he selected to be part of his seventh-floor team, however, and I didn't want my retirement to be sullied by their presence at an official farewell. One of Porter's most notorious personnel decisions was to remove Buzzy as executive director and replace him with a long-serving CIA support officer, Dusty Foggo. Dusty had worked in the logistics field, providing timely and much-needed support to CIA operational and covert-action missions abroad. Garrulous and backslapping, Dusty served in a variety of headquarters and overseas assignments, leveraging his powerful procurement authorities to befriend wealthy contractors and the politically well-connected in the corridors of Congress. During my last year at NCTC, my relationship with Dusty was tense but not hostile, as he slow-rolled CIA support to the center in deference to his pals in the Directorate of Operations. Two years after I retired, Dusty was charged in a thirty-count indictment for fraud, conspiracy, and money laundering. He subsequently was sentenced to thirty-seven months in prison after pleading guilty to one charge of fraud. In the immortal words of Forrest Gump, "That's all I am going to say about that."

On the Monday following my retirement, I started work as president and CEO of The Analysis Corporation (TAC), a small northern Virginia firm that provided classified technical and analytic support to the intelligence and law enforcement communities. I toyed with the idea of pursuing a totally new line of work in retirement but quickly realized that the only marketable skills I possessed were related to national security matters. I had become familiar with TAC during my time in NCTC and was impressed with the quality of its employees. TAC had started as a woman-owned company in the 1990s and had supported the Department of State for many years with very good reviews. I decided to join TAC rather than take a very attractive offer from the giant beltway contracting firm Booz Allen Hamilton. Although TAC was a subsidiary of a larger privately held company, I believed that the president and CEO role would give me greater opportunity to shape the company's future and to lead a workforce once again. Besides, TAC offices were located immediately adjacent to NCTC's Liberty Crossing compound in McLean, which meant that I could continue to use well-known commuting shortcuts to avoid northern Virginia's increasingly congested main roads.

Almost immediately when I retired, my life changed in three principal respects. First, I was no longer in constant 24-7 mode. I had to gear down psychologically and physically, which was difficult. For virtually my entire Agency career, and especially over the preceding decade, I had been on call any hour of the day or night, as a breaking national security development had the potential to demand my immediate engagement or presence whether I was at CIA headquarters or posted overseas. My role at TAC was much more routine and unexciting. I certainly enjoyed the people with whom

I worked and learned a lot about the business world and financial statements, but I soon found myself going through the motions of running a private-sector company. About eighteen months after I joined, TAC and its parent company were bought by a private British firm, Global, which introduced me to the world of acquisitions and mergers. It also gave me insight into the mechanisms used to protect classified work being done in companies owned by foreign firms. While TAC was supporting important national security programs, I found it difficult to get excited over the prospect of winning a government contract that would provide more revenue and profit to TAC and its parent company. For the first time since leaving graduate school, I was no longer directly involved in our country's national security mission.

Second, Kathy and I were now able to breathe more easily on the personal financial front. My starting salary at TAC was significantly higher than what I was making at the CIA when I retired. With my TAC salary augmented by annual bonuses and a government pension, we were able to steadily climb out of the rather deep financial hole that we had dug for ourselves during my days at the CIA. After twenty-five years of government service, our credit cards were maxed out, and I had lost count of the number of times we had refinanced the mortgage on our house in Herndon. While I did not feel guilty about our newfound financial windfall, I did find it rather incongruous that I was making so much more money for a job that entailed far fewer hours, had much less responsibility, and was not nearly as consequential from a national security standpoint as any of my jobs in government.

And third, I was soon able to walk once again without pain when I finally bit the bullet and had both of my arthritic hips replaced. The intensity of work in the years following 9/11 led me to believe that I could not take time off for surgery and follow-up physical therapy. Foolishly, I also thought that I could literally run through the pain by jogging several days a week despite the increasing discomfort I felt with each step. Once I retired, Kathy quickly brought me down to earth, telling me I no longer had an important job and therefore no excuse for not getting the surgery.

Since I knew that TAC alone was not going to be enough to keep me intellectually and professionally stimulated, I pursued additional opportunities while I was out of government. In late 2006, I was asked to become chairman of the board of the Intelligence and National Security Alliance (INSA), a not-for-profit organization dedicated to strengthening and professionalizing the relationship between the government and private sector, which revolved around the multibillion-dollar contracting environment. I was quite familiar with INSA, having attended several of their conferences and events, including as a featured speaker when I was at NCTC. I was impressed with the quality of the substantive reports INSA periodically published on national security matters. Moreover, very senior retired U.S. military officers who had led intelligence community agencies—including former director of the Defense Intelligence Agency (DIA) Jim Clapper, former director of DIA and NSA Ken Minihan, and former director of NSA Mike McConnell—had been chairmen of INSA and its predecessor organization, the Security Affairs Support Association (SASA) over the previous decade. When McConnell was tapped by President Bush in 2006 to replace Ambassador John Negroponte as director of national intelligence, I was humbled by the invitation to become the new INSA chairman. I greatly enjoyed my two-year tenure at INSA, as it allowed me to meet and get to know many senior private-sector officials involved in supporting the national security community. Many had found successful second careers in business after retiring from government and military service. With their top-secret security clearances and their firsthand government experience, they didn't have much trouble finding lucrative jobs in the contracting community, especially among the thousands of large and small companies dotting the D.C., northern Virginia, and southern Maryland landscape.

I also found other substantive outlets during this time. In the summer of 2006, CBS News reached out and asked if I wanted to be an on-air commentator on intelligence and national security matters for the network. In April of that year, CBS had staged a business coup when it signed the NBC *Today* show's Katie Couric to be the new *CBS Evening News* anchor. To enhance the network's substantive bench, I was added to their stable of former intelligence practitioners to provide context and historical perspective on terrorism developments. I met Katie in person a few times, but most of my interactions with her took place over the airwaves, as she would broadcast from New York while I was in the CBS studio in Washington, D.C. I also was interviewed several times on camera at TAC headquarters in McLean. Katie was unfailingly polite and very well prepared each time I was on her show.

I traveled to New York a few times to appear on CBS's *The Early Show*. One such appearance was on November 2, 2007, with Harry Smith as the anchor. During the interview, which was broadcast live, a video was shown that depicted a simulated yet graphic waterboarding of a blindfolded individual wearing an orange jumpsuit with his hands tied. Harry quoted President Bush saying that the United States does not torture, asking what that means in the context of waterboarding. I responded by saying that the CIA had used enhanced interrogation techniques on about a third of the one hundred individuals it had detained after 9/11 and that only a small proportion were subjected to the harshest techniques such as waterboarding. "And you say that some of this has borne fruit?" Harry asked me. I knew that question was coming. I told Harry that the Agency had been able to obtain a lot of information from those interrogation sessions.

"It has saved lives," I said. "And let's not forget. These are hardened terrorists responsible for 9/11 who have shown no remorse for the deaths of three thousand innocents."

I tried to stay factual in my comments, not wanting to get involved in a televised debate about what constitutes torture. I've watched the interview several times over the years, and, like most of my TV interviews, I feel that I could have done a better job. For instance, I should have said that all of the procedures were deemed lawful and authorized by the Department of Justice and that I was not claiming there was a cause-and-effect relationship between the application of the techniques and the information that was subsequently obtained from the detainees. I also failed to take advantage of the opportunity to say that I believed the techniques were unnecessary, inappropriate, and wrong. This interview would be used by my detractors a year later to argue that I didn't deserve to be President Obama's CIA director because of my stance on the CIA's interrogation program.

I also published several op-eds while I was out of government, mostly on intelligence community reform and on terrorism. The most consequential op-ed was one that I drafted but never submitted for publication. It was on Saturday morning, October 28, 2006, when I was en route to my TAC office in McLean and had the radio tuned to the local all-news station, WTOP. The president's weekly radio address came on, and I listened in disbelief when President Bush made what I considered to be inaccurate claims that Saddam Hussein and al-Qa'ida had been working closely together on the terrorism front. I knew from my years of service that this was simply incorrect. I immediately recognized that those within the White House and the National Security Council staff who had advocated for the Iraq war were working overtime to have President Bush publicly justify the disastrous military invasion that was dragging down the administration's political standing and poll numbers. With ten days to go before the critical midterm elections, the president's Saturday morning address was an obvious political advertisement to bolster Republican electoral prospects.

I was still hot when I arrived in my office. With no pressing work on my TAC agenda, I quickly banged out an 850-word draft op-ed on my computer entitled "You're Wrong, Mr. President," which proceeded to lay waste, at least in my mind, to President Bush's false commentary. As I typed, I angrily recalled the meetings I had attended in the White House Situation Room with George Tenet during which Secretary Rumsfeld, supported subtly but powerfully by Vice President Cheney, overstated the threat to U.S. national security interests posed by Saddam Hussein in order to make the case for invading Iraq. On that October 2006 morning, it took less than thirty minutes to pour my heart out and to decide then and there to submit the draft to the CIA's Prepublication Review Board (PRB) for a classification review—a necessary step for all former CIA officers. Usually, I would wait at least twenty-four hours after drafting an op-ed before submitting it to the PRB. The delay was in personal recognition that my emotions sometimes compelled me to write something to let off steam but that probably should not see the light of day. In this instance, I did not hit my "pause" button.

On the ride home that afternoon, I tried to convince myself that the op-ed was the right thing to do, despite the fact that I had never before taken such a bold public stand against an administration policy, much less a president. I told myself that my time at TTIC and NCTC gave me the substantive chops to push back against a false narrative that clearly was motivated by a political objective—to win votes in ten days' time.

That's when it hit me.

Despite my hope that the op-ed would be read as an objective and nonpartisan riposte to a politically motivated radio address, I realized that it would be interpreted by many, if not most, as a partisan shot against Republicans and on behalf of Democrats on the eve of an important election. "Ugh!" I said to myself. "I hate politics." By the time I arrived home, I had resolved to inform the PRB first thing Monday morning that I had decided to stand down on submitting the draft for publication and therefore it did not need to undergo classification review.

I dutifully sent the email to the PRB early Monday morning to ensure that Agency staff did not waste time reviewing the draft. Shortly before noon, I received a call from Heidi Avery, my former chief of staff at NCTC and one of the most competent and hardworking officers with whom I had the privilege to work in government. Heidi was then serving as a director within the Office of Intelligence Programs at the National Security Council, which was responsible for supporting the president, vice president, and national security adviser on all matters dealing with intelligence, including covert action. Heidi said she was calling as a friend and was very concerned about the furor I was stirring up with the op-ed. As I listened to Heidi, I was confused by her remark and was racking my brain to remember what I said in the few op-eds that had previously been published.

"Excuse me, Heidi," I said, "Which op-ed are you talking about?"

"The one on Iraq," she responded.

Her words hit me like a ton of bricks. As a former chief of staff to the director and as a deputy executive director, I knew full well that any draft articles submitted to the Agency by former officers were supposed to be reviewed for classification purposes only. Still trying to figure out why the NSC would have a copy of the op-ed, I quizzed Heidi a bit more. "How do you know about the op-ed, and what trouble are you talking about?"

Heidi proceeded to tell me that the op-ed was the subject of discussion in the White House that morning and that she was concerned about the potential backlash I might suffer, which she could not specify. As she talked, I felt my blood pressure rising and my mind racing a mile a minute. Why would someone in the CIA send my draft op-ed to the White House? I thanked Heidi for contacting me and told her I would follow up with the CIA to get some answers to my many questions.

With the Porter Goss regime still in place at Langley, many of my former CIA contacts and colleagues had either retired or moved on, so I scanned my mental Rolodex for someone in a senior-level position whom I trusted. The name I immediately came up with was

John Rizzo, a highly respected CIA lawyer who was serving as the acting general counsel at the time (given the difficulty of gaining Senate confirmation for CIA general counsels, John had served as acting general counsel several times and, in totality, had served as the CIA's top lawyer longer than virtually any confirmed CIA general counsel). I had a rather animated conversation with John—on my part, not his—and he acknowledged that what happened with my draft op-ed was inappropriate. "Sorry, John. I don't know why it got down to the White House," he said, adding that he did not disagree with my charge that the incident smacked of dangerous politicization by someone at the CIA. I told John that the Agency needed to investigate what happened and take appropriate steps to guard against a recurrence. I was never told how the draft got down to the White House, and I let the matter rest. At least I thought I did.

A few months later George Tenet called me at home one night. He said that Mike McConnell, the former director of NSA who had become director of national intelligence, was looking for someone to be his principal deputy, since Mike Hayden had left the position to succeed Porter Goss at the CIA. Goss's leadership team at Langley had so alienated senior CIA officers that several resigned in protest, leading the President's Foreign Intelligence Advisory Board to conduct a review of his tenure and to recommend he be replaced. George said that he had mentioned my name to McConnell as a potential principal deputy to him but wanted to check with me before encouraging Mike to call me about the job. George knew that I had mixed feelings about the Bush administration—its policies as well as some of its senior officials—but he also knew that I longed to return to public service. "Mike is a really good guy," George said, "and I believe you would enjoy working with him. He's not political in any way, and he will try to protect the intelligence community from the knuckleheads downtown."

I had not worked closely with Mike McConnell but always had a very positive impression of him, so I told George I would think about it and would call him back the following day. That night, I talked to Kathy. She knew that if I returned to government, the evenings and weekends that I had been able to spend with the family would go by the wayside. I told Kathy that I had mixed feelings about returning to government, mostly because of the impact it would have on our personal lives. Try as I might, I apparently could not find the words to conceal my inner enthusiasm at the prospect of returning to the intelligence community. Kathy had known that I had long talked about how the intelligence community needed streamlining in order to make it more efficient, and serving as the principal deputy director of national intelligence would certainly have given me that opportunity. As McConnell's deputy, I would have responsibility for coordinating intelligence budgets, programs, and initiatives across seventeen intelligence agencies, far greater statutory authority and clout than I ever had previously. She looked at me with a smile and said, "Do you want the job, John?" I knew it was a rhetorical question. Kathy and I had been married for almost thirty years, and she knew me better than I knew myself. She also understood that I felt I had unfinished work to do in government.

I called George back that night. "If Mike wants to talk about the job, I certainly will listen to what he has to say," I said.

George laughed and said, "I'm surprised it took you so long to think about it." Next to Kathy, George has always been able to read me better than anyone else.

A couple of days later, Mike McConnell called. He explained that he was looking for an experienced intelligence officer who could help him run the intelligence community. He said that he had heard that I did a good job at NCTC and that my name had been recommended by several individuals he had contacted in his search for a deputy. "They say that you've given thought to the future of the intelligence community. I also like the fact that you served in the Office of the Director of National Intelligence when you were with the National Counterterrorism Center, so you know the challenges of herding the

intelligence community cats." Mike explained that he was not offering me the job, as he would need to work with the White House on
the selection of his deputy. "I just want to know if you are willing to
have me float your name," he said.

I told Mike that I was honored that he would think of me for
the position. "I always got along well with President Bush," I told
him, "even though I did not always agree with some of his policy
decisions, especially the invasion of Iraq. But my relationship with
others in the administration was a bit rocky at times," I confessed.
I then told Mike that I had taken President Bush to task the year
before in a draft op-ed that, while never published or even submitted
to any paper for publication, gave the White House a fair amount of
heartburn. Mike said that he didn't think it would be disqualifying
since I had pulled it back before publication. The conversation was
pleasant and brief, about five minutes or so. At the end, I told Mike
that he should feel free to raise my name at the White House and
that I would consider it a privilege if I were given the opportunity to
rejoin the intelligence community and to serve as his deputy.

"Okay," Mike responded, "let's see how it goes."

A week went by, and I had not heard back from Mike. By then,
I was getting increasingly excited as well as nervous about the prospect of rejoining the intelligence community. I called George to find
out if he had heard anything more from Mike. He hadn't. "These
things take time," he counseled. Mike reached out to me later that
day, probably at George's urging, to say that he was still working
with the Office of Presidential Personnel but that he was encountering some opposition. "I've not given up yet, John, so you shouldn't,
either." I told Mike that I was still very interested in being his deputy, but I sensed that the opportunity to return to government service
was steadily slipping away.

And slip away it finally did. Within days, Mike called to say that
he was unable to get my name through the system. "I do not know for
sure, but it looks like your draft op-ed is the reason." Mike expressed

appreciation for my willingness to rejoin the intelligence community, and he wished me well. At the time, I was angry, really angry. I felt that the decision to stop my nomination was unfair and political. Over time, however, I have found less reason to quibble with the decision. The op-ed clearly underscored the depth of my disagreement with President Bush's public rationale for one of the most consequential foreign policy decisions of his administration. If I had been nominated for the principal deputy DNI position and the draft op-ed somehow came up during my confirmation hearing, it would have provided Democrats very damaging political fodder to use against the administration. But even if the Democrats remained unaware of it, the sentiments I expressed in the piece undoubtedly were seen by the Office of Presidential Personnel and senior officials in the administration as a likely harbinger of my future outspokenness, even if only within government circles, in the event I returned to government service. It was a potential problem that was easily avoided by finding someone else to be McConnell's deputy.

My disappointment in being denied the opportunity to return to government was short lived. I knew that intelligence and national security were still very much in my DNA, and I hoped that I would have another chance to return to the profession I loved at some point in the future. Indeed, by early 2008, I became very grateful to whoever made the final decision to scuttle my potential nomination to be McConnell's deputy. If I had gotten the nod and subsequently been confirmed by the Senate, I would not have had a snowball's chance in a very hot hell of ever working at the White House for President Obama or becoming CIA director.

16

JOINING THE OBAMA TEAM

I was at the Four Seasons Hotel in Dubai, United Arab Emirates, in late January 2008 participating in a board meeting of TAC's parent British company when Illinois's junior senator, Barack Obama, won the South Carolina Democratic presidential primary. As I was packing my bags for my return to the United States, I turned on CNN and watched Senator Ted Kennedy and his niece Caroline Kennedy give a full-throated endorsement of Obama's candidacy for president. Ted Kennedy said that Obama brought to mind a young candidate from another time who challenged America to cross a New Frontier. And when the Lion of the Senate said that Barack Obama had "lit a spark of hope amid the fierce urgency of now," his words lit a fire in me. I had been following Obama's steady rise in the Democratic Party over the previous year and deeply admired his eloquent articulation of America's hopes and dreams, both at home and abroad. My cousin Tom also had extolled Obama during our frequent phone calls, but I was skeptical that the young and relatively inexperienced senator was ready for the challenges of the presidency. "He could use more seasoning in the Senate," I told Tom. "He would make a more formidable candidate in 2012 or 2016. He needn't be in such a rush."

When I saw Obama on that stage in South Carolina and could feel the momentum for his nomination growing, my reservations about his candidacy evaporated. I had always eschewed partisan politics and never registered as either Democrat or Republican, or with any political party, voting over the years for Republicans, Democrats, Independents, and, on a lark, one Communist. I wanted to remain politically unaffiliated, but as a private citizen who takes his civic responsibilities seriously, I decided then and there to do something other than just vote for a candidate for political office. As soon as I returned to the States, I shared my feelings with Kathy, who also sensed that Obama was on a steady rise in the polls. It didn't take us long to decide to make a twenty-three-hundred-dollar contribution to the Obama for President campaign, the maximum individual amount allowed at the time. I then called the most politically savvy person I knew—George Tenet. I told George that I was deeply impressed with Obama and that, in addition to making a financial contribution, I wanted to explore other ways to help him get elected. George agreed that Obama's fortunes were rising but that he would have a difficult time overtaking Hillary Clinton before the Democratic convention. "I realize that," I told George, "and I certainly am not opposed to Hillary getting the Democratic nomination. But there is something I really admire about Obama and am interested in helping if I can."

George doesn't let time go by when he has something he can do for a friend, which is why I wasn't surprised when Tony Lake, who had recently become involved in the Obama campaign, called the following week to invite me to lunch in the District. I had gotten to know Tony when I was President Clinton's daily intelligence briefer. As Clinton's national security adviser, Tony was always with the president when I provided the PDB. I very much liked and respected Tony, not only for his formidable intellect but also because he made sure that the intelligence community's insights and expertise were made available to President Clinton and were integrated into the national security decision-making process. My respect for Tony grew exponentially in 1997, when he was nominated to succeed John Deutch as director of central intelligence but bowed out when political sniping by Senator Richard Shelby and a few other Republicans intensified, making his confirmation look increasingly uncertain. I was in Saudi Arabia at the time and had been looking forward to Tony becoming my new boss. Although disappointed at his withdrawal, I cheered when I read his withdrawal statement, which denounced the "political circus" in Washington. "I hope that sooner rather than later," Tony wrote, "people of all political views beyond our city limits will demand that Washington give priority to policy over partisanship. To governing over gotcha." Unfortunately, that lesson has yet to be learned.

I had just arrived and taken a seat at the outdoor café near Dupont Circle when Tony rode his motor scooter onto the sidewalk. As he walked toward me, removing a cringeworthy, less-than-fashionable helmet, he broke out into his familiar smile. After catching up on what had happened in our respective lives over the past couple of years, Tony began to talk about Barack Obama. "He's the real deal, John, and it would be great if you could help his campaign by sharing your intelligence and counterterrorism experience." Tony went on to explain that he was reaching out to a variety of individuals in hopes of bolstering Obama's limited national security expertise. Tony was not specific on what my role would be, saying only that it would not take up much of my time. Conference calls, emails, and maybe a short paper or two on topical issues would be about the extent of it.

"Sure, Tony, I'll be happy to help out." I wasn't sure what I had just committed to doing, but it sounded interesting. I knew that becoming an adviser on a presidential campaign would require termination of my CBS contract, but I was willing to give up being a paid network commentator in exchange for the opportunity to be affiliated with the Obama campaign. The following week, Tony invited me along with a couple dozen of his other recruits to a cocktail reception at his Washington, D.C., row house. As I approached the steps to Tony's home, I chatted up another individual arriving at the same time. "I guess Tony recruited you, too," I said with a smile. We remained in conversation as we stepped inside and were handed glasses of white wine. I learned that my newfound acquaintance was a lawyer in a prestigious New York law firm and had served in the Clinton administration as general counsel for the air force. He impressed me as serious yet very personable, and I could understand why he had been recruited to help the Obama campaign. We talked a bit about prevailing national security issues and our shared interest in seeing Barack Obama win the election. When I departed the reception that night, I bade him adieu and said I hoped that our paths would cross again. At the time, I had no idea that I would have hundreds more conversations and extensive professional dealings with Jeh Johnson, with whom I would serve when he became the Department of Defense's general counsel and then secretary of homeland security.

About a week after the reception, I received a call from Denis McDonough, who introduced himself as someone who was working with Senator Obama on his presidential campaign. I had never heard of Denis and knew nothing about his background. Two minutes of conversation told me a lot about Denis and his personality. The cadence of his voice was upbeat and high energy, and his comments were self-effacing. He said that he was working with Tony and others on national security issues in the Obama campaign and asked whether he could reach out to me occasionally to seek my views on substantive matters. Unsure of exactly what Denis wanted me to do, I once again agreed to volunteer my services. "Sure, call me whenever you want."

In the months leading up to the election, I participated in email exchanges and conference calls with Denis and other Obama advisers to discuss policy positions on a variety of topical issues being worked on by the campaign. As a former intelligence officer, I had not previously engaged in policy advocacy, but I seized upon my new adviser role and wrote several unsolicited memos on intelligence, national security, and Middle East policy issues that I passed to Denis. Unsure if my memos were making their way to Obama, I decided to publish an article in July in *The Annals of the American Academy of Political and Social Science* entitled "The Conundrum of Iran: Strengthening Moderates Without Acquiescing to Belligerence," which took a rather conciliatory approach to both Iran and Hizballah. I called Denis to give him a heads-up on the article's call for the next American president to tone down the rhetoric, establish a direct dialogue with Tehran, encourage greater assimilation of Hizballah into Lebanon's political system, and offer carrots in addition to sticks to weaken Iran's historic support for terrorist activities. My explicit advocacy for "greater assimilation of Hezbollah into Lebanon's political system . . . to increase Hezbollah's stake in Lebanon's struggling democratic processes" generated the most controversy, even among Obama's left-leaning supporters. It was my view then, and remains today, that the most effective way to reduce an organization's resorting to violence is to make its use of violence counterproductive to its larger political ambitions. Ever the diplomat, Denis called my position "interesting."

Being even remotely affiliated with a political campaign on the eve of a presidential election felt, well, weird. In my interactions with Obama supporters, I avoided partisan discussions that took a politically polarizing "we" Democrats against "them" Republicans approach. While there were times during the campaign when I believed Obama had become far too partisan in his public denunciations of Bush-era policies, I agreed with his overall strategic approach to national security challenges. I remember being asked by another CIA retiree why I had decided to become an Obama adviser despite what I agreed were unfair criticisms of programs involving the CIA.

"I have never agreed 100 percent with any candidate I eventually voted for," I told him. "Although I disagree with Obama about 20 percent of the time," I added, "I disagree with about 50 percent of what McCain says. My math tells me to support Obama."

By the time Election Day rolled around, I had neither spoken to nor met Barack Obama. I also hadn't participated in any fundraising or get-out-the-vote activities, as they seemed far too political for me. I was content to be a long-distance adviser and to follow the news coverage of Obama's growing momentum in the national polls. It was with great excitement as well as relief that Kathy and I, along with a few of our neighbors, watched television coverage of the results on Election Night in our Herndon living room. Going to bed that night, I thought back to the race riots that wracked major American cities in the late 1960s, including several in northern New Jersey, not far from my North Bergen home. Only forty years later, it felt really good to be able to witness the election of America's first African American president.

Two days after the election, Denis called to invite me to Chicago to meet the president-elect. Denis didn't give a specific reason for the meeting other than to say that Obama wanted to extend his personal appreciation for my support to the campaign. "Wow," I said aloud, "that would be terrific." I was rather surprised that I was being invited to meet Obama. It had only been a few days since the election, and I was sure there were many people demanding his attention and plenty of things for him to do as he prepared for his move to Washington, D.C. What seemed particularly strange was that I had played only a very minor role in the campaign, and I wondered whether he was taking the time to thank personally everyone who was involved. In any event, I was excited by the opportunity and told Kathy and my family as well as a few friends in New Jersey—all of whom had been big Obama supporters—that I would have the opportunity to meet the president-elect in person.

After working out scheduling issues with a member of the

president-elect's team in Chicago, I made a reservation to fly round trip to the Windy City on the Monday after the election. I was told that I would be met upon my arrival at the airport and that arrangements had been made to get me to Obama's office in plenty of time. I arrived on schedule at O'Hare Airport shortly after noon. I headed through the "no return" security doors and looked around for someone to either greet me or to be holding a sign with my name on it. Nothing. I waited about ten minutes and then walked to the baggage terminal to see if I would have better luck there. Still nothing. I loitered for another ten minutes and asked two individuals who were obviously waiting for someone to arrive if they were looking for John Brennan. "Nope" came the same curt response from both.

It was close to 1:00 P.M. when I started to make phone calls. I had been given a number to call if there were any changes to my schedule, so I tried that one first. I called several times, and each time the phone just rang and rang. I then tried calling Denis and had the same result. I scrolled through the emails on my BlackBerry to see if I had misunderstood the directions I had been given. There were no emails. All arrangements for the trip had been made over the phone with individuals whose names I had scribbled on notes that I had left in my office at TAC. Ugh. I had been stranded at O'Hare for over an hour and a quarter and hadn't had any contact with anyone on Obama's staff since my arrival. My meeting with Obama was scheduled to occur in less than ninety minutes, or at least that was what I had been told. "Surely, this isn't a prank," I thought to myself. In a brief wave of panic, I envisioned Allen Funt and his camera crew appearing from behind one of the airport columns yelling "Surprise! You're on *Candid Camera,*" with my high school friends behind the camera laughing uproariously at my naïveté for thinking that I had a personal audience with the president-elect.

I tried to think logically. It was Denis himself who had told me that I would be getting a call to go to Chicago. "I'm supposed to be here," I reassured myself. "Something must have slipped through the cracks." I decided to start calling every number I had once again. Finally, I got through to Mike Froman, a former classmate of Obama's at Harvard who was on the transition advisory board. I explained my situation to Mike, including my fear that I was part of an elaborate joke. "No, John. We've been expecting you. It's been quite hectic here, so apologies for the miscommunication." Like everyone else on the Obama team with whom I interacted, Mike was cheerful and upbeat. I told Mike not to worry and that I would jump in a cab if he gave me the address and room number.

When I arrived at Obama's Chicago headquarters, I met Denis and Mark Lippert, another close adviser to Obama, as I was getting on the elevator. I had heard Mark's name many times before but had never met him during the campaign. Like Denis, Mark was nearly twenty years my junior and dressed very casually. Smiling profusely, Mark extended his hand and said, "Well, I finally get to meet the famous John Brennan!"

"You mean 'infamous,' don't you?" I responded. I knew that Obama had surrounded himself with advisers who were rather critical of the CIA and its Bush-era activities, so I figured that my CIA affiliation was a black mark against me in the eyes of some. Not so with Mark and Denis, I found out pretty quickly, as both had a healthy understanding of, and respect for, the Agency's mission and workforce.

After about ten minutes of small talk with Denis, Mark, and a couple of other folks in the office, I was informed that the president-elect was ready to see me. I looked at Denis, expecting that he would be joining me in the meeting. "You're on your own for this one, John," he said, with his trademark grin plastered across his face. I was then guided into a warm and modestly appointed empty office and was directed to take a chair across from where the president-elect would sit. I decided to remain standing, as I could feel the butterflies in my stomach starting to flutter. The feeling was remarkably similar to what I experienced when I met a president for the first time, a little more than eighteen years previously. Although I had met dozens of presidents, prime ministers, kings, and other world leaders in the intervening years, I was more nervous in advance of this meeting than any I could remember.

I had been in the office only a couple of minutes when Obama entered the room with a broad toothy smile that put Denis's Minnesota smirk to shame.

"Hi, John," Obama said in a full and friendly voice. "Thanks for coming all the way to Chicago. I hope your travel went well."

Obama's smile was captivating, and his demeanor had the effect of immediately neutralizing the butterflies. "Hello, sir. Thanks so much for the invitation." Losing all pretensions of formality, I proceeded to relate my experience at the airport, telling him that I thought my high school buddies had put Denis up to the ploy.

"Sounds like you went to school with the same type of classmates I had," he joked. I didn't think his smile could get larger, but it did.

After another minute or two of pleasantries, he got down to business. "I've read about your background, but maybe you can flesh out some of the highlights of your CIA career and tell me what you think about the role and responsibilities of the intelligence community, especially the CIA."

"Glad to, sir." I then spoke for about ten minutes. I started with an account of the summer I spent in Indonesia more than thirty years before, hoping to break the ice by referencing my brief visit to the country where he lived for four years as a teenager. I touched upon my study in Cairo and other life experiences and talked about America's special place and responsibilities in the world. I finished up with a quick list of the key national security challenges his administration would face, including on the terrorism front. At this point he interjected.

"Tell me what you think is the CIA's appropriate counterterrorism role."

On the flight to Chicago, I had mentally prepared for how I

would characterize the CIA's record and decided it was best to put all my cards on the table. "I was very proud to serve in the CIA for twenty-five years. I saw the good, the bad, and the ugly during that time. What I can say without reservation is that the CIA's work and mission are essential for America's safety and security as well as for global stability. But I also recognize that the CIA's history includes significant missteps, some of its own making and others at the direction of policy makers." I talked about my views toward the CIA's detention and interrogation program. I said that I was not in the chain of command for the program and that it never should have been undertaken by the CIA, which had no experience in detaining and interrogating individuals. I also explained why I did not use the term "torture" when referring to the enhanced interrogation techniques, since they were approved and deemed lawful by the Department of Justice. I could see that Obama was listening carefully to me, although he showed no visible reaction to my comments. I also talked about the importance of avoiding the loss of innocent lives during counterterrorism operations, which did bring a nod of approval from the president-elect. I then started to tick off a short scorecard on the CIA's successes and failures during my time at the Agency. Before long, however, I could see Obama's eyelids start to get heavy, as if they were in a race with the setting sun visible through his office window. I tried to enliven my remarks with hand gestures, which had no apparent effect.

I looked down at my watch and saw that I was at the thirty-five-minute mark of what was scheduled to be a thirty-minute meeting. I knew that Obama had been on a grueling schedule since Election Day, and it appeared to be catching up with him. Either that or I was more boring than usual. "Well, Mr. President-elect," I said in a louder-than-normal voice, "I really appreciate the opportunity to meet with you and to wish you well as you get ready for your inauguration." Obama straightened his slumping posture, smiled, and bid me a kind goodbye.

"Thanks for coming all the way out to Chicago," he said. "I hope to get to see you after I arrive in Washington."

I left Chicago that day not knowing whether the invitation to meet with Obama was simply a courtesy to say thanks for supporting his campaign or was a job interview. Before the meeting, I was outwardly agnostic but inwardly excited about a potential return to government service. My family and I had grown accustomed to the salary and the hours of private-sector life over the preceding three years, and I knew that letting it go would be difficult for all of us. When I called Kathy from the airport, however, she could already sense that I wanted to join the incoming Obama administration. "He's impressive," I said to Kathy. "He's really, really impressive. I think he will do great things for the country."

"Does this mean that you will accept a job if he offers you one?"

I knew Kathy was an even bigger fan of Obama than I was, so I turned the tables on her. "Would you like me to work for him?" I asked, already knowing the answer. I could sense her silent smile over the phone.

Denis called me the following day to ask if I enjoyed the meeting. "Absolutely. He's going to make a great president," was all that I could say. Denis quickly shifted to the real purpose of his call.

"There's a lot of work to do between now and Inauguration Day, and we need someone to take the lead on the intelligence portfolio for the transition team. Would you be willing to do that?"

Without asking what it would entail, I again readily agreed, telling Denis that I would be happy to do whatever I could to facilitate the transition. After several more conversations with transition folks over the next few days, I realized that joining the Obama transition team as a full-time member involved a variety of ethical rules and requirements that were designed to guard against any potential conflict-of-interest issues. Most significantly, I was informed that I needed to take an unpaid leave of absence from TAC as well as from INSA for the entire ten-week transition period, a loss in pay of nearly sixty thousand dollars. On top of the lost income from CBS News, Obama was fast becoming a rather expensive acquaintance.

With little understanding of what my transition duties would entail, I was very happy to hear that my former CIA colleague Jami Miscik had also been invited to be part of the effort. We quickly agreed that we would co-lead the intelligence transition team. Along with about a half-dozen other recruits, including a couple of Hill staffers, we were given workspace in the Office of the Director of National Intelligence at Liberty Crossing where we could review files, meet with intelligence officials, and prepare a report on the "state of intelligence" for the incoming Obama administration.

I also was given an office at the president-elect's transition headquarters, a building in downtown Washington that accommodated several hundred staff as well as the president-elect's most senior advisers. I was heading out of the building to my car at about 6:00 P.M. on Thursday evening, November 13, when I received a call on my BlackBerry from an unidentified number.

"Hello?"

"Hi, John, it's Barack."

"Hi, Barack . . . I mean hello, Mr. President . . . I mean Mr. President-elect." Getting personal calls from a future occupant of the Oval Office was new to me, and I didn't yet have the routine down, especially when answering an unexpected call.

Obama opened by saying that he enjoyed meeting me in Chicago and thanking me for my work on the transition. He then got to the point of the phone call. "John, I would like you to be my director of the CIA." The words had the effect of pushing my mute button, as I held my BlackBerry in stunned silence. "John? John, are you there?"

"Yes, sir. Sorry, sir. I'm just a bit speechless. I don't know what to say other than it would be the greatest honor of my life. Thank you, sir."

"Great," he said. "Obviously, you will need to go through the normal background check and a vetting process before an announcement is made, but I know that you've been through these things during your CIA career. Denis or someone else handling nominations will be reaching out to you in a few days on next steps."

To say that I was dumbfounded would be a vast understatement. I was deeply honored, more than I could express. It was an exceptionally surreal moment, and my thoughts quickly flashed back to when I started my CIA career as a newly minted GS-9 officer more than twenty-eight years before. And now I was being asked by the next president of the United States to be "the" CIA director.

Once the shock wore off, I immediately ducked into a nearby alley to call Kathy. "You will never guess who I just spoke to," I said. "Barack Obama! And he asked me to be CIA director!" A few shrieks and tears followed on both sides of the conversation. It felt so good to share the news with the person who made my career possible.

I had never been tapped for a position that required Senate confirmation. I had witnessed what George had to deal with when he was nominated to be deputy director of central intelligence, so I knew that it was going to involve very thorough scrutiny of my professional and personal life. I also remembered what happened to Tony Lake when he was nominated, but, unlike Tony, I was not affiliated with any political party and had a much lower public profile. "It might get a little bumpy," I acknowledged to Kathy, "but I should get through with only a few minor bruises."

I was advised by the folks handling presidential appointments to keep word about my conversation with the president confidential. "As you know, there has been no official offer extended yet," they warned. I understood. In addition to Kathy and our children, I told only my parents, siblings, and George, swearing them all to secrecy. As requested, I pulled together my tax returns, financial records, publications, nongovernment affiliations, and other material that would be relevant to a thorough FBI background investigation and submitted it to a law firm that was vetting presidential nominations.

It was only a couple of days later when I noticed a few mentions in the press that I was on a short list for a senior-level appointment in the Obama administration. Since I had been an adviser to the Obama campaign and was now on the transition team, I reasoned that the press was speculating, in this case correctly, that I was about to be selected for a top job. Rumors that I would be named CIA director started to gain some traction, which then generated commentary regarding my background as a CIA officer and questions on whether I was an appropriate candidate for the Langley job. Reference to my tenure as a senior CIA officer during the Agency's RDI program started to bring heavy criticism from the political left, which pointed to a perceived hypocrisy between Obama's strong criticism of Bush-era counterterrorism programs and my rumored appointment. My time as CIA's deputy executive director was used as evidence that I played a major role in what was widely referred to as a "torture" program. My comments during the CBS interview with Harry Smith that useful information was obtained from individuals subjected to enhanced interrogation techniques were used to claim that I had supported the Bush administration program.

I called Denis to discuss the growing public criticism about my potential appointment. I told him that maybe I wasn't the best choice to be CIA director, and I offered to bow out. "Obama doesn't need this problem right now," I told him. "He has more important issues on his plate. I understand if he changes his mind about offering me the CIA job."

Denis was unimpressed with my argument and laughed off my offer to bow out. "Don't worry about this, John. This is the usual flak that these appointments generate. The criticism will die down, and we'll get you confirmed. The president-elect wants you in the job."

I was reassured by Denis's positive tone. Denis knew the political waters of Washington, especially the ones that run through the corridors of Congress, much better than I did. He genuinely didn't seem concerned about the media stories. Buoyed by my conversation with Denis, I reassured Kathy that all was on track.

And then things started to go south rapidly. News coverage and commentary about my involvement in the CIA's "torture" program triggered growing opposition to my appointment among several Democratic senators, who started to kick up a fuss. They stoked negative commentary in the press and conveyed their objections to Obama's senior team.

Denis was still dividing his time between Washington and Chicago when he called me on Saturday, November 22, to ask that I meet him the following evening at transition headquarters in the District when he got into town. Denis was still my principal contact for transition matters, so I welcomed the opportunity to brief him on my interactions with the intelligence community, which I presumed was the purpose of the meeting. As soon as we sat down at transition headquarters, I mentioned that the criticism from the left had not yet died down as he had forecast. "I still seem to be in the crosshairs of the press." With a smile on my face, I added, "Are you sure you don't want me to bow out?"

I was expecting Denis to once again rebuff my offer. This time he just looked at me, paused for a moment, and then said, "Maybe it's the best thing, John."

Gulp.

I could feel my heart sink into my chest. His words hit me hard. It was as if I had been abruptly awakened from some fanciful dream that I was going to become CIA director. After a few moments of stunned silence, I said that I understood. I could see that Denis was as disappointed in conveying the news as I was to receive it, but the decision was made above both our pay grades.

I waited to get home to tell Kathy. On the drive home, I alternated between feeling sorry for myself and getting angry at what had happened. I felt that I had once again missed an opportunity to return to government service. I pulled myself together by the time I got home. "I have some bad news and some good news," I told Kathy with a smile on my face, as she met me at the front door. "The bad news is that I have been asked to pull out of consideration for the CIA director job, so I'm not going back to Langley." I blurted the words out quickly because they were painful to say.

I could see disappointment and tears begin to well up in her eyes. "That's so unfair," she said. "I'm sorry." After a few hugs and some silence, she remembered my opening line. "So, what's the good news?"

"The good news is that I will be working private-sector hours and getting private-sector pay next year, so our current life will continue as usual." It was the best I could come up with under the circumstances. I called George that night to explain what had happened. He was deeply disappointed with the news, seeing it as an unfair knock against me as well as against the Agency for its post-9/11 work. I had a difficult time sleeping that night. I knew there would be press stories in the coming days about how I was rejected for the CIA director job because of my purported role in a "torture" program. Rather selfishly, I felt personally aggrieved, and I didn't want my reputation further sullied as a result of mischaracterizations— intentional or otherwise—of my government service. I wanted to swing back.

I called Denis on Monday and said that I wanted to withdraw my name from consideration for the CIA appointment by writing a letter to President-elect Obama, which I subsequently would release to the press. I told Denis that I wanted to counter what had become a growing impression of my involvement in the CIA's detention and interrogation program. Denis said he understood but wanted to run the idea of a letter by the transition team's communications folks. He said that it was a bit unusual for someone who had not been nominated for a position to announce their withdrawal from consideration. I said I understood and would finesse the awkwardness. When he called back late that afternoon to say a letter would be fine, I told him that he would have it first thing in the morning.

I stayed late at TAC that night to write the letter, which I dutifully sent to President-elect Obama via Denis on Tuesday morning.

25 November 2008

Dear President-Elect Barack Obama:

I am honored to have been involved in leading your
Transition Team for the Intelligence Community, and I am
deeply committed to ensuring that your Administration is well
prepared to deal with the many challenges facing our Nation.
My transition responsibilities have led to speculation that I am
under consideration for a senior intelligence position in your
Administration. Quite unfortunately, this speculation has led
to strong criticism in some quarters prompted by my previous
service with the Central Intelligence Agency.

It has been immaterial to the critics that I have been a strong
opponent of many of the policies of the Bush Administration
such as the preemptive war in Iraq and coercive interrogation
tactics, to include waterboarding. The fact that I was not involved
in the decision-making process for any of these controversial
policies and actions has been ignored. Indeed, my criticism of
these policies within government circles was the reason why I was
twice considered for more senior-level positions in the current
Administration only to be rebuffed by the White House.

I am extremely proud of my 25-year record of intelligence
work, and I am prouder still of the courageous and heroic work
performed by the women and men of the CIA over the past 60
years. The Nation owes its CIA officers a tremendous debt of
gratitude for the sacrifices they have made for their country, and
they deserve strong and steady leadership in the years ahead.

Therefore, it is with profound regret that I respectfully ask that
my name be withdrawn from consideration for a position within
the Intelligence Community. The challenges ahead of our Nation
are too daunting, and the role of the CIA too critical, for there to
be any distraction from the vital work that lies ahead.

John O. Brennan

It wasn't the best letter I had ever written, nor the most precise. While I had been critical of some Bush-era policies, my letter gave the mistaken impression that I had actively if not strenuously opposed waterboarding and the application of other coercive interrogation tactics while I was in government. I did not. Although I was correct in saying that I was not involved in the decision-making process for any of these policies, I certainly didn't do as much as I could have and should have done when I was in the CIA to speak out against the interrogation program. A more candid letter would have included an acknowledgment of that shortcoming. I guess it was my frustration at having to bow out of consideration for the CIA job because of policies and practices beyond my purview and outside of my professional responsibilities that led me to overstate the extent of my opposition.

I tried to set aside my disappointment at having to step away from the CIA job by concentrating on my work with the intelligence transition team. Jami and I spent much of our time in meetings at Langley in an effort to learn as much as we could about ongoing intelligence activities. Covert action was one of our principal areas of inquiry, as any covert-action program under way at the end of the Bush administration would remain in force unless some affirmative action was taken immediately by the incoming Obama team to end or modify it. CIA Director Mike Hayden was very accommodating to all our requests, and he directed his staff to give us full and unfettered access to the CIA's most sensitive files. As former senior CIA officials, Jami and I were already aware of many of the Agency's most sensitive programs, which gave comfort to CIA officers who were given the task of briefing us and providing top-secret documents for our review.

Kathy and I were in Connecticut visiting family during the holiday season when Mark Lippert called to inquire whether I would be willing to join the administration in a position other than CIA director. Still hurting from the letdown of not becoming CIA director,

I demurred. "I don't want to go through that experience again," I told him. "And my CIA service will be a problem for whatever job you're thinking about."

"This one doesn't require Senate confirmation," Mark explained. "Obama would like you to be his assistant for homeland security and counterterrorism. You would be working at the White House."

I was driving at the time, and Kathy could hear both sides of the conversation. "I don't know, Mark, maybe it's just best for all concerned that I walk away once the transition is over." Aside from having lost my enthusiasm for rejoining the government after taking a battering in the media, I also had started to look forward to returning to my job at TAC.

"Well, give it some thought. Obama would very much like you to take the job."

Within the hour, Denis called with the same pitch, and he wanted to make sure that I understood that the position was at the "Assistant to the President" level—the highest personal rank of White House staff—and that I also would be a deputy national security adviser. "It's a great job, John, and we would love to continue working with you after Inauguration Day."

Kathy and I spent the drive back to Virginia going over, once again, the pros and cons of my return to the government, but this time the focus shifted to a White House job rather than taking the helm at Langley. "It would be a longer commute," I told Kathy, trying to think about the practical differences between the White House and CIA jobs, "and I don't exactly know what would be expected of me." By the time we crossed the American Legion Bridge into Virginia from Maryland, we had decided that I would call Denis back the next day and tell him that I would be willing to learn more about the job.

Within a few days, I had a meeting scheduled with retired marine general Jim Jones, whom Obama had selected to be his national security adviser. Jim was still working out of his office at the U.S.

Chamber of Commerce, next to Lafayette Park, directly across from the White House, and we spent about an hour together talking about national security matters. I had met Jim a couple of times when he was in the marine corps and I was in the CIA, but I really didn't know much about him aside from his stellar reputation as a strong leader and a thinking man's general. His professional bearing as well as his intellect and substantive knowledge were readily apparent during our conversation, and we had a common perspective on many of the national security challenges that the Obama administration would face in its first years in office. By the end of the meeting, I felt comfortable with the prospect of working with Jim and told him I looked forward to joining him in the Obama administration. I called Kathy and then told Denis I would take the job

My new homeland security and counterterrorism duties started about forty-eight hours before I took up residence in the White House, when an intelligence report surfaced about a possible terrorist attack on the National Mall on Inauguration Day. The credibility of the sources involved in the acquisition of the information had not been confirmed, but the plot reportedly was being hatched by the Somali insurgent group al-Shabaab, which was affiliated with al-Qa'ida. Bush administration officials took the report seriously and passed all details about the threat and their efforts to mitigate it to their Obama administration counterparts. On the evening before the inauguration, I was in transition headquarters when I received updated information on the threat from the CIA, which I shared with Denis and Mark. "We need to inform the president-elect," Denis said. I was impressed that Denis always referred to Obama with the formal title of "president-elect" even when talking with close colleagues.

"He's at Blair House now, but he will be taking off pretty soon to attend the pre-inaugural balls." Blair House is the official guest house of the president of the United States, located across Pennsylvania Avenue from the White House, which President Bush had graciously offered to the Obama family. Denis and Mark grabbed their coats and looked at me, saying "Let's go!" With Washington streets already in virtual gridlock in preparation for the following day's events, I had no idea how we were going to get to Blair House, which was about fifteen blocks away. As soon as we exited the building, Denis and Mark started to jog briskly through the falling snow and throngs of strolling revelers in various stages of insobriety toward Blair House. "C'mon, John, we have to hurry." With little choice, I started to jog behind them, hoping that I wouldn't slip and fall on the slick sidewalks.

The Secret Service had been informed that we needed to see the president-elect. As soon as we arrived, we were ushered into the limousine that was idling in front of Blair House. Obama entered the vehicle less than a minute later. I was perspiring and breathing heavily from the run, which Obama immediately noticed.

"Mr. President, I'm not sweating and out of breath because of the reported threat of an attack tomorrow. It's because Denis and Mark made me run fifteen blocks with my two artificial hips to get here."

I didn't realize it at the time, but that run was a harbinger of what my life would be like over the next eight years.

17

WORKING IN THE WEST WING

I watched the Clinton-Bush transition in 2000 and 2001 from my perch as George Tenet's chief of staff. My perspective, however, was limited to how the CIA and the intelligence community needed to transition their intelligence support from an outgoing administration to an incoming one. Once President Bush decided that George would remain as director, the interaction between intelligence officials and policy makers was a smooth one. The main challenge for the CIA, at least initially, was to ensure that the new cast of national security officials at the White House and elsewhere quickly understood the capabilities, limitations, and value of U.S. intelligence. At the time, I paid little attention to the broader government transition under way in the executive branch.

I had a much different role and vantage point during the Bush-Obama transition. No longer a CIA official, I was part of an incoming team of national security officials that would assume the reins of government authority upon the swearing in of the new president. The big unknown for me was whether the outgoing Republican administration would do its best to facilitate the transfer of power to an incoming Democratic administration. I wondered if candidate Barack Obama's harsh criticisms of many of President Bush's national security policies and controversial counterterrorism programs might have untoward implications for the transition. My biggest fear was that ideologues on either side might seek to undermine coordination and cooperation between the Bush and Obama teams.

My fear was unfounded. I was deeply impressed at how thoroughly and professionally the Bush administration worked to welcome and prepare the Obama team for its new responsibilities, especially on the national security front. In my almost daily visits and meetings at Obama transition headquarters, I sensed that my transition colleagues working in the domestic policy realm were receiving equally strong support from their Bush administration counterparts. In preparation for my forthcoming counterterrorism and homeland security position at the White House, I interacted with the incumbent homeland security adviser, Ken Wainstein, an accomplished and seasoned Department of Justice professional. I had some previous experience with Ken. My tenure at NCTC overlapped with his time at the FBI, when he served as general counsel and chief of staff to Bob Mueller. Once it was announced that I would be taking over his White House role, Ken and his deputy Tom Bossert did all they could to help me and the rest of the Obama team hit the ground running.

And we did.

The threat of a terrorist bombing on the Mall brought the senior members of the Bush and Obama teams together in the White House Situation Room early on Inauguration Day. I arrived on the White House compound at about 7:00 A.M. A White House motor-pool car had been dispatched to pick me up, as I needed to be escorted through the many roadblocks and police checkpoints that were set up to handle the throng of inaugural well-wishers. It was the first of several thousand trips I would take in motor-pool vehicles to and from the White House over the next four years. Ken arrived at about the same time and welcomed me to what would be my first day back in government after a hiatus of more than three years. The Situation Room started to fill up around 8:00 A.M., with Condi Rice, Steve Hadley, Mike Chertoff, Mike Hayden, Mike McConnell, Josh Bolten, Mike Mukasey, and Ken Wainstein from the outgoing Bush team, and Hillary Clinton, Jim Jones, Tom Donilon, Denis McDonough, Mark Lippert, Rahm Emanuel, and me from the incoming Obama administration. Also in attendance were those who would provide critical continuity by serving in both administrations—Secretary of Defense Bob Gates, Chairman of the Joint Chiefs of Staff Admiral Mike Mullen, and FBI Director Bob Mueller. This was not the first time this group had gathered, as we had participated the week before in a three-hour tabletop exercise organized by outgoing Bush administration officials on how the government was prepared to deal with a nuclear-related disaster in the homeland, the ultimate domestic security nightmare.

Over the course of the next four hours on Inauguration Day, the group received updates on the threat reporting and the security measures being implemented on the Mall, the inaugural parade route, and the areas around the White House. Some officials stopped by for only a few minutes before heading off to their Inauguration Day commitments, while others stayed for extended periods of time to share their thoughts as well as to discuss the latest intelligence. Throughout the morning, the conversation was highly professional, cordial, and downright friendly. Serious conversation about the threat and actions taken by federal agencies frequently was interspersed with laughs, including good-natured ribbing around the table about who would and would not be able to sleep late the following morning. There was never any hint of partisanship or political tension in the room.

I remember thinking at the time that I was bearing witness to one of the most remarkable features of our American democracy— the seamless passing of the governance torch from one administration to another following a presidential election. I give enormous

credit to President Bush and his national security team for overseeing a very effective and efficient presidential transition. Years later,
President Obama would repeatedly reference the example set by the
Bush administration when he issued guidance to his national security team on how to prepare for the presidential transition in January
2017. "We need to do as good a job as the Bush folks did," he told
us. "And if it's possible, we need to do even better." Unfortunately,
the incoming Trump team was neither well prepared to receive the
support, nor interested in it.

As soon as Barack Obama was sworn into office, at midday on
January 20, 2009, as the forty-fourth president of the United States,
I formally assumed the role of assistant to the president for homeland
security and counterterrorism. Ken headed out of what had been his
office that morning but was now mine, and he flashed a smile of relief and, with a bit of a smirk, told me the responsibility of keeping
the country safe was now mine. No longer a government official
and therefore not eligible for White House motor-pool support, Ken
later told me that road closures forced him to walk to his Alexan-
dria home, a rather abrupt transition to civilian life. As a wave of
anxiety washed over me, I spent the rest of the day in my new West
Wing office, monitoring intelligence reports, watching TV coverage
of the inauguration, and talking to the senior leadership and counterterrorism officials in the FBI, CIA, and NSA about the terrorist
threat. Fortunately, the terrorist attack we feared never materialized.
We later learned that the source of the information—an individual living in Africa who falsely claimed to have access to a terrorist
organization—had fabricated the threat, and the country remained
safe during my first day on the job.

The disappointment I felt at the beginning of the Obama administration at not having gotten the job of director of the CIA
quickly dissipated once the daily rhythm of White House activity
kicked in. My windowless office was far from glamorous—its low
seven-foot drop ceiling gave it the feel of a bunker in a war zone,

and the sound of White House rats occasionally scurrying inside the walls and ceiling was an added treat. But those office features were more than offset by its strategic location: about forty feet down the hall from the White House Situation Room and almost directly below the Oval Office. I could make it from my chair to the front of the president's *Resolute* desk in less than thirty seconds, which was not an infrequent occurrence. Mark Lippert and Denis McDonough shared an office in the same suite, and our staff assistants, files, and printers were crammed into a common foyer area.

I quickly realized that my daily proximity to the Oval Office gave me much more regular and direct access to President Obama than I would have had from the CIA director's office in Langley. As President Obama's principal homeland security and counterterrorism adviser, I frequently was in the Oval Office with him, participating in his daily morning PDB session as well as in subsequent national security discussions he held with senior staff and cabinet officials. Initially, I felt like a stranger living in another family's house. I really hadn't known or worked with the president or with the many other officials who had descended upon the White House. Even more disorienting was my new reality of being on the policy rather than the intelligence side of national security discussions. No longer in the role of teeing up national security problems, as I had with previous presidents, I quickly learned that I had assumed responsibility for helping a sitting president figure out what to do when confronted by daunting terrorism and homeland security challenges.

The counterterrorism dimension of my portfolio was quite familiar to me, given my CIA experience, but I had a steep learning curve on the homeland security front, which encompassed a whole lot more than preventing and responding to terrorist attacks inside the United States. I developed a close working relationship with Janet Napolitano, the former governor and attorney general of Arizona who was President Obama's first secretary of homeland security. In addition to our regular phone calls and meetings at the White House, Janet and I faithfully met once a month for an early and extended breakfast at the Diner, an unpretentiously named eatery in the multicultural Adams Morgan neighborhood of Washington, D.C. As Janet and I worked our way through our omelets, hash browns, and respective lists of homeland security items to discuss, sleepy-eyed Washingtonians would do double takes as they took notice of two familiar faces as well as Janet's Secret Service detail hovering nearby.

Janet was a blunt-talking, no-nonsense colleague whose legal background and state government experience were invaluable in the early days of the administration. Her tenure was not an easy one, as she was the principal cabinet official involved in what seemed like a never-ending series of homeland security crises in Obama's first term—the H1N1 influenza pandemic in 2009, the *Deepwater Horizon* oil spill in the Gulf of Mexico in 2010, the devastation of Hurricanes Irene in 2011 and Sandy in 2012, and illegal migration along the southern border every year. Since Janet only had statutory authority to direct the activities of her own department, she relied heavily on the White House to support her efforts to orchestrate the myriad activities undertaken by other federal departments and agencies as well as state governments that were beyond her jurisdiction. On more than a few occasions, I had to talk to cabinet members as well as to state officials to tell them that Janet was implementing presidential guidance and that President Obama would appreciate their cooperation.

The H1N1 flu pandemic was an early and serious homeland security challenge. The first cases were detected in Mexico, but not publicly announced, a few weeks before President Obama's April 16–17 visit to Mexico City. I accompanied Obama on that trip, but we didn't learn about the virus that was beginning to sweep through North America until we returned to Washington. We also were surprised when we found out that the director of Mexico's National Museum of Anthropology died from pneumonia and other complications from the flu less than a week after he gave us a personal tour of the museum. By the end of April, a public health emergency was declared in the United States, and an all-out government effort was under way to understand the nature and trajectory of the virus and how we could mitigate its impact, which had the potential to be significant. I was told that the virus was related to the H1N1 flu pandemic of 1918–19, known as the Spanish flu, which infected a third of the world's population, killing an estimated fifty million people, including nearly seven hundred thousand in the United States.

It was a baptism by fire for me on the medical front, and I quickly became an eager student of Dr. Tony Fauci, the director of the National Institute of Allergy and Infectious Diseases at the National Institutes of Health, and Dr. Richard Besser and his successor Dr. Tom Frieden, the directors of the Centers for Disease Control and Prevention (CDC). I quickly learned a lot about the science of the virus—its principal methods of transmission, morbidity and mortality rates, and which demographic groups were most susceptible to it (younger and healthy individuals were disproportionately affected, as more than one-third of people over sixty years of age had existing antibodies against the disease as a result of previous exposure to flu strains related to H1N1). I also became familiar with the challenges and long lead times needed to develop vaccines and the complexities associated with setting up national distribution mechanisms and prioritization of recipients for antiviral medication (Tamiflu was determined to have efficacy). This was a whole new world for me, and it was simultaneously fascinating and challenging.

As President Obama's homeland security adviser, I tried to coordinate federal government efforts, and I was very fortunate that two former governors, Janet Napolitano and newly minted Secretary of Health and Human Services Kathleen Sebelius of Kansas, had the lead for the Obama administration's response to the virus, including the engagement with state and local officials as well as with the health-care industry. The policy challenge was overwhelming. Orchestrating the capabilities and authorities arrayed across the departments and agencies of the federal government and integrating them with state and local counterparts as well as private-sector entities was a complex systems-engineering challenge for all involved. The questions were many—for example, what was available and how could we procure or manufacture what was not, how would items be paid for and distributed, and who would have priority?

Throughout this time, President Obama insisted that "science, facts, and data" drive administration policy and actions, and he encouraged homeland security officials to be forthcoming with the American people about the seriousness of the H1N1 flu, which subsided in the summer months but reemerged in the fall, ultimately infecting sixty million Americans and killing more than twelve thousand.

The strong teamwork I witnessed among the many players involved in confronting the H1N1 pandemic gave me confidence that the administration would be able to deal with other homeland and national security challenges that were yet to come. Looking back on it now, and watching the Trump administration's response to the coronavirus (COVID-19) crisis, I can attest that there was never a time when any of my colleagues or I felt even the slightest pressure to misrepresent facts, dismiss advice from medical experts, or heap public praise on the president for the actions taken by the administration. If any of us did, I am sure President Obama would have upbraided us for it.

It was not all smooth sailing for me during the crisis, however. In an early White House meeting on H1N1, the president turned to me and asked whether I thought the Stafford Act could be used to reimburse states for the cost of their H1N1 response efforts. Although I had heard of the Stafford Act and would eventually come to understand that it provides a mechanism for congressionally appropriated federal funds to be allocated to states for major disaster and emergency preparedness and assistance, I had no earthly idea at the time what was contained in the act. I took a few moments before responding, and then said to the president, "I don't know sir," and, remembering the advice I received as an intelligence officer to "go dumb early," I added, "and as soon as I find out what the Stafford Act is, I'll let you know."

Obama broke into a toothy smile and said, "Good idea, John."

Observing the daily coverage of the COVID-19 crisis eleven years later, it was apparent that the significant challenges of H1N1 paled in comparison, by an order of magnitude, to what we later would face as a country. Everything about COVID-19 is much more complex on the medical front and much more devastating for our national health, economy, and social well-being, testing the very mettle of our country. As I watch events unfold, I am deeply grateful for all the selfless work done by individuals nationwide across so many disciplines. Once again, I am very glad that Dr. Tony Fauci, an individual of exceptional medical acumen and dedication to his fellow citizens, is playing a prominent public role in explaining the seriousness of the threat posed by COVID-19 and the important actions to help mitigate its impact.

Cybersecurity was also in my homeland security portfolio, and it was the most complex and frustrating part of my White House job. Early briefings from some of the brightest technical and legal minds in the government convinced me of the daunting challenges facing any administration trying to make the digital domain more secure, reliable, resilient, and less vulnerable to cyberattacks and exploitation. "Mr. Brennan," one young and exceptionally talented digital expert told me, "while the government has the legal authority and unquestioned responsibility to secure classified and unclassified government networks, 85 percent of the digital domain is owned and operated by the private sector. There is no consensus on what the government can—or even should be allowed to—do when it comes to the .com, .net, .org, .edu, and countless other public domains."

No issue during my time at the White House—indeed, during my entire eight years in the Obama administration—brought the tension between the government's responsibility to safeguard our country's security and the privacy rights and civil liberties of American citizens into starker relief than cyber. I had numerous meetings with members of Congress, privacy advocates, national security professionals, private-sector technologists, and digital entrepreneurs, but I came away with few answers about how the sharp and legitimate differences of view on the appropriate role of government could and should be bridged. My frustration prompted me to repeatedly recommend to members of Congress that they should establish an independent bipartisan national commission—much as they did with the 9/11 and WMD Commissions—to bring together technologists, legal scholars, business people, national security professionals, futurists, scientists, academics, and other relevant stakeholders and cyber experts to undertake a strategic and comprehensive look at the dynamic challenges and opportunities presented by the digital domain. That recommendation was not taken up during the Obama administration, mostly due to congressional malaise. The 2019 National Defense Authorization Act established the Cyberspace Solarium Commission, a bicameral body chaired by members of Congress, which produced a report with several dozen recommendations on how the government could better address cybersecurity challenges, but more is needed. Unfortunately, it probably will take a massive cyberattack—similar to the triggering events that led to the creation of the 9/11 and WMD Commissions—to convince lawmakers that an independent national commission is essential to deal with the challenges of the digital domain.

During President Obama's first term, we made progress on developing a framework for determining how and when to respond to cyberattacks against the United States launched by foreign governments. With millions of cyberattacks taking place daily, we designed a process to identify cyberattacks that met an established threshold of national security, corporate, or financial impact as well as a level of confidence that the attack was attributable to a foreign government. Attribution was the most difficult aspect. During a visit to one intelligence community agency, I was shown a world map depicting the countries of origin of all cyberattacks against U.S. targets in the previous twenty-four hours. Over 90 percent emanated from somewhere in China, but only a handful could be attributed with confidence to the Chinese government. Despite the challenges associated with attribution, marathon meetings were held to establish the framework, which helped guide future decisions, such as U.S. government sanctions on North Korea in 2014 for its attack against Sony Pictures and indictments the same year by the FBI of five Chinese People's Liberation Army officials for stealing trade secrets and sensitive business information from U.S. corporations.

It was the potential for terrorist attacks against the homeland and American targets overseas, however, that consumed most of my time. Since President Obama insisted on close coordination of counterterrorism policies and programs across the administration, we scheduled a meeting every other week in the White House Situation Room to review terrorist threats and to discuss proposed actions to counter them. Referred to as a meeting of the "Counterterrorism Board of Directors," attendees included the president and vice president; the secretaries of state, defense, and homeland security; the national security adviser and deputy national security adviser; the directors of national intelligence, the CIA, and the National Counterterrorism Center; the chairman of the Joint Chiefs of Staff; and senior White House and National Security Council staff. I was responsible for developing the agenda for the meetings and for assigning briefing responsibilities. The sessions would run between thirty and sixty minutes, and they proved to be a very useful way to ensure a shared appreciation of the terrorist threat and senior-level awareness of actions that were under way to prevent terrorist attacks.

No one badgered me more about terrorism than President Obama's chief of staff Rahm Emanuel, who was a regular visitor to my West Wing office. Although short of stature at five foot seven—joking once that he liked visiting me because of what were, for him, high ceilings—he was a towering figure in the first two years of the Obama administration. An attendee at virtually all national and homeland security meetings I had with the president in the first two years of the administration, Rahm frequently asked probing and aggressive questions that had both substantive and political dimensions. While he had only limited experience on terrorism issues, he was obsessed about the potential consequences of terrorist attacks. Whenever a terrorist threat was raised with the president, Rahm would take a note card out of his shirt pocket and jot down a reminder to himself to ask me about it later in the day.

"When are you going to get that fuckin' bomb maker in Yemen?" Rahm asked when he appeared in my doorway one evening in September 2009. "What's his name again? Afriki?" Rahm's colorful language was legendary.

"No, Rahm, his name is Asiri, not Afriki," I said. I had just returned earlier that day from visiting Saudi Minister of Interior Prince Muhammad Bin Nayif in Jeddah. MBN (as he is known) had been injured the week before in a failed bombing attack carried out by the Yemen-based terrorist organization al-Qa'ida in the Arabian Peninsula, which we referred to as AQAP. Rahm was quite familiar with AQAP, having been present many times when the president received briefings on its plans to carry out attacks against U.S. targets. Rahm was eager to hear about my visit. The improvised explosive device (IED) used in the attempt to kill Prince Muhammad had been fabricated by Ibrahim al-Asiri, AQAP's ingenious and diabolical bomb maker. The would-be assassin was Ibrahim's brother Abdullah, who had been granted an audience with the prince after claiming that he had left AQAP and had important information to share. With an IED hidden in his undergarments—not inside his rectum, as some press accounts claimed—he sat next to the prince. Abdullah placed a call to his coconspirators in Yemen and then yelled "Allahu Akbar" before detonating the device, killing himself instantly but somehow only grazing the prince. At Prince Muhammad's insistence, I let him take me to the room where the attack took place, and he showed me the bloody residue and the hole in the ceiling where Abdullah's leg had lodged. Rahm cringed when I shared that story.

"I tell you, Brennan," Rahm said, "you need to get that fucker before he kills Americans."

Rahm's instincts were dead on.

A few months later I received a call at home on Christmas morning. "Mr. Brennan, this is the White House Situation Room. I hope I'm not disturbing you on your holiday." The voice belonged to one of the many dedicated young government professionals serving a tour in the West Wing's ground-floor nerve center.

"Not at all," I told her. "And thanks so much for being at the White House today." I knew well that pulling holiday and weekend duty was but one of the many sacrifices that national security professionals, whether stationed abroad or stateside, make throughout the year. "I hope things have been quiet for you so far."

"Well, sir, it was very quiet until a few minutes ago, when we received a call from the FBI about a passenger on a Delta flight from Paris that just landed in Detroit. It seems as though his pants caught fire when the plane was approaching Detroit International Airport."

I wasn't sure if I heard correctly, so I asked her to repeat what she just said.

"His pants caught fire, sir. They think he might have had some firecrackers on him that he tried to set off, causing the fire. He is being removed from the plane by airport security and the FBI is responding. That's all we know right now."

I struggled to process what I had just been told. "Okay, let me know as soon as you hear more," I told her. Firecrackers didn't make sense, I thought. And then I remembered Richard Reid, the British al-Qa'ida member who unsuccessfully tried to down an American Airlines flight during the 2001 Christmas season by detonating explosives hidden in his athletic shoes. Reid had trained in al-Qa'ida camps in Afghanistan and then bounced around Pakistan and Europe in the months following the 9/11 attacks before he boarded a flight in Paris bound for Miami. Fortunately, Reid's damp matches failed to ignite, preventing him from lighting the fuse.

The phone rang again. "Mr. Brennan. The FBI says the person with the fiery pants apparently had some type of IED on his body."

"Is he alive?" I asked.

"Yes, sir," came the response.

I breathed a sigh of relief when told he was conscious and was being questioned by security officers, as it was critical to try to get time-sensitive information from him about possible coconspirators trying to bring down other airliners. "Kath, I have to go to my office," I said, as I grabbed my coat and headed out the door. "I might not be home in time for dinner." I wasn't.

I had a two-track mind during the drive to the White House. Instinctively, I started to reprise my former intelligence officer role, searching my memory for any intelligence I might have seen that could have been remotely related to what was happening in Detroit. After coming up with nothing other than the numerous intelligence assessments I had read over the years highlighting al-Qa'ida's determination to bring down an aircraft over the United States, I focused on the second track—what did I need to do once I got to the White House? President Obama was not in Washington, having decamped to Hawaii only the day before. Most of his senior staff were either with him in Hawaii or scattered to other holiday destinations. I was one of the few senior White House officials still in town.

Arriving at the White House, I went straight to the Situation Room for an update. "I need to talk to John Pistole, ideally on the secure line," I told the staff on duty as I headed to my office.

FBI Deputy Director John Pistole had been a close colleague and friend for many years. When I was at the CIA and at the NCTC, we had worked closely together and had appeared alongside one another testifying in front of Congress and the 9/11 Commission. John was the consummate FBI professional—hardworking, competent, unflappable, and deeply knowledgeable about the Bureau's capabilities and mission, especially on the counterterrorism front. John's expertise and strong leadership skills were the reasons why President Obama selected him several months later to serve as administrator of the Transportation Security Administration, a position he ably held for four and a half years.

John told me that the individual aboard the aircraft was a twenty-three-year old Nigerian national named Umar Farouk Abdulmutallab who had tried to detonate plastic explosives hidden in his underwear. He was getting medical attention and being questioned in a holding room at the airport. In the months preceding the incident, there had been a fair amount of public debate about whether terrorism suspects arrested in the United States should be read their Miranda rights before being questioned. There were even false rumors circulating that the Obama administration was requiring the U.S. military to read Miranda rights to individuals captured on the battlefields of Iraq and Afghanistan. Contrary to claims made by critics of the Obama administration, Abdulmutallab was questioned before he was read his Miranda rights, based on a public safety exception as articulated in the 1984 Supreme Court ruling in the *New York v. Quarles* case, as well as after.

From my West Wing office, I was in constant contact with the Bureau, furiously trying to find out if a wave of al-Qa'ida attacks was again under way. I updated President Obama on a secure line with each bit of new information coming in. He agreed that I should inform congressional leadership immediately about what we knew about the threat, especially since it was being intensively covered in the media.

I proceeded to call key members of Congress, including the chairmen and ranking members of the Homeland Security Committees. With each call, I stressed the importance of keeping the details confidential, because we didn't know whether Abdulmutallab had any coconspirators who might be monitoring events, and we didn't want them to know that Abdulmutallab was cooperating. All the members of Congress whom I briefed said they understood and expressed appreciation for the call, including Representative Peter King (R-NY), who was the ranking member of the Homeland Security Committee in the House of Representatives. King was one of my last calls.

Less than ten minutes after my conversation with King, I was watching the news coverage in my office and saw King being interviewed live on CNN. Despite my admonition, and to my amazement, King began to share with the reporter and CNN's worldwide viewers details about the detention of Abdulmutallab that I had said were confidential. I went ballistic, and I immediately told the White House telephone operators to get King back on the line. As soon as we were connected, I tore into him. "You ignored my request. And now you have jeopardized our ability to handle this situation!" I think King tried to respond, but my Irish temper was having none of it. I told him that he would not get another such briefing from me after what he had done. I slammed the phone down, forever ruining whatever relationship two very stubborn and hardheaded Irishmen could have. Looking back on it now, I overreacted to King's public comments, which I am sure were not intended to compromise the ongoing investigation. King would become one of my most vocal critics, including when I was director of the CIA and even during my retirement, on numerous occasions falsely accusing me of leaking classified information.

Within days of the incident, the intelligence community was able to reconstruct Abdulmutallab's journey to Detroit from Yemen. They learned he had received direction from Anwar al-Awlaki, an AQAP senior official and U.S. citizen, and had obtained the IED from Ibrahim al-Asiri. Fortunately, the device's detonating mechanism failed, resulting in a fire rather than a blast. President Obama asked me to launch a review of how Abdulmutallab had been able to acquire a visa at the U.S. embassy in Sudan, despite existing derogatory information about him in U.S. files. The review was rather contentious, and it was completed in thirty days. I recommended to President Obama that several policies and procedures within the counterterrorism community be modified to improve information sharing and to ensure that a specific component within the counterterrorism community is assigned primary responsibility for following up on unresolved threat information. The president accepted the recommendations, and the National Counterterrorism Center, under the very able leadership of its director, Michael Leiter, a Bush administration appointee, was tasked with implementing them.

Less than a year later al-Asiri again tried to bring down two more aircraft over the United States. I was at a speaking engagement a few blocks away from the White House on Thursday evening, October 28, 2010, when I received an urgent call from Prince Muhammad. Speaking cryptically, he said he had information that was 100 percent reliable about an imminent terrorist attack against America. "John, it's that very bad guy to the south of us again, and it's very serious." This time the terrorists planted bombs in packages destined for Chicago that were sent air freight. Within minutes of the call, the Saudis passed to us through intelligence channels the shipping details, including the tracking numbers of the packages. The tracking numbers revealed that the packages were being transshipped through the United Kingdom and the United Arab Emirates. I talked to my British counterparts, who located one of the packages, which contained one of two computer printers that had been shipped. Their initial inspection, however, which included the use of sniffer dogs, failed to locate the bomb. It was only when they disassembled the printer after removing its expertly sealed plastic covering that they found the explosives. Security officials in the Emirates were notified of the concealment method, and the second bomb was discovered and defused.

Rahm was apoplectic when he learned about the plot—wondering whether the Chicago destination of the printers was meant to send a signal to the former U.S. senator from Illinois, President Obama—but

he gained new respect for Prince Muhammad's willingness and capability to prevent disasters on American soil. As a result, Rahm
supported my request that President Obama personally thank Prince
Muhammad in an Oval Office meeting the following year.

Tragically, there were times when brutal acts of violence were not
averted.

The morning PDB session on December 14, 2012, was well under way when the door opened, and the president's private secretary
said my senior adviser Nick Shapiro needed to pass a message to me.
The president looked up quizzically, as the interruption was more
than a bit unusual. Nick handed me a folded note that said, "FBI
reports active shooter incident at an elementary school in Connecticut. SWAT team on scene, individual with gun cornered in one part
of building. No word on whether there are any casualties. CNN
reporting story live."

"What's going on?" the president asked as I silently read the
note. I told Nick to tell the president what he had learned. The
tenor of the initial account provided by the FBI left the impression
that the situation was under control and that a tragedy had been
averted. Nick left the Oval Office, and the session with the president
resumed. As I was departing, the president called after me, "John,
keep me updated on the situation in Connecticut."

I returned to my office, where the TV had already been tuned
to CNN, which was reporting on what was unfolding at the Sandy
Hook Elementary School in Newtown, Connecticut. Details were
sparse, and there was no information on casualties. Cameras focused
on the students and teachers who had left the school building and
the SWAT team surrounding it. The images brought back memories of the mass shooting at Virginia Tech in 2007, my daughter
Jaclyn's first year at the school. Thirty-three students and teachers
were killed in that incident, including one of Jaclyn's best friends. I
tried to push any thought of a repeat of that tragedy out of my mind.

As I was watching the TV coverage, I received a call from FBI

Deputy Director Sean Joyce. "John, I have bad news," Sean said in a low voice. "We're inside the school, and it's carnage. It looks like over twenty have been killed," and then, with his voice cracking a bit, he added, "Most of them are little children."

I sat in stunned silence. The words "little children" struck a deep emotional chord in me, as I couldn't help but visualize what would have been a horrific scene.

After a few moments, Sean continued. "The shooter killed himself. But the challenge now is to identify the victims. And, John, it is really difficult for the police and school authorities to see the bodies, especially of the children, and not break down in grief and horror. This is going to take time to work through."

I couldn't say anything. I just listened in a state of shock.

Sean continued: "The school is being overwhelmed by distraught parents who know that there has been a shooting and are consumed with fear that their children have been killed or injured. But you and the president need to know that we have an unfolding national tragedy."

I thanked Sean for the call and then sat back in my chair. My staff entered the room to inquire about what Sean had shared, but I responded with only a blank stare on my face. I told them that I needed to see the president. I picked up the note cards on which I'd jotted down Sean's comments and headed out the door.

As I walked up the stairs, I tried to compose myself on the way to the Oval Office. The president was standing next to his desk when I entered the room. He was in the midst of reading something that made him smile.

I looked at him for a moment without saying anything, and he realized immediately that I had bad news. He walked toward me and could see that my eyes were red. "Mr. President, I've just learned from the FBI that there are over twenty killed at the elementary school in Connecticut." I then swallowed hard and said, "And most of them are little children."

The president just stared at me, trying to comprehend what I had just said. More than anything else I ever told him, the impact of my words was immediate and profound. He leaned onto the back of the sofa, and the tears started to well up in his eyes. It was at that moment that I felt we were reacting as fathers, horrified by the thought that little children could have their lives ended so suddenly, violently, and senselessly.

I gave the president some time to absorb the information and then told him the shooter was dead and that there would be no information coming out on casualties until families could be notified and consoled. My last comment made the president close his eyes, as the very thought of the pain that grieving parents would experience seemed too much for him to bear.

I am sure that President Obama wishes that he could have made more progress on some key issues during his presidency.

Gun control undoubtedly is among them.

18

TAKING LIFE TO SAVE LIFE

"I need to see the president as soon as possible."

Whenever I uttered those words to one of President Obama's highly competent and unflappable personal secretaries, who were seated a few short feet from the Oval Office door, they knew something was hot and that time was of the essence. My White House counterterrorism portfolio spoke for itself. "Sure, John," they would say. "He should be finished in a few minutes." Wondering whether President Obama's schedule was going to be blown up for the day, they would then ask with some trepidation, "How much time do you need?"

"Just ten minutes, fifteen minutes tops."

By the second half of Obama's first term, this was the normal routine whenever I needed to talk to the president about what usually was a fleeting opportunity to take lethal action—a term describing the use of offensive force intended to result in the loss of life—against a terrorist target abroad in order to save American lives. In the very early days of the Obama administration, the president's senior national security team had decided that any strikes against terrorist targets outside the hot battlefields of Iraq and Afghanistan would require presidential approval. Counterterrorism operations in those two war-torn countries were governed by in-country military chains of command according to predetermined rules of engagement and didn't require a presidential sign-off. As assistant to the president for homeland security and counterterrorism, I was the designated point of contact at the White House for all requests from U.S. officials for lethal action beyond the borders of Iraq and Afghanistan. It didn't matter if the strikes involved Tomahawk land-attack missiles (commonly referred to as TLAMs) launched from U.S. Navy surface ships or submarines, or laser-guided munitions fired from U.S. military aircraft or from remotely piloted vehicles (known as RPVs and drones) controlled by U.S. counterterrorism forces. If an action were to be taken against a terrorist target anywhere abroad except for Afghanistan and Iraq, I was the White House gatekeeper.

Before I would bring a proposal to the president, however, I first needed to satisfy myself that the request was ready for his decision. When time allowed, the seriousness of the threat and the request to strike would be the topic of discussion in several interagency meetings held in the Situation Room, where the intelligence would be thoroughly scrubbed and challenged, and rigorous debate would ensue on whether the target met the threshold for lethal action. Even after convening such meetings, I frequently would have private conversations with some of my main counterterrorism counterparts, such as Vice Chairman of the Joint Chiefs of Staff General James "Hoss" Cartwright or his successor, Admiral James "Sandy" Winnefeld, before I would be ready to bring the request forward to the boss. But when the threat appeared imminent, I would receive urgent secure-line calls heralding the imminent arrival of classified emails with attachments providing the nature of the threat and the proposal on how to neutralize it with a lethal strike, forcing me to decide quickly whether to bring it to the president's immediate attention.

While waiting to see the president outside the Oval Office, I would stand anxiously, looking through the floor-to-ceiling windows that frame the covered walkway connecting the West Wing to the White House residence. The few minutes I had before seeing the president gave me the opportunity to think through once more the intelligence I had been provided, the details of the strike proposal, and my confidence level in the recommendation I planned to make. I also would agonize over what questions the president would be likely to ask. If he posed a question that I failed to anticipate, it would be evidence that I hadn't prepared well enough for the briefing. And nothing bothered me more than not being prepared for a meeting with the president.

Without warning, the heavy wooden door would open inward into the Oval Office, releasing a stream of people carrying notepads and briefing books, chatting among themselves about some presidential guidance they had just received. If any stragglers stayed behind, one of the president's personal secretaries would peek in and announce, "Brennan's here," bringing an abrupt end to the conversation. The mere mention of my name would bring a look of seriousness and resignation to the president's face. I tried not to take it personally, as I figured he just knew that I was bringing either bad news or a counterterrorism "strike package," which would require a decision having life-and-death implications, whether by an action he authorized or one that he denied.

Joining us in the Oval Office, if their schedules allowed, would be the vice president, national security adviser, deputy national security adviser, the president's chief of staff, and the White House counsel, as their offices were given a heads-up that I would be bringing a strike request to the president. I would take my usual seat at the end of the sofa to the immediate left of the president's chair while the others settled into their customary seats. Wasting no time, I would dive into the intelligence that brought me to the Oval Office on such days. The following is an illustration of a typical such discussion— modified for security reasons:

"Mr. President, we have located one of the key operatives involved in a plot to blow up our embassy in Sanaa with a truck bomb. We have confirmation from human and technical sources that he is a member of AQAP. He has bedded down for the night at a compound about seventy-five miles outside the city. Earlier today, our drones observed a pickup truck at the same compound being loaded with a large amount of explosives. Based on previous terrorist attacks and plots we have uncovered, the analysts believe that the loading of the truck and its colocation with the operative make it likely that the truck will depart the compound tomorrow morning for the attack in Sanaa."

With his left elbow on the arm of the wood-framed chair, the president would rest his head upon his left hand, index finger pointing upward along the side of his cheek while his thumb and other fingers cradled his chin. The president always listened intently to my words in such briefings, his eyes fixed on mine, shifting them and moving his arm only when I handed him a map and a few photos showing the precise location and configuration of the compound of concern. He would let me continue without interruption.

"Mr. President, there are at least fifteen individuals on the compound, eleven of whom are noncombatants, including some women and children, so we are unable to strike the truck at this time. The Yemeni government has no military or security forces in the area. We recommend against notifying the Yemenis at this point, as AQAP has many moles inside the intelligence services and would likely be alerted that we have located the truck and operative. Moreover, any attempt by Yemeni forces to try to avert the threat by raiding the compound themselves would likely result in the death of most, if not all, of the others on the compound.

"U.S. special forces are not in a position to conduct a raid against the compound this evening. Even if they were, the assessment is that the risk to our forces would be too great, as AQAP has numerous compounds with many heavily armed fighters in the area.

"The bottom line, sir, is that there is no available option to conduct an on-the-ground disruption or capture operation.

"Mr. President, our drones are maintaining constant observation of the compound. The weather forecast calls for another twelve hours or so of clear skies before clouds start rolling in. If that holds, we should be able to see the truck and the operative depart. The analysts have mapped the most likely roads the truck will travel once it leaves the compound, and they have identified areas that would allow for a clean strike before the truck gets to the congested roads of Sanaa.

"Mr. President, all criteria for a strike have been met, and the lawyers have signed off on it. I recommend that you authorize a strike as long as it can be taken consistent with the standing guidance of near certainty of no civilian casualties. Our folks believe they can find a stretch of road that will allow them to take a clean shot." This would not be the first time I had recommended to the president that he authorize a strike against a moving vehicle. He knew the risks. Another vehicle could unexpectedly appear on the same road. If that happened the RPV pilots would "shift cold," redirecting the missile while in flight to land and explode in a safe location rather than risk killing innocent travelers who happened to be in the wrong place at the wrong time.

I would finish up with the final item on my checklist. "Our ambassador in Sanaa has concurred with the strike recommendation. And this situation is virtually identical to the hypothetical scenario I discussed with President [Abdrabbuh Mansur] Hadi when I visited Sanaa last month. He told me that we could take such strikes when there is an imminent threat to American life. Our ambassador will inform Hadi as soon as we hit the truck. If the strike is successful and no civilians are injured or killed, I am confident that the Yemenis will not object, although they might criticize it publicly for their own domestic political purposes."

The president would take additional looks at the map and photos. "What if we see someone else get into the truck with the AQAP guy? And what happens if the clouds roll in early and obscure our view, and we lose sight of the truck and the terrorist?"

The president would probably know what I would say, as we would have been through similar briefing sessions before. But he would want explicit reassurance that his previous guidance would be followed.

"Yes, sir. If anyone else gets in the truck, there will need to be near certainty derived from intelligence that the individual is AQAP or aware of the truck's true purpose. The operators know that they would need to contact us for further guidance if they cannot make a near certainty assessment. In the event we lose the truck because of extended cloud cover, the Yemenis will be immediately contacted and given details of the truck and the operative so that they can set up roadblocks on the edge of the city. Better to have the Yemenis informed at that stage, even if it leaks to AQAP."

"What about security around the embassy?" he would ask. "We need to get our folks out of harm's way."

"Yes, sir. We've drawn down our diplomatic staff over the past few weeks, and our ambassador asked President Hadi earlier today to strengthen and push out the security perimeter around the embassy given recent threat reporting that we have shared with the Yemenis. I'll call Hadi when I get back to my office to tell him that you are making the request personally."

"Okay. I approve the strike if there is near certainty there will be no civilian casualties. Keep me updated, including on the security situation around the embassy. Let me know when the truck leaves the compound and whether or not anyone other than the terrorist gets in it."

"Will do, sir. Thank you, Mr. President."

It would take me less than thirty seconds to get back to my office, where I would immediately relay the president's direction to the counterterrorism component that had made the strike request through its chain of command, such as General Cartwright, Admiral

Winnefeld, or, at times, Lieutenant General John F. Kelly, who was the senior military assistant to Defense Secretary Bob Gates and his successor, Leon Panetta. I usually would put a time limit on the approval. "You have authorization to strike if the criteria are met within the next twenty-four hours," I would say on the secure line call. "After twenty-four hours, you will need to provide an update and request an extension."

An early-morning strike in Yemen would take place an hour or two before midnight in Washington, which would allow me to call President Obama or visit him in the residence to give him a readout on what happened. If we took the strike, I usually would be able to report that it was carried out successfully and without any civilian casualties. But that wasn't always the case, especially in the first year of the Obama administration.

IT WAS WITHIN DAYS OF my arrival at the White House in January 2009 when I realized the full weight of the responsibility on my shoulders as President Obama's senior counterterrorism adviser. It had been more than three years since I was last in government and involved in the fight against al-Qa'ida, but my earlier engagement was solely on the analytic side. Although TTIC and NCTC assessments addressed the seriousness and imminence of terrorist threats, which were used to justify subsequent counterterrorist actions, I was never directly involved in the decision-making process on the use of lethal force. That changed dramatically when I assumed my White House role.

U.S. counterterrorism capabilities had grown increasingly sophisticated during my time out of government, especially on the technological front. One of the most significant advancements was improvements in the numbers and capabilities of RPVs, colloquially known as drones or by their General Atomic brand names, Predator and its more capable follow-up version, Reaper. These armed and unarmed aerial platforms, flown and controlled by American pilots at ground stations hundreds or even thousands of miles away, became an increasingly effective counterterrorism tool for technical intelligence collection, full-motion video observation, and lethal action in the hunt for al-Qa'ida. While RPVs were deployed to support U.S. military battlefield operations in Iraq and Afghanistan, they were especially useful in conducting counterterrorism strikes in countries where the United States had no combat forces and local governments lacked the capability or the will—sometimes both—to counter terrorist threats.

The Bush administration stepped up its use of armed RPVs during its last year in office. In my first weeks as President Obama's counterterrorism adviser, I received numerous briefings on the technical capabilities of the platforms, especially on the range and amazing accuracy of the laser-guided missiles they carried. I was impressed at the ability of the RPVs to dwell for extended periods of time over known and suspected terrorist compounds and to track the movement of terrorist operatives and vehicles in terrain that was beyond the reach of other intelligence collection efforts. Eliminating the risks associated with sending U.S. servicemen and women into harm's way to conduct combat operations against terrorists was a major advantage. While the technical briefings were comprehensive, I could find no accompanying White House guidelines regarding the need for a legal review of strike proposals nor any established operational criteria to be met before a strike would be authorized. Rather, the decision-making system seemed somewhat ad hoc, which was not surprising given the still-evolving nature of the program and the limited number of strikes that had been taken by the end of the Bush administration.

There was no question that the use of armed RPVs dramatically increased options for dealing with terrorist threats, but President Obama made it clear from the outset of his administration that he wanted tight control on their use. He did not want the increased availability and convenience of putting ordnance on targets to lower the standard of when such action would be authorized. President Obama and I had discussed the importance of avoiding the loss of any innocent life during counterterrorism operations when we first met in Chicago, and I knew that we needed to develop an interagency process and strike criteria to govern the use of lethal force in countries other than Afghanistan and Iraq. Creating such a process would take time, however, during which there would be no hiatus in terrorist threats or in proposals for lethal action being sent to the White House. During the first year of the Obama administration, I worked closely with NSC Legal Counsel Mary DeRosa and NSC Senior Director for Counterterrorism Nick Rasmussen to scrutinize the intelligence and strike options sent to the White House. When we deemed the threat serious and the options lawful and realistic, I would seek authorization for a strike during a meeting with President Obama and other senior White House officials working national security matters. It was during those early Oval Office meetings that I came to understand the conditions, circumstances, criteria, and considerations—which I referred to as the four Cs—that President Obama wanted taken into account before he was asked to approve a lethal strike.

We began to design a system that would optimize our ability to take effective lethal action against terrorist targets outside the United States to protect American lives. It was a lengthy and frequently contentious process. There was a wide range of views across national security agencies regarding how to assess the seriousness and imminence of the threat, the criteria to be met before taking lethal action, and, most especially, the confidence level needed to make a determination that civilian deaths or injuries would be avoided. Whenever a major terrorist operative was identified or located, a discussion ensued on the seriousness of the threat he posed and whether the threat could be mitigated only by lethal action. Frequently, the interagency discussions resulted in denials of proposed strikes against individuals due to insufficient intelligence about the imminence of the threat posed or the availability of other options to mitigate it. Lessons learned from each deliberation informed future discussions and decisions.

As the framework was taking shape, President Obama encouraged senior administration officials to talk publicly and as transparently as possible about U.S. counterterrorism actions.

While civilians were tragically killed in some strikes, the number was far fewer than the wildly exaggerated and unsubstantiated claims that were circulating in U.S. media accounts and, most especially, the international press. In addition to rebutting these inaccurate stories, President Obama also was keenly interested in establishing precedents and standards for the use of RPVs by other nations. "We can't criticize others for conducting such strikes if we don't explain how and when we use them ourselves," he said.

I felt a personal obligation to lean forward publicly and describe how President Obama was thwarting terrorist plans in a manner that was thoughtful, measured, and consistent with American values. I did so, however, with only mixed success in a series of speeches at the Center for Strategic and International Studies, the Council on Foreign Relations, New York University, Harvard Law School, Johns Hopkins University, and the Woodrow Wilson Center in Washington, D.C. I recognize now that, at times, my remarks were rather esoteric if not downright confusing, such as when I said in late 2009 that President Obama did not see counterterrorism as a fight against "jihadists." I pointed to Islamic teaching that refers to "jihad" as a holy struggle in pursuit of a moral goal and that terrorist attacks are neither holy nor moral. I was trying to make the point that "violence" and "jihad" were not necessarily synonymous, which ran counter to the prevailing view of most Americans.

I also argued that labeling terrorists as jihadists risked giving them "the religious legitimacy they seek but in no way deserve." I didn't win many converts with my thesis, then or since. And when I delivered public remarks in Arabic the following year and referred to Jerusalem by its Arabic name "al-Quds," conspiracy theorists ran wild—and continue to do so—with stories of how I was a prime example that the highest levels of the U.S. government had been infiltrated by Islamic extremists.

Undaunted, I continued to speak out and shared many details of the administration's counterterrorism policies and actions at these public fora. In late June 2011, I publicly stated that "nearly for the past year there hasn't been a single collateral death" in counterterrorism operations outside the hot battlefields of Iraq and Afghanistan, a claim that was widely disputed by critics of U.S. counterterrorism actions but which I stand by to this day. In April 2012, I stated publicly that the United States government conducted targeted strikes against specific al-Qa'ida terrorists using RPVs, an admission that, up to that time, the American government had refused to make. I considered such strikes the world's worst-kept secret and saw no reason to continue the charade. That unvarnished acknowledgment was accompanied by many other details, including how targeted strikes by the Obama administration adhered to the basic "law of war" principles of necessity, distinction, proportionality, and humanity; the strong preference for the capture rather than the killing of terrorists; the demonstrated ability of Article III courts to try and convict terrorists; and, the importance of congressional oversight of executive branch actions.

President Obama decided that we needed to do more. "I'm pretty confident that I'll win reelection," he told a small group of us in the Oval Office one morning in the spring of 2012, "but we owe the next administration an actual framework for deciding when it is appropriate to strike terrorist targets, whether the next president takes office in 2013 or in 2017. Let's take what we've done in practice and put it into a document that we can pass to our successors." As usual, President Obama's instincts were right. I certainly would have benefited if I had been given written guidelines on my first day in office that set out procedures that we could adopt or modify for our use of RPVs. Obama's direction prompted another intense round of interagency meetings among policy and intelligence officials and lawyers. During the discussions, it was decided that the document should address all U.S. direct action, which included capture operations by U.S. forces. We set our sights on finalizing the document by the end of 2012, but once President Obama won reelection, the process slowed and was not completed until the following year.

On May 22, 2013, President Obama approved a top-secret document entitled "Procedures for Approving Direct Action Against Terrorist Targets Located Outside the United States and Areas of Active Hostilities." As an illustration of the transparency the president was seeking, an unclassified White House fact sheet summarizing the document was issued the following day, and a declassified version of the top-secret document was later released as a result of a Freedom of Information Act (FOIA) request. I consider the procedures an enduring template for the conduct of lethal action against terrorist targets, whether carried out by the United States or another government. In addition to stipulating that lethal force must have a legal basis and only be used against targets that pose a continuing imminent threat, the procedures called for near certainty that (a) the terrorist target is present; (b) noncombatants will not be injured or killed; and (c) capture or other alternative to mitigate the threat, including by foreign forces, is not feasible.

According to press reports, the Trump administration decided early on not to follow the Obama administration's guidelines for taking direct action against terrorist targets. I do not know the criteria and procedures for striking terrorist targets abroad used by the Trump administration. I also find it surprising that there has not been more of a hue and cry by the press and human rights organizations about the much greater secrecy attached to counterterrorist operations in the Trump administration. While I fear that some White House officials have more relaxed standards when it comes to avoiding civilian injuries and deaths, I fervently hope that our counterterrorism professionals continue to carry out their responsibilities with the aim of doing their utmost to prevent the loss of innocent life, American and non-American.

President Obama's insistence on openness regarding counterterrorism actions continued throughout the remainder of his presidency. In early 2016, he directed the Department of Defense in coordination with the intelligence community to publish information on the results of lethal strikes against terrorist targets outside Iraq and Afghanistan. Accordingly, the Obama White House announced in July 2016 that from his inauguration on January 20, 2009, through December 31, 2015, a total of 473 strikes against terrorist targets resulted in the deaths of between 2,372 and 2,581 combatants and somewhere between 64 and 116 civilians. I was involved in the review of those statistics and believe they represent an accurate estimate of civilian deaths, although I believe that the number of civilian deaths is closer to 116 than to 64. Human rights organizations, which argued that the number of civilian deaths was much higher, understandably criticized our aggregate numbers, arguing that they couldn't be verified without an individual listing of the strikes and the methodology and sources used to determine them. But we were unable to do so because of concerns that full transparency would have revealed sensitive and classified sources, methods, and procedures that were used in the RPV program.

Without a doubt, my counterterrorism responsibilities in the Obama administration were the weightiest of my professional career, as they involved life-and-death decisions on a regular basis. An especially challenging case involved Anwar al-Awlaki, a U.S. citizen who was a senior leader of AQAP and instigator of terrorist attacks against U.S. persons and entities, including a mass shooting at Fort Hood, Texas, that killed fourteen and injured more than thirty as well as the attempted downing of an aircraft over the United States on Christmas Day 2009. There was incontrovertible intelligence in the summer of 2011 that Awlaki was involved in the planning and direction of additional terrorist attacks against U.S. persons, but he was burrowed deep inside Yemen, precluding a capture operation by either U.S. or Yemeni forces. The only option to eliminate the threat he posed was to launch a missile from one of our RPVs. Awlaki's U.S. citizen status, however, rightly prompted extended policy debate among national security departments and agencies and inside the White House on whether lethal action should or even could be legally taken against him. The discussion centered on the tension between the U.S. government's obligation to protect its citizens from terrorist attacks, including when those attacks are perpetrated by U.S. persons, and the right of U.S. citizens to due process under U.S. law. As a constitutional lawyer as well as the commander in chief, President Obama was seized with the issue and directed his national security team to work closely with senior government lawyers before bringing a recommendation to him.

The discussions were intense. There was no disputing the fact that Awlaki presented a serious threat to U.S. persons and interests, but there was significant concern about taking a strike with the specific objective of killing a U.S. citizen. While there were numerous cases over the years of U.S. citizens who had joined enemy forces and were subsequently killed on the battlefield as a result of U.S. military action, we knew of no previous instance when a U.S. citizen was intentionally targeted and killed by the U.S. government. The lack of precedent demanded that the matter receive an exhaustive review.

One option that was considered was whether there should be some review of the case outside the executive branch, such as by one or more former federal judges, before a decision is made about whether to strike a U.S. citizen. After many hours of deliberation, however, that option was discarded. It was deemed impractical from a timing standpoint, because such a review would take months if not much longer, during which time the threat would persist and likely grow. Even more significantly, a consensus emerged that it would be inappropriate and unethical to ask any individual outside the government to recommend whether a U.S. citizen, even one who joined al-Qa'ida, should live or die.

Ultimately, the Office of Legal Counsel in the Department of Justice authored a memo that concluded Awlaki posed a "continued and imminent threat of violence or death to Americans" and that taking lethal action against him, in the absence of other viable means to mitigate the threat, would be a lawful act of war covered under the Authorized Use of Military Force (AUMF), which was passed by Congress following the 9/11 attacks. With the highest legal advisory body in the executive branch posing no objection to the targeting of Awlaki, presidential authorization for the strike was granted. On September 30, 2011, an RPV-launched missile killed Awlaki in the Marib Governate of Yemen. He was the only U.S. citizen intentionally targeted during the Obama administration. Unbeknownst to U.S. intelligence, Samir Khan, a second U.S. citizen who was a member of AQAP, was with Awlaki at the time of the strike and also killed. Two weeks later, Awlaki's sixteen-year-old U.S.-citizen son, Abd al-Rahman al-Awlaki, who traveled to Yemen to join his father, was inadvertently killed in a strike targeting another senior AQAP leader.

At least four other U.S. citizens were killed as a result of RPV strikes during the Obama administration. Ahmed Farouq, Jude Muhammad, and Adam Gadahn were killed in separate strikes along the Afghan-Pakistani border that took place between 2011 and 2015. They were all members of al-Qa'ida and killed in authorized strikes, but their U.S. identities were not known until after they were killed.

Warren Weinstein, a U.S. citizen engaged in development work in the Afghan-Pakistani border region, was tragically killed in an RPV strike against a confirmed al-Qa'ida hideout in January 2015. At the time of his death, Weinstein had been held captive by al-Qa'ida for three and a half years.

Weinstein's death still haunts me. It was one of the most regrettable counterterrorism mistakes made during the Obama administration. I wish I could lessen the pain I am sure his family still feels. But I know that is impossible.

There is no denying that the death of Warren Weinstein and of every other noncombatant was tragic. There also is no doubt in my mind that if President Obama had not authorized strikes on al-Qa'ida targets, thousands more innocent individuals, many of them Americans, would have died as a result.

19

THE "PACER" OF ABBOTTABAD

The operation that killed Usama Bin Ladin was the most intense, secretive, well-planned, and successful operation I ever witnessed during my national security career. I knew from my work on the transition team that one of President Obama's highest priorities when he became president was to find Bin Ladin as soon as possible. His objective was twofold: to hold accountable the person responsible for the 9/11 attacks and, even more important, to deal a crippling blow to al-Qa'ida to further reduce its lethal capabilities and potential to kill more innocents.

To underscore his personal commitment to getting Bin Ladin, the president convened a meeting of the most senior members of his national security team in May 2009 to review the status of the pursuit. Leon Panetta, who had assumed the CIA director job only four months before, took the lead in the briefing. In efficient fashion, he walked through a series of briefing slides that acknowledged there was only scant and outdated intelligence on Bin Ladin's possible whereabouts. Included on the slides was information on several facilitators and couriers who reportedly were used by the exceptionally

security-conscious Bin Ladin to communicate with a handful of his
key al-Qa'ida lieutenants. Leon explained that CIA officers had been
involved in a tedious multiyear effort to find the individuals who
were in direct contact with Bin Ladin. "If we can find them," Leon
said, "we will be able to follow them to Bin Ladin." Like most attendees, I interpreted Leon's use of the word "if" to signal that the
CIA effort to find Bin Ladin was stuck.

President Obama appreciated Leon's honesty, but he was unsatisfied with what he heard. He wanted more done. On June 2, he sent a
memo to Leon directing that the CIA produce within thirty days "a
detailed operational plan for locating and bringing to justice Usama
Bin Ladin." Obama knew that the CIA was giving high priority to
the hunt, but he wanted to add an adrenaline boost and a signal of
support from a new president, especially one who had been sharply
critical of the CIA's detention and interrogation program during
the presidential campaign. Once again responding to a presidential
order—this time a noncontroversial one—a CIA plan to find Bin
Ladin was drafted and quickly approved by the president. The ener-
gized CIA hunt for Bin Ladin was on.

It was a little more than a year later when the CIA had meaningful new information to provide the president. In keeping with the
important symbolism of the 9/11 anniversary, Leon asked to meet
with the president on Friday, September 10, 2010, to provide an update on the search for the al-Qa'ida leader. CIA Deputy Director Michael Morell, a close colleague and friend whose intelligence acumen
I had admired when we worked together at Langley, called me in
advance of the meeting to emphasize the particular sensitivity of the
information that would be discussed and the need to have the fewest
possible number of White House staff present. To give weight to his
request, Michael said that the CIA had developed some potentially
very significant information regarding an individual whom CIA analysts assessed was Bin Ladin's courier. Michael and I agreed that in
addition to the president and vice president, Rahm, Jim Jones, Tom

Donilon, Denis McDonough, National Security Adviser to the Vice President Tony Blinken, NSC Legal Counsel Mary DeRosa, and I would be the only non-CIA attendees.

Arriving at the Oval Office with Michael and the head of the CIA's Counterterrorism Center, Leon was well versed in his brief. "A few weeks ago, we found and were able to follow an individual who we believe is a personal courier of Bin Ladin. The individual is living with his brother in a compound in Abbottabad, Pakistan." Leon's words that the CIA might have found the residence of Bin Ladin's courier had the effect of sucking the air out of the room. "We don't know much about the compound at this point, but this could be the breakthrough we have been waiting for." Leon cautioned that it was premature to get too excited, as there was still much to learn about the compound and its occupants. He then laid out the CIA's plan to collect more information on the compound without drawing the attention of the Pakistanis. Colorfully, Leon noted that Abbottabad presented significant challenges from a collection standpoint. "The goddamn Pakistan Military Academy is in Abbottabad, and it also is a goddamn retirement area for senior Pakistani military officers. This is going to be tough." The presence of the Pakistani military prompted animated discussion and speculation about whether Pakistani officials were aware of Bin Ladin's location or might even be harboring him.

"Good work, Leon," the president said, as the briefing concluded. "Tell your folks to keep at it. This has the highest priority. And let me know if you need anything at all to run this to ground." The president was clearly pleased with what he had just heard, and Leon left the office with an added bounce in his step. The rest of us stayed behind. The president looked at me and asked what I thought.

"If the CIA now has a bead on Bin Ladin's courier, it's the closest we have gotten to Bin Ladin since he slipped out of Tora Bora in December 2001," I said. Then, unabashedly, I exposed my CIA bias by bragging about the skill and dedication of the CIA officers hunting Bin Ladin, whether from their desks in Langley or in service abroad. "Mr. President, the CIA has the best experts in the world on al-Qa'ida. More than any other agency or department, they consider it their responsibility to find Bin Ladin, and they have been deeply frustrated for almost a decade at their inability to do so. This is very personal to them. If they believe the individual is Bin Ladin's courier, he almost certainly is. And they will move heaven and earth to find out everything they can about that compound and who lives there as soon as they can."

I was excited to sing the praises of the CIA that morning, as I had tremendous respect for the institution I once called home, especially the skills, dedication, and integrity of the overwhelming majority of the workforce. At the time of the briefing, Obama had been in office for nearly twenty months and had a much better understanding and appreciation of CIA capabilities than when he first assumed the presidency. Nevertheless, I felt that, unlike all his predecessors since President Truman, he had not yet experienced a "WOW!" moment as a result of something truly spectacular that the CIA was able to accomplish. Maybe this opportunity would develop into such a moment, I thought.

Over the next two months, Leon and his team kept us apprised of the few new developments on the collection front, including some intelligence derived from "exquisite" collection systems. These are technical collection systems that provide extraordinarily precise information and measurements but are also exceptionally sensitive. Progress on learning who lived at the compound seemed agonizingly slow, however, as the difficult operating environment of Abbottabad was everything Leon had forecast. I talked with Michael Morell practically every day, and the conversation inevitably would turn to the status of the CIA's knowledge about the compound. "John, we're doing everything we can," Michael would respond to my regular inquiries, "but we do not want to risk coming to Pak attention." I knew he was right, but I was still impatient.

On December 14, the president received the first detailed briefing on the Abbottabad compound from Leon and his CIA team. During the briefing, which again took place in the Oval Office, Leon provided many more details of the "unusually large and secure" compound and the surrounding neighborhood. The CIA had confirmed that the compound was the "bed-down" location of the Bin Ladin courier and his family. In addition, validated intelligence indicated that the courier had worked for two Guantánamo detainees who had served as Bin Ladin "gatekeepers" before they were captured. The detainees were al-Qa'ida operatives who had corresponded with Bin Ladin via the courier and then implemented the guidance they received, once again via the courier, from Bin Ladin. Leon told the president that the Agency knew that the two detainees had lied about the courier to protect Bin Ladin during their interrogations, which added to the CIA's confidence that the courier was the real deal. It was during this December meeting that the president was told for the first time that the CIA had obtained intelligence that an individual with physical features similar to Bin Ladin's, referred to as the "Pacer" due to his regular monotonous ambulations inside the compound's walls, was living there.

Although Leon and Michael were doing their level best not to prematurely raise hopes that the CIA had found Bin Ladin, there was an unmistakable sense of optimism in the White House, as 2010 was coming to a close, that the CIA pursuit of the al-Qa'ida leader had gained significant momentum. "If this looks like it's real," the president said to Donilon—who had succeeded Jim Jones as national security adviser two months earlier—McDonough, and me before he departed on his year-end holiday with his family to Hawaii, "I want folks to start thinking about our options to get Bin Ladin if he is at that Abbottabad compound."

The CIA was already thinking about a Bin Ladin "get" plan. While some CIA officers were eager to limit consideration only to those options that the CIA could develop and carry out on its own, Leon and

Michael, to their credit, quickly recognized that the U.S. military's broader set of capabilities needed to come into play. In early February 2011, the CIA asked for and received White House permission to bring Vice Admiral Bill McRaven, the commander of the U.S. Joint Special Operations Command, into the circle of knowledge on the compound and its possible inhabitants. Bill was asked to think about whether U.S. special forces could conduct a successful raid on the compound if the president decided to go that route. Recognizing that McRaven's superiors at the Pentagon needed to be brought into the discussion if he was going to develop military options, the White House agreed that Secretary Gates, Chairman of the Joint Chiefs of Staff Admiral Mullen, and his deputy, General Cartwright, also needed to be fully briefed. Soon thereafter, Secretary Clinton received her own briefing and became a member of the "briefed-in" group. Everyone was told that they could not discuss the matter with anyone else unless it was first authorized by the White House, meaning the president.

The pace of meetings, intelligence collection, and operational planning increased markedly by the end of February. At a March 4 principals committee meeting, the CIA brought a four-by-four-foot scale model of the Abbottabad compound into the White House Situation Room. The model, which was carried into the White House concealed in a large wooden case, proved exceptionally useful for the many subsequent discussions about the compound and the options available to get Bin Ladin. By the time of the May 1 raid, seventeen formal National Security Council meetings—at the deputies, principals, and presidential level—were held in the Situation Room on the subject. Unlike normal interagency meetings, these gatherings were unique in my experience. There were no meeting announcements, agendas, or read-ahead materials circulated to attendees in advance. Invitations were by name only and were conveyed cryptically and telephonically; no substitutes were allowed. No videoconferencing into meetings was permitted; indeed, all the camera lenses in the

Situation Room were covered during the meetings so there would be no inadvertent hemorrhaging of the subject matter via secure video. Maps and printouts of PowerPoint slides used in the discussion were distributed at the beginning of each meeting and retrieved from attendees before they departed. My administrative staff, unaware of the substance of the discussions being held, simply put "Mickey Mouse meeting" on my computer-based schedule.

The importance of secrecy was apparent to all, as the CIA continued to emphasize that any leak of information could undermine whatever chance there was to get Bin Ladin even before an operation got under way. It was therefore ironic and disconcerting when Leon mentioned at a meeting on March 4 that he had discussed the Abbottabad compound with some members of the Senate Select Committee on Intelligence (SSCI). I remember looking at the faces of others around the room as soon as the words left Leon's mouth. Like me, they were all stunned. Tom Donilon spoke up first, "You did what?!?"

"I told some senators on the committee about the compound," Leon responded. He then realized that Donilon was taken aback and clearly unhappy at the news, so Leon immediately started to push back. "It's my goddamn oversight committee. I need to keep them briefed on significant intelligence activities."

Tom interrupted Leon's spirited defense. "There's no 'activity' going on here, Leon. The president has not yet decided to do anything. We don't even know who is in that compound!" Other salty words were exchanged. Leon didn't relent, but he got the message: the president wanted this locked down, and leaders in Congress would be brought in at the proper time.

At a National Security Council meeting chaired by the president on March 14, the CIA started off with a comprehensive review of the intelligence. In the discussion, one of the CIA briefers said he was 70 percent confident that the "Pacer" was Usama Bin Ladin. The CIA briefer was a much-respected and longtime al-Qa'ida expert. The strength of his judgment was surprising, albeit welcomed, as it gave additional impetus and gravity to the subsequent discussions. Bill McRaven then briefed the meeting on the challenges associated with U.S. special forces conducting a raid against the compound. "We carry out this kind of assault with great success every single night in Afghanistan and Iraq. But we own the skies in those countries; we don't in Pakistan. If we do this on our own, the challenge will be flying our helos a hundred and fifty miles into Pakistan, carrying out the mission on the compound, and then flying back to Afghanistan. At some point, we're going to wake up the Paks, and they will be none too happy that we're in their country without their permission. I need to do some more homework on this, Mr. President, before I tell you whether or not I think it's doable." It was a sobering brief.

The president also was told that one option would be to launch joint direct-attack munitions (JDAMs) from B-2 bombers against the compound. The downsides of this option were readily apparent to all. In addition to killing everyone in the compound—including the women and children who had been observed living there—a strike using B-2 bombers would likely result in dozens if not hundreds of casualties in the surrounding area. No one in the room argued in defense of the morality of such a strike, even in an attempt to kill Bin Ladin. It also was recognized that the adverse reaction of the Pakistani government and people to U.S. missile strikes causing many civilian deaths would be extreme and likely volatile. Moreover, a standoff strike would not result in a definite determination that it was Bin Ladin who was observed at the compound and whether he was killed. Even if Bin Ladin died in the strike, al-Qa'ida could claim that he had escaped, which only would add to his already near-mythic status. The missile strike was discarded at this meeting.

With the CIA's increased confidence that Bin Ladin was on the compound, the president said he wanted planning to continue on the helicopter-assault option as well as on any other option that might be identified. "I want to meet again after deputies and principals thoroughly and quickly work through this. If Bin Ladin is in that compound, he won't be there forever." Obama had internalized what the CIA had said in numerous briefings: Bin Ladin and other senior al-Qa'ida members change their location periodically for security reasons. And the reality was that if Bin Ladin was indeed at the Abbottabad compound, we had no idea how long he had been there or was planning to stay.

Denis and I cochaired a very lengthy deputies meeting on March 22, during which we drilled down once again on all the available options to get Bin Ladin. Despite the risks associated with a helicopter-assault option, the deputies gave it the most attention and support. Several considerations came into focus during that meeting. First, the timing of a raid would be dependent on favorable weather conditions. Second, in order to cut down on visual observation by unfriendly forces on the ground, a raid would need to take place during a period of minimal moonlight, which occurs at the end of every lunar cycle. The first lunar window would present itself on April 2, with subsequent windows occurring every twenty-eight days. The president would need to be informed that the helicopter-assault raid option would only be available for a seventy-two-hour period, every four weeks. Third, contingency plans would need to be put in place if the assaulters encountered stiff Pakistani military opposition and were unable to extricate themselves safely from the compound. Finally, how would we deal with a helicopter that goes down inside Pakistan? Should the Pakistanis be informed before, during, or after a U.S. search-and-rescue (SAR) mission was under way? Deputies were instructed to prepare the necessary memoranda that the president and principals would need on these issues.

While strikes using B-2 bombers had already been ruled out, there was extensive discussion during the deputies meeting about the possibility of launching a tactical weapon with laser precision from an aerial platform to strike the Pacer during one of his walks. Notwithstanding the technical challenges associated with such a strike, this option had the same uncertainties regarding the inability to learn the true identity and even the fate of the individual struck. And, unlike the helicopter-assault option, striking the compound using B-2s or a tactical weapon would not provide the opportunity to seize material—known as SSE (sensitive site exploitation)—that Bin Ladin probably had at the compound. Nevertheless, deputies agreed that the tactical weapon option should be brought forward to the president. The meeting rejected any consideration of telling the Pakistanis about the Abbottabad compound. It was the unanimous view of the deputies that the Pakistanis would not agree to carry out a joint operation with U.S. forces on their soil or allow the U.S. to do so alone. Besides, we didn't know whether any Pakistanis in the government or military were involved in helping Bin Ladin hide out in Abbottabad and would inform him that his location was discovered. The deputies concluded that a unilateral U.S. operation was the only viable option.

Rather than wait until after the principals had an opportunity to reconvene, Obama chaired a National Security Council meeting on March 29. Once again, Leon started off providing the intelligence picture, which hadn't changed much in over a month. The president pushed Leon. "What is the likelihood that we will get more intelligence on the compound in the next few weeks that would raise our confidence that it's Bin Ladin?" Leon was never one to overpromise, and he was blunt in his response. "Not good. We have a few things under way, but I think this is about as good as it gets, unless we get very lucky." Leon's candor was one of the many reasons why Obama and the rest of those in the room liked and respected the CIA director so much.

It was then Bill McRaven's turn to brief on the homework he had done on a potential helicopter assault against the compound. Bill's reputation for being an outstanding briefer was on full display that day. Showing extensive knowledge of the tactics and logistics required for a risky compound raid deep inside Pakistan, Bill held the room's attention with his resonant voice and detailed and matter-of-fact presentation. He walked through how an operation would need to be conducted and the numerous dependencies of success. Like Leon, he was blunt in his comments to the president, acknowledging that he could not say whether a raid would be successful until he did more extensive planning. Obama listened closely, impressed by the expertise and obvious leadership skills of the legendary Navy SEAL. "How long will it take before you know if you can do it?"

"I'll have to pull a team together first, sir, and then we'll need to do a dress rehearsal. That should take us about three weeks." Obama instructed Bill to move forward with his plans, including the dress rehearsal. Bill then raised one of his principal concerns. "Mr. President, things could get rather 'sporty' when we get to the compound. The Pakistanis have a lot of security personnel on the ground in the area and they could try to prevent us from leaving the compound, whether we get Bin Ladin or not. I presume there would be some type of diplomatic intervention at that point to deescalate the situation so that we could get our team out of country." The visual Bill presented of U.S. special forces being surrounded by Pakistani soldiers landed like a thud in the middle of the table. We all knew that the risk to those carrying out the mission was significant, but the potential protracted nature of what would amount to U.S. special forces being held hostage by the Pakistanis was disturbing. After a few moments, the president broke the silence by firmly rejecting any notion of negotiating with the Pakistanis for the release of captive U.S. special forces.

"Bill, your team will need to be prepared to fight their way out if necessary." While Obama's words made clear that a nasty firefight with the Pakistanis might be necessary, everyone in the room was relieved that the United States would not be put in a position of bargaining with a foreign government for the release of its servicemen. Secretary Clinton, our nation's top diplomat, seemed most happy. "That's right," she said firmly.

Bill quickly responded, "Yes, sir!"

The president then widened the aperture of the discussion, asking about the broader implications and likely aftermath of a raid. Obama wasn't satisfied with what he heard. At the end of the meeting, he directed additional analysis to be done on the likely impact of a raid, whether it be a success or failure, on al-Qa'ida and its terrorist capabilities and intentions. He also asked for an assessment on the implications of a unilateral U.S. operation on our military and political objectives in Afghanistan. "I want to know how the Pakistanis are likely to react. Will they prevent us from using Pakistani airspace to supply our troops in Afghanistan? Will they release whatever partial hold they have on Haqqani fighters who are attacking our troops inside Afghanistan? What else might the Paks do to try to punish us?" As usual, the president was looking two and three chess moves ahead and wanted to be aware of and prepared for virtually any contingency.

That NSC meeting triggered a flurry of activity over the next three weeks. Bill pulled together his team of assaulters and conducted stateside rehearsals on April 7 and 13. Denis and I gathered deputies twice more in mid-April, so we could wrestle not only with the issues that had already surfaced but the many more that seemed to suddenly emerge. Among the questions we had to address were: Was this a kill-and-not-capture operation? What happens if Bin Ladin presents no discernible threat and wants to surrender? If captured, where would we take him? If he was killed, what would we do with the body? When would we talk to the Pakistanis to tell them about the raid, and who should be contacted first? Presuming that the operation would need to be publicly acknowledged, when would we do so and how? What should the diplomatic strategy be? What about congressional notifications? Who should the president call and in what order? The issues and outstanding questions kept piling up. After each deputies meeting, Denis and I would give a readout to Tom Donilon and the president and vice president at our morning Oval Office meetings. In one of those meetings, we agreed that we needed a detailed "playbook" that would be made available to principals, addressing all the decisions, action items, and responsibilities attendant to the raid and its aftermath. NSC Senior Director for Counterterrorism Nick Rasmussen, who also had attended all of the deputies, principals, and National Security Council meetings, was tasked to create a playbook with a "tick-tock," the White House euphemism for the operational timeline and the sequencing of all associated actions, as well as required talking points.

A principals meeting on April 18 was followed the next day by a National Security Council meeting that, in my mind, lit the actual fuse on the Abbottabad compound assault. Leon started off by saying that the intelligence picture remained unchanged. Leon said that the CIA was being creative in its attempts to have "up close and personal" interaction with the residents in the compound, but nothing had worked to date. DNI Jim Clapper provided the intelligence community's assessment of the likely Pakistani reaction, including the potential adverse implications for U.S. military operations in Afghanistan, and the impact of Bin Ladin's death on al-Qa'ida. The bottom line was that the likely fallout on the U.S.-Pakistan relationship was manageable if it was Bin Ladin who was killed, and civilian casualties were avoided. Bin Ladin's demise would be a significant symbolic, psychological, and organizational blow to al-Qa'ida, as Ayman Zawahiri, al-Qa'ida's number two, did not have Bin Ladin's leadership skills, operational knowledge, jihadi credentials, or charisma.

Bill McRaven then briefed us on the operational plan for the compound raid and the results of the rehearsals. He said he was confident his forces could conduct the compound assault successfully, with the next lunar window being the weekend of April 30–May 1. Secretary Gates and Admiral Mullen told the president that the helicopter assault represented the best military option available. I noted that the deputies unanimously recommended that the operation be approved by principals and authorized by the president.

The president told the assembled group to assume the operation was a "go" for planning purposes. He said that the playbook must be comprehensive, detailed, and completed before the end of the month. The president also said that he wanted a security plan for U.S. diplomatic facilities in Pakistan as well as for embassies and consulates worldwide considering the potential for protests and violence directed against U.S. interests and personnel.

In the ten days prior to the May 1 compound assault, another three deputies meetings, three principals meetings, and two National Security Council meetings were held. In addition, the president had a series of separate discussions with individual principals as well as with his White House senior staff. The playbook was fleshed out and constantly updated and amended. Intelligence assessments were written, briefed, and digested, and operational plans were refined. The assault force moved from its U.S. training base to Afghanistan.

In the last week of April, Mike Leiter, the director of the National Counterterrorism Center (NCTC), was briefed on the operation, and he offered to coordinate a "red team" assessment, which is a review conducted by a group of experts not previously briefed on the matter, on the likelihood that Bin Ladin was at the compound. After reviewing the intelligence for about seventy-two hours, a handful of NCTC al-Qa'ida analysts assessed the probability of Bin Ladin being at the compound as low as 40 percent, which Mike then briefed at deputies, principals, and National Security Council meetings. The NCTC assessment stimulated a new round of doubt about the intelligence foundation upon which a risky assault would be based. Recognizing that CIA's earlier 70 percent assessment as well as NCTC's red team assessment of 40 percent was based more on analytic instinct that on a rigorous quantitative methodology, the president shortened the discussion. "Listen. The odds are fifty-fifty; Bin Ladin is either at the compound or he isn't. Even if it's only forty percent, that's forty percent more than we've ever had before."

The last National Security Council meeting was held on Thursday afternoon, April 28. It lasted more than two and a half hours. The meeting started with an intelligence update on the compound and a status report on the plans for the raid. The only uncertainty on the operational front concerned the weather. The forecast for Sunday was slightly better than for Saturday. This was potential good news from a White House planning perspective, since the president and virtually all of Washington's political elite were slated to attend the White House Correspondents' Association Dinner on Saturday night. A presidential cancellation at the last moment would raise intense interest and speculation as to the reason for the president's absence, jeopardizing the veil of secrecy around the operation that had been kept firmly in place over the past several months. On the other hand, launching a life-and-death compound assault while the president provided comic relief to a room full of alcohol-fueled individuals decked out in black ties and gowns presented too many nightmare scenarios to imagine.

The president made clear that he wanted to hear everyone's recommendation on the compound assault. Leon dove in first, saying that he felt "very strongly" that the raid should go forward. In a firm and forceful voice, Leon said, "This is our best shot, and it might be the only shot we ever get." Jim Clapper and I spoke next and supported Leon's position with an equally strong endorsement. Having participated in virtually every Situation Room and Oval Office meeting on Bin Ladin and the Abbottabad compound over the previous many months, I was convinced that the intelligence picture was compelling and that an assault was merited. Secretary Gates, who had announced his decision to retire earlier that day, expressed serious concern about the risks associated with a helicopter assault, especially given the uncertainty that Bin Ladin was at the compound. Gates said that while a standoff strike with a tactical weapon was not a perfect option, it was his preferred option, because it would not risk the lives of two dozen American servicemen. Vice President Biden agreed with Gates, highlighting the importance of minimizing the potential loss of American lives. Biden frequently would strike a note of caution at NSC meetings, wanting to give Obama some breathing room when making a difficult decision. As frequently, Biden would seek out the president after NSC meetings concluded, which he reportedly did in this instance, when he recommended to Obama in the Oval Office that he should approve the operation. Secretary Clinton spoke the longest, reviewing aloud the pros and cons of each option before coming out in support of the helicopter assault. It seemed to me that she made up her mind as she spoke. "Okay," Obama said at the end of the meeting. "I'll make a decision tonight and let you know tomorrow whether it's a go or not."

On the home front, Kathy knew that something big was happening, since I had spent even more time than usual at the office over the preceding weeks. When I arrived home very late on Thursday night, I told her that I would need to spend most of the weekend at work because of an important counterterrorism matter that would consume my time. "Don't forget that Kyle's birthday is Saturday," she reminded me. "We'll celebrate at dinnertime, which should give you plenty of time at the office." Letting out a sigh, I looked at Kathy and said, "Sorry, but it's possible I might not get home in time."

I had spoken those words far too often to Kathy over the years. I also said them frequently to Kyle, Kelly, and Jaclyn to let them know that I might not be able to attend a school or sports event, or a birthday party. And like so many previous times, I couldn't tell Kathy or the children why I would miss a family gathering. I knew Kathy was disappointed and had every right to be, as she was too familiar with the role of a single parent because of my absences. I remember hoping that night that she would recall the words spoken to her several times by President Obama, who pulled her aside at White House functions to express his personal appreciation for the sacrifices she and so many others were making in the interest of national security. I benefited from the fact that she deeply admired

AUTHOR'S PERSONAL PHOTO

My grandparents Owen ("Odie") and Ann Brennan at their farmhouse in Mount Plunkett, County Roscommon, Ireland (circa 1960).

AUTHOR'S PERSONAL PHOTO

My grandfather Thomas Dunn *(on the right)* with his brother Frankie Dunn, known as the "Beer Baron of New Jersey," during a trip to Havana, Cuba, in January 1929. Frankie was tommy-gunned to death fourteen months later in Hoboken, New Jersey.

AUTHOR'S PERSONAL PHOTO

My parents during their honeymoon to Lake George, New York, in October 1952.

AUTHOR'S PERSONAL PHOTO

Posing with my sister Kathleen
for our Christmas photo in 1956.

AUTHOR'S PERSONAL PHOTO

Here I am, age eight, in my
Lion's Club Little League uniform
in front of my family's house in
North Bergen, New Jersey.

AUTHOR'S PERSONAL PHOTO

Kathy and me in my
parents' backyard shortly
before our wedding in the
summer of 1978.

AUTHOR'S PERSONAL PHOTO

I owned two suits when I joined the
CIA in 1980. When I wore this light
suit with no overcoat on a cold winter
day during a winter surveillance
exercise, I was spotted immediately.

With my Yamaha motorcycle in September 1982. It was a sweet bike!

AUTHOR'S PERSONAL PHOTO

AUTHOR'S PERSONAL PHOTO

Our twin daughters Kelly and Jaclyn, who were born prematurely at twenty-eight weeks in 1988.

The note I wrote my not-quite-five-year-old son Kyle after telling him about the U.S. bombing of Iraq at the beginning of Desert Storm in January 1991. I'm not sure why I wrote it, but we both signed the paper.

On the evening of 16 January 1991 Kyle and I discussed the bombing of Iraq, which is currently underway. I explained that the man in charge of Iraq is a bad man, who has hurt a lot of people and has taken over another country. I explained that war is very serious and very sad, because a lot of people get hurt and some die. Kyle said he understands.

John Brennan

Kyle

PHOTO TAKEN BY AUTHOR

CIA PHOTO

Kathy, Kyle, Kelly, and Jaclyn joined me at CIA headquarters in July 1996 when I was promoted into the Senior Intelligence Service (SIS).

CIA PHOTO

George Tenet has been a professional mentor and one of my closest friends for over twenty-five years. If I had not met George, I am sure that I never would have worked in the White House or become director of the CIA.

GEORGE H. W. BUSH PRESIDENTIAL LIBRARY AND MUSEUM

My first visit to the Oval Office was on August 30, 1990, to brief President George H. W. Bush and Secretary of State Baker on the implications of Iraq's invasion of Kuwait.

President George W. Bush was keenly interested in the capabilities of the National Counterterrorism Center, prompting his June 10, 2005, visit to the center's Liberty Crossing headquarters.

PHOTO BY ERIC DRAPER, COURTESY OF THE GEORGE W. BUSH PRESIDENTIAL LIBRARY AND MUSEUM

Kathy, always a huge fan of President Obama, at the Obamas' first State Dinner.

SAMANTHA APPLETON/THE WHITE HOUSE

PETE SOUZA/THE WHITE HOUSE

Rahm Emanuel and I accompanied President Obama to Louisiana in early May 2010 to check on cleanup following the *Deepwater Horizon* drilling rig explosion.

With President Obama on Martha's Vineyard, where we met daily during his summer vacations. The setting and our attire were casual, but our focus on domestic and international developments remained intense.

PETE SOUZA/THE WHITE HOUSE

PETE SOUZA/THE WHITE HOUSE

Dozens of meetings were held in the White House Situation Room to finalize preparations for the raid in Abbottabad, Pakistan, to get Bin Ladin.

I joined *(from left to right)* Denis McDonough, Bill Daley, and Tom Donilon in the White House Diplomatic Room on the morning of April 29, 2011, when President Obama gave the "go" order on the raid that killed Bin Ladin two days later.

LAWRENCE JACKSON/THE WHITE HOUSE

With King Abdullah of Saudi Arabia at the White House in May 2010. I always enjoyed brushing up on my Arabic whenever we met.

PETE SOUZA/THE WHITE HOUSE

My homeland security and counterterrorism portfolio kept me in regular contact with my close colleagues at the FBI, Director Bob Mueller and Deputy Director Sean Joyce.

PETE SOUZA/THE WHITE HOUSE

President Obama met with beleaguered Yemen president Abdrabbuh Mansur Hadi on the sidelines of the United Nations General Assembly in New York in September 2012.

PETE SOUZA/THE WHITE HOUSE

It was a privilege to work with Secretary of State Hillary Clinton, one of the hardest-working and most diligent members of President Obama's national security team.

PETE SOUZA/THE WHITE HOUSE

PETE SOUZA/THE WHITE HOUSE

Informing President Obama that more than twenty little children and teachers were killed at Sandy Hook Elementary School in Newtown, Connecticut, on December 14, 2012, was the most emotional experience during my time at the White House.

Despite my running battle with Senator Dianne Feinstein over the Senate Select Committee's study on the CIA's Rendition, Detention, and Interrogation program, I always had enormous respect for her commitment to our national security.

CIA PHOTO

CIA PHOTO

Vice President Biden joined my family (*from left to right:* me, Kathy, daughter Jaclyn, son Kyle, my father Owen, my brother Tommy, and daughter Kelly) at CIA headquarters in April 2013. Director of National Intelligence Jim Clapper is on the far left and CIA Deputy Director Michael Morell is on the far right.

I refer to this as my visit to the woodshed, as President Obama summoned me to the White House to talk about a CIA activity of questionable merit. I agreed with him.

Avril Haines, who served as my deputy at CIA and as principal deputy national security adviser, and Denis McDonough, who was deputy national security adviser and chief of staff, were two of my closest colleagues during my eight years with the Obama administration.

President Obama welcomed children into the Oval Office. Here he is with my two-year-old grandson, who is attempting to reprise John Kennedy Jr.'s famous desk crawl.

My adorable grandson stole the show during my farewell event at CIA headquarters in January 2017. It was an exceptionally bittersweet moment for me to bid a final farewell to a CIA family I had worked with for over three decades.

Obama and was willing to do what she could to support my work at the White House.

The president was scheduled to travel to Alabama and Florida on Friday morning, April 29. Before departing, he asked to see Tom Donilon, Chief of Staff Bill Daley, Denis McDonough, and me in the White House Diplomatic Room. Dutifully, the four of us gathered to the sound of the whirring helicopter blades of Marine One, which had just landed outside on the South Lawn to take the presidential party to Joint Base Andrews. The president joined us at 8:10 A.M. He was dressed casually, as he and the First Lady were scheduled to visit areas in Alabama that had been badly damaged by recent storms before heading to Cape Canaveral to watch the launch of the space shuttle *Endeavour*. We all remained standing, and the president waited for each of us to speak. In turn, we each said we supported the raid. It was evident he needed no convincing. "It's a go," he said, and then he told Tom to contact Gates, Mullen, and Panetta and tell them that he had approved the operation. The president said that weather should be the determining factor in the decision whether to launch Saturday or Sunday, adding, "McRaven needs to be the one to make that decision."

Principals convened in the Situation Room on Friday afternoon to go over final details of the raid and to review steps that would be taken to protect U.S. personnel and facilities from post-raid reprisals. An updated weather forecast confirmed that conditions would be more favorable on Sunday, and Bill McRaven sent word that he recommended the raid take place on that day. The president's authorization was then given for the compound raid to take place at 3:30 P.M. Sunday, Washington time, which was 12:30 A.M. on Monday, May 2, Pakistan time. Aside from avoiding the complications related to Saturday night's White House Correspondents' Dinner, the decision also allowed me to join our family dinner celebrating Kyle's birthday.

Once the president made the final "go" decision, Tom, Denis, and I decided it was time to brief a few other senior officials on the impending assault. I am not sure whether I drew the long or the short straw, since we didn't know how these officials would react to being kept out of the loop on such an important national security matter until then. Ultimately, I was tapped to conduct individual briefings in my office that weekend for Attorney General Eric Holder, Homeland Security Secretary Janet Napolitano, FBI Director Bob Mueller, and Susan Rice, who was then our ambassador to the United Nations. In each briefing, I explained the intelligence assessment that put Bin Ladin at the compound and the decision to go forward with the raid on Sunday afternoon Washington time. With each sentence, I watched their eyes grow in disbelief. I also swore them to secrecy, telling them they could only tell their deputies that a major counterterrorism operation would take place and that their key staff needed to be on call. Eric and Bob said they completely understood the need for absolute discretion. Janet expressed understandable concern that she didn't have adequate time to prepare for potential untoward developments in the United States following either a successful or failed raid. Despite being somewhat upset, she showed her true professionalism when she said, "Okay, John. I got it. I need to get to work." Susan Rice's reaction to the briefing was simply to increase the size of her smile as I spoke, interjecting several times, "Way to go, CIA!" I think she also sprinkled in a few exclamatory four-letter words, as was and remains her wont.

The schedule for the weekend was tightly scripted. On Saturday, deputies and principals convened yet again, and the contents of the playbooks were finalized and produced in three-ring binders by Nick and the few members of his NSC staff who were aware of the pending operation. President Obama called Bill McRaven that afternoon to pass along his personal best wishes and to reiterate his confidence in the ability of the assault team to conduct the mission. All tours and visits to the White House that were scheduled for the following day were canceled. I found it very difficult to sleep that night. I tossed in my bed quite a bit, worried that I had missed or forgotten an important detail. I wondered whether everyone else who was aware of the operation felt the same way.

On Sunday, deputies gathered in the Situation Room at 10:00 A.M., reviewing once more the underlying intelligence, the details of the raid, and the actions to be taken in its aftermath. Vice President Biden, Secretaries Clinton and Gates, and Chairman of the Joint Chiefs of Staff Mike Mullen arrived at 1:00 P.M. and President Obama joined the group at 2:00 P.M., the same time the helicopters and assaulters took off from their base in Afghanistan for the ninety-minute flight to Abbottabad. Leon and Michael Morell remained at CIA headquarters and teleconferenced into the Situation Room for the duration of the operation.

During one of our earlier NSC meetings, it had been decided that we needed a secure means of receiving immediate updates on the day of the operation that could be passed to the president and the national security team gathered at the White House. As a result, Air Force Brigadier General Brad Webb was deployed to the White House with a communications package that allowed him to be in real-time contact with Bill McRaven, who was directing the operation from Jalalabad, Afghanistan, and to monitor a video feed of the compound. We thought about having Webb set up his coms and join us in the Situation Room's main conference room but decided against it, as we didn't want to do anything that could distract Bill and General Webb from focusing on their operational responsibilities. Instead, Webb set up shop in a small anteroom only steps away from the main conference room. Initially, some of us would wander over to the anteroom to get an update from Webb about the status of the helicopters zeroing in on the compound, which we would relay to the rest of the group.

At 3:30 P.M., we received word that the helicopters were minutes out from the compound. One by one, we crowded into the anteroom

and watched the operation unfold. Webb was on his computer, texting with Bill and describing what we were witnessing—one helicopter pulled down hard onto a compound wall by the backwash of
its propellers, gunfire and explosive blasts knocking down steel doors,
and assaulters storming the residence. We watched mostly in silence,
with an occasional question asked about what we were observing but
not understanding. I don't think anyone realized at the time that Pete
Souza, the chief official White House photographer, slipped into the
room and took what would become one of the most iconic photos of
Obama's presidency. We waited for news about what was happening
inside the residence, and it seemed like an eternity before General
Webb received word at 3:50 P.M. from Bill. "Geronimo!"—Bin Ladin
was dead.

There was no jubilation or high-fiving in that small anteroom
that afternoon. There was no bravado and no applause. And there
wasn't any when we made our way back into the conference room.
Rather, there was a shared sense of relief and satisfaction that America had finally realized the long-held promise that the threat posed
by the mastermind of the 9/11 attacks would one day be eliminated.
Bin Ladin's death in that Abbottabad compound was the culmina-
tion of nearly a decade of determined work by many thousands of
individuals—in the intelligence, law enforcement, military, and diplomatic communities—who felt a strong obligation to those who
died in al-Qa'ida's many terrorist attacks. Those of us gathered in the
White House that day understood that we happened to be the latest
caretakers of that effort.

While getting Bin Ladin was the objective of the operation, we
knew that the mission would not be a true success unless all our special forces were able to return safely back to Afghanistan. This was
the most harrowing part of the entire ordeal for me. By the time the
assault force destroyed the downed helicopter and was ready to depart
the compound with Bin Ladin's body along with the numerous computers, documents, and other items for exploitation, we had received

word that Pakistan's air defense forces and national command authority were aware that something very unusual was happening in Abbottabad. The Pakistanis had scrambled some fighter jets, and the airspace between Abbottabad and the Afghan border was considered a much greater risk than it had been for the incoming trip. Having been a passenger in many nighttime helicopter flights at low altitude in Afghanistan and Iraq courtesy of the U.S. military, I have always considered our chopper pilots among the most talented, courageous, and dedicated members of the U.S. armed forces. They never proved it more than they did that night. At 6:00 P.M., we received word that all U.S. personnel were safely back in Afghanistan.

With our special forces out of Pakistani airspace and the strong likelihood that it was Bin Ladin's remains that had been flown back to Afghanistan, we began to implement action items in the playbook. The first action to be taken was Admiral Mullen's call to Pakistan's chief of army staff, General Ashfaq Kayani, at 8:02 P.M. The Pakistanis were perplexed over what had just gone down inside their country, and Mullen's task was to explain to Kayani that the extreme sensitivity and national security significance of the target demanded that it be done unilaterally. Based on everything I learned prior to and after the raid, I do not believe any senior Pakistani military or civilian official knew that Bin Ladin was hiding under their noses in Abbottabad. I do not know whether Bin Ladin received protection from lower-level Pakistanis. When I received confirmation from the Situation Room that Mullen was on the telephone with Kayani, I asked to be connected to Saudi Arabia's minister of interior, Prince Muhammad Bin Nayif. It was my responsibility to tell Prince Muhammad that Bin Ladin was dead and to ask him if Saudi Arabia wanted his remains. As soon as I got on the line, Prince Muhammad launched into his usual polite pleasantries. "Hello, John. How are you? How is your family? How is the president?" After assuring him that everyone was well, I delivered the talking points that I had written down for myself.

"Your Royal Highness, the president asked me to call you to re-lay some very important information. A few hours ago, U.S. special forces conducted a raid on a compound in Abbottabad, Pakistan. We had intelligence that Usama Bin Ladin was living on the compound, and he was killed during the raid. His body is now in Afghanistan and has been positively identified."

At this point, Prince Muhammad interrupted. "Congratulations, John. Well done! How are the boys who carried out the raid? Is ev-eryone okay?"

"Yes, Your Royal Highness. They are all safely back in Afghani-stan. Now that Bin Ladin is dead, I am calling to discuss what should be done with his body. I know that your government revoked his citizenship several years ago, but he was a Saudi by birth, and the Bin Ladin family still lives in Saudi Arabia. Therefore, we are asking if you would like his remains returned to Saudi Arabia. If not, we will ensure that they are buried in strict conformance with Islamic law."

"Yes, yes, John. We trust you to take care of his body. Do as you say. There is no need to send his body here." It was the response we had fully anticipated, as there would be no upside for the Saudis tak-ing Bin Ladin's remains.

"Okay. We'll handle it," I told him. "One last thing, Your Royal Highness. The president is going to make an announcement shortly. Please tell King Abdullah that President Obama wanted him to know about the raid and Bin Ladin's death before his public state-ment." I knew that Abdullah would be very pleased with the news. In the several private meetings I had had with the king, he spoke with great disdain about Bin Ladin. He had become emotional when talking about how Bin Ladin and al-Qa'ida had violated Islamic law and had tarnished Saudi Arabia's reputation in the eyes of many Americans.

With my playbook responsibility taken care of, I next called Kathy. I told her that President Obama would be making a televised announcement in a couple of hours, and I encouraged her to watch it, as it would be very good news. "So, I presume it's about what you couldn't tell me," she said, as the excitement in her voice steadily rose. She had been on the counterterrorism journey with me during my years at the CIA and the White House, so she knew the difficulty of the hunt for Bin Ladin and would appreciate the enormity of the achievement. I sensed the extent of her happiness when she said that I could stay at work as long as I wanted, which was not her usual parting phone comment.

The rest of the evening was spent getting the president ready for his speech to the nation and the world. Deputy National Security Adviser Ben Rhodes, who was President Obama's main speechwriter on national security matters, did his usual outstanding job putting into poignant words the historic event that had just occurred and its significance. After reviewing the remarks in the Oval Office, the president, Tom Donilon, Denis McDonough, and I loitered in the hallway outside the office to talk for a bit. Pete Souza was chronicling the day's events and captured that moment. The relaxed looks on our faces were in stark contrast to the worried expressions we wore just a few hours earlier when the fate of the operation and of our assault-ers was far from certain. The large framed photo of the four of us was given to me as a gift from President Obama. It has hung in my office—at the White House, at the CIA, and in my home—ever since.

I stood about thirty feet from the president in the East Room when he delivered a historic nine-minute televised address shortly before midnight. He got right to the point. "Tonight, I can announce to the American people and to the world that the United States has conducted an operation that killed Usama Bin Ladin, the leader of al-Qa'ida." Listening to his words, I thought about the thousands of individuals, including those I knew, who had perished because of the evil of Bin Ladin. By the end of the president's remarks, I felt phys-ically exhausted and emotionally drained. After chatting a bit with the few others who had assembled to hear the president, I returned to my office and called for my car. "I'll be out in ten minutes," I said, as I gathered a few things to put in my briefcase, which I then locked for the ride home.

When I walked out of my office and toward the ground-floor exit of the West Wing, I could see that the outside of the White House was far brighter than usual for 1:00 A.M. Even more surprisingly, I could hear the roar of voices and horns, first faintly and then more loudly, as I approached the door. When I got outside, I turned and walked in the direction of Lafayette Park, where I could see a crowd gathering. The lights in the park were on, and people were roaming about in a celebratory mood. And then, in virtual unison, chants of "USA, USA" and "CIA, CIA" broke out, as did the goose bumps on my arms and on the back of my neck. And, for the first time that day, the tears started to flow down my cheeks, as they still do every time I tell that story.

20

FACTORING IN FOURTH-ORDER EFFECTS

In the weeks leading up to President Obama's inauguration in 2009, I carefully read his books *The Audacity of Hope* and *Dreams from My Father,* which I had only cursorily scanned when they were first published. Aside from the high quality of the writing, I was struck by the deep thought he had given to national and international issues long before he actively pursued the office of the presidency. Nevertheless, with only four years in the U.S. Senate and eight years as a state senator in the Illinois General Assembly, President Obama had limited national security credentials and even less leadership experience when he became our nation's forty-fourth commander in chief and chief executive.

I was one of a small handful of individuals to serve in senior national-security-related positions during Obama's entire eight-year term of office. In my four years as Obama's homeland security and counterterrorism adviser and four years as CIA director, I participated with him in well over a thousand meetings that were held in the Oval Office and White House Situation Room on national security and foreign policy matters. During that time, I was able to closely watch how Obama quickly became very knowledgeable on national security issues and grappled with the diverse array of challenges and opportunities he confronted on the global stage. I also could see how his approach and priorities evolved over time. In many hundreds of meetings with Obama, I never saw him lose his temper or speak to anyone in a derisive manner, although he was quite proficient in using body language or a steely-eyed gaze to convey frustration or disapproval. After my first few months at the White House, I understood why the "no-drama Obama" moniker was attached to the young president. It was an apt description of the calm, patient, yet intense demeanor that seemed to come quite naturally to him, even when confronting issues of national significance. I also sensed an unspoken confidence in him that he would have eight years to make his mark, which undoubtedly reinforced his inclination to be patient during his first term in office.

From the very beginning of his administration, Obama took a very orderly and structured approach to national security issues, and he wanted an effective and well-organized support system that could help shape and guide his ultimate decisions. Accordingly, during my first month on the job, I was tasked to study whether the separate staffs in the Executive Office of the President supporting the work of the National Security and Homeland Security Councils should be consolidated. The two staffs, comprised mostly of government officials on rotation from their home agencies along with a far smaller number of outside experts newly hired as political appointees, were responsible for organizing interagency discussions and developing policy options for administration approval. The bifurcated organizational structure was designed by the Bush administration to highlight the importance it attached to homeland security after 9/11. It was not an unwise decision at the time, since the newly created Department of Homeland Security relied heavily on the work and support of officials at the White House. As DHS matured and in light of the intersection of many homeland and national security issues such as terrorism, cyberattacks, and nuclear security, I recommended to National Security Adviser Jim Jones that personnel supporting the two councils be combined into a single national security staff. Jim agreed, and President Obama accepted our joint recommendation in full.

Much more daunting than any organizational issue was the sheer challenge of dealing with the substantive breadth and complexity of the U.S. government's worldwide national security portfolio. Obama recognized that he had a steep learning curve, and he worked hard to understand the underpinnings of complex issues so that he could find the best or, frequently, the "least worst" option available to advance U.S. interests and prospects for global peace and security. Over time, I watched Obama's strong innate streak of idealism be tempered by a steadily growing pragmatism. The change was born out of presidential experience on the limits of America's ability to use its political and economic influence as well as its military might to shape developments abroad. As president, he was an advocate of evolutionary change rather than revolutionary upheaval.

There were several common features of all major national security decisions during the Obama years. First, a strong and multilevel interagency process undergirded all significant policy deliberations and decisions. The Obama administration retained the overarching framework for interagency discussions that was used by previous administrations, albeit with some minor changes in nomenclature.

- Policy discussions usually were initiated at the Interagency Policy Committee (IPC) level, which was a gathering of assistant secretaries or their equivalents from relevant departments and agencies, including the Office of the Director of National Intelligence and the CIA. Some issues would start at the sub-IPC level, which brought together deputy assistant secretary–level officials. These meetings were chaired by a senior director or director of a functional or regional office in the National

Security Council staff, which is part of the Executive Office of the President.

- Sub-IPC and IPC meetings prepared discussion papers and policy options to be taken up at a deputies committee (DC) meeting and, subsequently, at a principals committee (PC) meeting, which were comprised of the deputies and heads of departments and agencies respectively. DC meetings were chaired by a deputy national security adviser, and PC meetings were chaired by the national security adviser. The vice president was a member of the principals committee. Meeting attendees were each allowed to bring a plus-one, who, along with National Security Council staff members, became "backbenchers" at the meetings held in the White House Situation Room.

- Although some policy decisions were made at either the deputies or principals level, many issues required presidential review and approval. At such times, the president chaired a National Security Council meeting, attended by the vice president; heads of relevant departments and agencies—at a minimum, secretaries of state, defense, and treasury as well as the attorney general; chairman of the Joints Chiefs of Staff; the directors of national intelligence and the CIA; and the national security adviser and deputy national security adviser and senior NSC staff.

When I worked at the White House, I attended deputies, principals, and National Security Council meetings. When I became director of the CIA, I attended principals and National Security Council meetings.

Second, all interagency meetings started off with an intelligence briefing by whoever was representing the director of national intelligence and/or the CIA. Frequently, both intelligence representatives weighed in at the beginning of the meeting, which was invariably the case at principals committee and National Security Council meetings when I was CIA director and Jim Clapper was the DNI.

The intelligence briefing often provoked extended discussion, which at times amounted to admiring the problem longer than necessary and delaying the policy debate and decision. The NSC legal counsel or his or her representative also attended interagency meetings to advise on the legal basis for policy options under consideration. On important or controversial national security matters, the NSC legal counsel chaired interagency lawyers group meetings so that the perspectives of lawyers from national security departments and agencies could be considered during deputies committee, principals committee, and NSC meetings. The White House counsel always attended NSC meetings and often described the constitutional or statutory authority underpinning proposed options for a presidential decision.

Third, President Obama was exceptionally well prepared for NSC meetings. He closely read and extensively marked up memos provided to him in advance by his National Security Council staff that described in detail the issues to be discussed as well as policy options, implications, and recommendations. By my recollection, Obama never started off an NSC meeting by signaling his preferred policy outcome. Rather, he was eager to hear the views of others, and he actively elicited comments, especially when he sensed that someone held a different view from his own or appeared to disagree with something said at the meeting. I found it difficult to maintain a poker face when it came to national security discussions, and my not-infrequent furrowed brow or noticeable scowl would prompt Obama to call upon me or to simply lift his chin in my direction, signaling that I should speak up. In this way, Obama reminded me of George W. Bush, who also never seemed to want unspoken dissents to linger.

And fourth, Obama had an uncanny, and sometimes quite frustrating, ability to see potential second-, third-, and fourth-order effects of national security decisions. It was as if he was always playing a multidimensional chess game, carefully considering how each move available to him on one chessboard could lead to subsequent scenarios on other boards, with vastly different consequences and implications for U.S. interests. His questions and comments frequently illuminated potential ramifications of policy options that were teed up to him. He had an insatiable thirst for more information and more analysis, which sometimes delayed policy decisions but, in my view, often led to better decisions.

His decision not to provide Ukraine lethal weapons in the face of Russian annexation of Crimea and aggression in eastern Ukraine during his last two years in office was a case in point. Given the political and geostrategic importance that Putin attached to Ukraine, Obama assessed that U.S.-supplied weaponry would prompt Russia to escalate further its military involvement, just as Moscow did in Syria when a regime it had long supported with military and economic assistance faced increased pressure from rebel forces that were backed by sympathetic foreign benefactors. Ukraine's military had suffered from years of poor leadership as well as the adverse effects of Russian manipulation and penetration, and Obama believed that stepped-up Russian military activity in response to U.S. provision of lethal assistance would have overwhelmed already besieged Ukrainian defense forces. In such a scenario, Kiev almost certainly would have made a desperate plea for even greater U.S. military support, leading to either a major proxy conflict between the United States and Russia on Russia's border or an ignominious U.S. political retreat, neither of which appealed to Obama. "It's not yet time for lethal aid to flow," he said at the conclusion of one NSC meeting, adding, "We can provide other types of military assistance while we keep international and economic pressure on Moscow." In the years since, U.S.- and European-provided assistance and training have allowed the Ukrainian military to rebuild itself and to rid itself of Russian influence. I was therefore pleased to see, and privately applauded, the 2017 decision by the Trump administration to provide lethal assistance, including Javelin missiles. The time had come to provide lethal assistance to a revitalized Ukrainian military that had stabilized its defenses in eastern Ukraine without fear that advanced

U.S. weaponry would fall into the hands of the Russians or provoke a dangerous Russian reaction.

U.S. military engagement overseas was a principal focus of Obama, as it was for every president I served. Obama entered office with the goal of ending sometime during his presidency the U.S. military presence in Afghanistan and Iraq that he inherited from the Bush administration. U.S. military deployments in both countries were tackled early and often in Obama's first term, with what seemed like a never-ending series of interagency meetings at all levels that exhaustively debated the pros and cons associated with potential troop surges, reductions, redeployments, withdrawals, and mission adjustments. Rarely was there a consensus among key players—from the White House, State, Defense, Joint Chiefs of Staff, and intelligence community—about the prevailing conditions, much less the merits and implications of various policy options. There usually was a consensus, however, among White House officials, including Obama, that the U.S. military's otherwise admirable can-do attitude was coloring its perspective, resulting in its glass-more-than-half-full assessments of progress on the ground and its requests for maintaining if not increasing U.S. military presence.

I did not anticipate the decision announced in October 2011 that the U.S. would withdraw all its military forces from Iraq by year's end. In the months prior to the October 2011 withdrawal announcement, numerous interagency meetings at the deputies and principals level were held to consider options that called for several thousand U.S. troops to remain in Iraq beyond the December 2011 deadline for the departure of all U.S. forces, as stipulated in the U.S.–Iraq Status of Forces Agreement signed by President Bush in 2008. The policy options we evaluated focused heavily on maintaining U.S. counterterrorism and "advise and assist" support to the still fledgling Iraqi military and security forces. At the time, I was aware that negotiations with the Iraqis were ongoing about a status of forces agreement granting U.S. forces continued immunity from prosecution under Iraqi law—referred to as "privileges and immunities"—and I knew that the Baghdad government was raising objections. I was confident, however, that we would be able to convince the Iraqis that some continued U.S troop presence would be in their best interests. But that did not happen.

The pullout of all U.S. forces from Iraq was publicly attributed to Baghdad's unwillingness to extend immunity for U.S. forces, but I have always felt that the Obama administration did not press the Iraqis on this issue nearly as hard as we could have and should have. Rather, I believe that the ultimate decision not to push the Iraqis more forcefully was the result of successful lobbying of President Obama by administration proponents of a complete withdrawal, either because they had a genuine interest in getting our soldiers out of harm's way as quickly as possible (a position advocated strongly by Vice President Biden) or because they saw it as politically advantageous for the 2012 presidential election. Whatever the reason, and with the benefit of twenty-twenty hindsight, the withdrawal of all U.S. troops had major adverse implications for Iraq's stability. Although there were many factors that contributed to the subsequent explosive growth and devastation caused by the Islamic State of Iraq and Syria (ISIS), the absence of U.S. military forces played a major role in ISIS's ability to overrun Iraqi defenses in many parts of the country and to establish its violent caliphate.

Afghanistan was a different story. Unlike the flawed rationale for invading Iraq in 2003, the provenance of the U.S. military presence in Afghanistan was legitimately anchored in the U.S. response to the 9/11 attacks and the quest to prevent al-Qa'ida from using that country and neighboring Pakistan to stage follow-up attacks. But eight years had passed since the first U.S. boots had arrived on Afghan soil, and Obama made no secret of his intention to get all U.S. troops out of Afghanistan by the time he vacated the White House.

"One more year, one more year. I keep hearing that we just need one more year to turn things around." This was one of Obama's most repeated comments to the series of generals who took the helm of Central Command, which had responsibility for Afghanistan, and those in charge of U.S. and NATO forces in Afghanistan during his eight years in office. Obama's refrain became shriller after it was apparent that his 2009 decision to raise the number of U.S. troops in Afghanistan to more than one hundred thousand did not spell the collapse of the Taliban nor give the Afghan fighting forces the time, training, and experience he was told was needed for U.S. troops to pull out. I saw Obama evince more frustration during discussions on Afghanistan than he did for any other national security issue. Most annoying to him, I believe, was the inability of his administration to get the Afghan government to root out the pervasive political corruption, incompetence, and malfeasance that impeded virtually every U.S. goal in the country, especially the departure of U.S. troops.

I used my several trips to Afghanistan during the Obama years, both while working in the White House and later when I became CIA director, to press Afghan presidents Hamid Karzai and Ashraf Ghani and their intelligence and security chiefs to honor their commitments to meet agreed-upon milestones for progress on the security front. I also wanted to make sure that I was correct in my assessment that U.S. intelligence capabilities in Afghanistan and along the terrorist-infested Afghanistan-Pakistan border rested upon continued U.S. military presence and support, which I had endorsed in every deputies, principals, and NSC meeting I had attended. During each visit, including during my first time traveling abroad as CIA director in April 2013, I visited several of the forward operating bases scattered throughout the country where brave women and men of the U.S. military and intelligence community were working at great personal risk to uncover and disrupt plots to conduct attacks against targets inside and outside Afghanistan. And every visit convinced me that U.S. intelligence presence and capabilities in Afghanistan were essential to prevent the region from once again becoming a wellspring of terrorist activities directed against the United States.

A 2015 visit to Khost, after I became CIA director, was one of the most solemn and profound of any I took during my government service. It was in Khost on December 30, 2009, that seven CIA employees—two women and five men—were killed and another six injured by a concealed bomb worn by a Jordanian intelligence source who turned out to be a double agent working for al-Qa'ida. A Jordanian intelligence officer and an Afghan security officer also were killed in the attack. As I stood in front of the stone marker and visualized the explosive effects of that bomb—the shrapnel marks were still in evidence in nearby structures—I felt terribly conflicted. I knew that eleven children had lost a parent in that bombing and that thousands of other children also would never feel the loving embrace of a parent who had given his or her life elsewhere in Afghanistan in service of their country. A big part of me that day wanted the United States to be forever rid of these foreign commitments that put American life and limb at great risk. At the same time, I didn't want the sacrifice of the CIA officers who died at Khost—Jennifer Matthews, Scott Roberson, Darren LaBonte, Harold Brown, Elizabeth Hanson, Jeremy Wise, and Dane Paresi—as well as of so many other courageous Americans, nor the pain of their family members, to be in vain.

As I departed Khost that day, my thoughts were with the many U.S. troops, diplomats, and intelligence officers who had been killed in the line of duty, in Afghanistan, Iraq, and many other countries around the world, to prevent a recurrence of 9/11. I reflected on the times that my duties called on me to travel to a U.S. airport to honor fallen officers who returned home for the last time.

EACH TIME THE LARGE CARGO *plane would be visible from miles away as it slowly descended and approached the airport. It almost always would arrive after sunset, as the cover of darkness helped shield the identities of those who had gathered to be with their fallen colleague. They were there to accept the dignified transfer of remains of an American who had taken their last breath in a faraway land while serving the country they loved.*

Immediate family members would be lined up next to CIA officers in silent tribute as the plane rolled to a stop in front of them. The large door in the belly of the aircraft would open, allowing an honor guard to escort the casket off the plane. Grief and sadness were always present as the casket made its way past those gathered, but so too was a deep sense of patriotism and a solemn recognition that freedom has its price. When circumstances allowed, my deputy and I would join the escort. It was the most emotionally draining as well as the most important role I had as director.

In the days that followed, Kathy and I, along with other CIA officers, would meet the husbands and wives, mothers and fathers, sons and daughters, and sisters and brothers of the fallen in my office. I always felt that my words of condolence were woefully inadequate, as it was impossible for me to feel the full depth of their pain. Our first few minutes together would be a time for tears and for painful mourning, but smiles, gentle laughs, and palpable pride would usually follow when family members told stories of their loved one's accomplishments as well as their humanity. Never once did I hear a word of anger directed against the Agency or about their loved one's chosen profession.

My trips to the airport and the opportunity to spend time with the families of the CIA's fallen heroes served as one of the greatest sources of inspiration during my time as director. My chief of staff at the CIA during my last two years was a paramilitary officer who had served in harm's way with several CIA teammates who were killed in action. His gift to me as I departed Langley was a wristband with the initials of the CIA employees who died on my watch. I have worn it every day since, and it will always serve as a constant reminder of the sacrifices made by the members of the CIA family.

•   •   •

BY THE TIME MY PLANE landed back in Kabul, I was convinced that we needed to maintain a U.S. military presence in Afghanistan at least through the end of the Obama administration so that the intelligence community's mission would endure. That was the position I took in principals and NSC meetings during the remainder of my time as CIA director.

Obama's national security team fully anticipated having to deal with the challenges of Iraq and Afghanistan, but the fast-breaking events of the Arab Spring presented an unexpected series of policy choices and foreign policy dilemmas that lasted until the end of Obama's presidency. For many years, the intelligence community, especially the CIA, had provided intelligence and analysis about widespread poor governance, corruption, and political repression throughout the Middle East. But those ongoing conditions rarely sparked opposition that could not be quickly and effectively suppressed by authoritarian regimes. When a Tunisian fruit vendor, fed up with rampant corruption, set himself on fire in December 2010 and died the following month, however, it triggered massive and bloody unrest across the Middle East against the repressive rule and arrogant complacency of Arab strongmen living in luxury. Tactical warning from the intelligence community about the combustibility of Arab streets at the time and the potential that a single incident of self-immolation could set them ablaze would certainly have been welcomed, but such prescience is all too rare.

When the Arab Spring was developing, it brought back memories of the start of the Palestinian intifada in 1987, when I was working on Arab-Israeli issues in NESA. The death of four Palestinians in a traffic accident of suspicious origins in a Gaza Strip refugee camp provoked a rolling wave of massive riots and civil disobedience in Gaza and the West Bank that killed two thousand Palestinians and nearly three hundred Israelis over the next five years. Social media, which provides good insight into popular attitudes and activities, had not yet surfaced when the Palestinian intifada erupted in

1987, but it had taken hold in many parts of the Middle East by 2011. Sometimes, intelligence and security agencies are a bit slow to accept the reality that publicly available information can provide sought-after insight more readily than elaborate, risky, and expensive clandestine human and technical collection activities. There were indicators on social media throughout the Middle East that the region was a tinderbox and might ignite quickly given the right spark. The intelligence community, in my view, failed to tap into social media sufficiently, depriving it of important information on the depth and extent of popular disaffection with authoritarian leaders.

After President Ben Ali was driven out of Tunisia and took refuge in Saudi Arabia in mid-January 2011, U.S. government attention turned swiftly to the brewing political storms in other Arab countries. Obama paid closest attention to the situation in Egypt, which teetered on the brink of wholesale chaos and bloodshed as millions of Egyptians took to the streets to call for President Hosni Mubarak's ouster. Obama was most concerned that Egyptian security forces would mow down the protesters in an effort to preserve Mubarak's thirty-year authoritarian rule. I was in the Oval Office when Obama spoke to the Egyptian leader and strongly urged him not to use lethal force against the demonstrators, a plea that Mubarak mercifully heeded. When it became apparent that the Egyptian masses would not be satisfied with anything less than a change in leadership, Obama told Mubarak that it was time for him to step aside, which he did. It was the right call. If Mubarak had tried to ride out the quickly building political firestorm, I am certain that many thousands of Egyptians would have been killed in the resulting melee.

As I watched cable news coverage in the Situation Room of mobs rejoicing in the streets of Cairo when Mubarak resigned, I was struck by what I thought were very unrealistic expectations among some of my White House colleagues that democracy was virtually certain to flourish in Egypt and in other Arab countries once longtime rulers were pushed aside. Political reform in the Arab world was long over-due, and I joined my colleagues in hoping that the wave of populist activity would lead to more enlightened leadership, but I had my doubts. "Democracy is not a light switch that you can just flip on, especially in the Middle East," I said to muted reaction during one meeting in the Situation Room. Aside from the potential significant loss of life, I was concerned that a protracted period of political un-rest in countries throughout the Middle East would be detrimental to important U.S. national security interests and could redound to the benefit of our adversaries, namely Russia and Islamist extrem-ists. Intelligence community analysts participating in White House meetings agreed that it likely would be a long and ugly struggle between the street and authoritarian governments.

And it was.

A dizzying array of protests broke out in other Arab countries in the following weeks and months, prompting constant back-to-back-to-back meetings in the White House Situation Room, including on most weekends. In an NSC meeting on the growing crisis in Libya in early March 2011, I joined Secretary Gates and then–deputy national security adviser Denis McDonough in opposing U.S. mil-itary participation in a NATO-led international coalition to strike Libyan government military forces, but we held a minority view. It was not that I favored the Qadhafi regime in the quickly escalating Libyan civil war, and I was revulsed by the many reports of atrocities being committed by the Libyan government against the rebels. But I was most concerned that the proposed bombing campaign would lead to a complete collapse of the government and its security forces, ushering in a protracted period of political chaos and bloodshed that would serve to strengthen violent Islamist extremist groups in the region. At the time, we knew very little about the composition of the ragtag anti-regime forces that were steamrolling toward Tripoli from the eastern part of the country, and it seemed like a high-risk bet to wager Libya's future on them. And while I understood that it was difficult to formulate a post-air-campaign plan, I had my doubts that the Europeans would be either willing or able to make good on their pledge to help rebuild Libya afterward.

I do not recall if Obama made his decision at the end of the meeting or if he said that he would think about it overnight. If there was a lack of consensus at NSC meetings, especially on issues involving the use of military force, Obama frequently would take additional time to process the discussion and to weigh the pros and cons of the differing views raised. At times, he would convene a follow-up meeting with his senior White House staff or reach out individually to them or to one or more of the NSC attendees as he worked his way toward a decision. Whether it was at the end of the meeting or the following day, Obama decided that the United States would join the coalition. To this day, I do not know whether it was the right decision. Tragically, political instability, civil strife, and bloodshed have been prominent features of the Libyan landscape ever since Qadhafi was killed by rebel forces and his government fell in October 2011, which was a direct result of foreign military intervention. It will forever be unknowable whether fewer people would have been killed and Libya would be better off today if the air campaign had never taken place.

Less than a year after Qadhafi's fall, a U.S. diplomatic compound and annex in the eastern Libyan city of Benghazi were assaulted on the eleventh anniversary of the 9/11 attacks, resulting in the deaths of U.S. Ambassador Chris Stevens and fellow Americans Sean Smith, Tyrone Woods, and Glen Doherty. When I reviewed the closed-circuit video footage taken on the night of the attack of the compound, I was struck at how the unfolding scene was unlike any other act of terrorism carried out by a terrorist group in the Middle East. The footage clearly showed that the initial small-scale attempt to penetrate the compound perimeter was quickly followed by a mob scene wherein many dozens of individuals looted office equipment, personal items, and clothing and then set fire to the building, causing the deaths of Stevens and Smith. The follow-up attack against the annex where Woods and Doherty were killed, however, was a deliberate and sustained terrorist attack to kill Americans carried out by the well-armed Islamist extremist militia group, Ansar al-Sharia.

Much ado has been made about public statements by Hillary Clinton, Susan Rice, and others about the nature and genesis of the Benghazi attacks. In the aftermath of the events, there was great uncertainty, including within the intelligence community, about who was responsible and whether it was a spontaneous violent reaction to the film *Innocence of Muslims,* which depicted the Prophet Muhammad in a very unflattering light. Hours before the tragic events in Benghazi, several thousand protesters gathered outside the U.S. embassy in Cairo in response to calls by radical Islamist activists to denounce the film. It was not an unreasonable judgment at the time, nor is it still, that the attack in Benghazi was, at least in part, a violent reaction to the film; news reports about the protests against the U.S. embassy in Cairo were broadcast in Benghazi. The subsequent allegations made by Republican members of Congress, most notably then-congressmen Mike Pompeo and Trey Gowdy, that Obama administration officials intentionally misrepresented events in Benghazi were nothing more than an unconscionable partisan attack to score points against political rivals in Washington.

I visited Libya less than five weeks after the events in Benghazi, mainly to understand the threat environment and security posture of the remaining U.S. official presence in the capital city of Tripoli. In the aftermath of the Benghazi attack, evacuation plans became a priority, and, after several briefings and a tour of the U.S. embassy and housing facilities, I felt comfortable that U.S. diplomats, military officers, and intelligence officials had sufficiently enhanced security measures to handle multiple scenarios of deteriorating security conditions and terrorist attacks. Still, as I flew over and was driven through the war-torn streets of Tripoli, I was left with an uneasy feeling that the type of attack that took place in Benghazi could easily play out very quickly in the Libyan capital. My meetings with Libyan officials, including the then–head of state, President of the General National Congress Muhammad Magariaf, while cordial and marked by promises to help track down the perpetrators of the Benghazi attack, did not allay my concerns about the fragility and uncertain future of the country.

My departure from Libya was memorable. Minutes after my military plane took off from the Tripoli airport, my senior adviser, Nick Shapiro, realized that our passports, which had been given to U.S. embassy officials for safekeeping, had not been returned to us when we were shuttled from our armored SUVs to the tarmac. "We need to go back!" Nick shouted to the pilots, who looked at him quizzically but agreed to turn the plane around so that we could continue with our multicountry travel (yes, even senior White House officials and CIA directors have to present a valid passport when entering a foreign country and when returning to the United States). We were the only aircraft landing and departing that day, so the nonexistent air traffic control at the Tripoli airport presented no impediment to the quick U-turn. "If you are going to forget your passports," our pilot told us, "this is probably the best place to do it, as it would take a hell of a lot longer to do a quick unscheduled landing and departure at any other airport in the world." The Tripoli airport was completely (as well as eerily) deserted by the time we touched down; it reminded me of the scene in *The Godfather* when the hospital of the gravely injured Vito Corleone has been cleared out by would-be assassins. Fortunately, Nick was able to phone our embassy contact, who drove back through the streets of Tripoli to deliver our passports to us. Such selfless actions by U.S. personnel are carried out every day in challenging security environments around the globe, all in the interests of their government and fellow citizens.

Confident of the professionalism of the U.S. personnel on the ground in Libya and recognizing the importance of maintaining local contact with Libyan officials, I returned to Washington and recommended to Obama that our embassy remain open. Two years later, in July 2014, it was with reluctance but with a greater sigh of relief that I concurred with the decision to withdraw all U.S. personnel from Libya and to move embassy operations to Malta (and later Tunisia) because of heightened security concerns.

Libya certainly was not a success story, but much worse were the many years of bloodshed and devastation in post–Arab Spring Syria. Throughout much of my time at the White House and the CIA, I was engaged in what ultimately proved to be a futile effort to bring an end to widespread bloodshed and destruction of a country rich in history, culture, and sectarian conflict. Syria had been an early focus of Obama. In early 2010, he canceled a long-standing Department of State advisory warning Americans traveling to Syria about security risks. It was an effort to improve bilateral relations and pave the way for constructive Syrian engagement in a peace process with Israel. Those hopes were dashed the next year, when major anti-government protests erupted throughout Syria during the Arab Spring, a reflection of forty years of pent-up anger against the brutal and repressive authoritarian rule of Syrian presidents Bashar al-Asad and his late father, Hafiz al-Asad. When several thousand Syrian security and military forces refused to fire on protesters and defected to form the Free Syrian Army, the Obama administration steadily increased its support for the rebels. President Obama publicly called for President Asad to step down in August 2011, hoping that it would strengthen the ranks of the opposition and quicken what many in his administration mistakenly believed would be Asad's inevitable fall. I was among them.

There was a consensus within the Obama administration in late

2011 that the Free Syrian Army should receive political, financial, and even security support from the United States. A change of government in Damascus had many potential upsides. The Syrian government, which the United States had labeled a state sponsor of terrorism for more than thirty years, had long been regarded as a potent military threat to Israel, including its worrisome possession of chemical and biological weapons. Unlike Libya, Syria had a functioning government, well-established political institutions, and large armed forces that we assessed almost certainly would survive the toppling of its leader. Moreover, the composition of the Free Syrian Army appeared to be secular in political orientation, with Syrian nationalists, both Sunni and Shi'a, in leadership positions. Nevertheless, there was still deep unease about formally siding with the rebels in the early days of the Syrian uprising without a better understanding of their goals and their ultimate ability to gain the support of the Syrian people. In addition, the Asad regime was an important vassal state of Russia, and there was no one in the Obama administration who argued that Moscow would be likely to stand idly by if its decades of political, economic, and military investment were at serious risk. With twenty-twenty hindsight and having witnessed the tremendous destruction of Syria and enormous loss of life that have occurred, I deeply regret that we did not take bolder action at the beginning of the uprising to support the Free Syrian Army.

The Free Syrian Army's early battlefield successes raised hopes in Washington that the Arab Spring might notch an important success in Damascus, but policy decisions regarding the extent of U.S. support for the rebels became more complicated by late 2012. When al-Qa'ida in Iraq joined forces with al-Qa'ida in Syria (al-Nusrah) to form the Islamic State of Iraq and Syria (ISIS), Syrian opposition forces in many parts of the country took on an extremist Islamist cast, which only increased over time. Before long, the horrific atrocities and widespread killing by ISIS undercut international support for anti-regime forces in Syria, and internecine fighting that pitted

Free Syrian Army forces against ISIS fighters redounded to the regime's benefit.

In August 2012 Obama said that if the Syrians used chemical weapons in the civil war it would be a "red line" for the United States and would change his policy calculus. A year later the U.S. intelligence community assessed with high confidence that the Syrian government had used sarin to kill hundreds of people. But instead of launching military strikes, Obama seized an opportunity to build support for getting the Syrians to destroy their chemical-weapons stockpile. I do not know if Obama regrets his "red line" statement, but I suspect he wishes he had warned about the consequences of using chemical weapons without using the term "red line," which implied an automatic trigger for U.S. military action. I recall Vice President Biden warning at the time that "big nations can't bluff," an adage with which I agree. Nevertheless, the "red line" term ultimately was instrumental in convincing Moscow that the best way for Syria to avoid U.S. military action once chemical-weapons use was confirmed was for Damascus to agree to destroy its large inventory of chemical-weapons material and equipment. That agreement allowed the intergovernmental chemical-weapons watchdog, the Organization for the Prohibition of Chemical Weapons, to inspect Syrian facilities and to verify the destruction of the chemical weapons and associated infrastructure. After working on Middle East issues for many years, I knew that the elimination of Syria's stockpile of chemical weapons, which was one of the largest in the world, would remove a serious potential threat to Israel's security and regional stability. In addition to lacking the authorization of Congress or the UN Security Council to carry out U.S. military action against a sovereign state, the decision to forgo strikes was quintessential Obama. As was his custom, Obama was concerned about potential second-, third-, and fourth-order effects, such as the dissemination of lethal chemical plumes as a result of military strikes, an increased use of chemical weapons by a desperate Asad regime, and a sharp escalation of tensions with Russia. Obama saw the chemical-weapons destruction agreement as being far more advantageous to U.S. strategic interests and likely resulting in less loss of life than would have occurred had he authorized U.S. military strikes.

In the last five years of the Obama administration, I had countless meetings with U.S. and foreign officials, traveled extensively throughout the Middle East and Europe, offered ideas and recommendations, and carried out presidentially authorized activities that were designed to weaken the Asad regime, bring an end to Syria's bloody conflict, and bolster prospects for the emergence of a more representative and less repressive government in Damascus. While there were some tactical successes and failures along the way, Russia's steadily increasing military support and its direct military involvement in the conflict in late 2015 ultimately turned the tide of battle and preserved the rule of Bashar al-Asad. Unfortunately, I am unable to address many important aspects and details of U.S. policy toward Syria during the Obama administration because they remain highly classified.

I will always consider the Joint Comprehensive Plan of Action (JCPOA), which reversed Iran's determined effort to obtain nuclear-weapons capabilities, to be one of the Obama administration's crowning achievements. The agreement was a tremendous boon to Israel's security and regional stability, as the specter of a nuclear-armed Iran had been among the most serious national security concerns of U.S. policy makers for at least two decades. When negotiations with the Iranians started to move forward in earnest at the beginning of Obama's second term, I had serious reservations about whether Tehran would ever make the concessions necessary for a deal. My doubts were reinforced when the Iranians initially offered only a minimal reduction of centrifuges and uranium stockpiles and no inspections of its nuclear-related facilities by the International Atomic Energy Agency (IAEA) other than what had been previously agreed, which sent a clear signal that the negotiations would be long, contentious, and possibly futile. It was only because of the unwavering efforts of Secretary of State John Kerry, Secretary of Energy Ernie Moniz, and their very able policy and technical assistants, combined with Iran's increasingly desperate financial straits, that Tehran ultimately made the concessions necessary for a deal.

In the National Security Council meetings I attended, President Obama made it clear that an agreement to stop Iran's nuclear-weapons program was the highest priority. He saw an agreement as essential not only for regional stability but also to strengthen the influence of Iranian moderates, especially Iranian president Hassan Ruhani and Foreign Minister Mohammad Javad Zarif, and to provide economic incentives for Tehran to engage in negotiations with the United States on other important issues. Obama strongly believed that the initial agreement, from a practical standpoint, would need to be limited to the nuclear-weapons program. In an NSC meeting in early 2015, Obama specifically counseled American negotiators not to expand the parameters of a potential deal by trying to include language related to a reduction in Iran's ballistic missiles inventory. Obama argued, correctly in my view, that straying into conventional-arms-control issues would jeopardize the growing prospect of a nuclear-weapons deal by making negotiations much more complex and protracted. "The Iranians will immediately press for a reciprocal reduction in missiles in Gulf Arab states," he said, "and good luck with those talks."

I am certain that Donald Trump did not understand or even seek to learn the details of the JCPOA when he announced that the United States would withdraw from the agreement, which I consider a major U.S. foreign policy blunder. Even if Trump and his national security advisers were genuinely concerned about the time limits on some of the restrictions on Iran's nuclear-related activities—despite Iran explicitly affirming in the JCPOA that it "will never seek, develop, or acquire any nuclear weapons"—additional negotiations could have been launched to extend the duration of key restrictions.

And if Trump and JCPOA naysayers believe that the Iranians will negotiate away a potential nuclear-weapons program without receiving anything meaningful on the economic/financial front in return, they are even more delusional and foolish than I already believe them to be.

21

SECOND SHOT AT THE
BEST JOB IN GOVERNMENT

While disappointed I didn't get the CIA director job in 2009, I was pleased that President Obama named Leon Panetta, someone with deep Washington experience, to lead the CIA. I had known Leon only slightly when I was a PDB briefer at the White House and he was President Clinton's chief of staff. My recollections of Leon were positive. He impressed me as being serious-minded yet very affable, with a hearty laugh. Though he was an occasional participant in the PDB sessions with President Clinton, the press of his duties meant that Leon often entered or departed the Oval Office in the middle of a briefing rather than being present throughout. If he had to interrupt a briefing to share some urgent information, President Clinton always gave Leon his undivided attention.

Despite Leon's limited familiarity with the intelligence community—he had served in army military intelligence in the mid-1960s—his intellect, congressional and executive branch service, wonderful smile, broad name recognition, and well-honed skills as a politician won him immediate support and admiration among his CIA constituency. As the Obama administration's national security team was getting off the ground, Leon's already established gravitas ensured that the CIA would be an early major player within the Obama administration's national security team.

At the start of the Obama administration, retired U.S. Navy Admiral Dennis Blair was tapped to succeed Mike McConnell as director of national intelligence (DNI). I knew Blair well from the time we served together on the CIA's seventh floor in the mid-1990s, when he was the senior military representative at the Agency and I was executive assistant to then–deputy director George Tenet. Denny, as he is known to his friends and senior colleagues, impressed CIA officers as a very bright, hardworking, and no-nonsense naval officer. But he had a reputation for sometimes being curt and abrasive in interactions with the CIA's rank and file, especially when dealing with CIA officers who did not give appropriate deference to his military rank and views. Nevertheless, I liked and got along well with Denny during our days together at Langley, and I admired his efforts to enhance the relationship between the U.S. military and the CIA. He retired from the navy in 2002 after a very successful tour as commander of U.S. Pacific Command and then worked in the private sector, mainly in support of the defense industry.

I knew that it was going to be critically important for Leon and Denny to have a good working relationship. During the Bush administration, Mike McConnell and Mike Hayden made the best team of directors of national intelligence and the CIA. Both were longtime intelligence professionals with significant leadership experience in the intelligence community. Each had been director of the National Security Agency, and Mike Hayden had served as principal deputy director of national intelligence under the first DNI, John Negroponte, and continued in that role when McConnell became the second DNI. They liked and respected each other and had a very collaborative working relationship. Although McConnell had made known his intention to depart government upon the change of administration, Mike Hayden wanted to remain at the CIA. When I was on the Obama transition team (and after I pulled myself out of contention for the director of the CIA job), I recommended that Mike Hayden stay at the CIA at least for the first year of the new administration, believing that continuity of leadership at the CIA would be helpful to the incoming national security team. My recommendation didn't fly, however. President-elect Obama's principal advisers wanted a clean break with the intelligence controversies and officials of the Bush administration era. I made another push for continuity in leadership at the CIA during periods of presidential transition several years later when I was director of the CIA. I sent draft legislation to the White House in 2015 that called for CIA directors to serve seven-year terms, taking the selection of a new director out of the presidential election cycle. (Since 1976, FBI directors have been confirmed for ten-year terms.) My proposed legislation was not embraced by Obama's senior advisers, who believed that the covert-action authorities of the CIA director made it important for a president to have his or her own person in the job. I didn't agree but lost the argument. Foolishly, I thought a term appointment would make it unlikely a president would remove the leader of an important national security agency before their term expired; Donald Trump's politically motivated dismissal of Jim Comey in 2017 proved me wrong.

Unfortunately, the relationship between Denny and Leon was rocky from the start. Denny interpreted the language in the 2004 Intelligence Reform and Terrorism Prevention Act that created the DNI position as giving him exceptionally broad authority on virtually any intelligence activity, including those that traditionally had been the preserve of the CIA. Leon, on the other hand, viewed the Office of the DNI as a bureaucratic annoyance that got in the way of the CIA's mission as well as its relationship with the White House and with foreign intelligence services. This was a widely shared view within the Agency.

In multiple White House Situation Room meetings throughout

2009, it was evident that there was little to no consultation in advance between Denny and Leon or their staffs, and substantive disagreements between them on intelligence issues were frequent. Leon seemed unbothered by the tension, and he continued to win admirers in the White House and among his national security colleagues for his leadership at the CIA. Denny, however, appeared to resent Leon's rising fortunes, and made two mistakes in early 2010 that eventually sealed his fate. First, he tried to wrest away from Leon the ability of CIA directors to select chiefs of station, the individuals responsible for overseeing U.S. intelligence activities abroad. Denny sent out a directive announcing that he was taking control of the appointment process. Leon then sent out a message to his subordinates essentially saying: "Oh no he's not." Second, Denny ignored very specific guidance from National Security Adviser Jim Jones regarding how to handle a very important relationship with a European intelligence service. Aside from incurring the strong displeasure of Jim Jones and Deputy National Security Adviser Tom Donilon, Denny's actions were viewed by the CIA as another indication that he was trying to diminish Langley's influence.

By the end of May 2010, the situation had become untenable. Jim Jones, Tom Donilon, and I recommended to President Obama that he make a change and ask Denny for his resignation, the first member of Obama's national security team to depart the administration. Although Denny had rough sailing during his sixteen-month tenure as DNI, it in no way diminished his record of exceptional accomplishment as a naval officer who served his country ably and with great dedication and talent throughout his military career.

The morning after Denny's resignation, Jim Jones, Tom Donilon, Denis McDonough, Tony Blinken, and I were in the Oval Office following a morning PDB session when the president asked for ideas about who should be the new DNI. Tom Donilon mentioned Jim Steinberg, the deputy secretary of state under Hillary Clinton, who was widely admired for his intellect and strong national security background. Jim was a major player during the first eighteen months of the administration, and he effectively used his membership on the principals committee, the result of an unusual deal for a deputy secretary that he cut when he joined the administration, and frequent participation in National Security Council meetings to shape foreign policy. Jim had let it be known that he was looking to leave the number-two job at State, and Donilon and other senior officials were interested in keeping him as part of the national security team. I liked and admired Jim, but I didn't believe he was right for the DNI job. Jim had never served in the intelligence community, and his strength was substance rather than management of a large organization. I also thought that the Panetta-Steinberg personalities might clash—just as the Panetta-Blair ones had—and the combination would not lead to an improvement in the relationship between the CIA and the Office of the DNI.

The president looked at me, waiting for my reaction to Donilon's suggestion. "I vote for another Jim. Jim Clapper," I said, hoping to steer the discussion away from Steinberg. "Clapper's intelligence community résumé is second to none, and he understands the role and responsibilities of the DNI position. Most important, I am confident that he would get along with Leon and that Leon would get along with him. Jim Clapper is one of the few people in Washington who has no ego, even though he has every right to one." Jim Clapper's name did not seem to ring a bell with most of those in the room, including the president, so I recapped his lengthy career. "He was a marine before joining the air force, where he rose to be a three-star general. He was the director of the Defense Intelligence Agency in the Clinton administration and the director of the National Geospatial-Intelligence Agency during the George W. Bush administration. And he is now Bob Gates's undersecretary for intelligence at the Pentagon." For good measure, I added one more of his qualities. "And he had the honor of being fired by Don Rumsfeld for being appropriately insubordinate."

Obama seemed impressed. "I'll talk to Bob about it," he said. Later that day, Bob Gates gave Jim Clapper a ringing endorsement, and the nomination was announced within the week. As the Senate took up Jim Clapper's nomination, Dianne Feinstein, who was chairman of the Senate Select Committee on Intelligence, called me one evening when I was on the way home to ask for my views about Jim's nomination.

"John, do you know this General Clopper?" she asked. "I am very concerned about a military takeover of the intelligence community. Blair didn't work out, and now I'm concerned that we're going to make the same mistake with Clopper."

"Dianne, it's Jim 'Clapper,' and he is a longtime intelligence professional, and someone I think you will like and respect very much." There were many reasons why I admired Senator Feinstein, and her insistence that I and other government officials call her "Dianne" was one of them. I then shared highlights of Jim's intelligence experience and encouraged her to meet with Jim at the earliest opportunity. She soon did and liked him right away, paving the way for a 15–0 vote in the committee and a unanimous vote in the full Senate in favor of his confirmation. I have long considered my recommendation to President Obama that he select Jim Clapper to be his second DNI to be one of the signature achievements of my national security career. For nearly six and a half years, Jim provided outstanding leadership as director of national intelligence, launching a series of initiatives that enhanced cooperation and interaction among the seventeen member agencies of the intelligence community. Nonpartisan, honest, and having deep personal integrity, Jim also shrugged off, much better than I ever did, unfair criticisms levied against him by some members of Congress and the media. For example, he was sharply criticized by Democratic senator Ron Wyden in 2013 for responding to a question while testifying in an open hearing that the National Security Agency did not "wittingly" collect any data on millions of Americans. During the hearing, Jim said that he was very uncomfortable discussing sensitive intelligence matters in an unclassified setting, and he corrected his response, which he acknowledged was erroneous, soon after the hearing. Unfortunately, Senator Wyden, who is one of the most liberal members of the Senate, too often engages in public "gotcha" tactics in his dealings with the intelligence community. I believe he would be much more effective if he dealt with intelligence community leaders in a more straightforward manner.

It was only a year later that Leon Panetta was tapped to replace the retiring Bob Gates as secretary of defense. Unlike the DNI vacancy, I was not asked who should be nominated to fill the vacancy at Langley. Since I had been Obama's initial choice to be CIA director, I wondered if I might be asked if I was interested in being considered. But no one asked, and I was surprised when I heard National Security Adviser Tom Donilon say one morning outside the Oval Office that General David Petraeus would be the nominee. I tried to stifle my surprise, not that I thought David was unqualified. Quite the opposite. He had all the necessary qualifications for the job—stellar military record, strong leadership skills, deep experience in national security matters, and intimate familiarity with the many trouble spots that dotted the Middle East and South Asia. I just thought that someone would have let me know privately that David was getting the nod.

In the weeks that followed, I heard three separate explanations from colleagues in the White House about why I was not selected. The first was that President Obama wanted to keep me at the White House, as he was pleased with my work on counterterrorism and homeland security issues. I would like to think this explanation had the benefit of being true. The second was that David Petraeus actively petitioned the president for the CIA director job, as he had long been an admirer of the CIA workforce and mission. A third explanation I was given by a White House insider, however, involved heightened anxiety among President Obama's political advisers that

Petraeus was under consideration to be the candidate for vice president on the Republican Party ticket in 2012. Those advisers pushed to give Petraeus the CIA job, according to this explanation, so that a popular military hero would be taken out of the mix for the Republicans. I have no idea whether the third explanation had any basis in fact.

As President Obama's first term was drawing to a close, Kathy and I began to make plans for my second exit from government service. I was pretty confident that Obama would be reelected in 2012 and defeat Mitt Romney, so I felt no urgency in figuring out exactly when I would leave the administration, much less what I would do afterward. The beginning of Obama's second term seemed to be a good break point for me, and I started to send signals to some of my White House colleagues before the November election that I would be departing sometime in early 2013. I felt that four years in the White House on top of my previous twenty-five years at the CIA was more than enough. I was tired. The long and often erratic hours in the White House had shattered what had been my regular exercise routine, as there always seemed to be too much work to do in too little time. I even shunned physical therapy sessions after undergoing knee and hip replacements while working at the White House (one of my hip prosthetics was recalled, necessitating a new one), leaving me with a pronounced limp ever since.

A Washington, D.C., inner-city high school class was taking a tour of the White House one day in late 2012, and I was asked to speak to about two dozen students who had assembled in the Situation Room. Introduced by a White House escort, who embellished my record by saying I was a former CIA "spy" who did a lot of "cool" things during my career, I gave the students an overview of what life was like working in the White House for President Obama. After fielding several questions, a student raised his hand and said, "Mr. Brennan, what hobbies do you have? What do you like to do when you're not at the White House?"

I was stumped. I hadn't been asked that question in many years, and I had had little time for anything other than work and family since I started working at the White House. I started to stumble through an answer.

"Well," I said in resignation, "I guess my only hobby has been replacing body parts."

Although I had a smile on my face at the time, I could see that my words had an immediate chilling effect on the young man as well as on the other students in the room. Realizing that my response was being interpreted as my having been engaged in some type of sordid medical practice that I employed on others, I quickly added, "My own, my own body parts. I replaced my knee and my hip recently. I mean, I didn't replace them myself, my doctors did. And they were replaced in the hospital, not in the White House." It seemed to be going from bad to worse, and I wasn't sure if I had allayed fears that I was a modern-day Dr. Frankenstein. I decided to take no more questions, finishing up by encouraging the students to study hard so that they, too, could one day work in the White House, maybe even in the Oval Office.

Whatever plans Kathy and I had for our future were jettisoned almost immediately after Barack Obama's reelection on November 6, 2012. Two days after the election, Jim Clapper and FBI Deputy Director Sean Joyce arrived at the White House with the stunning news that David Petraeus was under active FBI investigation for disclosing classified information to his biographer, Paula Broadwell, with whom, it had been learned, he was having an affair. Within twenty-four hours, David resigned, and the CIA director position became vacant once again.

"So, what do you think, John?" Denis McDonough asked me, as he dropped by my office late one evening the following week. "Would you like to be considered for the CIA job?" Denis was the principal deputy national security adviser at the time, and he was on track to become Obama's fourth and final chief of staff in another two months. He also had been my closest friend and colleague at the White House over the previous four years.

I equivocated for a moment, prompting Denis to say, "Well, you better think about it, because the boss wants to talk to you first thing in the morning."

Kathy and I discussed it that night. I told her that I didn't think I would suffer the same fate as the last time my name was floated, and the administration would not go forward with the nomination unless it was confident I would be confirmed. We agreed that I wouldn't turn down the job if the president asked me to do it a second time.

In the Oval Office the following morning, I told President Obama that CIA Deputy Director Michael Morell, a close friend and outstanding intelligence professional who was then serving his second stint as acting director of the CIA, deserved the opportunity to be a confirmed director. "He really is terrific, sir. He has served in a series of senior-level positions in the Agency for thirty years, and he knows the intelligence profession and the workforce exceedingly well. He would make an excellent director."

"Are you saying you don't want the job, John?" President Obama asked.

"I would never say no to being director of the CIA," I responded. "It's the best job in government, but I still think Michael would be a great choice."

I found out later that Michael, in a meeting with the president, had endorsed me for the job. I guess Michael was more convincing—he had always been a better briefer than I ever was—because the president decided to nominate me as his next CIA director on January 7, 2013.

As the confirmation process proceeded and it appeared increasingly likely that I would be confirmed, I decided that I wanted to place my hand on something other than a Bible when sworn in as director of the Central Intelligence Agency. I knew I would take flak from the religious right for not affirming my oath on a Bible, but

I wanted to signal in some manner that I would be faithful to the laws of the United States as CIA director. The best way to do so, I thought, would be to take my oath with my hand firmly placed on the Constitution of the United States. But I didn't want a run-of-the-mill copy of the Constitution; I wanted a special copy. "See what the National Archives can do for us," I said to my staff, as I awaited the final vote in the full Senate. Within twenty-four hours, I received word that on the day of my swearing-in ceremony, the Archives would be willing to escort to the White House an original draft of the Constitution dating from early 1787 that had George Washington's personal handwriting and annotations on it. "Terrific," I said, "let's do it!"

As it turned out, Senator Rand Paul delayed a confirmation vote by launching one of his frequent publicity-seeking spectacles—a nearly thirteen-hour-long filibuster demanding an administration pledge not to use a drone to kill noncombatant American citizens inside the United States. The thought of such an attack is absurd, of course, but Paul wouldn't relent until he received an answer. Rather than endure more of Paul's delaying tactics, the administration responded with a pithy letter from Attorney General Eric Holder, which read, "It has come to my attention that you have now asked an additional question: 'Does the President have the authority to use a weaponized drone to kill an American not engaged in combat on American soil?' The answer to that question is no." Eventually, I was confirmed by a 63–34 vote in the Senate on March 7. Thirteen Republicans voted in support of my nomination, while Democratic senators Pat Leahy and Jeff Merkley and independent Bernie Sanders joined thirty-one Republicans in opposition.

The swearing-in ceremony was held in the Roosevelt Room of the White House the following day. Vice President Biden administered the oath of office with President Obama looking on. Kathy, Kyle, and Kelly were at my side, while Jaclyn, who was in Paris on a graduate fellowship, was there in spirit. Raising my right hand, I placed my left hand on the 226-year-old document and took what would be my final oath of office in the U.S. government. Following the ceremony, White House press spokesperson Josh Earnest issued a statement that noted I had taken my oath on the historic draft of the Constitution to show my commitment to the rule of law as I prepared to take on my CIA duties. Predictably, my critics saw nefarious intent on my part. They claimed that I swore allegiance on a draft Constitution without amendments, including the Bill of Rights, as an intentional show of disdain for the right to due process (Fifth Amendment) and the right to trial by jury (Sixth Amendment), both key issues in the debate over drone strikes. For good measure, they also said that I refused to be sworn in on a Bible because I had converted to Islam when I was stationed in Saudi Arabia. I had not.

There's no accounting for knuckleheads when it comes to politics and partisanship in Washington.

And so, the stage was set for my return to Langley.

22

STIRRING THE CIA POT

The tail end of a late winter nor'easter was passing through the Washington, D.C., area in early March 2013, when I became the twenty-first person to lead the women and men of the CIA. As my armored SUV drove onto the snow-covered compound shortly after taking my oath of office at the White House, I thought about the first few times I proudly displayed my prized CIA badge, as I passed through the front gate of the Langley campus more than thirty years before. Ever since those early days of my career, I had considered it a great honor to be part of an organization that helped keep our country strong and fellow citizens safe in ways that the American public would never know, nor even imagine. At times, that pride was leavened by the realization that the CIA as an institution, and CIA officers as individuals, had made some serious mistakes. Although I never doubted the necessity of the CIA, I frequently disagreed with some of its activities and approaches to national security challenges and wondered whether it was living up to the solemn responsibility entrusted to it by the American people. Feelings of both pride and concern intensified over the course of my intelligence and national security career, and I felt them acutely on that Friday afternoon when I caught sight of the CIA's original headquarters building for the first time as director.

Close colleagues told me that the reaction to my confirmation within the CIA's ranks was not uniformly positive. Indeed, a significant number of Agency officers were quite concerned about what I might do during my tenure. The policies I advocated and positions I adopted while serving at the White House and at TTIC/NCTC—stricter limits on covert action and greater information sharing among intelligence and law enforcement agencies—were seen by some Agency officers as inimical to CIA interests. Those fears were not unfounded. I had made no secret, including while I was George Tenet's chief of staff and deputy executive director, that I was not a fan of the Agency's stovepiped organizational structure nor of various aspects of its culture. While I had the opportunity to make some changes during my earlier CIA career, most were modest in terms of scope and impact. As CIA director, I would no longer be so constrained.

I was the fifth director to have previously served as a CIA staff officer; Richard Helms, Bill Colby, Bob Gates, and Porter Goss were the others. By the time I became director, I already had significant insight into what I considered the CIA's strengths and weaknesses, gained not only from my time working in multiple CIA components but also from my experience working directly with the CIA while serving in other government roles. Unlike most previous directors, who needed time to understand the inner workings of the Agency and to become familiar with its senior officials, I was able to hit the ground running and even call bullshit when I saw it. It was a real plus having a talented deputy like Michael Morell, with whom I had worked closely for many years and whose views on the intelligence profession usually matched my own. And after more than four years at the White House working on all national security issues involving the CIA, I had a strong substantive grasp of major CIA programs, including on the covert-action front. As director, however, I would need to dig into the details of all CIA activities in order to explain and defend them to the White House as well as to Congress.

In the weeks leading to my confirmation, I promised myself that I would not be a caretaker director who simply would ride herd over existing CIA activities. Rather, I wanted to leverage my knowledge of CIA authorities, capabilities, and mission to help the Agency adapt to the national security opportunities and challenges of a technologically driven twenty-first century. I felt that it was my responsibility to build upon the work of previous directors by taking a comprehensive and strategic approach to organizational issues and making changes that might be disruptive in the short term but would pay dividends over time. Accordingly, I identified people, cyber, organizational structure, culture, and ethics as my five principle priorities to tackle as director during the almost four years that remained in the Obama administration.

It was not lost on me that I was the latest in an unbroken line of white males to become CIA director; the history of CIA deputy directors was no different. Since its birth in 1947, CIA had only partially shed its reputation as a bastion of white male dominance. Although important progress had been made on bringing more women and minorities into the CIA, much more needed to be done to overhaul internal policies and practices to ensure equal opportunity for all CIA employees. As I awaited confirmation as CIA director, former secretary of state Madeleine Albright—a member of the CIA's External Advisory Board—called to ask if I wanted her to continue with the project she was spearheading on women in leadership at the CIA, which David Petraeus had launched before he left the Agency. I strongly encouraged her to do so. In my first full week on the job, the study arrived on my desk as a classified document, which was unsurprising given traditional CIA bias to overclassify virtually any information dealing with its work or workforce. I directed that the entire report be declassified and publicly released so that the CIA could be held to account. It was far from the last time

I had to direct the declassification of a CIA document that had been unwarrantedly classified. Although the report indicated that women had made steady statistical gains in terms of employee numbers and promotions inside the CIA over the previous several decades, it identified a variety of systemic obstacles that stood in the way of further progress.

Almost immediately, I had to make an important personnel decision that brought the issue of women in leadership to the fore. Shortly before my arrival as director, the deputy director for operations (DDO), the CIA official responsible for overseeing all CIA clandestine collection, covert-action, counterintelligence, and foreign-liaison activities, had retired. The acting DDO was Gina Haspel, who eventually would be appointed CIA deputy director and then CIA director during the Trump administration. Gina was one of several candidates I considered for the DDO position, and there was anticipation within the Agency that I might select her as the first female DDO in CIA history. And I struggled with the decision, because I knew that picking her would send a powerful signal to women in the Agency, which I would have welcomed. While Gina was an accomplished officer, I was not convinced that she was the best candidate for the job, so I convened an outside panel of former senior Agency officers who interviewed a half dozen senior Directorate of Operations officers, Gina included. Based on the comments of the panel members, I selected Frank Archibald, a very experienced and widely respected operations officer whom I considered the most qualified and best fit for the job. It was the right decision, and Frank did a terrific job leading the CIA's clandestine collection activities and covert-action programs over the next two and a half years.

When Michael Morell announced his retirement in June, I had yet another important personnel decision to make. I selected Avril Haines to be my new deputy, the first woman to hold the deputy director position. I had worked closely with Avril at the White House, where she served as legal adviser to the National Security Council

and was a constant source of sage advice on covert-action and counterterrorism matters. I did not select Avril because she was a woman,
although I was glad to be able to send a clear signal to women in
the Agency that one more glass ceiling had been broken. I selected
Avril because she had a wealth of national security knowledge and
the perspective of an outsider who could take a fresh and objective
look at CIA activities. Having grown up in the CIA myself, I wanted
a partner with a different background than mine who could readily
challenge traditional practices and policies of the CIA. In addition,
Avril was a terrific role model and mentor to scores of CIA women.
She remained so even after Susan Rice stole her from me a short eighteen months later to make her the principal deputy national security
adviser at the White House. When Avril left the CIA, I continued
the practice of selecting an exceptionally talented outsider with deep
national security experience—David Cohen from the Department of
the Treasury—as her successor and my new deputy.

I also had an early opportunity to make an important change in
CIA operational practices. In July 2013 I spoke at the annual conference of the investment bank Allen & Company LLC in Sun Valley,
Idaho. At breakfast on the first day, I sat next to Bill Gates, who also
was a conference speaker. As soon as we started to chat, Gates raised
his deep concern about widespread press reports that the CIA had
used a vaccination program in Pakistan as a ploy to gather DNA evidence in the effort to find Bin Laden. Gates said that, regardless of
the veracity of the reports, the mere suspicion that the CIA was engaged in such activities was having a significant deleterious impact
on vaccination programs in developing countries. As the conference
was about to begin, Gates underscored the depth of his concern and
asked me to look into the matter. His final comment to me was,
"Please see what you can do about this very serious problem." I told
him that I would follow up on it.

Gates was right. If rumors of CIA involvement in vaccination programs were deterring people from receiving important vaccines, a long-standing U.S. commitment to improving global health and eradicating deadly diseases was being undercut. Something needed to be done. The following month, I issued new policy guidance that the CIA would make no operational use of vaccination programs or vaccination workers and that the CIA would not seek to obtain or exploit DNA or other genetic material acquired through such programs. The directive applied to worldwide CIA operations and to U.S. and non-U.S. persons alike. Shortly after I issued the directive, I called Bill Gates to inform him of the change. He was delighted.

The report on women in leadership encouraged me to dig into the experience of other demographic groups in the Agency. In a series of meetings with CIA employees, I heard heart-wrenching stories of Agency officers who tearfully described how their professional opportunities and contributions within the CIA were constrained as a result of discrimination, harassment, or simple intolerance of their faith, race, ethnicity, physical disability, or sexual orientation. Hearing these accounts, I turned to another member of my External Advisory Board, civil rights icon Vernon Jordan, to lead a study on diversity in leadership at the CIA. Commissioned in January 2014 and completed in June of the following year, the report was harshly critical of the CIA's record on diversity, finding a "failure of leadership in making the engagement and development of every officer an equal priority; a general lack of accountability in promoting diversity; the absence of an inclusive culture; a consistent failure to integrate the management of talent; and a deficient recruiting process." Again, I directed that the final report be declassified and publicly released, despite the warnings of some CIA officers that the report's strong criticisms would be highly controversial within the CIA. Avoiding controversy was no reason to classify the report and conceal its rebuke of the CIA record on diversity. Like the study on women in leadership, the report on diversity included a series of recommendations and action plans, which were implemented and briefed to the CIA workforce, the White House, and congressional oversight committees.

One CIA demographic group that my deputies and I felt especially privileged to support was the LGBTQ community. Throughout my career, I saw too many CIA colleagues live in fear of having their sexual orientation exposed and their intelligence careers ended, either officially or, equally devastating, informally. LGBTQ officers in the CIA often were considered a security risk because of the perceived potential for blackmail by foreign intelligence services. This happened despite an executive order signed in 1995 banning the previous intelligence community policy of withholding security clearances based on sexual orientation.

Acceptance of LGBTQ orientations was still controversial when I returned to the CIA in 2013. As part of Gay Pride Month in June of that year, I authorized an exhibit of large-format photographs on the main floor of CIA headquarters showcasing LGBTQ officers and their families and the importance of diversity and inclusion at the Agency. While most feedback from the workforce was very positive, I received at least a half-dozen notes from employees, most sent anonymously, that strongly criticized my decision to allow the celebration of what was referred to as "abnormal," "destructive," and "immoral" behavior. I was not surprised by the notes. The CIA, after all, is a microcosm of American society, which remains divided on many social issues, including sexual orientation. Recognizing the importance of walking the talk, Avril, David, and I, along with other senior CIA officers, wore our Agency badges on rainbow lanyards that were distributed by ANGLE, the Agency Network for Gay, Lesbian, Bisexual, and Transgender Officers and Allies. During my time as director, well over one hundred officers stopped me as I walked through the halls and corridors to say that seeing rainbow lanyards on senior officers gave them confidence that LGBTQ officers were respected members of the CIA family and would have the opportunity to thrive professionally. I hope that is still the case.

Michael, Avril, David, and I participated in as many diversity events inside the Agency as our schedules allowed, and we were very pleased to see some of the Agency's most respected senior officers, from all directorates, take leading roles in promoting diversity initiatives. Some of my critics have claimed that I was more interested in advancing liberal social agendas such as diversity inside the Agency when I was director than in carrying out the CIA's intelligence mission. It is a specious and illogical argument, since there is no U.S. government agency that can make a better business case for diversity than the CIA, which serves as our nation's eyes and ears across a richly diverse globe. If the CIA cannot embed diversity and inclusion in its DNA by tapping into the melting pot known as America, I am certain it will fail in its mission as an intelligence organization responsible for helping keep our nation safe.

The first major substantive issue I tackled at the Agency was cyber. Fresh off my experience wrestling with hydra-headed cyber challenges while at the White House, I decided to initiate a review of CIA cyber authorities, capabilities, and expertise. To lead the review, I selected my longtime CIA colleague Sue Gordon, who would become principal deputy director of national intelligence and then acting director of national intelligence in the Trump administration. (Donald Trump's decision not to nominate Sue for the permanent DNI role upon the departure of Dan Coats in 2019, despite the strong bipartisan support Sue enjoyed in Congress, was a badly missed opportunity to have a competent female professional take the helm of the intelligence community). Sue and a small team of technical experts did a fine job identifying the many CIA components engaged in cyber-related activities and proposing several options to streamline and rationalize their work. Each of the options, however, involved a complex series of organizational changes that would bring their own set of challenges and bureaucratic controversies.

Sue's study provided the impetus I needed to launch a comprehensive review of the entire CIA organization that would prompt a major restructuring that I believed would enable the CIA to carry out its mission more effectively and efficiently in an increasingly complex, fast-paced, and technologically advanced world. In September 2014, I selected nine highly experienced and talented CIA officers from across the organization with whom I had worked during my career to comprise the study group. They worked full-time for ninety days on the project, dubbed the "modernization effort," digesting Sue's cyber study, interviewing current and former CIA officers and policy makers, and reviewing best practices across the public and private sectors. To lead the effort, I chose Greg Vogle, a tough-as-nails DO paramilitary case officer, whose integrity and commitment to the CIA mission during his thirty-year career were second to none. Greg had near legendary status in the CIA in part owing to his years of service in post-9/11 Afghanistan, which included saving the life of future president Hamid Karzai when a bomb exploded near them. As soon as I announced the review, many CIA officers became quite vocal in their opposition to what they anticipated might be a change to the traditional headquarters array of four separate directorates— Operations, Intelligence (Analysis), Science and Technology, and Support. Greg was the battle-hardened DO veteran that I thought could best take what I expected to be withering bureaucratic fire.

I think I shocked the group when I first brought them together and said that I wanted a comprehensive review of CIA's organizational structure. "If at the end of the ninety days you come back and tell me that the CIA is organized and functioning exactly as it should be, you better be prepared to work hard at convincing me, because I currently do not buy it." To encourage them to think big, I told them what I thought would be an ideal way to restructure the Agency. "The 1986 Goldwater-Nichols Act reorganized the Department of Defense in a most profound and exceptionally impactful way," I said. "It integrated the military services into regional and functional combatant commands and put in place unified and streamlined command structures. I believe the CIA needs to take a similar approach to our intelligence mission by bringing together capabilities in regional and functional units." It was a radical idea, but it was one that I had harbored for many years and wanted the group to think about as a potential model. Aside from the counterterrorism, counterintelligence, and weapons-proliferations centers at headquarters and CIA stations and bases in the field, the Langley headquarters structure was largely balkanized. The clandestine service was in one directorate. The analysts in another. And neither often mixed with the science and technology or support folks. I did not consider this a recipe for cooperation or success.

Designing and implementing the TTIC model more than a decade earlier was very challenging, but far less complex than overhauling the entrenched organizational structure, chain of command, and internal work processes of the CIA that had developed over the course of nearly seventy years. While the study group consisted of exceptionally gifted CIA officers of various professional disciplines, none was steeped in the craft of organizational change. For that expertise, we secured the services of a major outside consulting company with deep expertise and experience in numerous restructuring efforts in both the public and private sectors. The company's participation was crucial to helping guide the work of the review group.

During the ninety-day study, I found it difficult to communicate sufficiently or often enough with the workforce about the need for the Agency to undergo organizational change. I frequently heard the question, "What's broken that you're trying to fix, John?" I usually responded by saying that the CIA, like all other organizations, needed to continuously adapt to the evolving realities, challenges, and opportunities of the twenty-first century. I often mentioned that Kodak had once had a monopoly on the photographic industry but failed to anticipate and adjust to the transformative changes taking place in technology and in its commercial market, which pushed it into bankruptcy. I then would pivot to the reason why a matrixed rather than a stovepiped organization would work best for the CIA. The intelligence profession and the environment within which the CIA operates had also fundamentally changed as a result of technological innovation that had occurred since the CIA's founding. I believed it would be a dereliction of our responsibility if we did not bring together the tremendous expertise, knowledge, capabilities, tools, and skill sets scattered throughout the Agency to achieve success. To win converts, I would conclude with a warning, saying that none of us wanted the CIA to become the intelligence community equivalent of Kodak.

Along with Avril and then David, I met regularly with the study group to assess its progress and to react to its preliminary findings and leanings. At the end of the ninety days, the review group presented its recommendations, two of which were unanimously supported by the group. The first recommendation called for a major investment in developing talent and leadership across the CIA, which was the number-one issue raised by the workforce with the study group. The second recommendation called for the creation of a new Directorate of Digital Innovation—the first new directorate in more than fifty years at the Agency—to accelerate the integration of cyber and digital capabilities in all CIA mission areas. Superior capabilities and creative excellence in the digital domain were deemed imperatives for the CIA by the study group, and the historic establishment of a new directorate was designed to highlight its enterprise-wide role.

The study group's last recommendation offered two options to consider for organizational change. One called for a modest pilot program that would integrate the headquarters components working on a single geographic region. This option was favored by several of the study group members who thought it would be a good test of the integration principle and be less disruptive and less controversial than the second, more sweeping option, which was the CIA equivalent of the Goldwater-Nichols Act. This option involved the restructuring of CIA headquarters components into ten mission centers—six regional and four functional—with each center integrating the expertise and capabilities that previously had been dispersed in the four (and soon to be five) directorates. Each mission center would be led by an assistant director of the CIA, who would be responsible for overseeing all CIA activities related to the geographic region or functional issue, reporting directly to the CIA deputy director and director. Much as the army, navy, air force, and marines are force providers for the U.S. military's combatant commands, this option called for the directorates to be responsible for the standards of professional tradecraft and the training, career development, assignment, and promotion of CIA officers in the more than sixty specialized professional disciplines in the CIA.

The study group did great work, and the members were not surprised that I endorsed their recommendations, deciding on the comprehensive reorganization option despite the major bureaucratic antibodies it would immediately generate. It was partially for this reason that I didn't opt for the pilot program, as I knew that it would have been suffocated and made to look like an abject failure by opponents of change hoping to prevent wider implementation.

One of the strongest opponents of major organizational change was the person I had selected two years earlier to be my deputy director for operations, Frank Archibald. Frank had been consistent in his personal opposition to a major reorganization. I knew that Frank was channeling the views of a large portion of the DO, which interpreted the reorganization as an attempt to weaken what was long perceived to be the DO's paramount place in the Agency. I understood their concern, as they not only had rightful pride in the Agency's espionage mission but also wanted to avoid major organizational change that could disrupt their ability to carry it out. I explained to Frank and to other DO senior officers that I wanted to strengthen operations as well as other Agency missions by ensuring that all CIA officers and components benefited from the skills, insights, knowledge, and tools that exist in other parts of the CIA. Many were unswayed by my argument, Frank among them.

On the day before I announced my decision about the reorganization, I called Frank into my office and told him that I planned to move ahead with the comprehensive "Goldwater-Nichols" option. I then explained that I needed a deputy director for operations who believed in the merits of the reorganization and that I had too much respect for him and his views to ask him to be part of something he did not support. I told Frank that I had decided it was time for new leadership of the DO and that I would be replacing him. With the professional demeanor he had exhibited throughout his career, Frank said he understood and wished me well and hoped that the restructuring of the Agency would succeed for the good of the mission. I then called Greg Vogle into my office and told him that I wanted him to be the new DDO. I figured that if Greg was able to survive the ninety days leading the study group, he probably also could withstand whatever flak he was likely to take from his DO colleagues as he directed them to get on board the reorganization train.

I had no choice but to make a change in the leadership of the DO, despite my great admiration for Frank Archibald (sadly, Frank passed away in early 2020, less than five years after he retired from the Agency). A lesson I repeatedly learned throughout my career was the importance of having a full airing of competing views in the run-up to making an important decision. Once a decision is made, however, especially ones involving organizational matters, it is essential to have a leadership team that rows together in the same direction. Otherwise, failure is a certainty.

It would be an understatement to say that the process leading up to the reorganization annoyed some members of the CIA's oversight committees, both Republicans and Democrats. Committee staff seemed most upset. Although we informed the committees of the creation and purpose of the study group and kept them apprised of its work, there was significant heartburn that I did not ask the committees for approval before moving forward with the study and deciding on the outcome. I did not want to ask Congress for permission. When I was deputy executive director, Buzzy and I tried to implement a "pay for performance" system throughout the Agency, only to be hamstrung by oversight committee members and staffers who created roadblocks at every turn. I was not going to go through that experience again. If I had done a "Mother may I" with Congress, I am sure the initiative would have been significantly watered down if not scuttled completely. Committee members and staff would have been lobbied hard by CIA employees opposed to the reorganization and by influential Agency alumni, a generally change-averse group.

When I was called to appear before the committees to defend my actions and decisions related to the study group and the ultimate reorganization, I told them that I had an obligation as CIA director to lead and manage in a manner that I believed best enabled the CIA to fulfill its mission over time. I said that I needed to function much like a public-sector CEO. "You are my board of directors, and I know that I ultimately need your support for the organizational changes I have approved. But I am the chief executive of the CIA, and you need to allow me to lead the organization in the manner I deem best." The more thoughtful and serious-minded Senate and House intelligence committee members and staffers were supportive of the reorganization once they gained an understanding of the reasoning behind it and the anticipated benefits. Complaints from the committees also softened once they received assurance that the costs associated with the reorganization, such as the construction of new office spaces, could be absorbed within the existing budget.

The last twenty-two months of my tenure were used to implement what was referred to as the Agency's "Blueprint for the Future," which I described in a March 2015 statement to the CIA workforce. The new Directorate of Digital Innovation, the ten mission centers, and the resources and new processes to develop talent and leadership in the CIA's workforce were well established by the time I departed in

January 2017. According to several of my former CIA colleagues, my successor, Mike Pompeo, had pledged to undo the reorganization soon after he was confirmed as director, perhaps to demonstrate to Mr. Trump that he also would dismantle any work done in the Obama administration. But once the details and merits of the reorganization were explained to Pompeo and CIA officers strongly advocated against upending the new organizational structure, only minor tweaks—such as the addition of more mission centers—were made.

One of the benefits I envisioned from the reorganization was a decrease in the pockets of insularity, parochialism, and arrogance that I had encountered too many times inside some Agency components. Too many Agency officers had spent their entire professional careers in the critically important but narrow slice of the intelligence profession, espionage. As a result, some CIA officers viewed the clandestine collection of intelligence from human sources as the be-all and end-all of national security, and they had little understanding and even less appreciation for the importance and role of other disciplines and capabilities outside the espionage world. Over the past several decades, there has been a dramatic increase in the amount of national-security-related information that can be obtained by sophisticated technical means, frequently made possible by espionage successes, or from publicly available sources, including in the digital domain. As a result, the recruitment and running of sensitive human sources, who often put their professional careers and even their lives at risk by working for the CIA, should be reserved for obtaining needed national security information that is neither accessible by other means nor already available elsewhere in the intelligence community. It has been my experience that bringing together professions, expertise, data, and technical tools in integrated components, rather than relying on stovepiped and parallel work units, is a much more effective way to tackle increasingly tough intelligence challenges. Moreover, the existing counterterrorism, counterintelligence, and weapons-proliferation centers had already proved that integration inside the CIA could be done without compromising very sensitive sources and methods, including the identities of human assets.

As director, I tried to dispel what I thought was the image of the CIA as a lawbreaking organization, and I believed that some of the terminology used inside the Agency was part of the problem. My efforts met with less-than-resounding success. In a February 2016 NPR interview, correspondent Mary Louise Kelly pressed me on several alleged CIA programs involving clandestine technical collection, aggressive counterterrorism actions, harsh interrogation tactics, and the covert arming and training of foreign rebel forces. She then made a passing reference to the CIA being in the business of "stealing secrets." I never liked how some CIA officers cavalierly used the term "stealing," which, perhaps because of my strict Catholic upbringing, I always associated with wrongdoing. When she mentioned the stealing of secrets, I became frustrated, concerned that Kelly's listeners would get the sense that the CIA routinely skirted U.S. law. I immediately overreacted and interrupted Mary Louise, saying, "We don't steal secrets. Everything we do is consistent with U.S. law. We uncover, we discover, we reveal, we obtain, we elicit, we solicit."

Despite the extensive substantive observations I provided on other major national security issues during the interview, my comment that CIA doesn't "steal" secrets made banner headlines and was mischaracterized as an admission or mistaken belief that the CIA was not in the espionage business. Nothing could have been further from the truth. Espionage will always be a central part of the CIA's mission, but the clandestine collection of foreign intelligence, like all CIA activities, *must* be in conformance with its statutory authorities and U.S. law, notwithstanding the violations of foreign law that are inherent in all forms of espionage. Unfortunately, there is a surfeit of individuals, including current and former CIA officers, who cannot divorce themselves from what I consider the misleading term, "stealing secrets." And more than a few CIA retirees who espouse very hawkish views on intelligence and national security issues have aligned themselves with ultraconservative political organizations and news outlets, which provide them a ready opportunity to criticize and misrepresent my CIA record.

Some of my other views and policy positions also generated opposition inside CIA components. For instance, I adamantly opposed during my time in the White House and as CIA director the intentional dissemination of false information by any U.S. government department or agency, even if done so clandestinely or covertly. I knew full well that the spreading of disinformation was a time-honored intelligence practice used, including by many Western services, to discredit adversaries and to shape public perceptions. However, I argued in several National Security Council meetings that the United States should be able to advance and advocate for its policy positions by utilizing the truth rather than by creating falsehoods, even when confronting adversaries like Russia, North Korea, and Iran. I argued that, from a practical standpoint, any revelation that the U.S. government had been responsible for purposely propagating false information—a distinct probability in a leak-prone digital world—would raise legitimate questions about the veracity of other U.S. government information. The resultant impact on international support for U.S. policy positions could be devastating. Moreover, I opposed the use of disinformation on the principle that it was inconsistent with America's democratic values and what should be our government's unwavering commitment to the truth.

President Obama shared my view on disinformation, so it usually wasn't difficult to prevail in debates, even though some colleagues disagreed with my absolutist position. I also supported President Obama's view that covert action should be undertaken only when there is no viable diplomatic, military, or other option available *and* when the hand of the United States needs to be hidden for national security purposes, not for political reasons. Opting for covertness because of its availability, convenience, or simply to avoid public accountability or embarrassment for U.S. actions were not sufficient justifications for President Obama or for me. This position also was not widely embraced by those at Langley who believed the CIA's covert-action capabilities should be more widely used to shape global developments.

23

A TORTURED SENATE REPORT

Of all the issues I dealt with during my tenure as CIA director, none was more complex, challenging, distracting, and time consuming than the continuing fallout from the Agency's Rendition, Detention, and Interrogation (RDI) program. It was the source of tremendous tension and even acrimony between me and many Democrats in Congress, especially those on the Senate Select Committee on Intelligence (SSCI). Things got so bad at one point that two Democrats on the committee—Senators Mark Udall and Martin Heinrich—publicly called for me to be fired for allegedly impeding and spying on the committee's work. I did not impede or spy on the committee's work, but such is life in the highly partisan waters of Washington.

The RDI program was moribund by the time the Obama administration came into office in January 2009 and long before I became CIA director more than four years later. The CIA had started to scale back its interrogation activities by late 2006 and transferred the last of its detainees to Department of Defense custody at the U.S. naval facility in Guantánamo, Cuba, in April 2008. Nevertheless, the

RDI program was the focus of strong criticism by the Democrats throughout the 2008 presidential campaign. Obama himself was a frequent critic, publicly referring to CIA practices as "torture" and vowing to end the program forever if he were to be elected. Making good on his promise just two days after he was inaugurated, Obama signed Executive Order 13491, which stated that the CIA "shall close as expeditiously as possible any detention facilities that it currently operates and shall not operate any such detention facility in the future." On that same day, he signed Executive Order 13492 that said detention facilities at Guantánamo Bay "shall be closed as soon as practicable, and no later than 1 year from the date of this order," a wildly optimistic goal that proved unattainable even a decade later. Despite having been on the intelligence transition team, I was surprised that these executive orders had already been drafted by others on the transition team and were ready for signature when I took up my duties at the White House.

Notwithstanding these early actions by the Obama administration, many Democrats in Congress were not satisfied with simply turning the page on the past. They wanted to do more, and I detected several motivations at play. Without a doubt, there was genuine and deep outrage among many members of Congress over what they said were human rights violations carried out by CIA officers under the cloak of covert action during the George W. Bush administration. Democrats as well as some Republicans believed that the RDI program involved torture and other acts of cruel, inhuman, or degrading treatment prohibited by U.S. law and the UN Convention Against Torture, irrespective of Department of Justice memos that deemed the program lawful, and they wanted to find a way to prevent the program from ever being reconstituted. As part of this effort, some Democrats, who seemed to have selective memories on what was briefed to them and their reaction to it when the program was started, sought to hold the Bush administration publicly accountable for the most controversial aspect of the program—the CIA's use of enhanced interrogation techniques

(EITs). These techniques were borrowed from the U.S. military's Survival, Evasion, Resistance, and Escape (SERE) training for servicemen and -women who might be captured and subjected to hostile interrogation. Waterboarding, one of the SERE techniques, was used only by the U.S. Navy in its training.

In addition to moral indignation, however, I quickly sensed upon my return to government that there also was strong partisan interest on the part of many Democrats to rake the previous Republican administration over the coals in order to score political points that could be cashed in during future elections. This is the way of Washington politics, and I have witnessed both parties engaging in such efforts over the years. In this instance, the Democrats recognized they had very limited ability to go after individuals who had served in the White House and had authorized the program, so they decided to use the Senate's oversight authorities to dig into the CIA program itself. Within six weeks of Obama's inauguration, a formal investigation was launched under the new chair of the SSCI, Senator Dianne Feinstein, who, along with her predecessor Senator Jay Rockefeller, had been outspoken in decrying the tactics employed in the RDI program. The Republicans on the committee, under Vice Chairman Kit Bond, reluctantly agreed to support the investigation initially but withdrew from it in September 2009, citing concerns that the committee's work could interfere with a Department of Justice investigation, announced the month before by Attorney General Holder, that was looking at possible criminal liability of some CIA officers. While Republican concerns about getting crosswise with Department of Justice investigators were well founded, the decision to withdraw turned out to be a very consequential one. With Republicans no longer involved, a few very partisan Democrat members and staffers were able to shape the investigation and the resultant written report to meet their political and ideological goals rather than conduct a thorough, fair, and apolitical review of a controversial CIA covert-action program.

In the early months of the Obama administration, my former

intelligence community colleagues would often reach out to me to discuss sensitive and controversial matters. One afternoon, a former colleague from the CIA called to flag a potential problem. "John, we love Leon. We really do. But he just made a very bad decision that is going to hurt us all. He agreed to let the SSCI have direct access to all our operational files for its RDI investigation. He's basically turning over everything to them."

"Huh?" I was trying to get my head around what I was just told, and "huh?" was the most eloquent comment I could muster.

"That's right, John," he said. "Leon has agreed to provide all information related to the program, including compartmented operational cables, for review by committee staff. The scope and the nature of the access being granted to the committee is mind-boggling. And there's even more," he blurted out. "Leon also agreed to a committee request that we build a computer system for committee staffers, using CIA funds and equipment, so they can read and review everything on a searchable digital database in a CIA-provided SCIF located outside CIA headquarters ["SCIF" is the acronym for a special compartmented information facility, which is a tightly controlled room where the most sensitive intelligence can be securely stored and discussed]. This has never happened before. The Democrats will turn this into a political donnybrook."

"No, no, no," I uttered into the phone. "He should never have done this. Didn't folks tell him it is a big mistake?"

"We sure did, but he wouldn't listen."

At the time, I was focused solely on the precedent-setting nature of Leon's decision to give the SSCI a staggering amount of the CIA's internal, privileged, deliberative, and operational documents wholesale. I later found out that Leon also had agreed to provide the committee with the personnel records, including background investigation reports and polygraph results, of CIA officers involved in the RDI program, an unprecedented intrusion by Congress into the private lives of American citizens working at the CIA. In his memoir

Worthy Fights, Leon says that he didn't believe he had a basis to refuse the SSCI's request and that his proposal to set up a reading room would allow the CIA to retain some control over the material, an offer that was not first cleared with the White House.

In my twenty-five years at the CIA, I had never heard of such a thing ever being contemplated, much less done. I immediately recognized the likelihood that the Democrats would use whatever gory details of the interrogations they could find to drag the CIA and its officers through politically charged mud in order to smear the Bush administration. At the time, I hadn't considered the very messy implications of Leon's agreement to allow the SSCI to use CIA computers for the committee's investigation and to have the CIA be responsible for the network's upkeep and security. And I certainly had no premonition that this arrangement would become a source of tremendous conflict between Democrats on the committee and a future CIA director, namely me.

As soon as I hung up the phone with my Langley contact, I went to see Denis McDonough and explained the downsides of breaking what had been a long-standing practice of not turning over the CIA's internal operational files to Congress. "The only time CIA has shown operational cables to the oversight committees was when there was a narrow request for very specific information, not for a congressional hunting expedition." I explained that even in the cases when operational cables were shared, the CIA retained control over the material. "If the CIA's oversight committees are going to be given unfettered access to operational cables in order to score political points—and if it happens in this case, Denis, it will happen in others, including in programs currently under way—you can kiss goodbye any incentive for CIA officers in the field to provide a full and honest readout of covert-action programs. Why the hell would they if partisans in Congress will use them for political fodder?"

Denis could see that I was hot, and we agreed that we should talk to Rahm Emanuel. As I explained the situation and the implications of Leon's decision, Rahm quickly grasped the problem. I told Rahm that it didn't matter whether it was the Democrats or the Republicans who were spearheading such oversight activities, the White House needed to defend the principle of separation of powers between the executive and legislative branches and to protect the CIA from congressional overreach. "Otherwise," I said to Rahm, "the CIA will interpret decisions like Leon's as being done by one political party in order to retaliate against the other. And the CIA will feel like the proverbial meat in a political sandwich. This will not endear the Obama administration to a CIA that is already feeling under the gun. Leon's agreement to the SSCI's request will result in a fishing expedition that will be cherry-picked to death." Mixing metaphors had always been a bad habit of mine whenever my blood pressure rose, and my blood pressure was steadily rising as I spoke.

Since a principals committee meeting was scheduled for later that morning, we agreed to talk to Leon outside the Situation Room as soon as it was over. As the principals started to scatter after the meeting concluded, Rahm grabbed Leon before he could depart. Rahm was his usual subtle self. "What the fuck did you do, Leon? You can't just turn over CIA's operational files to the committee. That's fuckin' ludicrous."

Leon was similarly undiplomatic. He glared at Rahm and in a louder voice said, "Don't tell me what I can and can't fuckin' do. It's our oversight committee. I have no choice."

"Of course, you do, Leon. Just say NO!" In *Worthy Fights,* Leon remembers Rahm saying that President Obama had his "hair on fire" over Leon's decision. Rahm was being hyperbolic, but he was not incorrect in channeling Obama's pique over the issue. In White House discussions about the RDI program in early 2009, Obama sent clear signals that he had no interest in punishing CIA for carrying out directives that were deemed lawful at the time they were issued by the Bush administration, irrespective of his personal revulsion over the tactics used.

There were several more volleys that went back and forth between Leon and Rahm, with neither giving an inch. Leon and I also got into a heated exchange, but it was too late. Leon had already given the order, and he was not going back on his word to the committee. Besides, CIA components had already started to carry out his wishes. A massive search had been launched at Langley to identify all CIA documents responsive to the SSCI request, and CIA information technology specialists were quickly designing a computer network system, dubbed RDINet, for use by SSCI staffers who would work in a CIA-leased building in northern Virginia. The CIA provided all the furniture, equipment, security arrangements, and computers at the facility and agreed to provide ongoing IT support.

RDINet was a stand-alone system—a small network of less than a dozen machines (computers and printers). The CIA transferred documents to SSCI staffers across a firewall, which was a software feature that granted access to information in the network according to a user's SSCI or CIA designator. As soon as the CIA-leased facility was up and running, the Agency started to push what eventually would be millions of pages of highly classified and very sensitive documents over the firewall for SSCI review. Democratic committee staffers, under the direction of Daniel Jones, who had spent a few years working for the FBI, quickly went to work. Using a unique and powerful search engine the CIA provided, the staffers combed through terabytes of data that had been accumulating in the CIA's digital and hard-copy files to find graphic details that could be presented as evidence of "torture," abuse, excesses, and wrongdoing. No stone was left unturned from a document-review perspective, as the CIA fulfilled its obligation to make available to the SSCI review team everything in its files that was covered by the committee's mandate. There was one hiccup before I became director, when the CIA pushed a significant number of CIA documents over the firewall in 2011 that were outside the agreed-upon time frame of the approved SSCI document request. When the CIA discovered the mistake, it unilaterally and without advance notice retrieved the documents from the SSCI side of the firewall, angering the committee and prompting a contrite CIA to pledge to never again take such action without first consulting the SSCI. The incident foreshadowed what would be a much more contentious exchange between the CIA and the committee several years later.

By the end of 2012, Jones and his team had drafted a dense, richly detailed, and extensively footnoted sixty-three-hundred-page report replete with the most graphic examples of the CIA's application of enhanced interrogation techniques and the conditions under which detainees were held. The "study," as it was called, contained twenty conclusions and twenty supporting case studies. It liberally and selectively pulled text from cables to support the overall thesis of alleged extensive CIA wrongdoing, with virtually no acknowledgment of how the CIA's worldwide counterterrorism work, including in the RDI program, uncovered and disrupted al-Qa'ida's many plans to carry out follow-up terrorist attacks, including against the homeland. The study was far from balanced. Most telling of the Democrats' lack of interest in presenting a fair, objective, and comprehensive report was their decision not to interview any former or current CIA officers who were involved in the RDI program. The Democrats stuck to this course even after the Department of Justice closed its criminal investigation in August 2012 without pressing any charges against CIA officers. Indeed, I believe the department's decision not to pursue any criminal charges against CIA employees infuriated the more ideologically driven members and staffers on the committee and made them more determined to use their report to exact their version of justice on CIA employees they deemed guilty. Even some of the most ardent critics of the RDI program inside the CIA were taken aback by the draft report, with one former colleague telling me, "As we feared, it is a one-sided and very partisan and inflammatory account of CIA misdeeds that reads like an aggressive and zealous prosecutor's brief."

The CIA received a draft copy of the study in December 2012 for review and comment. At the time, I had been nominated to be CIA director but was still working at the White House. I was pressed hard by Senate Democrats during my confirmation hearing and pre-confirmation courtesy calls to commit to the eventual declassification and release of the study. However, I decided to wait until after my confirmation to read it along with the CIA response to it, as I strongly suspected that the study's portrayal of events might be politically skewed and at odds with the facts. While my opposition to EITs had hardened over the years as I learned more details about how the program was implemented, I was unwilling to become a pawn in the Democrats' partisan blame-and-shame game that was being directed against the CIA. Throughout this period, no White House official, up to and including the president, ever tried to color my views of the study or to encourage me to embrace it publicly. One of the greatest votes of confidence I ever received from President Obama was when he pulled me aside before my confirmation hearing for a chat in the Oval Office. Referencing the committee study and my need to respond to it, he said, "John, I nominated you to be CIA director because I know that you will do what you think is right. Don't worry about the politics of the SSCI study. We'll sort that out."

By the time I was confirmed as director in early March 2013, the CIA was already engaged in an intense review of the study. Along with my deputy Michael Morell, I met frequently with the CIA officers who were reviewing the draft study, all of whom were seasoned, senior analysts and none operationally involved in the RDI program itself. We instructed them to be as rigorous as possible in their work—accepting what the SSCI got right but also identifying any factual errors in the study's analysis or presentation. At the same time, we told the review team not to take issue with any part of the study because of concerns that it might cause embarrassment for the CIA or for former and current CIA officials. The team was given directions to prepare a detailed written response that we could submit as soon as possible and that I could discuss with SSCI members. Michael and I carefully reviewed and made comments on the review team's response, which provided analysis on the study's twenty conclusions and twenty case studies. We also worked with the review team to refine eight action items on how we planned to prevent systemic problems identified in the CIA's conduct of RDI activities from occurring in other covert-action programs. On June 27, I sent the Agency's formal comments on the study to the committee along with a cover letter to Feinstein and Senator Saxby Chambliss, who had become SSCI vice chairman upon Senator Bond's retirement in 2010. In the cover letter, I explicitly acknowledged the significant weaknesses of the RDI program, and the many mistakes made by the Agency, including:

- a lack of preparations and core competencies to conduct detention and interrogation activities.
- failure of management at multiple levels to monitor the program.
- conflict of interest on the part of Agency contractors who designed the program and were involved in determining the effectiveness of the techniques.
- failure to perform comprehensive and independent analysis on the effectiveness of the interrogation techniques.
- detaining some individuals under a flawed interpretation of the authorities granted to CIA.
- insufficient accountability for poor performance and management failures by Agency officers.

In addition, I stressed my unequivocal opposition to the program in the letter by stating, "I personally remain firm in my belief that enhanced interrogation techniques are an inappropriate method for obtaining intelligence and that their use impairs our ability to continue to play a leadership role in the world." To reassure the committee that the program would not be restarted, I said, "it is my resolute intention never to allow any Agency officer to participate in any interrogation activity in which enhanced interrogation techniques would be employed." But I also went on record objecting to "the Study's unqualified assertions that the detention and interrogation program did not produce unique intelligence that led terrorist plots to be disrupted, terrorists to be captured, or lives to be saved." The CIA response included detailed comments on the unique intelligence that was elicited from detainees, including from those who were subjected to the harshest interrogation tactics. I did not, however, claim that there was causation between the application of EITs and the acquisition of worthwhile intelligence, writing: "The Agency takes no position on whether intelligence obtained from detainees who were subjected to enhanced interrogation techniques could have been obtained through other means or from other individuals. The answer to this question is and will forever remain unknowable."

As in my confirmation hearing, I refused to call EITs "torture"—in that memo or in any subsequent written or oral statements on the program—which greatly rankled the more zealous, ideological, and partisan of my Democratic critics. My argument has always been that "torture," which is defined in U.S. law, is laden with legal liability for anyone involved in the program. I firmly believed then, and continue to believe, that Agency officers who carried out their covert-action responsibilities consistent with the guidelines issued by the Department of Justice for lawful interrogation procedures, by definition, were not involved in the unlawful activity of "torture." Those Department of Justice guidelines have been roundly criticized by legal scholars, but the CIA officers were obliged to rely upon them when they were carrying out the EITs. I knew that the Democrats were going to be left unsatisfied and annoyed by my memo, which I felt was an honest and apolitical representation of my position and the position of the CIA's professional leadership team. To highlight my determination to steer clear of policy issues and political considerations, I noted in the memo that "as Director of CIA, it is not my role to engage in a debate about the appropriateness of the decisions that were made in a previous Administration to conduct a detention and interrogation program of suspected terrorists following the attacks on 11 September 2001."

The June 27 memo was received less than enthusiastically by Democratic SSCI members and staffers, as many saw it as a deliberate attempt by the CIA to subvert the study's findings and its eventual declassification and public release. In follow-up conversations with Senator Feinstein, I told her that the CIA's review team would be happy to meet with committee staffers to go over the report and our comments in hopes of being able to make the study more accurate. I knew it was an exercise in futility to get the Democrats to make the study more objective and less partisan, as they were clearly determined to make the report as damning as possible of CIA actions and, by extension, the Bush administration. But, I thought, perhaps we could correct some factual mistakes in the study and get some of the more egregious misrepresentations removed.

While SSCI staffers and CIA review team members were meeting to resolve outstanding differences, we started to receive questions, first from the staff and then from committee members, about what would become known as "the Panetta review." While the exact origins of the Panetta review are unclear, in terms of who authorized it and when, it was a CIA initiative undertaken while Leon Panetta was director to learn what was in the CIA's voluminous operational files that the SSCI was about to review. The rationale was that the CIA needed to be prepared to deal with the eventual SSCI findings and criticisms. It was not a formal CIA "fact-finding" effort, which would have involved interviews of employees or even an investigation by the inspector general. Rather, it was simply a review conducted by a handful of CIA officers, most of whom were between assignments and none of whom were counterterrorism analysts, of whatever documents they pulled from the corpus of data provided to the SSCI. It would not surprise me if the Panetta review had been initiated shortly after Leon and Rahm had their curse fest outside the White House Situation Room in 2009.

The CIA officers involved in the review were instructed not to draw their own conclusions but only to identify issues and actions as recorded in CIA files that had occurred during the RDI program and that could become the focus of SSCI interest and concern. The officers produced their own monthly written reports and made handwritten marginal comments on printed documents, which were not reviewed for accuracy, appropriateness, or quality-control purposes by senior CIA officials. Contrary to the directions they had received, some of the officers made personal comments reflecting their individual outrage and disgust about what they read. Those monthly reports and handwritten notes constituted the totality of what is known as the Panetta review, all of which was created after the RDI program had ended and after the time frame identified in SSCI's document request that was approved by Leon Panetta. As a result, it was not authorized to be shared with the SSCI staff.

The Panetta review group had been up and running for several months when the order came down from the CIA's seventh floor to cease its work following the announcement in August 2009 that the Department of Justice had launched a criminal investigation into the actions of some CIA officers involved in the RDI program. The reason for the stand-down order, I have been told, was that senior CIA officials, including lawyers in the Office of General Counsel, made the decision that it was inappropriate to create new documents on the past RDI program while the Department of Justice was conducting a criminal investigation. When the cease-and-desist order was given, all the work product of the members of the Panetta review was collated and filed, in hard copy and digitally. At the time, the CIA was being roundly criticized as well as investigated for its 2005 decision to destroy videotapes of interrogation sessions involving the use of enhanced techniques. By 2009, there was no longer any question in the CIA about the imperative to retain all uniquely created material, this time from the Panetta review.

The entire issue became much more complicated on Wednesday evening, January 8, 2014. My deputy, Avril Haines, and I had invited Senators Feinstein and Chambliss to dinner at the CIA. While the SSCI report was one of the topics we discussed, a range of national security issues and CIA-specific matters also were on our agenda. The discussion was very substantive and wholly apolitical, which is the way engagements between the leaders of the intelligence community and oversight committees should be conducted. As we walked the senators to their cars, Avril and I told them that we very much enjoyed the evening and that we looked forward to future get-togethers.

Seconds later, Nick Shapiro, who had become my deputy chief of staff at the CIA, approached. Almost breathlessly, Nick exclaimed, "It looks like the committee has the Panetta review on its side of the RDINet firewall in the SCIF." He said that CIA officers who told him about it had no idea how the committee obtained the document.

I figured there must be some mistake, because there was no record that the Panetta review was ever given to the committee even though the committee, which somehow had learned about the review, had made several recent formal requests for the document. As I thought more about it, it occurred to me that the SSCI's requests for the Panetta review might have been a clever feint to conceal the fact that staff had somehow obtained it but needed an authorized copy so that its contents could be officially incorporated into its study. I remembered the conversations I had had in the preceding

few months with Feinstein and with Senator Mark Udall, one of the
most liberal and ideological of the SSCI Democrats, who were in-
sistent that the committee receive a copy of the Panetta review. My
experience with Udall had not been good, as I found him to be disin-
genuous if not worse in his dealings with me. Udall and I talked on
the phone a few times about differences between the committee and
the Agency on the study, and each time we seemed to reach an understanding about the way ahead. Those understandings lasted only
until he hung up the phone, as he and his staffers quickly followed
up with public criticisms and comments to the press that misrepresented the CIA position and my comments to him. In September
2013, Udall had raised the Panetta review in an open hearing on the
nomination of Caroline Krass to be the CIA's general counsel, saying
that the review was at odds with the CIA's formal response to the
SSCI study and that the committee wanted a copy. "I bet Udall is a
part of this," I said to myself, as I went off to sleep the night of the
January 2014 dinner with Feinstein and Chambliss.

I was briefed the following day on why the CIA believed the Panetta review resided on the SSCI's side of the firewall. Over the preceding weeks, SSCI staff had made very specific comments to their CIA
counterparts about the contents of the Panetta review that could only
have been made if they had seen the document. As a result, the CIA
officers responsible for RDINet grew increasingly suspicious that
SSCI already had the document, and, on their own initiative, they
conducted a generic search of the CIA-owned network to determine
whether the document was in the system. It was a forensics search
for a specific binary code sequence of 0's and 1's denoting a unique
string of words contained in the Panetta review. That search revealed
that the binary code of the Panetta review was, indeed, on the SSCI
side of RDINet. Nothing other than 0's and 1's was identified in that
initial search.

The briefing was compelling. "I want a thorough check of all
Agency records," I said, "including a forensics check of the network

to confirm that the Panetta review was never formally or inadvertently passed by the CIA to the SSCI." I also said that CIA lawyers needed to determine in advance that all actions to be taken were consistent with CIA authorities and computer security responsibilities. As soon as the briefing was over, CIA officers conducted an intense legal review as well as an administrative review of the initial arrangements between the SSCI and the CIA when RDINet was first established. Those reviews determined that the CIA could proceed with the limited forensic check as long as the SSCI's work product on RDINet was not exposed or examined in any way.

I engaged in a back-and-forth with our computer experts and lawyers on Friday and over the weekend about what we could do to find out conclusively whether the Panetta review had already been obtained by SSCI staff. We all agreed that our actions should in no way infringe upon SSCI authorities and prerogatives or violate any strictures, legal or otherwise, on CIA actions. On Tuesday morning, I convened a meeting in the director's conference room to get an update, as I had told my staff that I wanted to reach out to SSCI leadership as soon as possible to discuss the matter with them. When I entered the conference room, I saw the many lawyers and IT specialists with whom I had been dealing over the preceding days, but I was surprised to notice that the head of the CIA's Counterintelligence Center (CIC) was also in attendance. Calling the meeting to order, I asked for the latest information on what had been learned since I had been briefed the night before. Surprisingly, it was CIC's chief, a senior and very experienced operations officer, who began to brief. I don't think he got two sentences out of his mouth before I cut him off, saying, "Wait a minute. Why is CIC involved in this?" I was intimately familiar with CIC's mission and its superb analytic, operational, and technical work, but it was in the business of catching spies, not investigating possible congressional misdeeds. "This is not a counterintelligence matter," I said emphatically, only to be told that the IT forensics and audit experts trying to determine how the

Panetta review got to the SSCI side of the firewall were attached to the CIC. "Everybody stop!" I said, as my heart skipped a few beats. "I want no more action taken until I discuss this with the SSCI." With the CIC involved, I found intolerable any potential insinuation that someone on the SSCI staff might be a spy. I left the meeting in a bit of a huff, not knowing exactly what had transpired on the forensics front and recognizing that the CIA's problem-solving proclivity might have gotten ahead of me.

A meeting with Senators Feinstein and Chambliss was set up in the Senate Hart Building for the following day, January 15. The senators were told only that I had a very sensitive matter to discuss and that they could each bring a single senior staffer. I read through my talking points verbatim, making sure that I used language that CIA lawyers and IT experts had agreed was an accurate description of how we found out that the Panetta review was on the SSCI side of RDINet and the reason for our very serious concerns. I emphasized that the entire RDINet computer network was a CIA system and that the CIA had a statutory responsibility to ensure that it was secure, especially in light of the extremely sensitive operational and covert-action information it contained. "If there is a vulnerability in RDINet, we need to find out immediately, not just to secure RDINet but also to determine whether the same vulnerability exists in similar CIA networks." In recognition of this being an unprecedented issue involving prerogatives of both the executive and legislative branches, I concluded my presentation by proposing that CIA and SSCI security personnel conduct a joint inquiry into what happened.

Feinstein, Chambliss, and their staff directors listened closely to my points, asking me once or twice to repeat a sentence so that they could understand exactly what I was saying. I was not confrontational, but I was firm in my determination to get to the bottom of a very disturbing development. The senators seemed genuinely surprised and taken aback by what I told them. They knew that I was upset at what we had discovered, and they said they would consider the proposal to conduct a joint security review. Feinstein turned to her staff director, David Grannis, and asked whether he had heard anything about the Panetta review and RDINet. David responded meekly: "Kind of, but not really."

By the end of the meeting, both senators pledged to follow up on the matter. I was pleased that Feinstein seemed genuinely unaware of the existence of the Panetta review on the SSCI side of RDINet. Despite my frequently strong disagreements with Feinstein over the years, I never had any doubt about her integrity, honesty, and ethics. Her public service and dedication to our national security have been second to none. I did not have the same confidence in and respect for everyone on her staff.

By the following day, Feinstein's demeanor had changed. She claimed that the CIA had no right to conduct the search on RDINet, and she flatly turned down the offer of a joint security review. It was clear that her staff had convinced her to take a hard line against any effort to find out how the Panetta review got on the SSCI side of RDINet, which I believe would have revealed wrongdoing by committee staff. Under normal circumstances, senators have little choice but to rely on their staff to ascertain facts and to provide recommendations. In this instance, however, staff members working on the RDI study had a direct conflict of interest that Feinstein should have recognized and taken into account. A bitter standoff between the committee and the CIA ensued, with both sides retreating to their respective corners in the following weeks. The situation worsened when I asked the CIA inspector general to conduct a preliminary review of CIA actions—it had no authority to scrutinize the actions of SSCI staff. The IG decided to make a criminal referral to the Department of Justice to determine whether the CIA had violated any laws when it conducted the forensic search of RDINet, since the network was being used by a separate branch of government. In turn, the CIA's acting general counsel, after being briefed on the matter by CIA officers and the CIA inspector general, made a criminal referral to the Department of Justice about a possible criminal violation by SSCI staff when it acquired and retained an unauthorized copy of an internal CIA document, the Panetta review.

While I had reservations about the wisdom and likely implications of the CIA making a criminal referral to Justice about SSCI staff, I recognized that it was the acting general counsel's decision. As a CIA director appointed by a Democratic president, there was no way I was going to stop the Agency's top lawyer from making what he believed was a prudent criminal referral about the alleged actions of Senate Democratic staffers. If I had prevented the referral from going forward, I am sure that some within the Agency would have questioned whether I did so for political reasons. Looking back on it now, I wish I had taken a more activist role in trying to stop the referral, as it had the very unfortunate effect of pouring gasoline on an already raging fire. As soon as the acting general counsel made the referral to Justice, I called Feinstein and Chambliss separately to tell them. Senator Feinstein expressed deep indignation but was relatively measured in her immediate response. Chambliss lamented the escalating tensions and counseled me to find a way to repair relations with Feinstein and the Democrats. "Boy, I sorely wish I could," I told him.

To this day I do not know how the Panetta review got on the SSCI side of RDINet, but I am certain that Dan Jones, the lead staff member on the study, knows. Jones or another staffer might have actively exploited a vulnerability in the RDINet system, or the Panetta review might have inadvertently been passed across the firewall. In any event, SSCI staff who accessed the review would have recognized immediately that they were not authorized to have it based on its markings as well as its date, which was outside the time frame of documents approved for passage to the SSCI. Dan Jones also knew that he was committing a serious security violation when he printed the top-secret code-word document and carried it to SSCI spaces in

the Hart Building in Washington, D.C., as he publicly acknowledged in an interview with *The Guardian* in 2016.

A feud between the Democratic chair of the Senate intelligence
committee and a CIA director appointed by a Democratic president
did not make for good politics, and the White House grew increasingly nervous about where things were heading. On March 11,
Senator Feinstein took to the Senate floor and in a scathing speech
publicly claimed that the CIA engaged in "illegal and unconstitu-
tional breaches" in attempts to spy on the SSCI. That same morning, I spoke at a Council on Foreign Relations event in Washington,
D.C., and said, in response to a question, that allegations about the
CIA hacking into Senate computers "couldn't be further from the
truth." As tensions rose, Avril did her best to find a way to get things
on a better track and recommended to the White House that Vice
President Biden get involved. Avril had been deputy chief counsel
for the Senate Foreign Relations Committee when Biden was chairman, and she knew he had a special knack for bridging differences
between warring parties.

Vice President Biden jumped at the opportunity to mediate, and
a meeting was scheduled for March 24 at the vice president's official
residence, the U.S. Naval Observatory in Washington, D.C. I arrived
about fifteen minutes before the scheduled 3:00 P.M. meeting time.
Senator Feinstein arrived promptly at three o'clock and was met on
the front porch by Vice President Biden, who had just trotted down
the stairs from the second floor of the residence with his usual genial
flair. As soon as I heard their voices, I walked toward the parlor to
join them. The senator returned the vice president's warm welcome
with a smile and said, "Hello, Joe." Upon my entrance, her smile
disappeared as she eyed me. "Hello, John." Her tone was somber, if
not sullen.

The distinct chill in the air confirmed my instinct that I would
have my work cut out for me in the meeting. I tried to lighten things

up and said cheerily, "Hi, Dianne, it's good to see you." Cheery she wasn't, and my greeting didn't have any noticeable effect on her grim look. Noticing the dark attire she was wearing, I wondered whether she had purposely selected her outfit in order to give the impression that she was attending someone's funeral, my own. Glancing at the vice president, I noticed his dark gray suit and dark tie, which made me worry even more.

We made our way to a room on the first floor and took our seats. The vice president started off the conversation. "The reason I asked you both to come here today is that it pains me—it really does—to see two people I like and respect so much fighting with one another. The president feels the same way. I don't need to tell you it is not good when the head of the Senate Intelligence Committee and the director of the CIA are engaged in a rather public spat. We've got to fix this, folks, for the good of the country. We really do. And I don't want us to leave here today without agreeing to do so."

Feinstein kept her head bent, lips pursed, and hands clasped in her lap during the vice president's remarks. Since I was the junior member of the group, I looked to her to speak first. She waited an uncomfortably long time before thanking the vice president for his initiative and agreeing that there needed to be a resolution to what she referred to as a "dispute between the committee and the CIA."

"I was shocked, Joe, shocked, when I found out that the CIA went into our computers. It happened once before, and the White House and CIA promised that it would never happen again. But it did, and I'm very disappointed in John for allowing it to happen." She spoke in a low and steady voice, consistent with the demeanor of an aggrieved party. "It just shows that the CIA is doing whatever it can to prevent the committee from issuing its report on the Agency's interrogation program. The CIA has fought us at every turn, and its latest actions violate the separation of powers between the executive and legislative branches of government."

She paused for a moment, but before I could speak, she continued.

"And now the CIA has made a criminal referral to the Department of Justice about the actions of committee staff, who have done absolutely nothing wrong. I am giving my own money to a fund that has been set up so that staff members can retain lawyers to protect themselves. I tell you, Joe, things are in an awful state."

The vice president winced as he looked at me. I was unsure how familiar he was with the history of the interaction between the committee and the CIA since the investigation had begun more than five years before, but I knew that this wasn't the time to get into the sordid details. I also didn't want to get into a "he said, she said" argument with Feinstein, as that would only get us mired down in competing versions of the facts. I tried to take the high ground and focus on the way ahead.

"Dianne, it is very unfortunate that things have gotten to this point." I added that I wanted a good relationship with her and the committee, and I wanted the committee to be able to finish its report on the CIA's detention and interrogation program—the sooner the better. "The CIA is absolutely not trying to prevent you from carrying out your oversight duties," I said, thinking about the millions of pages of CIA documents that had been passed to the committee in RDINet. Feinstein stared at the coffee table in front of her as I continued. "It is clear that we each believe wrongdoing was done, Dianne. We differ, however, on whether wrongdoing was done by committee staff or by CIA officers. But let's face it. Neither of us knows for certain who did what to those CIA computers that were being used by the committee. We only know what our staffs told us they did and didn't do." I wanted to make explicit reference in front of the vice president to the fact that the computers were CIA computers, not committee computers, as Feinstein had stated. I could see that my unwillingness to accept her version of events, which held the CIA wholly culpable, was making her uncomfortable. At this point, the vice president was about to interject, so I quickly got to my punch line.

"Dianne, we both need to find out the facts. As you know, the IG is completing its review of CIA actions. If it is determined that any CIA officer did anything inappropriate or wrong, I will personally apologize to you and hold those individuals to account. I give you my word on that. And, since Majority Leader Harry Reid has asked the Senate sergeant-at-arms to review the actions of committee staffers, I fully expect that you would tell me if any staffers engaged in inappropriate conduct and that you would take appropriate action." I knew that it was a long shot to expect her to acknowledge, much less apologize for, any misdeeds of her staff, but I wanted to press for a fair and equitable resolution with each side held to the same standard.

Sensing an opening, the vice president chimed in. "We have to get this behind us, folks. There are too many important national security matters that the committee and the CIA need to work on together. Dianne, I know that John will find out what his people did. He'll tell you exactly what happened and will apologize to you if an apology is called for."

The prospect of an "apology" resonated with Feinstein, and she slowly started to emerge from her mournful demeanor. Looking up, she talked a bit about the report and its importance, and she underscored her determination to prevent the CIA from ever detaining and "torturing" terrorists again. "The program is a blight on our nation's soul. I want to make sure that it will never be repeated, under a Democratic or Republican president."

"That's for damn sure," the vice president said, as he rose from his chair, signaling an end to the gathering.

"We're all in agreement on that point," I said, as we walked toward the front door.

Bidding me goodbye on the front porch, Feinstein offered up her only smile of the afternoon. We both promised to be in touch. As I headed back to Langley, I felt that the vice president had helped push the "pause" button in the war of words between the committee and the CIA. Although the respite in Panetta-review-related tension was much needed, I knew the fight was not over and ultimately would transition to arguing over the SSCI study itself.

In the months that followed, my relations with Democratic committee members and staffers remained quite chilly. As far as I am aware, the Senate sergeant-at-arms never conducted any investigation of the actions of Senate staffers as was directed by Senator Reid, and no serious effort was made by committee members to find out how the committee staff had gained access to the Panetta review on RDINet. The one positive development during this time was the decision by the Department of Justice not to launch a criminal investigation of the actions of either SSCI staffers or CIA officers, which helped calm nerves in the Senate and in the CIA.

In July, the IG completed its review of CIA actions. When I was briefed on the IG's findings, I learned for the first time that CIA technical experts during a forensics search had inappropriately accessed the content of four internal messages written by SSCI staff on the RDINet. It didn't matter that the substance of those messages was minimal and benign. Accessing the content of those messages was wrong, even if done inadvertently. "Well, I owe the chairman an apology for this," I said to my senior staff. "That's what I promised to do when we met at the vice president's house." I knew that the Senate sergeant-at-arms investigation of SSCI staffers' actions was likely to remain stillborn, so there was no likelihood that I would ever hear anything close to an admission of wrongdoing, much less an apology, from Senator Feinstein. Nevertheless, I needed to honor my pledge, and my senior staff agreed.

On Thursday, July 31, I met with Senators Feinstein and Chambliss in SSCI spaces to try to bring some closure to the contretemps over the Panetta review. Once again, I pointed out the CIA's solemn responsibility as well as its statutory authority to safeguard the IT systems that process and protect CIA information, even when those systems are being used by non-CIA individuals who happen to be

SSCI staff. Since the senators would soon receive the IG report, I decided to walk through its key points, focusing on the circumstances surrounding the inappropriate access of the staffers' messages by CIA employees. "The access to the four messages was wrong, and never should have happened. I apologize to the two of you and to the committee for this inappropriate action by the CIA. I will convene an accountability board to determine whether some disciplinary action is warranted for the CIA employees involved." Feinstein listened intently to my words, and her blue eyes teared up when I said, "I apologize."

"Thank you, John. Now we can move on and get our work done."

I knew that my apology would quickly become public knowledge, so I authorized the release of a statement that said I apologized for CIA employees acting "in a manner inconsistent with the common understanding" between the SSCI and the CIA when RDINet was set up. The statement was intentionally brief and nonspecific because we didn't want to compromise the ability of the accountability board to conduct its own review and to determine whether CIA officers knowingly acted in an unethical or even unlawful manner. But in retrospect, the language of the statement also was ambiguous and confusing. Rather than explaining that the actions taken by the CIA were appropriate and warranted with the single exception of accessing the content of four internal SSCI messages, the vagueness of the statement allowed false narratives about the CIA purposefully and illegally "hacking" into Senate computers to flourish.

In the months that followed, rather than having CIA officers sit in judgment on fellow Agency officials, I asked former Democratic senator and SSCI member Evan Bayh and former White House counsel Bob Bauer to cochair an accountability board. I recused myself from any role in acting upon the board's recommendations to eliminate any appearance of conflict of interest. The board was directed to provide its findings and recommendations to Avril, who would consult with Director of National Intelligence Jim Clapper on any accountability actions that might need to be taken. I found the board's work to be exceptionally thorough—much more so than the IG's quick initial review—and I was very pleased when the board determined in December 2014 that no CIA officer had acted in bad faith and recommended against taking any administrative actions. Despite the public release the following month of the board's final report and its clear articulation that the CIA forensic search of RDI-Net was appropriate, prudent, and lawful, the myth that "the CIA spied on Senate computers" continues to this day.

While the accountability board was doing its work in the fall of 2014, the committee forwarded its nearly six-hundred-page executive summary of the RDI study to the CIA for a classification review. Senators Feinstein and Udall, Dan Jones, and other SSCI advocates said they believed that the entire document was unclassified and ready for public release. It was not. Far from it. A rigorous CIA review revealed hundreds if not thousands of passages, names, and terms that foreign services could have quickly exploited to reveal sensitive U.S. intelligence sources and methods. Prodded on by Dan Jones, Feinstein was outraged by CIA objections, and she appealed immediately to the White House, claiming that the CIA was simply trying to prevent the study's release.

By this time, Denis McDonough and Lisa Monaco, my very capable successor at the White House, had become intimately familiar with the contentious back-and-forth between the CIA and SSCI Democrats. They challenged CIA redactions and assumed the roles of arbiters, seeking to reach an accommodation on the executive summary that would satisfy Feinstein yet protect CIA secrets. On the sidelines of a White House meeting, Denis asked me a very direct question. "John, I need to know from you whether CIA concerns about the executive summary are legitimate and significant. Dianne is furious, and she will not rest until the study's executive summary is released."

"The concerns are valid and very serious, Denis, and we are representing not just our objections but also those of State, Defense, and others, including foreign governments. But don't take my word for it," I told him. "Take a briefing from my folks, and they will show you what a foreign intelligence service would learn by taking the information contained in the current version of the SSCI executive summary and then using it to search against a very small portion of the Internet to reveal the CIA's sources and methods. It absolutely will blow your mind." I had received the briefing the week before from Sean Roche, a brilliant senior CIA officer who was leading the classification-review team of wicked-smart data scientists and data-curation specialists. I knew that their analysis would convince Denis of the legitimacy of CIA concerns, which is exactly what happened in a briefing the following day at CIA headquarters. Denis subsequently hosted a session in the White House Situation Room, where Sean and his team gave the same briefing to Senator Feinstein and Dan Jones. Unfortunately, it took another four months of negotiations and numerous modifications before the CIA determined that the revised draft executive summary of the study was unclassified and posed no objection to its public release.

On December 9, 2014, the SSCI publicly released a 525-page executive summary of the full 6,700-page study, the latter remaining classified to this day. The release of the executive summary resulted in a media feeding frenzy, as its gory details of the interrogation program were widely disseminated and roundly denounced. With condemnations of CIA actions growing, I felt that I needed to address the issue publicly, so I held a press conference two days later in the lobby of CIA headquarters, the first time a director had done so. Since the committee study made virtually no mention of the CIA's heroic actions in the aftermath of 9/11, I opened my remarks by talking about how the CIA responded to the national tragedy and the many accomplishments and sacrifices of CIA officers in the fight against al-Qa'ida. Although I criticized the committee's investigative process as flawed and noted several areas of disagreement with the study, I also highlighted what the study got right and what the CIA did wrong. After my prepared remarks, I took about a dozen questions from the assembled reporters, which prompted Donald Rumsfeld to send me a handwritten note about a week later praising my willingness to do so. Or maybe he was just pleased that I didn't begin any of my answers with the phrase, "to be honest."

By the time my first full year as CIA director was coming to a close, I fervently hoped that I would be forever rid of everything and anything related to the RDI program and the RDINet brouhaha. No such luck. In late 2019, a movie entitled *The Report* was released (thankfully to less-than-stellar reviews) that purported to portray actual events related to the SSCI investigation into the CIA's RDI program. The movie contained numerous factual errors, fictional events, and intentional misrepresentations of CIA actions, the most egregious of which was a scene showing CIA officers breaking into SSCI workspaces to steal documents and computer disks related to the Panetta review. That is patently false. Even the insinuation in the movie that a CIA officer physically handed off a hard copy of the Panetta review to Dan Jones is belied by the fact that the document was on RDINet and was printed out in the SCIF. Like the SSCI study itself, the movie mischaracterizes the motives and actions of many CIA officers and does a great disservice to the historical record. Nevertheless, I thought Annette Bening did a wonderful job playing Dianne Feinstein. And I was less than shocked to see that the actor who had portrayed a deranged serial killer in the film *The Silence of the Lambs* was selected to play me.

In mid-2014, while the SSCI study was still under way, Dan Jones had told colleagues that he intended to make a movie about the SSCI investigation and the interactions between the committee and the CIA. Unfortunately, Dan Jones let his ideological zealotry and personal interests skew what should have been a fair, objective, and much-needed Senate review of one of the most controversial chapters of CIA history. And while CIA officers made some serious mistakes in their efforts to stop al-Qa'ida's murderous agenda, demonizing and fictionalizing their actions in a movie is simply way beyond the pale.

24

OH, THE PEOPLE I'VE MET

As a kid growing up in New Jersey, I longed to meet someone famous one day. My father and I would take the bus and train to Yankee Stadium several times a year in the 1960s, and each time I would implore him to get seats near the field so that I could be as close as possible to Mickey Mantle, Roger Maris, or another hulking Bronx Bomber. Although we were only able to afford tickets in the nosebleed section of the stadium, my father would take my hand around the seventh inning and we would casually wander down to the box seats. Once there, a few dollars passed to an obliging usher would put us in a couple of just-vacated seats near the field, from where I could see the facial expressions and even hear the voices of my boyhood heroes. There was something very special about being that close to greatness.

I never had the good fortune to meet any of the Yankees from the legendary championship teams of the 1960s, although I did get to throw out the ceremonial first pitch at a game at Yankee Stadium on September 6, 2016 (I believe I caught the corner of the plate for a strike). Nevertheless, I felt like a wide-eyed little kid during the

Obama administration when I met Baseball Hall of Famer Hank Aaron, football great Peyton Manning, moonwalker Buzz Aldrin, singer-songwriter James Taylor, Supreme Court Justice Antonin Scalia, civil rights icon John Lewis, and so many other Americans that I had admired over the years. And when Kathy and I traveled to Houston, Texas, on a couple of occasions to dine with former president George H. W. Bush and former first lady Barbara Bush, I would think back on those nights in the Bronx when my father and I were able to catch just a quick glance of fame. Only in America.

I eventually discovered that fame and greatness do not always go hand in hand, especially in Washington's political circles. Unfortunately, I have met many well-known politicians, on both sides of the aisle, who decide their every move based not on integrity and honor, but on the perceived impact on some combination of their personal political fortunes, fundraising prospects, and partisan agendas. Sometimes, they even admit to it. When I served at the White House as President Obama's counterterrorism adviser, Denis McDonough, Avril Haines, and I paid visits to key members of the Senate and House of Representatives to argue for language in the pending National Defense Authorization Act that would allow the transfer of Guantánamo detainees to the United States for trial and incarceration. It turned out to be a futile exercise, with unfounded congressional fears of security challenges ultimately torpedoing Obama's goal of closing the Guantánamo detention facility during his presidency. Senator Lindsey Graham, an influential member of the Senate Armed Services Committee, was one of the members we went to see. As we sat in the waiting area of his office, we watched C-SPAN coverage of Senator Graham speaking live in the Senate, misrepresenting Obama administration counterterrorism policies and lambasting me by name. When the senator returned to his office and realized we had watched his misleading soliloquy, he laughingly responded by saying, "Oh, don't pay any attention to what I say on the Senate floor. It doesn't mean anything. It's just politics." Ever since, Senator Graham's frequently vacillating public statements always ring hollow to me, as I wonder what he actually believes and what he says simply for the sake of craven politics. Increasingly, the latter seems to be his forte.

Notwithstanding the tactics of Senator Graham, I have met many individuals of integrity in Congress, and I bet that Senator John McCain never said anything on the Senate floor that he disavowed or dismissed in private. I say this as someone who frequently was on the receiving end of angry and emotional McCain diatribes. My last exchange with Senator McCain was much like others I had with him. It was in late 2016, at a closed hearing of the Senate Select Committee on Intelligence (SSCI) on the Middle East. While I was in the process of responding to a question from Senator Marco Rubio, Senator McCain interrupted, saying sternly, "Bullshit, Mr. Brennan, bullshit!" His profanity was directed at a reference I made to administration policy on the conflict in Syria, not anything related to CIA activities or the intelligence assessment I was providing. It was quite evident that violating committee protocols by interrupting another senator's time was nothing new for Senator McCain, because the other senators remained silent as McCain's face got redder and redder. After glancing briefly at Senator McCain with a rather startled look on my face, I proceeded answering Senator Rubio's question, but McCain was not to be deterred. "Bullshit, Mr. Brennan, that's bullshit," he said once again. With that, he got up from his chair and left the committee room. Despite his outburst and what I believed was his misdirected ire, I could never get angry at Senator McCain. He had sacrificed so much for our country, especially during his years as a prisoner of war in Vietnam, and I admired his unyielding determination to do what he thought would keep America strong and safe. In this instance, I knew that he fervently believed that a more forceful U.S. response to Russia's military escalation in Syria was in America's best interests, not his own political interests—an all-too-novel position among politicians.

Senator Saxby Chambliss also was a vocal critic of mine, but he eventually warmed to me. Immediately before the Senate's 63–34 vote confirming me as CIA director in March 2013, Senator Chambliss, who was then vice chairman and soon to be chairman of the SSCI, took to the Senate floor and gave a blistering denunciation of my nomination. He said that I was unfit to be CIA director and was too political for the responsibility given my White House position. Considering the relatively few interactions I had had with Chambliss over the previous years, I was surprised at the vehemence of his words. As soon as the Senate vote was over, I phoned Senator Chambliss and told him that I heard what he said and that I would prove him wrong. "Well, let's hope you do, John," he said. "Let's hope you do."

About two years into my tenure as director, Senator Chambliss pulled me aside after I had finished a briefing for his committee. "John," he said, "do you remember that conversation we had after the Senate voted to confirm you?"

"You bet I do, Mr. Chairman. I remember exactly what we both said."

"Well," Chambliss replied, "you're proving me wrong, and I am very glad that you are." His words were most appreciated, even if they were prompted by my frequent fights with Democrats on his committee. It was the only time any member of Congress ever told me they were wrong about something. Senator Chambliss and I didn't always agree on substance, but we developed a mutual respect that I believe served the CIA-SSCI relationship well. When Chambliss retired from the Senate, I asked him to serve on my advisory board at the CIA. His perspective and Republican credentials complemented nicely the views of another advisory board member, former Democratic senator and SSCI member Evan Bayh.

It was the world stage, however, that presented the greatest opportunity for me to see and interact with figures of history, both good and bad. During the first part of my career, I was usually a note taker or simply an attendee at senior-level meetings, which allowed me to witness the implementation of U.S. foreign policy and the way various U.S. and foreign officials carried out their responsibilities. After I joined the Obama administration, unless I was accompanying the president or vice president, I frequently was the principal U.S. official in meetings with foreign heads of state and government, cabinet ministers, and chiefs of intelligence and security services during my travels abroad. It was initially a very intimidating experience, although always fascinating and with many memorable moments.

From a national security and intelligence perspective, I had most in common and the deepest respect for my counterparts in allied countries, especially the United Kingdom and Australia. Not only were our international policy goals and national security interests closely aligned, there also were near-identical professional standards and extraordinarily close intelligence-sharing arrangements that created strong bonds of mutual trust. Along with Canada and New Zealand, the United Kingdom, Australia, and the United States comprise "The Five Eyes," an informal yet unbreakable constellation of intelligence and law enforcement agencies that have pledged since World War II to share among themselves their most sensitive secrets and to never spy on one another. I developed especially close ties to Jonathan Evans and Andrew Parker, the successive directors general of MI5, and John Sawers and Alex Younger, successive chiefs of MI6, the British rough equivalents of the FBI and CIA respectively. There was virtually no intelligence that I wouldn't share with them, at times to the dismay of some of my CIA colleagues who viewed all intelligence activities as a competitive sport. I also established a very close working relationship with Olly Robbins, who was the UK's deputy national security adviser and my British counterpart when I served as President Obama's homeland security and counterterrorism adviser. My position in the White House and as director of the CIA also gave me access to British Prime Ministers David Cameron and Theresa May, both of whom were substantively strong as well as consistent advocates of close cooperation between British and American intelligence and security services. Another of my closest foreign colleagues was Nick Warner, my main Australian counterpart, whose decades of intelligence experience gave him unrivaled substantive knowledge, professional expertise, and direct access to senior government officials around the globe. Nick was an especially astute observer of global geostrategic developments, and I actively sought out his insights, including his views on the impact and efficacy of U.S. foreign and national security policies.

While I enjoyed and benefited from working with many other services, notably those of the Dutch, Norwegians, French, Italians, Japanese, and South Koreans, it was during my many years living and traveling in the Middle East and South Asia that I had the most intriguing and captivating engagements. The CIA always has had a very close relationship with Israeli intelligence and security services, and I regularly interacted with the directors of Mossad and Shin Bet to discuss our respective organizations' views on regional affairs and to explore areas of mutual operational interest. The Israeli services are among the world's most innovative, technically proficient, professional, and effective, and they have a strong track record of uncovering and thwarting threats to Israel's security. I enjoyed my meetings with Mossad and Shin Bet leaders far more than my meetings with Prime Minister Bibi Netanyahu, whose politics and policies have been very detrimental to prospects for a two-state solution to the Israeli-Palestinian "problem." Whenever I would visit Israel, I also would meet in Ramallah with Palestinian Authority leaders and intelligence officials. My Israeli counterparts strongly supported my meetings with Palestinian officials, as they heavily depended on the Palestinian services to carry out their important responsibilities irrespective of the political and Islamist extremist winds that might blow in the region. In each visit I paid to Ramallah, I explained that the CIA would continue to support Palestinian intelligence and security components as long as they maintained their professionalism and steered clear of engaging in political activities. Despite the political headwinds generated by Netanyahu, I had confidence that the Palestinians were living up to their obligations.

During the Obama administration, I probably spent more time with Saudi officials—kings, princes, and technocrats—than with any others. King Abdullah of Saudi Arabia was one of my favorite interlocutors. I had about a half-dozen meetings with him, and each time he impressed me as a mensch (yes, I know it might seem a bit incongruous that I am using a Yiddish word to describe a Saudi king, but I am sure that Abdullah would have appreciated the irony). Unlike many Saudi officials, including other kings, Abdullah never hesitated to provide a direct response to a question and to volunteer his candid comments and criticisms of U.S. policies. His honesty and candor gave him a reputation for being far less pro-American than his predecessor, King Fahd, and other senior princes, but I found his straightforward remarks refreshing and never reflecting any weakening of his admiration of America.

In a March 2009 meeting, Abdullah strongly praised the leadership of President Obama but criticized the U.S. practice of releasing some Guantánamo detainees, which had begun under President Bush and continued under Obama. Abdullah was most concerned that some of the released detainees would seek to join al-Qa'ida even if they had not been terrorists before their capture, and he offered his suggestion about how to follow their subsequent movements. "You could implant microchips in their bodies and track them with Bluetooth," the octogenarian monarch said with a satisfied look on his face. "We do it all the time with horses, camels, and falcons so that we can find them when they take off into the desert." A bit startled, I responded with the first thing that came to mind. "Well, Guantánamo detainees have better lawyers than your horses, camels, and falcons so we can't implant microchips in their bodies." Abdullah just smiled.

In many of our meetings, Abdullah spoke angrily about Usama Bin Ladin and al-Qa'ida. "They are not Muslims. They are heretics, murderers!" he would say. In addition to the many thousands of deaths caused by al-Qa'ida, Abdullah expressed deep concern about the adverse impact terrorism had on the reputation of Islam and Saudi Arabia in the United States and in other countries around the world. In one meeting, Abdullah ruefully acknowledged that he was the Saudi official who had turned down a Sudanese government offer in 1996 to deport Bin Ladin, who had been living in Khartoum for the previous five years, to Saudi Arabia. "I deeply regret that decision," he told me. At the time of the decision, Abdullah was crown prince and acting regent as a result of a debilitating stroke suffered by his half brother, King Fahd, the year before. Abdullah didn't say why he had rebuffed the Sudanese offer, although I suspect that he was adhering to what had been Fahd's strategy of avoiding potential problems whenever possible. Also left unsaid in the meeting was the likelihood that the events of 9/11 might never have happened if he had decided otherwise.

I was especially close to Prince Muhammad Bin Nayif (MBN), a favorite nephew of King Abdullah who was Saudi Arabia's minister of interior and then crown prince during my years in the Obama administration. I had dozens of meetings with MBN in Jeddah and Riyadh, which usually involved initial discussions with our respective teams followed by an elaborate dinner, which left no one unsated. Afterward, MBN and I would retire to his private quarters for a couple of hours of cigarette-smoke-filled discussion about counterterrorism cooperation, regional conflicts, and the kingdom's future. MBN was an advocate of political and social change in Saudi Arabia, telling me once that he believed Saudi Arabia should become a constitutional monarchy, with Saudi citizens playing a much more influential role in government. MBN was an outstanding counterterrorism partner and a close friend.

When King Abdullah died in January 2015 and his half brother Crown Prince Salman ascended to the throne, most Saudi watchers anticipated that Salman's son, Prince Muhammad Bin Salman

(MBS), would play an increasingly influential political role in the kingdom's affairs. They were not wrong, although they probably underestimated the extent to which MBS would consolidate his political power. I first met MBS in 2014, when he was chief of staff to his father, then the crown prince, and I was struck by the significant role MBS played in the meeting. As Salman and I conducted our discussions seated next to each other in a large tent outside his palace, I could see MBS on the far side of the room typing on his laptop. Whenever MBS stopped typing, a message immediately would show up on a laptop positioned in front of his father, who appeared to include whatever substance he read in his comments to me. In the years since, I have thought many times about that scene while I've watched MBS perfect his skills as the power behind the throne. He cleverly engineered the sacking of his father's first two crown princes—Prince Muqrin, a half brother of King Salman, and MBN—to position himself as his father's successor. And by arresting and seizing much of the wealth of more than a hundred princes and technocrats in late 2017, MBS further solidified his political influence and grip on power.

As CIA director, I had several meetings with MBS. He came across as well read, intelligent, energetic, cunning, and politically savvy, but also extremely unrealistic when it came to Saudi Arabia's ability to influence events in the region. I met with MBS shortly after he was appointed minister of defense in early 2015. He was organizing the start of a Saudi-led military coalition to fight against Houthi rebel forces that had ousted the Saudi-supported government in Yemen. "We'll finish off the Houthis in a couple of months," he said confidently. "And then we'll turn our attention to cleaning up the situation in the north," an apparent reference to Syria and Iraq. I looked at him with a rather blank stare and wondered to myself what he had been smoking. That was more than five years ago. Yemen is still racked by civil war and continued Saudi bombing, and Syria and Iraq are far from cleaned up.

MBS has taken some positive steps since he assumed the role of Saudi Arabia's principal decision maker. Making it legally permissible for women to drive, relaxing harsh social strictures against the mixing of men and women in public places, and opening up the kingdom to previously verboten entertainment opportunities have allowed the kingdom to begin to emerge from its ultraconservative cocoon. Continuing along this path is essential to undercutting the cultural and radical religious influences in Saudi Arabia that have spawned terrorism by extremist groups that purport to be Islamic. While enacting these important reforms, however, MBS has opted for the authoritarian's preferred course of action, ordering the arrest of political activists and suppressing political dissent, brutally if necessary.

Saudi citizen and *Washington Post* columnist Jamal Khashoggi was a particular irritant to MBS. Khashoggi was widely known and respected inside and outside the kingdom for his literary talent, political acumen, and principled opposition to MBS's increasing authoritarianism and arrogance. When I read about Khashoggi's horrific murder and dismemberment at the Saudi consulate in Istanbul, Turkey, in October 2018, I knew immediately that MBS bore responsibility. Based on everything I have learned over the past forty years about Saudi intelligence and security services and the way the Saudi government operates, I am certain that such an audacious operation occurring inside a Saudi diplomatic mission against a high-profile journalist working for a U.S. newspaper would have required the direct authorization of Saudi Arabia's top leadership. Nothing in King Salman's background suggests he would have authorized the murder; MBS's background does. And press reports saying that the CIA assessed that MBS was responsible reinforced my conviction. The subsequent failure of the Trump administration to hold the Saudi government to account for MBS's role in the murder of Khashoggi was one of the most egregious examples of unprincipled leadership I have ever witnessed in the U.S. government.

My trips to Saudi Arabia frequently also involved travel to Yemen, which I visited ten times while I worked at the White House and was director of the CIA. My trips often focused on gaining Yemeni government support for U.S. counterterrorism actions against al-Qa'ida in the Arabian Peninsula (AQAP), and I always would meet with Yemen's presidents during my visits. President Ali Abdullah Saleh was a most intriguing individual, having run the country with an iron hand for nearly twenty years by the time I started working at the White House in 2009 (Saleh had been president of North Yemen for a dozen years before the unification of North and South Yemen in 1990). A former army colonel, the rather diminutive Saleh was the Yemeni equivalent of a New York City mafia don. He received me either in his presidential office or his outdoor gazebo, flaunting his manicured fingernails and wearing his gold Cartier sunglasses, Rolex wristwatches, Gucci shoes, and finely tailored Giorgio Armani suits. He always had at least four phones at his side, which he would pick up and use intermittently during our conversations. His restless leg syndrome was ever present, as were his many attendants who replenished our tea, coffee, and juice every few minutes.

By the time the Arab Spring reached Yemen's shores in early 2011, I had met and spoken with Saleh on numerous occasions and thus became the administration's point person on Yemen. As thousands of protesters clogged the streets of the capital city of Sanaa for weeks on end, resulting in dozens dead and hundreds injured, I was in regular telephone contact with Saleh, warning him not to use lethal force against the demonstrators. With some prodding, Saleh finally agreed in April to step down in favor of his vice president, Abdrabbuh Mansur Hadi, only to renege on the commitment within weeks. A bombing seriously injured Saleh in early June and he went to Saudi Arabia for medical treatment, and I visited him in a Riyadh hospital the following month. He was visibly scarred and wearing medical gloves on his injured hands. "You're not rid of me yet, Mr. John," a seated Saleh said to me as I walked into his room.

"I know," I responded, "you're the cat with nine lives. And I think you're only on your fourth or fifth." Smiling seemed a bit painful for him, but he broadly smiled, nonetheless.

I next met with Saleh in January 2012 in New York City, where he was receiving follow-up medical attention. His return to Yemen from Saudi Arabia the previous September had been met with more violence and hundreds more killed, and we once again discussed the transfer of power to Hadi, which he reluctantly agreed was inevitable. "What will I do in retirement, Mr. John?" he asked me.

"Maybe you should write a book about your life and your views on Middle East politics, or teach at Sanaa University," I told him, knowing full well that he would never withdraw from Yemen's political scene. Within four weeks of our meeting, Saleh relinquished the presidency.

I subsequently developed a close relationship with President Hadi, whose haberdasher and manicurist were far less busy than Saleh's. Hadi was a bit of a reluctant political warrior, although he became increasingly determined to lead Yemen out of its Arab Spring convulsions. He also was a very good counterterrorism partner. Hadi was very supportive of U.S. missile strikes and broader counterterrorism efforts to dismantle AQAP's extensive presence in the country, especially since it had taken firm root in the southern part of Yemen, which was Hadi's homeland. When I became CIA director, I continued to shuttle back and forth between Saudi Arabia and Yemen in hopes of easing Yemen's many political, economic, and security challenges and facilitating cooperation between the two countries. Hadi was an honest politician without a strong political base, which ultimately led to his overthrow in early 2015 by Iranian-supported Houthi rebels, who had forged an alliance with the opportunistic and still politically influential Saleh. Hadi became and remains a political exile in Saudi Arabia, and Saleh was felled by a Houthi sniper bullet in December 2017 while he was in the process of switching sides, once again, in Yemen's tragic odyssey of internecine warfare. I guess he had used up his nine lives.

Along with Syria, Yemen is one of the great tragedies of the twenty-first century. A beautiful country with a rich culture and wonderful people, it has been decimated by years of bloodshed, malnourishment, corrupt leadership, extremist religious influence, and foreign intrigue. If any country deserves consideration of massive and sustained economic assistance and infrastructure development, it is Yemen. Along with Somalia, Yemen would be a country to consider for some form of international "receivership," wherein the United Nations or other multilateral institution would take custodial responsibility for dealing with its financial obligations, overseeing its budget, and implementing an economic recovery plan. Maybe it is a far-fetched idea, but I see no recourse to reversing the downward spiral of failed and failing states like Yemen without some form of aggressive international engagement.

With memories of my student days in Cairo forever etched in my mind's eye, I loved returning to Egypt during the Obama administration. The closest I came to an Egyptian leader when I was a student at AUC in the mid-1970s was when Anwar Sadat's motorcade sped past me one afternoon on its way to the airport, and I caught a glimpse of Sadat's pharaonic profile through the rear door window. In my subsequent visits to Egypt as a U.S. official, my time as a student in Cairo often became a subject of conversation with my Egyptian interlocutors, including the current president of Egypt. Abdel Fattah al-Sisi was director of military intelligence when we first met in 2010. He was an engaging dinner partner, and I found him to be a sophisticated observer of regional and world events. His comments, while sometimes critical of U.S. policies, were devoid of the usual polemics I encountered when meeting Arab officials for the first time. At dinner, al-Sisi cited and gave me a copy of a paper he wrote in 2006 while studying at the U.S. Army War College entitled

"Democracy in the Middle East." The paper was surprisingly critical of the Mubarak government's control of the media, tolerance
of blatant economic inequality, politically repressive security forces,
and responsibility for Egypt's high illiteracy rate. In the paper, al-
Sisi also advocated for less U.S. military support to governments in
the Middle East and for more U.S. investment in education. I found
the paper and al-Sisi's comments very refreshing, and I hoped that he
would play an even more important role in Egypt's future.

He has.

I met al-Sisi again many times in the aftermath of the Arab Spring,
when he became minister of defense, then deputy prime minister, and
ultimately president of Egypt in June 2014. We had extended conversations each time about the difficult challenges facing his country,
and I conveyed messages from President Obama about the importance
of al-Sisi's support for peaceful political reform in Egypt. Al-Sisi usually nodded in agreement as I went through my talking points, but
he would become quite animated and angry when he talked about
takfiris—violent Islamist extremists—whom he claimed had taken
his religion hostage. Frequently, he cited verses of the Quran as evidence of his strong personal faith and the apostasy of the *takfiris*.

I had three very memorable meetings with al-Sisi. The first was
when I traveled to Cairo in late 2012 to push President Muhammad
Morsi, who had been elected a few months earlier with the support
of the Muslim Brotherhood, to cooperate on a specific counterterrorism initiative. Morsi had selected al-Sisi to be his minister of defense,
and al-Sisi participated in my meeting with Morsi, which was held in
the presidential palace while angry demonstrators were gathering and
chanting outside the palace walls. Al-Sisi was appropriately deferential
to Morsi during the meeting, but I could tell from al-Sisi's demeanor
and the subtle comments he made to me beforehand that all was not
well between the two. Sure enough, al-Sisi spearheaded a palace coup
less than a year later, jailing the increasingly unpopular Morsi, who
remained incarcerated until he collapsed in a Cairo courtroom while

standing trial on espionage charges in June 2019. He subsequently died suddenly, according to Egyptian officials, of a heart attack.

Al-Sisi and I met again in February 2014 as the Egyptian government was preparing to hold a presidential election following the overthrow of Morsi. At the time, al-Sisi was held in high public regard for taking bold action against Morsi to de-escalate rising tensions and avoid bloodshed, and he was widely rumored to be on the verge of announcing his candidacy for president. After initial pleasantries and the obligatory several rounds of sweetened tea, al-Sisi asked me pointedly, "Do you think I should run for president, Mr. Director?" I was taken aback by the directness of his question. I certainly was not going to give him political advice, but I took the opportunity to highlight the magnitude of the many political, economic, and security challenges facing the next Egyptian president. "Anyone who decides to run for president of Egypt needs to have their eyes wide open about just how difficult the job will be, especially on the economic front," I said to him. "You have earned a very strong reputation for your accomplishments as a military officer, which is much different than being president. Your decision on whether to run for president is a very personal one, and one that you need to think deeply about." Not wanting to be drawn further into a political discussion, I shifted topics.

My last meeting with al-Sisi was in January 2016. He had been president for eighteen months, and there were widespread reports of Egyptian political activists being jailed by his security forces. There were other signs of al-Sisi's reliance on authoritarian measures to crack down on opposition elements, and I was sent to Egypt to underscore the Obama administration's growing concern about actions being taken under his watch. "Remember what you wrote in your War College paper," I said to him as he walked me outside when our meeting concluded. "Don't do the same things for which you criticized Mubarak."

Unfortunately, al-Sisi has opted to be an authoritarian leader rather than a bold and wise one, making it a question not of if but when another wrenching and likely bloody Arab Spring will return to the Egyptian streets.

Authoritarianism was alive and well when I visited Havana, Cuba, in August 2015, but I had reason to believe at the time that political reform might be in the offing. Full diplomatic relations between the United States and Cuba had been restored in July, and Secretary of State John Kerry visited the island nation two weeks before me. I had had a meeting in the United States earlier in the year with Alejandro Castro, the son of then-president Raúl Castro and overseer of Cuba's intelligence and security services. That meeting was part of the Obama administration's multiyear effort to normalize relations with Cuba, and the purpose of my visit was to explore intelligence cooperation and information sharing with the Cubans on terrorism, narcotics smuggling, and human trafficking. Having grown up in Hudson County, New Jersey, where many thousands of Cuban émigrés had settled in the aftermath of the 1959 revolution, I jumped at the opportunity to go to Cuba. Not only did I have many Cuban childhood friends who closely followed and discussed events in their former country, I also had grainy black-and-white photos of my mother's visit to Cuba in the late 1920s with her father and rum-running uncles.

As far as I know, I was the first CIA director to set foot on Cuban soil since the Agency's ill-fated 1962 Bay of Pigs invasion, and it didn't take long for that fifty-three-year-old seminal event in U.S.-Cuban relations to come to the fore during my visit. I arrived in Havana by plane on a rainy afternoon, and I marveled at the beautiful Cuban countryside and the vintage cars in pristine condition that I saw on the road during the drive into the city. I met Alejandro Castro the following morning at his headquarters. I was accompanied by members of the just-opened U.S. embassy in Havana and several CIA colleagues who traveled with me from Langley, and Alejandro was joined by about a dozen Cuban officials. Each team was lined up on its own side of a very long conference table, and Alejandro and I took turns making brief opening remarks on behalf of our respective delegations. Alejandro then embarked on what turned out to be a meandering year-by-year exegesis of the history of relations between Cuba and the United States (made longer by the need for English translation), with heavy emphasis on the heroic actions of his ailing uncle Fidel and his father Raúl in the face of U.S. transgressions. The Bay of Pigs fiasco was given special and lengthy attention. Before arriving, I was informed by my Cuba watchers that Alejandro would be likely to engage in some catharsis, but he was going well beyond what was even remotely reasonable. As I looked at the faces of his colleagues at the forty-five-minute mark, I noticed several of them rolling their eyes and wincing in seeming embarrassment at Alejandro's performance. It was at this point (and Alejandro had only reached the 1970s) that I interrupted him, saying we each had our own perspective on history. "We need to focus on the future, Alejandro," I said, "not on the past."

It took another ten minutes or so before he ended his remarks, which allowed us to have some worthwhile discussions about a framework for cooperation on issues of mutual concern. Despite the rocky start, I was very interested in reaching agreement on tangible next steps. The Cuban intelligence service is quite competent—as the CIA unfortunately has found out all too often over the years—and the Cuban intelligence officers I met that day and at dinner that evening were impressive and highly professional. They did not adopt the same ideological stance as Alejandro, and they seemed much more worldly in their understanding of broader geostrategic trends under way around the globe. I wanted the CIA to be able to tap into their knowledge and expertise despite Alejandro, who apparently did not think the lengthy harangue in the conference room was sufficient. When we adjourned for a late lunch in his dining room, where a garlic-and-lemon-flavored roasted pig and Cuban rum awaited us, he presented me with an inscribed copy of his book *The Price of Power,* a 289-page screed detailing the "contradictions, intemperance, and vice" of the United States toward Cuba and other worldwide "victims" of American imperialism. A Pulitzer Prize winner it is not.

That night, I walked the historic streets of Old Havana, peered into Ernest Hemingway's favorite watering holes, and toured the city's famed rum distilleries. And as my plane took off the next day and I watched the beautiful city of Havana recede in the distance, I was hopeful that Cuba's repressive security practices, political oppression, and socialist economy would also soon fade from view, which was the ultimate goal of normalized relations as envisioned by President Obama. Unfortunately, the Trump administration's abrupt decision to halt America's diplomatic rapprochement with Cuba and the Havana government's failure to take much-needed steps to open up its economy and enact political reforms have undermined the progress that was made in the last few years of the Obama administration.

My boyhood dream of someday meeting famous and powerful people has been more than realized by the opportunities I have had while serving in government. Sadly, I found out that few of the individuals I have met have been as heroic as Mickey Mantle and Roger Maris appeared to my youthful eyes.

25

DEALING WITH RUSSIAN INTRIGUE

During my first decade at the CIA I had no direct interaction with Soviet or Russian officials. As an analyst on the Middle East, I carefully tracked Moscow's efforts to expand its influence in the region and watched with keen interest throughout the 1980s its failed occupation of Afghanistan and the steady demise and ultimate collapse of the Soviet Union. It was during my stint in CTC that I first met Russian intelligence officials, at a hastily called counterterrorism exchange in Washington in 1992. With the Russian government struggling to steady itself after the many political dislocations of the previous two years, the CIA was encouraged to extend an intelligence olive branch to the successor organizations of its principal global adversary, the KGB. The symbolism of the get-together far outweighed the paltry substance of the exchange, and it did not trigger any real improvement in U.S.-Russian intelligence relations.

I subsequently made three visits to Russia, all to Moscow. Each time I arrived on a hulking, dark gray U.S. military transport aircraft that made an unmistakable "America has arrived" statement as it touched down at Sheremetyevo International Airport. The planes were always directed to park at a far corner of the airport, lest too many locals set eyes upon a visible symbol of America's military might. Whenever the military planes I traveled on overnighted at an airport overseas, armed U.S. military guards maintained 24-7 presence and vigilance to prevent any funny business by aggressive host-country intelligence and security services.

My first visit to Moscow was in August 2000, when I was George Tenet's chief of staff. The drive from the airport along the tall tree-lined highways into Moscow city center immediately brought to mind the images and musical score of the movie *Doctor Zhivago*. The overcast skies and the monotonous drab concrete apartment buildings of Soviet-era vintage—known as Khrushchyovka, for Russian Premier Nikita Khrushchev, who initiated their construction—gave a bleak if not foreboding impression of the local environment even before I entered the city center.

When I traveled with George, I didn't have much time to myself, and my first Moscow trip was no exception. His Moscow visit was replete with official meetings accompanied by a dizzying number of vodka toasts, excellent caviar, and very mediocre other food—but I usually remained holed up in our "control room" in the Ritz-Carlton Hotel. It was my responsibility to read and prepare intelligence reports related to the trip as well as to stay in close touch with CIA headquarters on all other matters of national security concern. During our visit, we were tracking frenzied Russian efforts to recover their nuclear-powered submarine *Kursk,* which sank in the Barents Sea from an internal explosion just four days before our arrival, tragically killing all 118 personnel on board. To stymie inevitable Russian attempts to use their sophisticated technical collection capabilities against our visiting delegation, an opaque tent had been set up inside the hotel control room so that our team could securely handle classified material without observation from Russian cameras that might be hidden in the ceiling or walls. This is standard practice for any overseas travel by agency and department heads who bring classified documents or computer systems with them.

Not being a Russia specialist, I did not know if I was ever going to make it back to Moscow, so I was determined to do some sight-seeing at the crack of dawn and late at night, before and after carrying out my official responsibilities. It was the one and only time I was able to wander around Moscow, a truly beautiful city, without an accompanying U.S. security detail. Like any other U.S. official visiting or living in Russia, I assumed that I picked up a Russian intelligence tail as soon as I left the hotel. A series of bombings by Chechen separatists from the Caucasus, targeting a shopping mall and apartment buildings in and around Moscow the year before, made me wary of loitering at any one location for too long. Flashy Western-style stores selling luxury goods and expensive fashions from Paris and Milan dotted the downtown landscape, although a good deal of homelessness and poverty could be seen as well. Less than a decade after the collapse of the Soviet Union, my first visit to the Russian Federation reinforced my general impression that the country still had a long way to go before it could emerge from the political, so-cial, and economic consequences of its Communist past.

I had periodic routine interactions with Russian diplomats and intelligence officials during my subsequent work at the National Counterterrorism Center and in the White House. In the aftermath of 9/11, I briefed visiting Russian counterterrorism delegations in an effort both to thwart terrorist attacks against Russian interests as well as to encourage the Russians to share terrorism-related threat information with us. My American colleagues always complained that our intelligence exchanges were wholly lopsided, with Russian offerings paling in quantity and quality compared to what we provided them. While I agreed that the information flow was mostly one way, I saw the disparity more as a reflection of the vastly more extensive and capable U.S. collection and analytic capabilities that were directed against terrorist organizations, especially al-Qa'ida, than an intentional Russian effort to withhold threat information from us. "Let's show them how good we are," I said to my skeptical teammates, "and maybe some American professionalism will rub off on them." My hope was that the Russian services would reorient a greater share of their sophisticated intelligence apparatus away from American targets and toward terrorist groups. This would turn out to be another one of my unmet aspirations.

I made my second visit to Russia, and first as CIA director, in June 2013. Mikhail Fradkov, the head of Russia's Foreign Intelligence Service (SVR) had invited me to visit Moscow when we spoke shortly after he called to congratulate me on my confirmation as CIA director. The SVR is the CIA's principal Russian counterpart and has responsibility for recruiting spies and collecting intelligence outside Russia. An economist and trade specialist by educational background and training, Fradkov worked his way to the upper echelons first through the Soviet bureaucracy and then in the fledgling Russian government. He was serving as Russia's representative to the European Union when, in March of 2004, President Putin unexpectedly appointed him prime minister. This was considered a safe choice by Putin, as Fradkov had earned a reputation as a competent, albeit unremarkable, functionary without a personal political power base. When Fradkov was selected to head the SVR in late 2007 as part of a government shake-up, it was once again seen as a crafty move by Putin, who undoubtedly preferred someone without intelligence experience or political ambition to serve as the nominal head of his old organization.

By the time I had arrived in Moscow as CIA director, Fradkov had already been politically damaged as a result of the embarrassment of the 2010 arrest and expulsion from the United States of ten deep-cover Russian intelligence officers—referred to as "illegals"—who had burrowed into American society using false personas (the factual basis for the TV show *The Americans*). One of the most challenging aspects of that case was deciding how to handle the timing and announcement of the arrests so as not to scuttle a scheduled visit to the United States by then–Russian president Dmitry Medvedev. It was decided after lengthy discussions among senior national security and counterintelligence officials that the arrests would take place immediately after Medvedev's U.S. visit and his meeting the following weekend with President Obama at a G20 gathering in Canada. Participating in many meetings on the illegals, I found it fascinating to see how the timing and public acknowledgment of law enforcement activities—in this instance a counterintelligence operation—can be adjusted but not compromised to avoid undermining important foreign policy objectives.

I found the discussions in Moscow with Fradkov and his SVR team rather stuffy and unnourishing and wouldn't be surprised if they did as well. Each side took turns giving rather generic presentations on terrorism and nuclear proliferation—topics agreed upon beforehand given the general commonality of U.S. and Russian interests on both topics. The scripted briefings required translations on both sides, belaboring the pain. Although Fradkov spoke only in Russian, he demonstrated a good understanding of English—undoubtedly developed during his diplomatic postings in Europe. Several times he corrected a very nervous and not very competent SVR translator. It was only in our brief one-on-one conversations on the sidelines of the group meeting and following the dinner when he spoke in near-fluent English to me. Despite his formal manner, Fradkov was by no means an unpleasant fellow. He was a gracious host with a refined bearing and demeanor, which stood in stark contrast to his subordinates, whose rumpled and ill-fitting suits along with crass manners gave away their KGB lineage. I came away from my meetings with Fradkov with a strong sense that he was going through the motions of being SVR director, avoiding organizational or operational risks that might further diminish his political standing. I very much liked the idea that Russia's principal foreign intelligence agency was being led by this rather uncharismatic and cautious individual.

As head of the SVR, Fradkov was my official host and counterpart, but I was most interested in meeting Alexander Bortnikov, the head of Russia's internal security organization—the Federal Security Service (FSB). The FSB is frequently described as the Russian equivalent of the FBI, but that comparison does a great injustice to the Bureau. When the KGB was disestablished in 1991, the FSB assumed responsibility for monitoring, suppressing, and, at times, eliminating domestic threats to the Russian government. The FSB is a brutal, thuggish, and thoroughly politicized organization dedicated to doing whatever the higher-ups in the Kremlin want done, up to and including torture and murder. The FSB's counterintelligence authorities have given it free license to track and disrupt activities by Russians and non-Russians alike, including the many foreign diplomats residing on Russian soil. Indeed, it was Bortnikov's FSB that gave me the most heartburn after I returned to government service. At the White House and the CIA, I consumed a steady diet of State Department cables and intelligence reports about heavy-handed actions carried out by the FSB against domestic Russian dissidents and, at times, even U.S. diplomats and private U.S. citizens living, studying, and working in Russia.

Our ambassador in Moscow at the time was the very accomplished Mike McFaul, a preeminent Soviet and Russian specialist who took an extended sabbatical from his professorship at Stanford University in order to join the Obama administration. Before becoming ambassador, Mike had served as the senior director for Russian and Eurasian affairs on the National Security Council staff, where he was Obama's principal adviser on Russia and the planned "reset" in relations. Mike and I had a very good working relationship when we served together in Washington, and he encouraged me to come to Moscow at my earliest opportunity, seeing it as a way to enhance communication and understanding between senior U.S. and Russian officials. By the time of my visit, Mike had been ambassador in Moscow for about eighteen months and was an increasingly outspoken critic of Putin's autocratic style and policies. Mike and I had several conversations about my trip before my Moscow visit, and we agreed that I should confront Bortnikov directly and tell him that the FSB needed to desist from its harsh tactics.

Like Fradkov, Bortnikov greeted me at the entrance of his building upon my arrival. Unlike Fradkov, Bortnikov welcomed me with a smile on his face. Shorter and slighter than Fradkov, he showed an affable and relaxed style and an easy demeanor that belied his organization's brutish reputation and behavior. I did not return the pleasant look nor the warm greeting, as I wanted to demonstrate from the outset my displeasure with the actions of his organization. Once we were settled in the FSB's conference room and introductions were made by both sides, Bortnikov gave brief opening remarks, welcoming my visit and emphasizing the importance of improved relations between the United States and Russia, including between its intelligence and security services. Throughout his remarks, the soft-spoken Bortnikov maintained his smile and even tried to lighten the atmosphere with some levity. Russian humor is an acquired taste, however, and one that I have never really developed.

With Ambassador McFaul at my side, I slowly walked through my talking points. I agreed that improved relations between Russia and the United States were in the best interests of both countries and would enhance the prospects for peace and stability in many parts of the world. I said that my visit was intended to send such a signal to senior Russian officials and that I hoped that there would be more such visits—by both sides—in the future. I then launched into a recounting and corresponding stern rebuke of the numerous FSB transgressions that were directed against Americans in Russia. Citing one especially egregious example that involved a physical assault, I termed such incidents "unacceptable" and said that, if continued, they would be met by a stiff U.S. response. Some of the FSB officials who were seated at the conference table shifted uncomfortably if not angrily in their seats as I delivered what I had hoped would be received as a figurative two-by-four upside the head. Throughout my presentation, Bortnikov kept his eyes focused on me and took only a few notes. His smile dimmed only somewhat when I detailed the incidents of most serious concern, but he showed no outward sign of being perturbed by my remarks.

None of us on the American side of the conference table knew how Bortnikov was going to react to my presentation. After a slight and seemingly pensive pause, Bortnikov began to speak in a measured and unemotional manner. He expressed appreciation for my candor and once again reiterated the importance of better relations between Washington and Moscow. He then countered my opening thrust by saying that Russian citizens and diplomats in the United States had been continuously harassed by U.S. intelligence and law enforcement agencies for many years. He termed such incidents contrary to the words of U.S. government officials who claimed they wanted better relations with the Russian government. Bortnikov's return volley about alleged mistreatment of Russians in the United States was a trite talking point used by Russian officials in both Washington and Moscow. The FBI, thankfully, has routinely kept an up-close-and-personal watch on known and suspected Russian intelligence officers in the United States, which I am sure the Russians consider harassment. Moreover, Bortnikov needed to say something that would soothe the bruised feelings of his FSB underlings in the room, who had to suffer in silence during my opening gambit. Indeed, their dour faces perked up when he went on the offensive, albeit a relatively mild one.

Bortnikov then took a tack that foreshadowed virtually all my subsequent dealings with him, which was to avoid confrontation and to lessen whatever tension might be in the air. He said that some of his officers might have gotten a bit "carried away" when they were conducting their professional duties. "It happens in all organizations," he noted. With that, he gave me a Cheshire-cat smile, as if to say, "this is the type of business we're in and sometimes things like this happen on both sides." Bortnikov never apologized for any of the harsh tactics employed by FSB officers, and the remainder of the day's discussion focused mainly on terrorism issues and recent developments in the Middle East. By the time I climbed back aboard the U.S. military aircraft that awaited me at Moscow's international airport the next day, I had a strong sense that it was more important for me to cultivate a working relationship with Bortnikov than with Fradkov. As head of the internal service, I knew that Bortnikov had the ability—to the extent allowed by Putin—to dial up or down the pressure applied on U.S. citizens and diplomats, which was my principal area of concern. Moreover, Bortnikov's self-confidence and willingness to talk freely in front of his subordinates indicated to me that his position was secure, suggesting he had a stronger relationship with Putin than did Fradkov. By the time we took off for my next stop, I had decided that I would make an extra effort to cultivate a personal relationship with Bortnikov.

I would meet with Bortnikov twice more and talk on the phone with him about a dozen times during the remainder of my tenure as CIA director. When Bortnikov was tapped to head Russia's delegation to attend a White House–sponsored summit on countering violent extremism in February 2015—another indication of Bortnikov's favored position in the Putin government—I saw it as a good opportunity to meet Bortnikov on my turf. I had spoken to him periodically since my 2013 visit to maintain a personal connection, even though relations between Washington and Moscow suffered another serious downturn in 2014 as a result of Russia's invasion and annexation of Crimea. Despite the stated discomfort of some senior CIA operations officers who did not favor Bortnikov visiting Langley headquarters, I extended an invitation to him through established liaison channels. Bortnikov quickly responded in the affirmative.

There was something quite surreal as well as personally satisfying in greeting the head of Russia's internal security service in the lobby of CIA headquarters in full view of the large and famous Agency seal that adorns the marble floor. It was one of the many times in my career when I was struck by how much my life had changed from my days growing up in my blue-collar neighborhood of New Jersey and how honored I was to represent my government as director of the CIA. Bortnikov was his usual smiling self, and, as there had been no incidents of outrageous FSB actions toward U.S. diplomats in Russia since our last meeting, I returned the smile. We spent a few minutes talking in front of the Memorial Wall and then met for over an hour in my office. I delivered an official and what was by then an oft-repeated U.S. government démarche on Crimea and Ukraine that had been heard and dismissed by countless Russian officials in the preceding year. The remainder of our discussion focused on the continued political turmoil and sectarian fighting that was raging in Syria, Libya, and Yemen. During this meeting Bortnikov and I agreed to increase the frequency of our dialogue on Syria in light of the escalation of fighting between Syrian government troops and the patchwork of anti-government forces that spanned the country's wide secular-to-Islamist extremist spectrum.

Over the next twelve months, I had numerous phone conversations with Bortnikov. I called him once when I was in Afghanistan. We both lamented the tremendous loss of life among Afghans and non-Afghans that had occurred over the last several decades in the war-torn country. Most of our conversations focused on Syria. While I knew that Bortnikov was not responsible for Russia's policy in the Middle East, he was part of Putin's inner circle. He also demonstrated that he had direct and immediate contact with the Russian leader. During one National Security Council meeting on Syria in early 2016, I was asked to step out of the meeting and call Bortnikov in order to get a quick response from Putin on an issue related to cease-fire negotiations. Less than thirty minutes after I spoke to Bortnikov, he called me back with Putin's purported agreement.

It was in the spring of 2016 when the storm clouds portending the unprecedented scale and scope of Russia's interference in the U.S. presidential election started to come into focus for me. Russia, and before it the Soviet Union, had long been engaged in efforts to shape electoral outcomes in liberal democratic societies, especially in Europe, as well as in other parts of the world. Using intimidation, blackmail, and financial inducements, Russian intelligence services would seek to bribe and recruit political candidates who, if elected, would support Moscow's political and economic objectives. In addition, the Russians made extensive use of witting and unwitting sources in foreign media to disseminate political propaganda and disinformation designed to promote the electoral prospects of candidates they favored and to hurt the chances of those they opposed. Before the advent of the digital age, these activities were limited to only what was possible in the physical domain. With the explosive growth of the cyber environment in the early years of the twenty-first century, Russian intelligence services—indeed, intelligence services worldwide—exploited the new and readily accessible World Wide Web to ply their covert-influence efforts. And by 2016, the offensive cyber capabilities of Russian military, intelligence, and security services were among the world's very best—and most practiced— including, but not limited to, the pursuit of desired foreign election outcomes.

Russian interference in the 2016 U.S. presidential election took place against the backdrop of intense diplomatic interaction between U.S. and Russian officials on the increasingly chaotic situation in Syria, where the Arab Spring–inspired civil war had been raging for five years. In the summer of 2015, the mostly uncoordinated efforts of secular and Islamist extremist rebel forces in the northern part of Syria had combined to make important territorial gains, raising the specter of a possible insurgent breakthrough to the capital city of Damascus. A flurry of Russian diplomatic activity made it clear that Putin was concerned about the potential fall of the Bashar al-Asad regime, and he publicly contrasted Moscow's willingness to support its beleaguered Arab partners with what he claimed was Washington's abandonment of Egyptian president Mubarak. In September 2015 Putin deployed thousands of Russian troops as well as advanced combat aircraft and heavy weaponry to Syria to reverse the fortunes of Syrian government forces. Putin had calculated, correctly it turned out, that neither the Obama administration nor other governments that had been supporting Syrian rebel forces would match the sharply increased Russian investment. Within six months, Russian-led combat operations, which included long-range missile strikes from Russian land bases and naval vessels, altered the tide of the battle significantly and, ultimately, decisively.

In the spring of 2016, however, the Russians and Syrians were still frustrated at their inability to wrest control of the rebel-held eastern portion of the northern city of Aleppo, which had been Syria's most populous and prosperous before it was largely destroyed and bifurcated by conflict. As the result of an e fort to reunite the city under government control, Aleppo became the focus of an intense Russian and Syrian bombing campaign that sought to dislodge thousands of insurgents who had taken refuge in the city. While President Obama was unwilling to confront the Russians in Syria with U.S. military force, he was eager to stem the bloodshed and avert a humanitarian crisis among the more than three hundred thousand men, women, and children still holed up in the eastern part of Aleppo. The indefatigable Secretary of State John Kerry, after successfully negotiating the Joint Comprehensive Plan of Action on Iran's nuclear program and the Paris Agreement on greenhouse-gas emissions the year before, became heavily engaged in pressing the Russians to agree to a "cessation of hostilities" that would allow noncombatants and rebel fighters in eastern Aleppo to travel safely to areas still under insurgent control north of the city. Initial attempts to secure a cessation-of-hostilities agreement collapsed in the face of violations by both sides; even when the Russians seemingly agreed to the outlines of a cease-fire, Moscow routinely ignored the terms and allowed Syrian forces to conduct military operations against rebel forces in designated safe zones. Given in-depth CIA expertise on the many domestic factions and foreign actors involved in the Syrian conflict, I was asked by the White House to support Kerry's efforts by engaging directly with Russian officials.

In late March 2016, I traveled to Moscow to meet with senior Russian officials to push them to engage more seriously in negotiations that would allow at least a temporary halt to the bombing and the fighting in Aleppo. With the situation on the ground rapidly deteriorating, my trip was hurriedly arranged. In addition to my request to see FSB Director Bortnikov and SVR Director Fradkov, I also asked to see two other senior Russian officials whose portfolios included Syria. One was Putin's chief of staff, Sergei Ivanov, a longtime Putin ally and fellow former KGB officer who was widely considered to be the major architect of Russia's Syria policy. A former secretary of the Security Council, first deputy prime minister, and minister of defense, Ivanov was one of Putin's closest policy advisers. If anyone other than Putin had the ability to shape Russia's Syria policy, including on the siege of Aleppo, I believed it would be Ivanov.

Accompanied by McFaul's successor, U.S. Ambassador John Tefft, and an embassy translator, I met with Ivanov and his translator in the Kremlin. Ivanov was personable but formal. We didn't spend more than a couple of minutes on introductory pleasantries; discussion on Syria dominated the forty-five-minute meeting. Ivanov demonstrated a strong understanding of the history of the civil war, its multiple factions, and the military situation on the ground around Aleppo, confirming my assessment that he was deeply involved in Russian policy formulation on Syria. He asked good questions and evinced—or I should say feigned—an interest in Russia's signing on to a cessation-of-hostilities agreement that would avoid further bloodshed. His biggest concern was the increasingly large

ISIS representation within the Syrian opposition. "American policies are allowing the Islamists to gain strength in Syria and throughout the Middle East. You are supporting terrorists," he claimed with apparent conviction. This had been the Russians' primary argument over the previous two years and was being used by Moscow to justify what amounted to wanton atrocities by Syrian regime forces against all opposition groups.

I explained that the Syrian opposition was highly fractured, and I disputed his allegation regarding U.S. support to terrorist groups. "We agree that ISIS presents a grave threat to regional stability and needs to be crushed. But supporting authoritarian leaders and their brutally repressive tactics is not the way to weaken ISIS's popular support." Ivanov frowned as he listened to me, but I pressed on. "It is important for the United States and Russia to work together to halt the bloodshed. If we don't bring down the level of violence, there is no way that meaningful negotiations can take place between the Syrian government and the opposition." By the end of the meeting, it was apparent to me that the Russians would remain steadfast in their support for Asad. I found the meeting interesting but unproductive in bridging differences of view.

I also requested a meeting with the newly appointed director of Russian military intelligence (the GRU), Igor Korobov, whose predecessor had died suddenly the month before while on a foreign trip. With heavy Russian military involvement in Syria, the GRU had the intelligence lead for the Russian team involved in cease-fire negotiations. When I met with Korobov and his GRU Syrian experts, we had a detailed exchange of information on what each side considered viable for a durable cessation-of-hostilities agreement. My impression of Korobov was that he was overwhelmed by his appointment and a bit unsure of himself, and even a bit nervous, during our exchange. What I didn't know at the time was that the GRU, just one week before my visit, had used a simple but highly effective spear phishing attack to access the computer—and more than fifty thousand emails—of John

Podesta, Hillary Clinton's campaign chairman. Maybe Korobov was nervous during our meeting because he wondered whether I knew at the time that his organization had successfully conducted its first round of election-related cyberattacks. I wish I had known, but I didn't. The following month, the GRU stepped up its efforts and gained access to the servers of the Democratic National Committee (DNC) and the Democratic Congressional Campaign Committee (DCCC), infecting at least thirty DNC computers with malicious malware.

I departed Moscow with only the barest of hopes that the Russians would work in earnest to forge an agreement among the warring Syrian factions that would allow safe passage out of Aleppo for anyone wanting to leave. Those slim hopes were dashed in subsequent months, however, as the Russians and their Syrian cocombatants steadily battered the eastern section of the city into a very bloody and costly submission. The death and dislocation of millions of Syrians and the destruction of much of the country during the civil war was one of the most painful chapters of the Obama administration. I deeply regret that we failed to prevent the escalating cycle of violence.

It was in early 2016 when the U.S. intelligence community uncovered cyber efforts by the Russians, Chinese, and other intelligence services to hack into the networks of U.S. presidential campaigns. Those attempts, reminiscent of similar efforts in the run-up to the 2008 and 2012 campaigns, were neither surprising nor overwhelming. Foreign governments, especially adversarial ones, have always been eager to learn who has influence as well as what policy positions are being advocated within the campaigns of aspiring presidential candidates. Most often, the cyber activities were designed to collect politically sensitive information that could be exploited when a new administration took office. In an early sign of the major trouble that was looming, the Office of the Director of National Intelligence publicly acknowledged in May that "foreign intelligence services have been tracking this election cycle like no other." Jim Clapper emphasized the point in a public appearance at the Bipartisan Policy Center in Washington the same month, prophetically saying that "we'll probably have more" cyberattacks before the election.

When DCLeaks.com (a website later identified as a front for Russian cyber-espionage efforts) and Guccifer 2.0 (a persona later identified as being operated by the GRU) released thousands of stolen emails from the Democrats in June, it became readily apparent that the cyber theft of emails was not simply an intelligence collection effort designed to gain advanced insight into the inner workings of the major presidential campaigns. Rather, the public release of the emails signaled an intentional effort to embarrass and politically hurt the Democratic candidate, Hillary Clinton. And when nearly twenty thousand stolen emails from the Democratic National Committee were released on July 22 by WikiLeaks, which already had an established reputation for disseminating information received from Russian intelligence services, I became convinced that Moscow had embarked on an unprecedented campaign to interfere in the election. But what I didn't know at the time was whether the Russians were simply trying to bloody Hillary Clinton so that she would be weakened politically if she won the November election, as was predicted by most polls, or making a serious effort to get the Republican candidate, Donald Trump, elected.

In many respects, both objectives made sense. Putin had a rather frosty relationship with Clinton when she was secretary of state, blaming her for helping spark protests in Moscow in December 2011 with her public call for a full investigation into reports of fraud and intimidation in the just-concluded Russian legislative elections. Putin viewed her comments as a direct effort to undermine him. Putin also had long harbored a grudge against former president Bill Clinton that dated back many years. Not only did Putin feel that the

Clinton administration had not done enough to facilitate Russia's political and economic transition in the years following the dissolution of the Soviet Union, the Russian leader also felt that President Clinton intentionally slighted him at the United Nations General Assembly in September 2000. It was Clinton's final address as U.S. president, and he gave an inspiring farewell speech to an auditorium overflowing with diplomats, dignitaries, and members of the press who had gathered to hear the parting words of the respected statesman. Clinton left the auditorium immediately after speaking, prompting many of those in attendance to do so as well. The next speaker was the newly inaugurated president of Russia, Vladimir Putin, who delivered his speech to a half-full auditorium, a development he blamed on Clinton.

As a businessman without any government or foreign policy experience who was well known for being more interested in making deals than for taking principled positions on policy issues, Trump was an attractive candidate to Moscow. Putin had good experience cutting deals with businessmen who had become heads of government—Italy's Silvio Berlusconi being a prime example—and his goal of ridding Russia of U.S. sanctions imposed after the annexation of Crimea would take quite a bit of deal making. It also was no secret that Trump and Putin were openly flirting with one another, as each made flattering public comments about the other over the preceding year.

By the time of the WikiLeaks email dump in July, CIA officers working on Russia, cyber, and counterintelligence issues had grown increasingly concerned about the potential scale and scope of Russian activities focused on the November election. There had been numerous press reports about suspected Russian efforts over the previous months, but some of the more insidious and potentially damaging Russian activities were known only to a small number of intelligence and law enforcement professionals responsible for tracking clandestine Russian activities. As the telltale signs of Russian-intelligence tradecraft related to the election started to come into starker relief, concerns steadily rose in Langley.

When I arrived in my office on Monday, July 25, I told my staff that I wanted to read everything relevant to Russian interference in elections. I had great confidence in the CIA officers working on the issue, but I wanted to absorb as much information as I could in anticipation of a discussion I would need to have with senior administration officials, including President Obama. I asked to see "raw" intelligence, which is the actual information obtained from human and technical sources before it is subsequently processed and turned into finished intelligence reports that are disseminated outside the CIA. As a former analyst, I wanted to have as complete and thorough an understanding as possible about the Russians' capabilities and what they might be up to so that I could field whatever question might be directed my way. Over the course of that last week of July, I consumed a wide variety of raw intelligence, finished intelligence reports, and analytic assessments relevant to Russian intelligence activities in and against the United States. My reading was supplemented by meetings with the CIA's world-class Russia, cyber, and counterintelligence experts, and I also reviewed several seminal CIA and FBI studies and assessments that had been done on major Russian espionage cases. I had been involved in many counterintelligence investigations involving Russian spying activities over the course of my career and was quite familiar with the tactics the Russians used to cultivate relationships with unsuspecting individuals who fell prey to their spy craft. In particular, I reviewed closely the case of the ten Russian "illegals," who were arrested and deported in 2010, when I was working at the White House. The exposure of that Russian SVR program gave me good insight into the techniques and mechanisms used by Russian intelligence operating inside the United States.

By early Thursday morning, July 28, I was done with my reading and internal discussions and called my deputy, David Cohen, into my office. David also had been reviewing his own set of documents and reports related to Russian intelligence activities, and it was time to do a gut check with him. I greatly valued David's counsel and insight, as he had routinely proved to have an exceptionally good eye for detail when reviewing intelligence reports. His Yale Law School training obviously had paid dividends. He sat down and looked at the conference table in my office, which had piled on it large three-ring binders, writing tablets, and individual documents, all of which were extensively tabbed and highlighted in yellow marker.

After comparing notes, we agreed that the threat was serious, and I told him I had decided to talk to the president about it.

I picked up my secure line and, unable to reach the national security adviser, Susan Rice, I spoke to Avril Haines, who was Rice's principal deputy. I was cryptic in my comments. "Avril, I need to see the president. It is really important that I do so today." I told her that the CIA had uncovered some very disturbing developments related to the November election. "This sensitive information must be restricted to just the core national security group. That's it."

When I received word that my appointment with the president would be at 1:45 P.M. that day, I reached out to Jim Clapper to let him know that I had requested to talk to the president and that he could join me if he was available. Jim was out of the office and was busy the entire day, so I told his principal deputy, Stephanie O'Sullivan, that I would be meeting the president and would give Jim a full readout afterward.

When I arrived at the White House, Avril told me that only she, Susan, and Denis would be joining the discussion with the president. The vice president and Lisa Monaco had other commitments. We entered the president's dining area adjacent to the Oval Office, where he was seated at the small table awaiting his lunch. White House photographer Pete Souza snapped a few photos of us seated at the table and then was excused. I started off with an overarching statement before getting into the specifics.

"Mr. President, it appears that the Russian effort to undermine the integrity of the November election is much more intense, determined, and insidious than any we have seen before." I went on to share the details of what we knew, how we knew it, and why I was so confident in the assessment. "President Putin has authorized these activities, which appear to be designed to hurt Hillary Clinton and to boost the election prospects of Donald Trump." I gave a short review of Russia's history of interfering in foreign elections, especially in Europe, and explained how the explosive growth of the digital domain gave Moscow many more opportunities to shape electoral politics abroad. "Unfortunately, the Russians are exceptionally capable when it comes to cyber activities, and it looks like Putin has unleashed his intelligence services in advance of the election."

President Obama listened carefully while he methodically consumed the lunch of soup, garden salad, and iced tea that had been set in front of him. The "Obama stare" kicked in soon after I began talking, so I knew I had his attention. As soon as I finished speaking, questions started to fly. "Can the Russians get into the electoral infrastructure? Could they change vote tallies? What about money going into campaigns?" I answered a few questions and punted on others, promising to provide follow-up responses.

"We're trying to figure this all out," I said. "We have experience with Russian interference in European elections, including the use of money to buy off members of the media, politicians, and political parties. The FBI can provide details on what the Russians have done in previous U.S. elections."

I told the president that I would discuss the way ahead with Jim Clapper, Jim Comey, and Mike Rogers at NSA. "The CIA, FBI, and NSA need to work together on this. I would like to pull together a joint team to coordinate the collection and analysis of the intelligence so that we can provide regular coordinated updates to you and others who will need to be briefed on this." A discussion then ensued about the options available to counter Russian activities. It was agreed that we first needed to understand as much as we could about the Russian attack plan. Once the picture became clearer, we could then identify and decide on the options available.

"What are you planning to do on the congressional front?" Denis asked. Although I knew we would need to brief Congress, I hadn't yet thought through a congressional game plan. Damn.

"Well," I started speaking as I was thinking. "The most sensitive intelligence should be limited to the Gang of Eight. They have a good track record of keeping sensitive intelligence matters secret. We can't afford leaks. They would be devastating, and our ability to learn more about Russian plans and capabilities could dry up in an instant." Hmmm . . . that wasn't a bad off-the-cuff response, I thought.

The president nodded and directed me to pull together a briefing for the Gang of Eight. "What about the campaigns?" he said. "They need to know what the Russians are up to." The president remembered well the briefings on cyberattacks that he, his advisers, and his campaign IT specialists received from the FBI in the run-up to the 2008 election, when the Chinese were particularly aggressive against networks used by the Obama and McCain campaigns. Denis responded immediately.

"I'll work with John to coordinate the outreach to Congress. FBI has the lead to brief the campaigns about cyber threats, so we'll work this with Jim Comey."

The discussion lasted about thirty minutes. By the time I climbed back into my waiting SUV outside the West Wing, I felt that everyone in the room understood the seriousness of the issue and that next steps were agreed upon. "Now the hard part starts," I thought. "What can we do to stop the Russians?"

Early the next morning I met with Jim Clapper at his Liberty Crossing office to tell him about my discussion with President Obama. When I returned to my office at Langley, I spoke to Jim Comey on the secure line for about fifteen minutes to give him a similar readout. We discussed our shared concern about the picture of Russian meddling in the November election that was steadily emerging. I told Comey that the CIA would provide the Bureau everything we learned about Russian activities, including anything about the possible witting or unwitting involvement of Americans. I also spoke at some point that day or the next to Mike Rogers at NSA. Clapper, Comey, and Rogers all agreed that we needed to keep the intelligence in strict confidence, in light of the exceptionally sensitive counterintelligence equities and privacy concerns at stake.

Following up on my conversation with President Obama, Jim Comey, Mike Rogers, and I decided to send some of our Russia, cyber, and counterintelligence experts to be part of a "fusion cell" that could cross-check and share information being collected by the three agencies. I did not want excessive compartmentalization and bureaucratic walls to inhibit necessary information sharing among the CIA, FBI, and NSA on such a serious matter. I had witnessed previous instances of institutional rivalries during my career that had inhibited mission success, and I decided to take tangible steps to prevent it from happening again. Within days, the FBI and NSA augmented the staff they already had in residence at the CIA, and the fusion cell was up and running.

Despite being in the throes of a frantic effort to uncover and help thwart Moscow's attempts to interfere in the presidential election, I still had to deal with the Russians on Syria as well as on other developments as required. One such development had occurred in June, when a uniformed Russian FSB guard tackled and tried to prevent a U.S. diplomat from entering the front door of our embassy in Moscow. In the struggle, which was captured on one of the embassy's security cameras, the diplomat's shoulder was dislocated. In the aftermath of the incident, I asked to speak to Bortnikov to denounce, once again, the thuggish and violent behavior of the FSB. The call was postponed several times, probably because he anticipated what

I was calling about. Eventually the call was scheduled to take place on Thursday, August 4.

As I was reviewing my talking points for the call the evening before, I decided that it would be appropriate—indeed, important—for me to raise Russia's election meddling directly with Bortnikov. I called Avril and explained why I wanted to raise it with him, hoping that she would then try to convince others at the White House that it was the prudent thing to do. "I can cite the press stories about the stolen emails and reported Russian involvement," I told her, "and I can do this without revealing the extent of our knowledge and jeopardizing sensitive sources and methods. There is just no way I want to have a conversation with the head of Russia's premier security service, who happens to be one of Putin's closest confidants, and not say anything about ongoing Russian efforts to interfere in our election. What message would we be sending to the Russians if I say nothing? We need to tell them in no uncertain terms that they need to knock it off. My call with Bortnikov gives us an opportunity to brush them back now with a high hard one." I was not sure if Avril understood my baseball metaphor, but I was on a roll. "I'll clear it with Clapper and Comey, and I am sure that they will be supportive." Avril agreed with my argument and asked for the talking points that I would propose to use. With some effort and cajoling, she convinced others at the White House, some of whom were uncertain whether I should be the first administration official to raise the issue with the Russians, to sign off on my proposed talking points by the following morning.

I had three topics for my call with Bortnikov. First, I discussed Russia's continued failure to prevent repeated Syrian violations of the cessation-of-hostilities agreements on Aleppo that had been forged among the warring factions. I dispensed with this issue rather quickly, as I knew that Bortnikov would just relay my points to Foreign Minister Sergey Lavrov, who had assumed Russia's diplomatic lead on Syria negotiations along with Chief of Staff Ivanov. I next hit Bortnikov hard on the injured American diplomat. "This is in direct contravention of your personal assurances to me that American diplomats would not be physically mistreated by your officers." While I didn't threaten retaliatory treatment, I did mention that the FBI had never engaged in physical altercations with Russian diplomats and that we expected reciprocal treatment. Bortnikov disputed the facts and claimed that the U.S. diplomat attacked the FSB guard. I simply told him that he was wrong and that we had videotapes to prove it.

I then turned to my election talking points, which went along the following lines:

- There is widespread press reporting about Russian attempts to interfere in our upcoming presidential election. Some reports claim that Russian intelligence services are involved in the hacking of computer networks affiliated with the Democratic Party and the subsequent public release of stolen emails.
- If these reports are accurate, Russian intelligence services should stop such activities immediately. Any further attempts to interfere in the election would seriously roil U.S.-Russia relations and prevent cooperation between our governments on important bilateral and multilateral issues for many years to come.
- Interference in our election will backfire. All Americans would be outraged at any Russian attempt to interfere in the most solemn foundation of our democratic system of government—the right to choose our elected officials, including the president, without outside interference.

Bortnikov's response was as anticipated. "Mr. Director, Russia would never dream of interfering in any foreign election, especially a U.S. presidential election. We are ready to work with whomever the America people choose to be the next president. This is just another example of Russia being blamed for something that it is not responsible for."

"Alexander," I said sternly. "I ask that you convey these points to President Putin immediately. It is important that he understand the seriousness of this issue and the consequences of Russian interference in our election." While it was the GRU and not the FSB that was the primary Russian service involved in hacking into Democratic networks, I was sure that Bortnikov was fully aware of what was going on. I also was confident that Bortnikov would relay my talking points to Putin. I never heard back from Bortnikov. In fact, my conversation with him that day about Russian interference in the presidential election was the last conversation I had with him or any other Russian official.

Consistent with presidential guidance, the CIA's Office of Congressional Affairs contacted the offices of all Gang of Eight members during the first week of August to let them know that I needed to speak to them personally about an important and sensitive matter. Both the Senate and the House were already on their summer recess, so we deferred to the members on when and where they wanted to schedule the briefings. We said that each member could have one senior staffer with the requisite clearances in the briefing.

Three briefings took place in August and five in September. For each briefing, I used carefully prepared talking points that described what we knew and didn't know about the extent and the nature of Russia's attempts to interfere in the election. I provided a high-level explanation of the provenance of our knowledge and said that we judged that the interference was designed to undermine the integrity of the election, hurt Secretary Clinton, and enhance the electoral prospects of Donald Trump.

For all in-person briefings, Neal Higgins, the director of the CIA's Office of Congressional Affairs, accompanied me and took notes. Adam Schiff was the first to be briefed. He had a previously scheduled visit to the CIA in early August on a separate issue, and he stopped by my office while at Langley for the briefing. Nancy Pelosi was next; I met her in a SCIF on Capitol Hill. Both Schiff and Pelosi quickly grasped the gravity of the information and asked to be kept informed of additional intelligence that might become available.

Harry Reid's office was told that I wanted to do the briefing in person, but his staff said that he was in Nevada and would not be back in D.C. until September and wanted to be briefed by secure phone as soon as possible. I agreed, although I said that I would not be able to discuss some of the most sensitive details over the phone, even on a secure line. I had developed a good relationship with Senator Reid as a result of the in-person quarterly intelligence updates I provided separately to him and to his Republican counterpart, Senator Mitch McConnell. Reid always showed strong intellectual curiosity during the updates, McConnell less so. A phone call was arranged for mid-August, and Reid took my secure-line call at the FBI field office in Las Vegas. As I had with Schiff and Pelosi, I walked through the key points of the briefing, leaving out some of the more sensitive aspects regarding how some intelligence was acquired. When I was finished, Reid told me that he had recently received other information regarding the Russians and the Trump campaign that had deeply disturbed him. He said he was in the process of writing a letter to Jim Comey to encourage the FBI to investigate what he had been told. "John, can I include the information that you just shared with me in my letter to Comey?" he asked. "I want to make sure Comey understands the urgency. The letter will be classified."

"Sorry, sir," I told him. "I must ask you not to reference any of my information in your letter." I had no idea who would see Reid's letter before and after he sent it to Comey, and I wanted to avoid any leaks. "Jim Comey is fully aware of everything I have told you, but what I shared with you is exceptionally sensitive and shouldn't be included in any correspondence. But you certainly can discuss the information directly with Jim."

Numerous right-wing pundits, social-media activists, "Brennan critics," and even members of Congress—including Congressman Devin Nunes—have publicly claimed that I told Harry Reid during this phone call about the now infamous "dossier" compiled by former British intelligence officer Christopher Steele. That is flat-out wrong. When I spoke to Harry Reid in August, I had not seen nor was I even aware of the dossier. I didn't know anything about it until late September, when Tom Brokaw, Richard Engel, and a couple of other journalists approached me on the sidelines of a conference in Aspen, Colorado, and asked me whether I had heard about some salacious reporting circulating among media types involving alleged sexual escapades of Mr. Trump in Russia. Although I am not sure, their query might have been related to the Steele dossier. I told them I had not seen any such reporting. I would not see the Steele dossier until mid-December, when I received a copy from the FBI in advance of a discussion on whether a summary of the dossier prepared by the FBI should be included or appended to the classified intelligence community assessment of Russian interference in the election that was being drafted at the time. It was appended.

I briefed the five other members of the Gang of Eight on Tuesday, September 6, the day after Labor Day. All the briefings were done individually in congressional spaces. The first briefing was for Senate Minority Leader McConnell, and it was the most noteworthy. Tom Hawkins, McConnell's senior staffer, greeted Neal and me as we arrived at a Senate secure conference room. While I did not always agree with the substantive and policy views that Tom had advocated in previous meetings, I considered him one of the most competent and dedicated staffers on the Hill. Given the importance of the issue, I was glad he would hear the briefing.

McConnell entered the conference room with his usual poker face and sat down at the table. "Okay, what's up?" he said. I walked through the same points I had used in my other sessions, highlighting the fact that the Russian activities were ongoing, and that the CIA, FBI, and NSA were attempting to uncover the full range of Russia's

intelligence operations. When I concluded, McConnell stared at me
and said dryly, "One might say that the CIA and the Obama administration are making such claims in order to prevent Donald Trump
from getting elected president." I was completely gobsmacked by
his comment. Here was the Republican leader of the Senate dismissing intelligence delivered personally by the director of the CIA
about Russian interference in a presidential election that was only
two months away. By suggesting that the CIA was part of a plot by
the Democrats to win the presidential election, McConnell showed
his own strongly partisan political instincts. I could feel myself getting mad, but I suppressed a very strong urge to tell him in very
colorful terms what I thought of his offensive comment.

"Well, Senator," I said with a glare, "I certainly hope that *you* are
not suggesting anything of the sort, as I would take great umbrage
at your insinuation that CIA is abusing its statutory responsibilities
by engaging in partisan politics." He knew I was angry, and I was
glad he did. At that point, Tom Hawkins made a comment or asked a
question to defuse the obvious tension that had filled the room. Neal
also jumped in, hoping that I was not going to do a "full Brennan"
(a phrase my staff and friends used to describe those occasions when
I would tell individuals what I really thought of them). Within minutes, McConnell excused himself, without saying anything more.
Tom stayed behind and asked a few more questions related to the
level of confidence in the information. "I'm very confident, Tom," I
said. "Otherwise, I would not be wasting McConnell's time."

"Okay, I'll talk to him," was his response.

My subsequent meetings with Senators Feinstein and Burr as well
as with Speaker Ryan went much better. They all expressed strong
interest and deep concern about what they heard, and they were encouraged to hear that the CIA was working closely with the FBI
and NSA to understand more fully what the Russians were doing.
They asked for regular updates. The briefing for Devin Nunes, the
chairman of the House intelligence committee, was notable for his

general lack of substantive curiosity or concern about what I had just told him. "Boy, oh boy," I said to Neal on the way out. "It's times like this that I really miss having Mike Rogers as House intelligence committee chairman." (Rogers—not to be confused with former NSA director Mike Rogers or Alabama congressman Mike Rogers—was a Republican congressman from Michigan who decided not to run for reelection in 2014). "I had had my run-ins with Mike, but he was smart and genuinely interested in national security. Unfortunately, Nunes is neither." Nunes has proved my point ever since.

26

WHAT THE HELL JUST HAPPENED?

The fusion cell of CIA, FBI, and NSA experts set up in early August prepared regular updates and analysis on the status of Moscow's efforts to interfere in the election, which I used to brief President Obama and his national security team throughout September and October. The CIA, FBI, and NSA have complementary operational authorities that cover the waterfront of human sources, technical collection, and law enforcement authorities, and the agencies have a strong history of working collaboratively on counterintelligence cases. The investigation demanded the utmost discretion, and I wanted only individuals with an absolute need to know to be involved. To protect extremely sensitive intelligence sources and methods, I purposely kept the fusion cell limited to the three agencies, which traditionally have been the workhorses of counterintelligence investigations.

This was the most complex and politically fraught counterintelligence investigation I had ever encountered. It involved what appeared to be Russian interference in an upcoming U.S. presidential election, with Moscow seeking to hurt the Democratic candidate while helping her Republican rival. Moreover, U.S. persons, including some affiliated with the Trump campaign, appeared to be caught up, wittingly or unwittingly, in the Russian scheme. During their authorized collection activities directed against foreign targets, the CIA and NSA sometimes also would pick up information on U.S. citizens and entities, which is referred to as "incidental collection." When the information collected involved a possible violation of U.S. law by Americans, that information would be passed immediately to the FBI for follow-up action as appropriate. In light of the potentially volatile nature of this information in the political realm, I was determined to prevent this information from being widely circulated within the intelligence community or, even more damaging, leaked publicly.

With the counterintelligence investigation and intelligence collection effort well under way, the White House held regular meetings at the deputies, principals, and National Security Council level to review policy options to disrupt Russian interference. President Obama repeatedly told attendees that the Russians needed to be deterred, but that he wanted nothing done by the U.S. government that could unintentionally affect November's vote in even the slightest way. "We need to prevent the Russians from affecting the vote itself without doing anything that might somehow help them achieve their goal of undermining the integrity of the election," he said at one meeting. "Let's not make this situation worse." At the time, I interpreted his comment to mean that an overreaction by U.S. intelligence or law enforcement agencies—such as more aggressive and potentially controversial collection and disruption activities directed against Russian interference in the election—could lead to a widespread impression that Obama administration actions made the results of the November election invalid, not Russian interference.

Consistent with the president's guidance, there was strong consensus among senior national security officials that we should follow up on my early August phone call with Bortnikov by warning the

Russians again privately as well as publicly about the consequences of interfering in the election. Accordingly, a grim-faced
President Obama spoke to Putin on the sidelines of the G20 summit in St. Petersburg in September and again by phone at the end
of October, with Putin cavalierly dismissing the allegation each
time. A public statement that highlighted Russian responsibility
for the theft of emails from the Democratic Party to interfere in
the presidential election was released by Secretary of Homeland
Security Jeh Johnson and Director Clapper on October 7. Quite
unfortunately, the now infamous *Access Hollywood* tape, in which
Donald Trump made misogynistic and lewd remarks about his interactions with women, was released the same day as the Johnson-
Clapper statement. No government memo, no matter how well
written, is going to get much traction when competing for media interest with a recording of a presidential candidate bragging
about his penchant for grabbing women in a crude, offensive, and
lascivious manner.

Despite the lack of public attention, our governmental efforts
to deal with the potential election crisis continued. The most intense national security policy debate revolved around what action
the United States should take to deter Russia from additional attempts to interfere in the election. We did not know if the Russians
planned to launch an Election Day attack, but several states had detected probes of their voting-related computer systems by a Russian
company. While the administration had assessed that it would be
extremely difficult for the Russians to alter actual vote tabulations
because of a variety of redundancies and safeguards in the decen-
tralized nationwide election system, there was concern that Russian
intelligence services could cause localized havoc and simply prevent
people from voting by disabling computer-based voter-registration
rolls. To address this potential scenario, Secretary Johnson made personal offers of federal assistance to state and local officials to help

them monitor their election networks for cyber intrusions and enhance their computer hygiene capabilities.

One option would be to send an unmistakable signal to Moscow that Washington had its own formidable cyber capabilities that it could unleash in response to further Russian interference. Over the years, I have been asked numerous times why Russia and China have better cyber capabilities than the United States. They simply do not. The United States government possesses tremendous cyber capabilities, including on the offensive front, and it could have used them against Russia in the fall of 2016. The dilemma, however, was that, regardless of the subtlety or forcefulness of a U.S. cyber action, it was unknown whether a cyber response by the United States would prompt the Russians to recoil or to step up their election interference campaign, making matters worse. The specter of an escalatory spiral of cyberattacks between the United States and Russia on the eve of a hotly contested U.S. presidential election tipped the balance for me against a cyber response. I continue to believe it was the appropriate decision.

I did not envy President Obama's dilemma in the weeks leading up to the November 8 presidential election. As chief executive, commander in chief, and titular head of the Democratic Party, he watched his fellow Democrat and former secretary of state do battle against an inexperienced and unprincipled opponent who enjoyed—and publicly welcomed—the active support of Russia, America's principal adversary. It was on July 26, 2016, when Trump publicly stated that he hoped Russia would be able to find Secretary Clinton's emails and share them with the press (according to the Mueller Report, Russian GRU officers "targeted for the first time Secretary Clinton's personal office" five hours after Trump's comment). Trump also raised eyebrows in the White House and throughout the U.S. intelligence and law enforcement communities when he repeatedly praised Putin and WikiLeaks during his campaign appearances and

publicly rebutted reports that Russia attempted to influence the
election by hacking into Democratic networks.

It was clear to me that President Obama and most White House
staff expected Hillary Clinton to win the November election, although there was a clear sense that the race was tightening and that
the result would be closer than earlier anticipated. Some people
wonder whether President Obama would have taken a more aggressive posture vis-à-vis Russian interference if he had believed at the
time that the election was a toss-up or that Trump actually might
win. The answer to that question is unknowable, but I believe he
would not have done anything inappropriate or unethical to help
Secretary Clinton's electoral prospects. President Obama's personal
integrity, adherence to the rule of law, and deep respect for the office
of the presidency would not have allowed it. At most, he would have
authorized a rattling of Russia's cyber networks in hopes of blunting
further Russian actions.

I often have been asked what I think about two decisions made
by Jim Comey prior to the 2016 presidential election that have
been the source of great controversy and speculation as to their
impact on the outcome of the election. The first decision was to
hold a press conference on July 5 to discuss the findings and recommendations of the FBI investigation into Secretary Clinton's use of
a personal email server when she was secretary of state. The second
decision was to notify Congress in an unclassified letter one week
before the election that the FBI had acquired emails "that appear
to be pertinent" to that investigation. In the letter, Comey said
that the FBI was taking investigative steps to determine whether
the emails contained classified information and to "assess their importance to the investigation." I have no doubt that Jim genuinely
believed both his decisions were the right things to do given the
extraordinary circumstances of the case. I also believe that he was
not motivated by political considerations when he made each decision. In all my dealings with Jim, he never once evinced any

hint of politicization in the conduct of his duties. Nevertheless, and recognizing that I was not in Jim's shoes at the time and do not know all the facts and advice available to him, I believe Jim's decisions were mistakes.

A press conference announcing the results of the FBI investigation on Secretary Clinton's emails was an extraordinarily sharp break from the standard FBI practice of providing the results of its investigations and its recommendations on whether criminal charges should be pursued to the Department of Justice. The Department of Justice was not consulted about Jim's plans to hold the press conference and found out about it only when it received press inquiries that morning. Moreover, and despite the FBI's recommendation against bringing criminal charges against Secretary Clinton, Jim publicly rebuked the secretary for being "extremely careless" in handling very sensitive and highly classified information. Jim justified his remarks at the press conference by saying that the high-profile nature of the investigation required an unprecedented amount of transparency. In his book *A Higher Loyalty,* Jim also said that he was aware of information that could cast serious doubt on Attorney General Loretta Lynch's prosecutorial independence, which would have lent credence, if exposed, to claims that her decision to not criminally charge Secretary Clinton was a political one. Jim indicated that the information was something other than the attorney general's widely criticized thirty-minute meeting with former president Clinton aboard her plane on the tarmac of Phoenix Airport the week before Jim's press briefing.

I believe Jim's decision to hold the press conference was problematic on three levels. First, Department of Justice guidelines clearly state that the Public Integrity Section of the department's Criminal Division should be consulted on matters regarding "the timing of charges or overt investigative steps near the time of a primary or general election." The investigation into the Clinton emails during the 2016 presidential election was a major national news story, and it was obvious that any official government announcement on it would have major political implications. The decision to ignore Department of Justice guidelines was a very consequential one that I do not believe should have been made unilaterally by an FBI director. Second, even if it was not election season, it is not the FBI director's prerogative to issue a public statement on the Bureau's recommendation to the Department of Justice on whether to bring criminal charges against an individual. By doing so, Jim essentially arrogated the authority of the attorney general and undermined the department's ability to make its own determination, which frequently takes place after discussions with the FBI. And finally, it is not up to an FBI director to decide when and about whom an accounting of FBI-assessed noncriminal activities—in this instance, reference to "extremely careless" handling of classified information—should be publicly released. Despite her public prominence, Secretary Clinton was entitled to the same treatment as any other American who was under FBI investigation but subsequently not charged with a crime.

Jim's decision to notify Congress about emails the Bureau obtained in October was similarly problematic. The department's guidelines about the need for consultation before any investigative steps are taken on the eve of an election applied with even greater temporal force, but they were once again ignored. Jim sent his letter to Congress before it was known whether the emails, which were on a laptop used by former U.S. congressman Anthony Weiner, contained any additional classified information or even if they all were already in FBI possession. Since Jim was told by his technical experts that it would take a minimum of several weeks to exploit the computer's contents (as it turned out, it took much less time than anticipated), he felt a notification was necessary because he had previously informed Congress that the investigation had been closed. Whether the acquisition of a laptop with contents of undetermined significance warranted a reopening of the case is a matter of conjecture.

Commentary about Jim's decision to reopen the Clinton email

case is accompanied frequently by criticism that he did not inform Congress or publicly disclose that the FBI had launched its Crossfire Hurricane investigation into whether individuals associated with the Trump campaign were coordinating "wittingly or unwittingly" with the Russian government. I believe that criticism is wholly unwarranted. At the time, Crossfire Hurricane was an ongoing and very sensitive investigation that had not been briefed to Congress, and it would have been a violation of investigation protocols and the privacy rights of U.S. persons as well as a highly suspect act of politicization had Congress been notified or a public disclosure made.

Evaluating the appropriateness and wisdom of Jim's decisions in 2016 with the benefit of twenty-twenty hindsight, including knowledge of the outcome of the 2016 election, is far different from having had to make the decisions at the time, as Jim did. As with many of my own decisions throughout my career, I would not be surprised if Jim would make different decisions if given another chance.

Once Donald Trump was elected president by dint of his electoral college victory, despite garnering nearly three million fewer popular votes than Secretary Clinton, the fusion cell began to wrap up its election-related work. Since the FBI's Crossfire Hurricane investigation was still ongoing, the CIA and NSA continued to collect foreign intelligence related to Russian activities in the United States and to pass any significant information incidentally acquired on U.S. persons to the FBI.

Denis McDonough called me on the secure line in early December and said that President Obama wanted a report produced on everything the Russians had done to interfere in the election. "The president wants a complete written record on what happened, John, but can it be done," he asked, "without compromising sensitive sources and methods?" I told Denis that pulling together a written record was an excellent idea and that the president should ask Jim Clapper to oversee the production of an intelligence assessment. I added one caveat.

"CIA can take the lead drafting the report," I told Denis, "but if the president wants a full record of what happened and still protect sources and methods, we will need to restrict the coordination process to ODNI, CIA, FBI, and NSA. They are the only organizations that have had full access to all the underlying intelligence." I knew that limiting involvement to the four agencies was not the standard practice for a formal intelligence community assessment, such as a national intelligence estimate, which reflects the views of all seventeen members of the intelligence community. But there was no way that I wanted to disclose exceptionally sensitive and politically charged counterintelligence information, including on U.S. persons, to potentially hundreds of additional individuals at those agencies.

I called Jim Clapper to give him a heads-up about the request. After talking through the modalities of the process, we agreed that there should be a comprehensive top-secret code-word document as well as an unclassified version derived from it that had the exact same findings and conclusions. Jim agreed that the CIA should be the lead drafter, and, contrary to various right-wing conspiracy theorists, I did not personally select the CIA officers who wrote the assessment (it not only would have been highly unusual for the director of the CIA to personally select the drafters of an assessment, it also would have been professionally unethical). Rather, I left it up to the CIA components responsible for Russia, cyber, and counterintelligence to select the relevant experts, some of whom had served in the fusion cell, to write the report.

The initial draft of the intelligence assessment was completed within two weeks. David Cohen and I reviewed the draft, raising a few questions but making no substantive adjustments. The bottom-line judgments of the written assessment—that President Putin ordered an influence campaign in the 2016 presidential election to undermine faith in the U.S. democratic process, denigrate Secretary

Clinton to harm her electability and potential presidency, and help Donald Trump's election chances—had not changed from the analysis done before the election. While the assessment was coordinated within the CIA, FBI, and NSA at the expert level, Jim Clapper, Jim Comey, Mike Rogers, and I had several conversations about it. One discussion among the four of us was held by secure conference call. I was in Mountainside, New Jersey, visiting my gravely ill father at the time and took the call in my SUV, which was parked outside my parents' assisted-living facility. The four of us agreed that the quality of the draft was strong and that the key judgments, at the time all at the high confidence level, were sound. One point of difference was that Mike Rogers of the NSA said that he personally did not believe there was sufficient intelligence to support a high-confidence judgment that the Russians were favoring Trump in the election. Having consumed virtually every bit of intelligence on Russian interference in the election in the preceding months, I told Mike that I agreed with the analysts. Jim Clapper and Jim Comey noted they also did. Mike said that he would revisit the NSA judgment on that one conclusion, and he subsequently decided that NSA would give it moderate confidence, one analytic level below high confidence. The NSA's moderate confidence on this one judgment eventually was noted in the final report.

Mike wasn't the only one who questioned the confidence level on the judgment in the assessment related to Russia favoring Mr. Trump's candidacy. Two senior managers in the CIA mission center responsible for Russia—one with extensive operational experience and the other with a strong analytic background—visited me in my office and said that they had the same view as Mike Rogers. After a long discussion, during which I came to the conclusion that the two officers had not read all the available intelligence, I said that I would not overturn the judgment of the CIA analysts who, as a team, were deeply familiar with all the relevant intelligence and had made the high-confidence judgment. I encouraged the two officers, who said that they raised their concerns with the drafters of the assessment, to discuss their concerns again with the authors.

The only other aspect of the assessment that was decided at the head-of-agency level was how to handle the Steele dossier. Since neither the substance of the dossier nor any of its sources and sub-sources were ever validated by U.S. intelligence, CIA analysts ada-mantly opposed using any of the information in the dossier when they drafted the assessment and decided on the key judgments. Jim Clapper and I supported that view. Nevertheless, Jim Comey and his deputy, Andy McCabe, pointed out that President Obama wanted the written record to be comprehensive, and the dossier was very much related to Russia and Mr. Trump. After reviewing the options available, it was decided that the Bureau would draft a one-page summary of the dossier and that it would be appended to the highly restricted top-secret code-word version of the assessment that would be provided to President-elect Trump. The dossier did not inform any of the analysis or the judgments in the assessment itself.

While the assessment was being drafted and finalized, we re-ceived numerous requests from members of Congress—Republicans and Democrats—for briefings on Russian interference. Unfortu-nately, an early December House Permanent Select Committee on Intelligence briefing by a member of the intelligence community who was not privy to the most sensitive intelligence understated sig-nificantly what was known about the Putin-directed influence cam-paign. The Republicans were already pushing back on reports that the Russians had been trying to help Trump win the election, and the increasingly partisan Devin Nunes, who had become a member of Donald Trump's presidential transition team, scheduled a com-mittee briefing for December 15. Nunes wanted the briefers to be Jim Clapper, Jim Comey, and me. I called Jim Clapper the morning before and said that we should not do any briefings on the issue un-til the intelligence assessment was completed, so that a thorough, accurate, and consistent accounting could be provided to Congress. I reached out to Nunes's office that afternoon to explain our position, but Nunes refused to take my call, opting instead to issue a public statement, blasting us, in what would become his dishonest fashion, for refusing to brief the committee. Nunes's antics were well known even back then to other members of Congress, so I called Speaker Ryan that evening to explain why we needed to postpone the briefing. In his usual accommodating manner, the Speaker said that he fully understood and told me not to worry about Nunes.

It was about this time that Democrats in Congress became increasingly concerned about what might happen to the intelligence reports that revealed Russian interference in the election once the Trump administration came into office. Senator Mark Warner, the vice chairman of the Senate Select Committee on Intelligence, called me in December to discuss the disposition of CIA information about Russian activities. "I'm really concerned about what might happen to CIA files after you leave," he said, "so maybe it would be best for the oversight committees to get copies of all relevant CIA documents to ensure they are preserved." Along with SSCI chairman Senator Burr, Senator Warner was a very strong supporter of the CIA, and I could tell that he was very worried that CIA files might somehow "get lost" when Trump and his national security team took over.

"I share your concerns, senator, about the incoming administration, but I have full confidence that CIA professionals will preserve and protect Agency files." Having lived through the painful aftermath of Leon's decision to provide the SSCI an unprecedented amount of CIA information, I was not going to accede to Warner's request, despite my belief that his intentions were noble. "But what I would suggest, senator, is that the committee should request information in CIA files that would help fill out your understanding of Russian activities." I had only recently become aware that the oversight committees were not provided any of the reports that we provided to the FBI on the incidental collection of information on U.S.

persons. "For instance, the committee might want to ask the CIA for copies of the reports we sent to the FBI that involved activities by U.S. persons that might constitute violations of U.S. laws." Why not, I thought. The committees were entitled to that information, given their CIA oversight responsibilities. It is my understanding that the SSCI subsequently asked for and received those reports.

I read through the fully coordinated top-secret code-word intelligence assessment the following week. As soon as I finished, I called Jim Clapper and told him that I felt that we could produce an unclassified version, with all of the key judgments and much of the same language intact, by surgically redacting all references to sources and methods. Jim agreed, and he praised the analytic tradecraft as well as the clarity of the writing in the assessment. By the end of December, the classified and unclassified versions of the assessment were ready for final production, and arrangements were made to brief its findings to President Obama, President-elect Trump, and the congressional leadership the first week of January.

This was a challenging time for me personally, as my father's health steadily deteriorated during the month of December. Kathy and I took four trips to New Jersey to spend as much time as we could with my mother, sister, and brother at my father's bedside. It was very painful to see my father slowly fade, but it was wonderful to be with him and my New Jersey family during his last days. And each time I was there, Washington's turbulent political waters seemed a million miles away.

There is something very serene, peaceful, yet heartbreaking when you hold a loved one's hand as death nears. On the morning of December 27, 2016, I held my father's hand for the last time. I told him I loved him and thanked him for his life's work.

I continue to do so every day.

27

UNDAUNTED

As the cold days of January 2017 slipped by, I felt like the final curtain was falling on my national security career at an accelerated rate. I had planned to leave government service at the end of the Obama administration regardless of the outcome of the election. If Secretary Clinton had won, I probably would have remained until a new director was confirmed, but I had no intention of staying, nor did I believe I would be asked to stay for even a day, when Trump was elected. Unlike my first retirement a decade earlier, I knew that I would never again return to public service. More than thirty-three years in the government was more than enough. I needed to make up for lost time with my family and, in the process, try to earn some money. Besides, there was no job in the government that could rival the challenges, opportunities, and institutional camaraderie that came with being director of the CIA.

As we prepared to take our leave of the CIA family, David and I paid dozens of parish calls throughout the Agency, thanking the women and men of the CIA for their selfless dedication to our national security. During our visits, we sought to strike a positive and optimistic tone about what the future would bring and how incoming Trump administration officials would quickly recognize the value of the CIA's work. While we didn't mention Donald Trump's public disparagement of the intelligence mission and of the just-completed intelligence community assessment of Russian interference in the election, Trump's publicly expressed sentiment was the elephant in every office we visited. "Your mission is vital," we said, "so don't let the political winds distract you from carrying out your responsibilities with determination and professionalism." I pushed back publicly against Trump's tirades, however, as I wanted the CIA's rank and file to know that they deserved a spirited defense. On the weekend before the inauguration, I appeared on *Fox News Sunday* and told Chris Wallace it was "outrageous" that Trump publicly alleged that intelligence agencies had leaked the Steele dossier and that he made reference to "living in Nazi Germany."

We heard from a significant number of officers concerned about Trump's misogynistic reputation and the potential that his administration would undo the many gains that had been made by women in the Agency, and more broadly within government. And it wasn't just women. We also heard from Muslims, African Americans, and members of the LGBTQ community who saw Trump's election as a harbinger of a retreat on the diversity and inclusion front that had been steadily gaining strength within the government over the past several decades.

During our last week at Langley, we held two sessions for Agency officers in the auditorium. There was a Martin Luther King Day celebration on Wednesday, which we used to highlight the important strides made in the Agency to ensure that all Agency employees had an equal opportunity to realize their professional goals irrespective of their gender, race, religious faith, ethnicity, sexual orientation, or disabilities. "Do not let progress be undone," I said to the workforce. "You know what is right. If you see that a colleague is not being treated fairly, speak up. If you believe that Agency leaders are not fulfilling their responsibilities to promote diversity and inclusion, speak out. You have the ability to shape the Agency's future. Seize it, and never let it go." Republican congressman Mike Pompeo of Kansas, an active and outspoken member of the House Permanent Select Committee on Intelligence, had already been nominated but not yet confirmed as the next CIA director. I knew Pompeo had a keen intellect and was familiar with the CIA's mission, but his highly partisan views and strong ideological leanings left me uneasy about whether he would support and defend the CIA's apolitical and truth-telling mission with Donald Trump in the Oval Office. My uneasiness was warranted, as Pompeo's time at the CIA and subsequent tenure as secretary of state solidified his reputation of putting loyalty to Donald Trump above commitment to country.

On Thursday, David and I bade farewell to the workforce in an all-hands session that was broadcast live to all Agency facilities and posts worldwide. It was an emotional event for me, as the two families that I loved for more than thirty-six years, on the home and professional fronts, were gathered one last time. At the end of the ceremony, I invited my two-year-old grandson to join me onstage. I got down on one knee when he walked toward me, and then I turned to the workforce as I put my arm around him. "This is why we are here and make the sacrifices we do. It is for our children and grandchildren, so that they will be able to enjoy the freedoms, liberties, and prosperity that we have experienced throughout our lives." But it was my adorable grandson, not me, who held the rapt attention of the hundreds of CIA employees in the auditorium that afternoon. And when he decided to emulate his "Pop-Pop" by taking a knee himself next to me, the auditorium erupted in applause and the tears started to make their way down my cheeks. It was the most bittersweet moment of my life.

On Inauguration Day, my last day as a U.S. government official, I skipped the gym and went into headquarters early to gather up a few remaining personal items in my office and to walk the halls as director one last time. Since it was a holiday in the national capital region, the corridors were mostly empty, but the components that stay open twenty-four hours a day, 365 days a year, were fully staffed. I walked through both headquarters buildings, past several of the offices where I spent many of my early years at the Agency, and reminisced to myself about the many wonderful experiences and colleagues I had during my intelligence career. Thirty-six and a half years had gone by much too quickly.

My last stop was the CIA's iconic main lobby. I had hoped to spend a quiet moment of reflection and commemoration in front of the star-emblazoned Memorial Wall. I could think of no better way to say goodbye to the Agency than to give silent thanks to the fallen, many of whose faces—some I had known in life and many others in death—would always be indelibly etched in my mind's eye. But as I neared the lobby, the din of hammers, folding chairs, and loud voices told me that a quiet final adieu was not to be. The CIA's able support cadre was already hard at work constructing the stage that would be used by Donald Trump the following day during his first visit to Langley. "It figures," I said to myself. "Trump has even found a way to disrupt my departure from the Agency."

David Cohen and his wife, Suzy, graciously invited Kathy and me as well as Jim and Sue Clapper, Avril and her husband, David, and Lisa Monaco to their house for brunch that day. After one last trip down the executive elevator to the garage, I jumped in the SUV at about 9:30 A.M. to hurry home to pick up Kathy before heading to the Cohens' house in Maryland. I continued to read intelligence reports, in hard copy and on the classified computer systems in my SUV, throughout the morning, as I would remain director until noon that day. Since Mike Pompeo had not yet been confirmed as the next director of the CIA, Meroe Park—the executive director and number-three official at the Agency—would serve as acting director for at least a few days. If anything significant happened overseas, I wanted to make sure that the Agency was prepared to support Meroe in carrying out her temporary duties.

The brunch was a wonderful opportunity to spend time with some of my closest colleagues from the past eight years. We never turned on the TV to watch Donald Trump take the oath of office. I do not recall anyone even suggesting it. When the noon hour struck and Jim, David, and I automatically returned to civilian life, our SUVs with their classified computer systems were driven away, replaced by ones without computers. On the way home, I read news reports of Trump's inaugural address on my iPhone. I shook my head in shock and disbelief at his references to "American carnage" and his haughty and baseless belittlement of the work and accomplishments of prior administrations. "If Trump plans to adopt a different tone as president than he did as a candidate," I said to Kathy, "he sure as hell is not showing it in his first remarks as president."

That night, I went to bed without any government responsibility for the first time in eight years. It felt strange, but I looked forward to sleeping in the following morning.

The next day, Kathy and I were at home and decided to watch TV coverage of Donald Trump's visit to CIA headquarters, which was broadcast live on cable news. I was very pleased that Trump decided to go to Langley on the first full day of his presidency. Well-crafted remarks highlighting his appreciation of the CIA's work and the importance of the intelligence mission would go a long way to soothing simmering concerns that were rippling through at least a portion of the workforce. Regardless of any personal political leanings they may harbor, all CIA officers want to know that their "first customer" values their contributions to national security.

It was gratifying to see Meroe, as acting director, welcome Trump and the other visitors, and I thought Vice President Pence's remarks expressing admiration for the work and sacrifices of the women and men of the CIA were very suitable for the occasion.

And then Trump began to speak, and it didn't take long before he went political.

My iPhone started to light up soon after Trump started to talk about his election victory and the size of his inaugural crowd with clear disregard for the solemn backdrop of stars on the Memorial Wall. My former colleagues, fellow retirees as well as serving CIA officers, began texting me, with many simply writing "WTF?" Other texts were not nearly as kind. As Trump was still talking, I told Kathy that I couldn't take it anymore. I felt physically nauseated watching and listening to him. "I'm going to the gym to blow off some steam," I said as I hurried out the front door before Trump finished speaking.

At the gym, I got on a stationary bike, where the TVs were replaying Trump's remarks. The more I heard, the angrier I got. When I received a text from a close CIA friend that said, "Trump just desecrated the Memorial Wall!" I knew I needed to say something publicly. But how? I no longer could ask the CIA's Office of Public Affairs to put out a statement, and I had no contact information for anyone in the press.

"Nick!" I said aloud. As I peddled, I tapped out a text message to my former White House colleague and deputy chief of staff at the CIA, Nick Shapiro. "Since you are known to your media friends to be a reliable source and a close friend of mine, feel free to share with anyone interested that "Former Director Brennan is deeply saddened and angered at Donald Trump's despicable display of self-aggrandizement in front of CIA's Memorial Wall of Agency heroes. He should be ashamed of himself."

Within minutes, Nick emailed about a dozen media contacts. Before I got off the bike, my statement was being widely reported on the cable news networks. "Well, so much for giving Trump the benefit of the doubt," I said to myself as I headed toward the weight equipment. I had a feeling at that moment that my ride into the sunset of retirement was not going to be as relaxing and as uneventful as I had hoped.

I missed going into Langley every day and working with my former CIA and administration colleagues, but I cherished the ability to spend time with Kathy and our children and to catch up on my sleep, my reading, and my long list of tasks to do at our Herndon house. I also traveled back and forth to New Jersey quite a bit to visit my mother, as she was without her life's partner after nearly sixty-five years together. In the weeks leading up to what would have been Owen's ninety-seventh birthday, on April 2, she frequently would ask us when it would be his birthday. "Soon, Mom," we would say. "Don't worry, we'll let you know when it's here." But we didn't have to let her know, as she took her last breath on Owen's birthday. Kathleen, Tommy, and I decided that Dottie had planned it so that she would surprise Owen by spending his birthday with him in the heaven they both so richly deserved.

Despite staying heavily engaged on the home front, I could not help but continue to be outspoken about what was happening in our government. Trump made no progress on the learning curve in either national security matters or in his public comments, and I spoke out whenever I felt the need to do so. My comments at the Aspen Security Forum in July 2017 prompted Mike Pompeo to reach out to me. I appeared alongside Jim Clapper at Aspen, where Jim and I were both critical of Trump's six-month record as president, during which he fired James Comey, continued to disparage U.S. intelligence and the media, and told President Putin at the G20 meeting in Germany that it was an "honor" to meet him despite Russian interference in the U.S. presidential elections only months before. My spirits had been buoyed two months earlier, when former FBI director Bob Mueller was appointed special counsel at the Department of Justice to look into Russian interference in the 2016 election, as I felt that there was still much to be learned about what happened and the extent to which U.S. persons might have abetted Moscow's efforts. I knew that Bob would have his work cut out for him, but I was hopeful he would be able to unearth the full scope of illegal activities undertaken by

Russian intelligence services and their accomplices. At Aspen I said that if Trump decided to fire Mueller, members of Congress should rise up and say, "Enough is enough!"

It was on my drive from Aspen to the airport in Denver when the head of the CIA's Office of Public Affairs called me. "Don't shoot the messenger, John," he said, "but Director Pompeo wants to talk to you about your remarks at the Security Forum."

"Happy to," was my response. I knew Pompeo was not calling to compliment me on what I said in Aspen, but I was very curious to find out what he was going to say and how he would say it. After Pompeo was nominated to be CIA director the previous November, I had had only one interaction with him. He came to CIA headquarters to meet with me in late November, and he expressed his deep admiration for the work of the Agency and his eagerness to begin his new job. I offered to meet with him at any time to facilitate the transition but never heard from him again until the day after my appearance in Aspen. The lack of contact was in keeping with the incoming Trump administration's general lack of interest in working with the outgoing Obama team.

When I returned home from Aspen and spoke to Pompeo the next day, he expressed two concerns. First, he said my remarks were "disrespectful of the president" and that, as a former CIA director, I should refrain from making such comments. Second, he incorrectly claimed that I came perilously close to revealing classified information in my forum remarks on Syria. I disagreed with him on both counts. On the matter of being disrespectful, I said that I believed many of Trump's reckless actions and irresponsible statements deserved strong criticism, even from a former CIA director, and that I would continue to speak out whenever I believed it appropriate. I told Pompeo that I was surprised that a current CIA director would be expressing dissatisfaction with the public comments of a private citizen. On Syria, I told Pompeo to check the transcript of my remarks, which he acknowledged he had not personally read, as they would confirm that I did not discuss anything classified.

I never heard from Pompeo again. But he showed his pettiness that December when he personally removed Kathy and me from the invitation list for the CIA's annual holiday party, the only time a former director and spouse—who are always invited to the party—have been disinvited from the event they once hosted. In recent years, members of the Trump family and White House political appointees have attended the holiday gathering at the CIA, so perhaps Pompeo didn't want to risk unpleasantness over the punch bowl. When I met with Gina Haspel, at her invitation, soon after she was confirmed as Pompeo's successor at the CIA, she greeted me by saying that I would be invited to future CIA holiday parties. That has not yet happened, as Kathy and I were not invited to the two holiday parties that Gina has since hosted. Not being invited to the CIA's annual holiday party is a trivial matter, but the fact that the guest list is adjusted to weed out what amounts to an administration "enemies list" illustrates the lengths to which some will go to satisfy the petulance of Donald Trump.

I kept up my criticism of Trump in the months after Aspen, as he provided almost daily opportunity for fresh criticism. In September, I decided to open a Twitter account in order to more directly respond to Trump's outlandish statements, lies, and grandstanding, much of which he was propagating in the Twittersphere. I had never joined a social-media platform previously, although I had long recognized the power of social media from a communications standpoint. It was for this reason that I authorized the CIA to set up its official Twitter account in early 2014 and selected, with great delight, the CIA's first Twitter posting: "We can neither confirm nor deny that this is our first tweet."

The stridency of my comments about Donald Trump's performance as president increased significantly in spring 2018, when he took tangible action to harm a former colleague and dedicated public servant, then–deputy director of the FBI Andy McCabe. I have known Andy for many years and was always impressed with his diligence and dedication to mission. Andy was a good partner of the CIA, and he was always well prepared and collegial whenever he represented the Bureau at interagency meetings in the White House Situation Room. Quite unfortunately, Andy joined James Comey as a target of Donald Trump's vituperative efforts to hit back against Bureau officials who had had the audacity to honor their professional responsibilities rather than pay blind fealty to Donald Trump. In keeping with his juvenile bullying tactics, Trump also attacked Andy's wife, Jill, a medical doctor who had run unsuccessfully for a Virginia State Senate seat as a Democrat.

As Andy approached his retirement date, Donald Trump repeatedly denounced him and applied strong public pressure on the Department of Justice to fire Andy for alleged infractions related to the Bureau's investigation of former secretary of state Hillary Clinton. I have no insight into the veracity of the allegations, which the Department of Justice decided not to prosecute. But when Andy was fired less than forty-eight hours before he was eligible to retire, I saw it as a blatant act of political retribution against Andy and his family that was engineered by Donald Trump. But even more than the firing, it was the instant glee shown by Trump in a tweet—"Andrew McCabe FIRED, a great day for hard working men and women of FBI—A great day for Democracy. Sanctimonious James Comey was his boss and made him look like a choirboy. He knew all about the lies and corruption going on at the highest levels of the FBI."

Maybe it was because it was St. Patrick's Day and my Irish dander was more easily ruffled, but Trump's comments made me see red. "He is evil, despicable, and vile," I said to Kathy as we had our morning coffee. She agreed. Without saying another word, I drafted and pushed "send" on a responding statement of my own on Twitter: "When the full extent of your venality, moral turpitude, and political corruption becomes known, you will take your rightful place as a disgraced demagogue in the dustbin of history. You may scapegoat Andy McCabe, but you will not destroy America . . . America will triumph over you." With that statement, which received 235,000 "likes," the battle was joined.

I knew that my caustic criticisms of Trump would trigger a sharp backlash from Trump supporters as well as from individuals who believe a former CIA director should not engage in such public denunciation of a sitting president. Soon after my St. Patrick's Day tweet, an offer to serve on one of Booz Allen Hamilton's advisory boards was rescinded. I was told that I was "too hot" considering my outspokenness and that the risk of blowback on the firm would be too great if I were to be affiliated with it. Speeches and other opportunities for financial remuneration also began to dry up, but I was determined not to let monetary considerations keep me from speaking out against Mr. Trump.

I continued to be outspoken on Twitter in the following months, calling Trump's self-adoration "disgraceful," his behavior "unprincipled and unethical," and his administration a "kakistocracy." Online dictionary searches of the word, which describes a government run by the worst, least competent, and corrupt of citizens, increased by 14,000 percent that day. While these statements on Twitter were hard hitting, they were mild compared to the many others I drafted but, upon further review and reflection, decided against sending. When Trump appeared at a press conference in Helsinki, Finland, in July and said he believed Putin's denial that Russia interfered in the 2016 presidential election, however, I blew my top. "It was nothing short of treasonous," I said in another posting on Twitter, seeing Trump's comments as a contemptible betrayal of his country. I said that Trump was "wholly in the pocket of Putin," and I ended my fusillade with, "Republican Patriots: Where are you???"

While I was unsurprised by the extent of Mr. Trump's incompetence, dishonesty, and cravenness, I was shocked at the willingness of the overwhelming majority of Republicans in the Senate and the House of Representatives to kowtow to his shameful behavior. They ignored and made excuses for Trump's lies, impulsive actions, crude behavior, and narcissism, which only served to encourage his petulance and recklessness. There had been times during my government career when I felt some Democratic lawmakers failed to live up to their oath of office as well as the standards of integrity that should be the norm for all public servants. The totality of those instances, however, paled in comparison to what I considered a near wholesale abdication of political norms, ethics, and decency by the mainstream Republican Party. Having respected many members of the Republican Party with whom I had previously worked, I was angry that someone of Trump's debased character could so quickly and completely eviscerate the party of Lincoln.

I was doing some work around our house in Herndon on August 15 when Nick Shapiro called. "John, the White House is revoking your clearances," he said breathlessly.

"Huh?" I said. Once again, it was Nick who was the bearer of bad news.

"Turn on the television," he practically screamed into the phone. "Sarah Huckabee Sanders is reading a statement that Trump is taking them away!"

The television was on in another room, and, as I walked toward it, I could hear Huckabee Sanders finishing up her statement. "Additionally, Mr. Brennan has recently leveraged his status as a former high-ranking official with access to highly classified information to make a series of unfounded and outrageous allegations—wild outbursts on the Internet and television—about this administration. Mr. Brennan's lying and recent conduct, characterized by increasingly frenzied commentary, is wholly inconsistent with access to this nation's most closely held secrets and facilities [*sic*] the very aim of our adversaries, which is to sow division and chaos."

Kathy had joined me in front of the television as Sanders was concluding her remarks. "I guess my stuff on Twitter got under his skin," I said to her.

"Can they do this to you?" The sound of her voice indicated that she was both mad and worried.

After my many years serving on the CIA's seventh floor, I have intimate familiarity with how security clearances are granted as well as revoked within the intelligence community. A security clearance revocation takes place only after the completion of a rigorous process involving a credible allegation that an individual has violated his or her security obligations, a formal review of the allegation, notification and usually an interview of the individual involved, and, in the event of a decision to revoke, the opportunity for the individual involved to appeal. At times, I was the CIA official who had to make the final decision to strip an individual of their security clearances. No such process preceded the White House announcement claiming that my security clearances were being revoked, and no basis existed to revoke them.

"No one has been in touch with me about it," I said to Kathy, "so I really don't know what's happening."

As had occurred when Trump spoke in front of the CIA's Memorial Wall the day after his inauguration, I was quickly inundated with text messages, emails, and phone calls from family, friends, and former colleagues expressing outrage at Trump's action. I told everyone that I was as clueless as they were but was unsurprised by the move. I knew that there was no basis to revoke my security clearances and that it was simply an effort to rebuke me publicly for my outspokenness and to try to intimidate others from criticizing Trump. The White House announcement, and my public statement that I might consider potential legal action to prevent Trump from politicizing security clearances, prompted Henry Kissinger to terminate a consultancy contract I had with his firm, Kissinger Associates Inc. As with previous administrations, Dr. Kissinger has had an ongoing substantive relationship with the Trump White House, offering his

perspective and recommendations on a wide variety of foreign policy matters whenever asked. I do not know whether White House
officials encouraged Dr. Kissinger to terminate my contract or if he
worried that he would be tainted by association with me, but the
timing of the termination certainly suggests it was one or both reasons.

One phone call I especially appreciated at the time was from former vice president Joe Biden. He expressed his deep disappointment in the White House announcement and then said some very
nice things about my service to country and our time together in
the Obama administration. I didn't expect the vice president to call
but was not surprised when he did. I had a very close relationship
with him when I served at the White House and as director of the
CIA. His vast experience on national security issues and his familiarity with the intelligence profession made him one of the most
active participants in the countless meetings we attended together
over eight years. President Obama actively sought out and deeply
respected Biden's perspective on every important issue, including on
how to deal with Congress on difficult and controversial policy matters such as the Affordable Care Act and the Joint Comprehensive
Plan of Action with Iran.

In addition to Biden's substantive breadth and political acumen,
he also was a constant source of optimism and encouragement during
White House meetings. "Come on, folks," he would say in his usual
avuncular manner if he detected that the mood in the White House
Situation Room was flagging as a result of some setback on the national security front. "We're the United States of America. We can
do this. We've been through tough times before, and we did just
fine, and we'll do so again." His words always seem to provide a
needed shot of adrenaline at difficult times, and I deeply appreciated
his personal involvement and deft touch when he hosted Senator
Feinstein and me at his residence in an effort to defuse tensions over
the Senate intelligence committee's RDI study.

But it was the vice president's phone calls to my parents on their birthdays, the forty-five minutes he spent with my father in New Jersey talking about their shared Irish roots, and the humanity and resilience he has shown at times of personal tragedy—in his life and the lives of others—that gave me most insight into his decency, character, and moral fiber. These are the qualities of Joe Biden I will most remember and cherish. They also are the qualities that should be in the DNA of every individual elected president of the United States.

In the days following the White House announcement, there was much commentary in the media for and against revoking my security clearances. I was deeply appreciative that so many of my former colleagues, including former directors and deputy directors of central intelligence, national intelligence, and the CIA, signed an open letter supporting my right to speak out, even if they didn't agree with all that I said, and decrying White House abuse of security clearances in its attempt to stifle free speech. And I was deeply touched and heartened when Admiral Bill McRaven, in retirement, wrote an op-ed in *The Washington Post* in which he said to Trump, "I would consider it an honor if you would revoke my security clearances as well, so I can add my name to the list of men and women who have spoken up against your presidency."

There has been significant debate and confusion over why I and other former CIA directors retain security clearances upon retirement and what benefits and entitlements are derived from their retention. Let me attempt to set the factual record straight.

First, there is a strong national security basis for former CIA directors to maintain their security clearances once they leave office. All CIA directors have been involved in exceptionally sensitive activities during their tenures, including interactions with foreign leaders and heads of intelligence and security services. The personal experiences, insights, and counsel of former directors can be invaluable to their successors and to serving CIA officers who want to have a deeper understanding of historical context, lessons learned, and previous initiatives and approaches that were successful and those that were not. During my tenure, I invited my predecessors back to Langley to engage in substantive discussions with me and with other CIA officers on several occasions. In addition, former CIA directors freely give of their time by participating in training courses and seminars, including those involving covert action. For all these interactions, security clearances are necessary for a free-flowing discussion on intelligence matters.

Second, from the time I left the CIA, on January 20, 2017, until the White House announced that my security clearances were being revoked, on August 15, 2018, I made no request to the CIA or to any other government agency for classified information for my own purposes. Many of my critics seemed to believe that my security clearances allowed me to access classified material whenever I wanted and that I was routinely receiving classified briefings. Not true. In fact, the only time I read or discussed classified material after leaving the CIA was when I was preparing for my open and closed testimony in front of Congress in 2017 on matters related to Russia's interference in the 2016 U.S. presidential election. And my only visits to the CIA and to other intelligence community agencies have been in response to official invitations, not at my initiative.

Third, the retention of my security clearances has provided no financial benefit to me. While some former Agency officers, including directors, require security clearances to serve on boards of companies that engage in classified work with the government, I never sought such appointments nor served on any boards requiring security clearances after I departed government service in January 2017.

Finally, it should come as no surprise that the White House announcement about the revocation of my clearances, like so many other of its public statements, was not true. As of the publication date of this book, my top-secret code-word clearances remain intact. I still have a CIA badge that allows me to access CIA facilities, which I have used more than a dozen times to attend retirement ceremonies and to participate in nonsubstantive meetings to which I have been invited.

Interestingly, though, I found out in November 2019 that Donald Trump personally issued a presidential directive in July 2018 forbidding anyone in the intelligence community from discussing or sharing classified information "with former CIA Director John Brennan." It is the first and only time any president has issued such an order. Given that Donald Trump issued the directive, it is yet another badge of honor for me.

On the day after the White House announced that Trump was revoking my clearances, I published an op-ed in *The New York Times* that said his claims of no collusion with Russia were "hogwash." Coincidentally, or maybe it was not just a coincidence given my previous experience, I had submitted the draft op-ed to the CIA publications review board at 9:14 A.M. on the day that the White House made its announcement, which took place that afternoon. Pointing to Trump's late July 2016 public call upon Russia to find the missing emails of Secretary Clinton, I wrote that he "was not only encouraging a foreign nation to collect intelligence against a United States citizen, but also openly authorizing his followers to work with our primary global adversary against his political opponent." For me, the questions that remained were "whether the collusion that took place constituted criminally liable conspiracy, whether obstruction of justice occurred to cover up any collusion or conspiracy, and how many members of 'Trump Incorporated' attempted to defraud the government by laundering and concealing the movement of money into their pockets."

When the Department of Justice released a redacted copy of Special Counsel Bob Mueller's final report in July 2019, I had three principal reactions to the section on Russian interference in the election. First, the report provided strong corroboration of the findings of the intelligence community assessment about Russian attempts to interfere in the election. It showed that Russia's social-media campaign and hacking operations coincided with a series of contacts between Trump campaign officials and individuals with ties to the Russian government and that Moscow perceived it would benefit from a Trump presidency and worked to secure that outcome. In addition, the investigation revealed that the Trump campaign expected it would benefit electorally from information stolen and released through Russian efforts. The report also provided detailed evidence that the Trump campaign showed interest in and welcomed the release of documents damaging to Secretary Clinton by WikiLeaks (a method known to be used by Russian intelligence).

My second reaction was surprise at how extensively and effectively the Russians had used social-media platforms in the United States, propagating their election interference activities by using false U.S. personas. Since the CIA has no legal authority to target its collection capabilities against U.S. social-media platforms, I was unaware of most of this activity when I was CIA director and found out about it only when I read the Mueller report. I will acknowledge that the CIA should have done a better job learning earlier about Russia's plans to use the Internet Research Agency and the tactics it employed to interfere in the 2016 election. Once Russian intentions were known, however, I tried to ensure that the CIA, along with the NSA, was providing all relevant intelligence and analysis to the FBI inside the fusion cell to assist the Bureau in its daunting challenge of uncovering Russian activities inside the United States, including in the social-media realm.

My third takeaway from the report was that the letter sent to Congress by Attorney General William Barr in March had intentionally and significantly misrepresented the actual findings of the investigation, giving the false impression that Trump and his campaign had been exonerated of wrongdoing. They were not. The report chronicled the numerous actions by individuals affiliated with the Trump campaign that were wrong, unethical, and designed to invite Russian interference in the campaign. The report also confirmed for me that, in his public testimony in front of Congress in April, Barr's questioning of the predication of the FBI investigation was unfounded. Moreover, Barr's claim that U.S. intelligence and law enforcement had engaged in "spying" against the Trump campaign during the counterintelligence investigation was highly prejudicial and very inappropriate. Barr is many things, but he is not sloppy in his use of terms, and he clearly intended to please Trump and fuel speculation that investigators were involved in criminal wrongdoing by using the word "spying."

The Mueller investigation *did not establish* that members of the Trump campaign criminally conspired or coordinated with the Russian government in its election interference activities. Unfortunately, the Mueller investigative team was prevented from gaining access to important financial records and conducting interviews of key individuals involved in the campaign, notably Mr. Trump, both of which might have provided further insight into whether criminal activity took place. Nevertheless, I accept the findings of the Mueller investigative team that the evidence it was able to uncover did not support a charge of criminal conspiracy.

The public release of the Mueller report only served to strengthen Mr. Trump's belief that he is beyond accountability for his actions, as he abused his authority almost immediately afterward by seeking a personal political favor from the president of Ukraine, withholding military assistance to Kiev as leverage, and then obstructing congressional investigation into his actions. Trump's subsequent impeachment in the House of Representatives and the Senate's failure to convict him in early 2020 underscored for me the willingness of every Republican member of Congress except Senator Mitt Romney to ignore and even encourage Donald Trump's trampling of America's democratic principles, norms, and laws. I fully expected Trump to retaliate against respected public servants, including military officers, for their truthful testimony to Congress or because they fulfilled their professional responsibilities and obligations related to the impeachment process. And when Trump took such actions, it reminded me of the many authoritarian rulers around the world I have seen retain power by eliminating political opponents and weeding out individuals in government suspected of less than absolute fealty to them.

The refusal of the CIA to grant my December 18, 2018, request to access the "records that I originated, reviewed, signed, or received while serving as Director of CIA" is in keeping with Mr. Trump's efforts to retaliate against his enemies, suppress their right to freedom of speech, and intimidate others from speaking out. While the lack of access to my records made the writing of this memoir more difficult and time consuming than it otherwise would have been, I was determined to not allow Donald Trump to prevent its publication. Accordingly, I submitted the draft to the CIA's Publications Classification Review Board on April 20, 2020. The board carried out its responsibilities in a professional manner and, after I made changes on portions of the manuscript that the Board identified as being of classification concern, completed its review in a timely manner.

I sorely wish that I had never felt compelled to speak out as vociferously as I have against a sitting president of the United States. It has given me no pleasure to do so. But, as long as Mr. Trump continues to trample the tenets of our democracy, lie to the American people, denigrate the office of the presidency, endanger our national security, and sully our reputation around the world, I will not relent in my criticism of him.

I have received many welcome words of encouragement from friends and strangers alike to continue with my public commentary. If, after thirty-three years of public service, I also must endure a steady stream of derisive and offensive comments, false allegations, and physical threats from those who are upset with me, so be it.

It is a path I have freely and willingly chosen.

I remain undaunted.

TRUTH MATTERS

I had just arrived at Penn Station in New York City after a pleasant three-hour ride aboard the Amtrak Acela train from Washington, D.C. As soon as I emerged from the underground station and heard the familiar hustle and bustle of the Big Apple, I decided to forego a taxi ride to my hotel on Fifty-second Street, about two dozen blocks away. It was a rather chilly November afternoon, and the appeal of a brisk walk through the busy New York City streets as the afternoon sun was beginning to set was simply too hard to resist. The opportunity to buy a large soft pretzel being warmed by a street vendor might also have entered my mind.

It had been nearly three years since I'd left my dream job as CIA director, and I enjoyed the opportunity to stroll alone, black roll-aboard in tow, taking in the sights, sounds, and scents of one of the world's truly great cities. The walk brought back memories of my days as a Fordham University student more than forty years before, when a commuter bus from New Jersey would deposit me in mid-Manhattan for my subway journey under congested city streets to Fordham's leafy campus in the Bronx. But those student days were long gone. I was now in New York City to talk with business leaders at a breakfast meeting the following morning about China's global rise before heading off to Lincoln Center to encourage Fordham University School of Law students to consider career options in national security. That I would be doing either as a former director of the CIA was simply unimaginable when I walked those New York City streets as a college student in the 1970s.

As I made my way up Seventh Avenue, I could sense that more than a few people recognized me as they passed, most likely from my appearances on cable news programs and photos in newspapers and magazines. No one could have accused me of being a recluse in my retirement. I had become used to encountering passersby who would offer smiles, sneers, and occasional comments, the tenor of which hinged on whether they were strongly supportive or deeply offended by my many tweets and public critiques of Donald Trump and his political acolytes. Silence was not an option for me as long as the unscrupulous Trump was ensconced in the White House, and my outspokenness had reverberations in my daily life.

At Thirty-ninth Street, my fellow pedestrians and I stopped at the corner and waited for the red light that had halted our progress to turn green. As a delivery truck heading west slowly passed in front of us, the driver, who looked to be in his late thirties, leaned out his window and pointed directly at me.

"Hey, Brennan! You suck, you fuckin' Communist!!!"

To punctuate his message to all within earshot, he banged several times on the outside of his truck door as he and his equally animated fellow front seat passenger pulled away.

The hurled insult certainly got the attention of those around me, some of whom nervously laughed while others shook their heads. Startled by the suddenness of the comment but unsurprised by the choice of invective, I directed my eyes forward, tightened my grip on the handle of the roll-aboard, and continued my trek to the hotel.

It was not the first time the epithet "Communist" was directed my way. I knew full well that I had only myself to blame for its initial airing in public discourse a few years before. My vote for Communist Party candidate Gus Hall in the 1976 presidential election, which I publicly acknowledged decades later to encourage Americans to pursue career options at the CIA even if they, too, did some crazy things in their youth, had spurred an ongoing narrative that I was a Communist. Trump's apologists and defenders in Congress, on TV networks, and in social media were quick to cite that vote as evidence that I was un-American to the core and undeserving of my previous government positions and the public's trust. It did not matter to them why I revealed that vote or that I cast it when I was a politically naïve twenty-one-year-old university student with a rebellious streak. Indeed, many of my critics decided to raise the stakes by sewing elaborate fictional coats onto the factual button of that single vote. For example, then Republican Congressman and current Florida Governor (and seeming presidential aspirant) Ron DeSantis said on Fox News that I was "a member of the Communist Party during the Cold War." On cue, social media trolls jumped at the chance to smear me and to discredit my public commentary about Trump's dishonesty, venality, and incompetence by quoting national political figures such as DeSantis in their often-crude tweets. I am not sure whether the truck driver even knew about my vote for Gus Hall, but he clearly was aware that I had been given the moniker of Communist.

After checking into my hotel and having dinner at a nearby restaurant that evening, I embarked on what had become my nightly routine of wandering through very busy (pre-COVID-19 pandemic) streets whenever I was in New York. With my hands warmly pocketed in my overcoat in the unseasonably cold weather, I casually strolled through the brightly lit walkways and plaza of Rockefeller Center, my thoughts consumed with the words of the truck driver. I think it was his visible anger that bothered me most, which prompted my own blood pressure to rise. I called Kathy to let off some steam. "I served my country for more than three decades, took some pretty tough assignments, and helped stop terrorist attacks against Americans worldwide," I said to her. "Now, I am scorned and cursed as a Communist on the streets of New York just because I cast a single throwaway vote in a presidential election more than forty years ago."

I eventually calmed down, thanks to Kathy's empathetic words and a stiff bourbon at the hotel bar before I went to bed. I didn't think much about the truck driver's words again until I was on the Acela returning to Washington the next afternoon. As the train made its way through New Jersey, I began to call the truck driver "Joe," as he looked like many of the people I had known growing up in Hudson County. I started to write Joe off as simply another crazy Trumper, but, after thinking about it for a while, I realized that giving him that label would be as inappropriate as the Communist handle he had publicly pinned on me on Seventh Avenue. I knew nothing about Joe, but I assumed that he was like many millions of other hardworking Americans who love their country dearly. Many have a visceral and knee-jerk dislike of anything that raises the specter of Communism—such as my vote for Gus Hall—and many more have taken great umbrage and become deeply angered at my strident public criticisms of Donald Trump. I will never know what motivated Joe to hold me in such disgust that day, but he clearly didn't want to pass up the unexpected opportunity to tell me off.

As my train wound its way through Pennsylvania, Delaware, and Maryland, I filled out Joe's profile in my mind's eye. I thought that he probably lived with his family in a modest house in a predominantly blue-collar neighborhood in one of Manhattan's many suburbs; my guess was Staten Island. I cast Joe as an avid reader of the *New York Post* as well as a regular watcher of nightly Fox News programs. His weekends likely were consumed with attending sporting events with his kids and gathering with extended family and friends at backyard barbecues when the weather allowed and in cramped, laughter-filled living rooms and basements when it didn't. As I imagined the life of Joe and his family, it increasingly resembled the family life of my New Jersey youth.

The more I thought about Joe, the more I wished I had been able to tell him that I was never a Communist and that I tried my best during my government career to serve my country and to keep my fellow citizens safe. I thought it would be a lot of fun to have a conversation with him about the foolish things we each did when we were twenty-one years old. I wanted to get to know Joe, to laugh with him, and to have the opportunity to share our life stories with each other. But I never got the chance.

The anger I initially felt toward Joe has long since dissipated, and I have often recalled that brief encounter and who, fairly or unfairly, I imagined Joe to be. I try my best now not to get angry at people who see me at my local grocery store or restaurant and tell me that I should be ashamed of myself, in jail, or subjected to far worse punishment for whatever transgression, illegal act, or mortal sin they believe I have committed. For all I know, they might have very legitimate and well-considered criticisms of the value, appropriateness, and effectiveness of the national security policies, programs, and actions that they associate with me. And that is fine. America's national security record is far from perfect, and I know I have made my share of mistakes, missteps, and misstatements during my life. I do not expect to be immune from criticism. On the other hand, some of my confronters might be like Joe, products of information environments that offer incomplete, skewed, and frequently fictionalized accounts of my life, professional career, and the intelligence world. Notwithstanding the questionable quality of the input they receive, I recognize that their American citizenship entitles them to express their views, even those I consider sorely misguided, as long as they do not trample upon my rights and the rights of others, break the law, or resort to violence.

My tolerance, however, does not extend to those who knowingly fill the minds of Americans with false and distorted information in order to shape attitudes, behaviors, and actions for their own selfish and corrupt ends. During my government career, I always believed foreign adversaries posed the most serious threat of undermining our democratic foundations by polluting America's information environment with propaganda. It was the seriousness of that foreign threat that prompted intelligence, law enforcement, and homeland security professionals to work furiously in the run-up to the 2016 presidential election to uncover Russian information operations that were designed to influence American voters. My colleagues and I knew full well that Vladimir Putin and his intelligence services regularly exploited the free and open information environments of the United States and other democratic societies to advance Russian interests, with the ever-expanding digital domain presenting far greater opportunities to do so than ever before. To this day, I remain unsure whether or not Russian information operations tipped the balance of the vote in several key states leading to Donald Trump's electoral college victory.

Now, though, I fear that the greatest and most insidious threat to our democracy comes from the many American politicians, TV and radio personalities, and social media influencers who intentionally and constantly spread disinformation on American airwaves. Driven by ideology, politics, money, or the craven quest for personal notoriety and power, the knowing purveyors of false and misleading information prey upon the fears, concerns, and misunderstandings of average Americans like Joe the truck driver. These domestic propagandists go far beyond the traditional embellishments, hyperbole, and exaggerations that have become an ingrained and accepted feature of our political landscape over the past 246 years. By vanquishing the truth, they have been far more effective than the combined efforts of foreign intelligence services in sowing anger, hate, and distrust among Americans, fraying our social fabric, eroding our democratic principles, and polarizing our body politic. Moreover, their lies make their underlying racist, xenophobic, and antidemocratic sentiments all too evident.

The danger of such incendiary disinformation came into stark relief on January 6, 2021, when Donald Trump's oft-repeated and unsupported claims of election fraud in the 2020 presidential election resulted in the violent assault and desecration of the United States Capitol. Thousands of individuals from all corners of America responded to the clarion calls of Trump and his coconspirators to march on Washington in support of what amounted to an attempted authoritarian coup against the United States government. Many of the individuals in that crowd undoubtedly were determined to overturn the election results regardless of known facts, but I am sure that a significant number of Capitol assaulters were duped into believing that Trump actually won the election as a result of the lies that were widely circulated by his active propagandists, including members of Congress.

On an even broader scale, domestic propagandists have been able to defy and dispute the overwhelming consensus of the world's scientific and medical communities on how to deal with the COVID-19 pandemic, causing an untold number of preventable deaths and serious illnesses among Americans. They unashamedly distribute false and misleading information on the virus's transmissibility, virulence, and prevalence; the efficacy of available vaccines; and widely discredited drug treatments and home remedies as vaccine alternatives. Many of our country's leading health professionals have endured baseless attacks on their integrity, medical acumen, and scientific competence; the ability of Dr. Tony Fauci, the dedicated and highly accomplished director of the National Institute of Allergy and Infectious Diseases, to withstand the withering onslaught against him has been nothing short of heroic. The harmful impact of many social media influencers on public attitudes and actions on how best to deal with COVID-19's evolving challenge has been significant. Their disruptive role raises the deeply disconcerting question of how our foreign adversaries will seek to exploit them as well as replicate their efforts when our country faces potentially more devastating health, national security, or environmental crises in the future.

Throughout the course of my life, I have looked to the individuals who are entrusted with the solemn responsibility and requisite authority to nurture, strengthen, and safeguard our country's democratic principles and system of government, especially during challenging times. Foremost within that group are the elected officials at the national, state, and local level whose oaths of office obligate them to fulfill their responsibilities with integrity, decency, and honesty, a combination that seems all too rare in today's political climate. While the Democratic Party certainly has engaged in some unsavory partisan politics over the years, the current state of the Republican Party is nothing short of surreal. It was once an important bastion of strong and rational conservative thinking on national security, government spending, and social issues. In recent years, however, it has increasingly become a political tool of dishonest demagogues, far right-wing ideologues, and shameless nativists who have no regard for the truth. I can only hope that Liz Cheney's and Adam Kinzinger's personal courage and political tenacity in exposing Donald Trump's corruption and decrying his corrosive impact on the Republican Party's moral compass bear fruit and followers.

As a career intelligence officer, I know that "truth" is often elusive. Despite the most exquisite and costly human source networks, technical collection systems, and analytic expertise that American taxpayers can afford, the capabilities, plans, and intentions of our foreign adversaries are cleverly masked in a complex web of deception and denial. Tragically, our domestic political, social, and cultural landscapes are also clouded over by the efforts of those with hidden agendas who purposely seek to conceal the truth from average Americans like truck driver Joe.

Over the last 42 years, I have passed through the iconic lobby of CIA's original headquarters building in Langley, Virginia, countless times. Most times, the saying etched at the top of the wall on the southeastern corner of the lobby would only peripherally catch my eye, but, like legions of former and current CIA employees and the citizens who visit, I always felt its influence. Its message is timeless. Its importance profound.

> "AND YE SHALL KNOW THE TRUTH
> AND THE TRUTH SHALL MAKE YOU FREE."
> —John 8:32

I hope that Joe the truck driver and his family are well and that they are enjoying all the happiness, opportunities, and rewards that our great country has to offer. As American citizens, they deserve no less.

ACKNOWLEDGMENTS

There are simply too many people who have had an influence on my life to acknowledge all of them by name, but I need to identify more than a few and will do so in rough chronological order. My parents, Owen and Dorothy; sister, Kathleen; brother, Tommy; and maternal grandmother, "Mamie," were the ideal nuclear family; they made growing up in the Brennan household a wonderful adventure of which I have only fond memories. Their love and support throughout my life have meant the world to me, and I have tried my best never to disappoint them. While my parents and Mamie have passed away, I look to Kathleen and Tommy, my many Brennan, McGuire, Murphy, and Diffley cousins—in America and Ireland—and my Pokluda in-laws for continued support and encouragement.

My classmates, lay teachers, coaches, Franciscan Sisters, and Christian Brothers from St. Joseph of the Palisades elementary and high schools all deserve a share of the credit or blame for what I have done with my life. I look back at my New Jersey school days and feel fortunate that I was raised in a community that reinforced the moral guidance I received at home. Joe Boucher, Gerry Boyle, Mike

Cahill, Frank Doty, Robert Keane, and Kevin Kiley are just a few of the many childhood friends who have made a deep and lasting impression on my life.

At Fordham University, Professor John Entelis and Professor John Banja instilled in me a lifelong interest in the Middle East and the pursuit of wisdom. If I had not been lucky enough to be their student at a very formative stage of my education, I am certain that my life would not have been as rewarding, fascinating, and challenging as it has been. Many years after my student days at Fordham, I was deeply honored when Fordham University president Father Joseph McShane asked me to give the commencement address to the 2012 graduating class. Father McShane has become a good friend and source of inspiration ever since. As a current distinguished fellow at Fordham University Law School's Center on National Security, I have been grateful for the support I have received from the center's director, Professor Karen Greenburg, and students Milana Bretgoltz, Raina Duggirala, and Nigel Frank, who assisted with the initial research for this memoir. Similarly, Professors Steven Slick and Paul Pope at the University of Texas at Austin have graciously allowed me to serve as a visiting fellow and to share my national security and intelligence experiences with their Longhorn students.

There are countless current and former CIA officers to whom I owe a deep debt of gratitude for the support, collegiality, mentorship, friendship, and guidance extended to me between 1980 and 2017. Although I am unable to provide many names due to cover or security considerations, I will cite just a few. From my first twenty-five years at the CIA, I am especially grateful to John Helgerson, Tom Elmore, Bob Ames, Bob Layton, Hal Wilcox, Jack Duggan, Karl Ruyle, John Lauder, Paul Metzger, Gordon Sund, Sten Schreiber, Paul Pillar, Martha Kessler, Tom Wolfe, David Carey, Carolyn Stettner, Jack Devine, Alan Fiers, Fred Turco, David Cohen (of subsequent NYPD fame), Doug MacEachin, John Gannon, Sandra Kruzman, Helene Boatner, Winston Wiley, Jami Miscik, Dottie

Hanson, John Edwards, Ken Levit, Michael Morell, Bill Harlow, Alan Wade, Cindy Bower, Mary Corrado, John Gordon, Jim Pavitt, Lloyd Salvetti, Marty Petersen, Buzzy Krongard, John McLaughlin, and George Tenet, as well as Special Assistants Mary, Theresa, Wendy, and Blondine. After I returned as director in 2013, there were thousands of colleagues over the course of the four years I served who provided me invaluable support and wise counsel and with whom I was honored to serve, most notably, my deputies, Michael Morell, Avril Haines, and David Cohen; Executive Directors Sue Bromley and Meroe Park; General Counsels Stephen Preston and Caroline Krass; Chiefs of Staff Rodney S., Deb B., Tanya P., and Brian C.; Director of Public Affairs Dean Boyd and Director of Congressional Relations Neal Higgins; and the dozens of CIA officers who served as my executive assistants and as the heads of the CIA's five directorates and ten mission centers, all of whom gave of themselves selflessly and unsparingly. My special assistants Lisa O. and Brenda C. have my deepest and everlasting appreciation for the patience, tolerance, and competence they exhibited while handling my schedule, peculiar work habits, and personality quirks.

I will be eternally grateful for having had the opportunity to work for eight years, including four years at the White House, for President Obama and Vice President Biden. I simply cannot say enough good things about their character, integrity, intellect, and love of country. My time working in the Obama administration was made all the more enriching by working closely with cabinet members and military leaders and alongside hardworking patriots like Jim Jones, Tom Donilon, Susan Rice, Rahm Emanuel, Bill Daley, Jack Lew, Denis McDonough, Mark Lippert, Tony Blinken, David Axelrod, Valerie Jarrett, Pete Rouse, Jim Messina, David Plouffe, Alyssa Mastromonaco, Pete Souza, Robert Gibbs, Jay Carney, Josh Earnest, Greg Craig, Bob Bauer, Kathy Ruemmler, Neil Eggleston, Mary DeRosa, Caroline Krass, Avril Haines, Lisa Monaco, David Kris, Nick Rasmussen, Liz Sherwood-Randall, Ben Rhodes, Mona

Sutphen, Nancy-Ann DeParle, Samantha Power, Gayle Smith, Heidi Avery, Nick Shapiro, Tommy Vietor, Terry Szuplat, Cindy Chang, Katie Johnson, Anita Decker Breckenridge, Ferial Govashiri, Dora, Jason, and so many more.

The women and men of the U.S. armed forces, intelligence community, diplomatic service, and law enforcement will always have my deepest respect and appreciation. I also want to acknowledge all the leaders of the intelligence community who came before me, as I tried to build on their many accomplishments during my career. Those who had the greatest influence on my career, either by example or by intercession, were Richard Helms, William Colby, George H. W. Bush, Bobby Ray Inman, William Webster, Bob Gates, Dick Kerr, John Deutch, George Tenet, John McLaughlin, Michael Hayden, Stephen Kappes, Leon Panetta, Michael Morell, and, of course, the inimitable Jim Clapper.

I never would have embarked on this literary journey were it not for the encouragement, wise counsel, and inspiration offered by my literary agent, David Black. David's persistence as well as his readiness to buy me top-shelf bourbon with a twist of orange ultimately convinced me to plunge headlong into writing my first book, but maybe not my last. I could not have found a better person with whom to work on this memoir.

Jamie Raab, the president and publisher of Celadon Books, a division of Macmillan, also has been an ideal colleague, guiding me patiently through the publication process and accommodating my many personal peccadilloes as well as the CIA's institutional requirements for prepublication classification review. Jamie's colleagues, including Adriana Coada, Elizabeth Catalano, Kelly Too, Christine Mykityshyn, and Cecily van Buren-Freedman, were a great publishing team, and I greatly appreciated their forbearance as well as their kindness while they worked with a very inexperienced and mistake-prone first-time author.

I want to extend my sincere appreciation to the CIA Prepublication

Classification Review Board, which carried out its responsibilities in a very professional and conscientious manner. I especially appreciated that the members of the board and the CIA officers who reviewed the draft manuscript did so at a time made more challenging by the COVID-19 pandemic and Washington's political environment.

I owe two individuals a special note of thanks. Bill Harlow has been a close friend and confidant for many years, and I will always be grateful for the tremendous support, guidance, and insight into the literary world that he provided throughout my writing journey. There is no doubt in my mind that I would have given up writing this memoir several times had it not been for Bill's much-appreciated, albeit frequently irreverent, words of encouragement. Like Bill, my former senior adviser at the White House and deputy chief of staff at the CIA, Nick Shapiro, has been a "Brennan whisperer" for many years. Nick's guidance on media and public-relations matters has always been spot-on, and his friendship has helped sustain me during difficult times both during and after my government service.

Finally, and despite the richness and beauty of the English language, there are no words that capture the depth of my love and appreciation for my wife, Kathy; children, Kyle, Kelly, and Jaclyn; and grandsons, Kaiden and John. My life has meaning because of them, and I will always be thankful that they made my time on this earth so wonderful, so worthwhile, and so rewarding.

GLOSSARY

AL-QA'IDA—Arabic for "the base"; the umbrella name for Usama Bin Ladin's Sunni Islamist group dedicated to driving Westerners out of the Gulf region and establishing a Muslim caliphate

AQAP—al-Qa'ida in the Arabian Peninsula; a branch of al-Qa'ida that is primarily active in Yemen and Saudi Arabia

AUC—American University in Cairo

CIA—Central Intelligence Agency

CIC—the CIA's Counterintelligence Center

COVERT ACTION—an activity or activities of the United States government to influence political, economic, or military conditions abroad, where it is intended that the role of the United States will not be apparent or acknowledged publicly

CTs—CIA career trainees

CTC—Counterterrorism Center; a component of the CIA made up of operators, analysts, and technical experts, responsible for carrying out the CIA's counterterrorism mission, including operations against terrorists worldwide

DC—deputies committee; NSC committee chaired by the deputy national security adviser and generally made up of the second-ranking person from the Departments of State and Defense, the Joint Chiefs of Staff, the Office of the Director of National Intelligence, the CIA, and other national security agencies as warranted

DCI—director of central intelligence; the head of the U.S. intelligence community and the CIA. Position established in 1947 and disestablished in 2005 with the creation of the position of the director of national intelligence.

DDCI—deputy director of central intelligence, a position disestablished in 2005

DDI—Directorate of Digital Innovation in the CIA, the Agency's fifth directorate established in 2015

DDO—deputy director (of Central Intelligence) for operations; head of the intelligence-collection arm of the CIA

DEXDIR—deputy executive director of the Central Intelligence Agency (renamed deputy chief operating officer in 2017)

DHS—Department of Homeland Security

DIA—Defense Intelligence Agency; the Department of Defense's intelligence organization, providing foreign military intelligence to the war fighter

EITs—enhanced interrogation techniques; a set of interrogation techniques approved by the Department of Justice for CIA use in questioning suspected high-value terrorist detainees. The techniques ranged from facial slaps to waterboarding.

EXDIR—executive director of central intelligence; third-ranking official in the CIA (renamed chief operating officer in 2017)

FBI—Federal Bureau of Investigation

FINDING—a legal document, signed by the president, granting specific authorities to the CIA and the intelligence community to conduct covert actions

FISA—Foreign Intelligence Surveillance Act; a 1978 law laying out specific authorities and procedures for the collection of physical and electronic foreign intelligence

FIVE EYES—an informal association of five English-speaking countries—the United States, the United Kingdom, Canada, Australia, and New Zealand—that cooperate closely on intelligence sharing and do not spy on one another

FSB—Federal Security Service of the Russian Federation; the domestic successor to the KGB in Russia

FSNs—foreign service nationals; non-Americans working for the U.S. government overseas

GANG OF EIGHT—the majority and minority leaders in the Senate, the Speaker of the House and minority leader in the House, and the Democratic and Republican leadership of the Senate and House intelligence committees

GID—Saudi Arabia's General Intelligence Directorate; the CIA's principal organizational counterpart, renamed the **GIP**—the General Intelligence Presidency

HPSCI—House Permanent Select Committee on Intelligence

ICA—intelligence community assessment; a document containing the analytic judgments of several intelligence community agencies that is produced under the auspices of the director of national intelligence

IPC—Interagency Policy Committee; a group of assistant secretaries and their equivalents from departments and agencies that meet under the auspices of the National Security Council to discuss and make recommendations on national security policy matters

INSA—Intelligence and National Security Alliance; a not-for-profit organization dedicated to strengthening the relationship between the government and private sector in the national security realm

IRTPA—Intelligence Reform and Terrorism Prevention Act of 2004; the law that created the position of the director of national intelligence (DNI), the National Counterterrorism Center (NCTC), and the Privacy and Civil Liberties Oversight Board

ISIS—Islamic State of Iraq and Syria, formed in 2013 by the combination of al-Qa'ida in Iraq and al-Qa'ida in Syria (al-Nusrah) to establish a caliphate in the region

JCPOA—Joint Comprehensive Plan of Action; an agreement completed in 2015 between Iran and the five permanent members of the United Nations Security Council, plus Germany and the European Union, providing a "road map" for Iran to work with the International Atomic Energy Agency (IAEA) to constrain Iran's nuclear program

JSOC—Joint Special Operations Command; a U.S. military organization charged with planning special-operations missions

KGB—Soviet "Committee for State Security"; the Soviet Union's premier intelligence service and CIA's main rival during the Cold War

MABAHITH—Saudi Arabia's internal security service

MON—memorandum of notification; a written update, approved by the president, to a previously authorized covert-action finding

MOSSAD—Israeli Institute for Intelligence and Special Operations, counterpart to the CIA in Israel

NCTC—National Counterterrorism Center; established in 2004 as the successor organization to the Terrorist Threat Integration Center to serve as the primary organization in the U.S. government for integrating and analyzing all intelligence pertaining to terrorism and counterterrorism and to conduct strategic operational planning

NE DIVISION—Near East Division of the CIA's Directorate of Operations

NESA—Office of Near Eastern and South Asian Analysis, a CIA component in the 1980s and '90s

NGA—National Geospatial-Intelligence Agency; provides exploitation and analysis of imagery and geospatial information to describe, assess, and visually depict physical features and geographically referenced activities on earth. Formerly known as the National Imagery and Mapping Agency.

NIC—National Intelligence Council; the intelligence community's component responsible for producing national intelligence estimates and other strategic assessments

NIE—national intelligence estimate. Produced by the NIC, the NIE is the intelligence community's most authoritative written judgment concerning national security issues. It contains the coordinated judgments of the intelligence community regarding the likely course of future events.

NSA—National Security Agency; U.S. cryptological organization that coordinates, directs, and performs highly specialized activities to protect U.S. government information systems and produce foreign signals intelligence information

NSC—National Security Council; the president's principal forum for considering national security and foreign policy matters with his senior national security advisers and cabinet officials. The NSC also serves as the president's principal arm for coordinating these policies among various government agencies.

PANETTA REVIEW—an uncompleted internal CIA document intended to identify important issues contained in the Agency's files turned over to Senate staffers as they related to the Rendition, Detention, and Interrogation (RDI) program

PC—principals committee; NSC committee chaired by the national security adviser and consisting of the vice president, secretaries of state and defense, chairman of the Joint Chiefs of Staff, director of national intelligence, director of the CIA, and heads of other departments and agencies as warranted

PDB—President's Daily Brief; a compilation of intelligence presented to the president and designated recipients six days a week

PREDATOR—a remotely piloted vehicle (RPV), also known as an unmanned aerial vehicle (UAV), used for surveillance and, post-9/11, capable of delivering Hellfire missiles on targets. A follow-up and more capable version of the Predator is the **REAPER.**

PTTR—President's Terrorist Threat Report; a daily document produced by TTIC and NCTC between 2003 and 2005 to provide the president and designated recipients information and analysis on key terrorist threats and what was being done to thwart them

RDI—Rendition, Detention, and Interrogation program; a covert-action program authorized by President George W. Bush after 9/11 giving the CIA authority to capture, transfer, detain, and interrogate suspected significant terrorists

RDINET—the CIA computer system containing documents about the RDI program that was made available for the use of SSCI staff

SSCI—Senate Select Committee on Intelligence

STEELE DOSSIER—a report created by former British intelligence operative Christopher Steele containing allegations of misconduct, conspiracy, and cooperation between the Trump presidential campaign and Russia

TTIC—Terrorist Threat Information Center, established by presidential directive on May 1, 2003. TTIC was renamed NCTC in 2004.

WMD—weapons of mass destruction

PRINCIPAL CHARACTERS

CIA

Robert Ames—legendary Near East Division operations officer; Director of Office of Near Eastern and South Asian Analysis; killed in the 1983 bombing of U.S. embassy in Beirut, Lebanon

Frank Archibald—Deputy Director for Operations (2013–2015)

William Casey—Director of Central Intelligence[1] (1981–1987)

David S. Cohen—Deputy Director (2015–2017)

John Deutch—Director of Central Intelligence (1995–1996)

Robert Gates—Director of Central Intelligence (1991–1993); Secretary of Defense (2006–2011)

Porter Goss—Director of Central Intelligence (2004–2005); CIA Director (2005–2006)

Avril Haines—Deputy Director (2013–2015); Deputy National Security Adviser (2015–2017)

---

1. All directors and deputy directors of central intelligence served simultaneously as directors and deputy directors respectively of the CIA.

Gina Haspel—Deputy Director (2017–2018); CIA Director (2018–present)

General Michael Hayden—Director of National Security Agency (1999–2005); Principal Deputy Director of National Intelligence (2005–2006); CIA Director (2006–2009)

A. B. "Buzzy" Krongard—Executive Director (2001–2004)

John McLaughlin—Deputy Director of Central Intelligence (2000–2004)

Jami Miscik—Deputy Director for Intelligence (2002–2005)

Michael Morell—Deputy Director and two-time Acting CIA Director (2010–2013)

Leon Panetta—CIA Director (2009–2011); Secretary of Defense (2011–2013)

General David Petraeus—CIA Director (2011–2012)

Mike Pompeo—CIA Director (2017–2018); Secretary of State (2018–present)

John Rizzo—Acting General Counsel on multiple occasions

Nick Shapiro—My deputy chief of staff at the CIA and previously my senior adviser at the White House

George Tenet—Deputy Director of Central Intelligence (1995–1997); Director of Central Intelligence (1997–2004)

Fred Turco—Chief of Counterterrorism Center in the early 1990s

Greg Vogle—Deputy Director for Operations (2015–2016)

INTELLIGENCE COMMUNITY

Admiral Dennis Blair, USN, Ret.—Director of National Intelligence (2009–2010)

Lt. Gen. James Clapper, USAF, Ret.—Director of National Intelligence (2010–2017)

Sue Gordon—Principal Deputy Director of National Intelligence (2017–2019)

Vice Admiral Mike McConnell, USN, Ret.—Director of National Intelligence (2007–2009)

Admiral Mike Rogers—Director of the National Security Agency (2014–2018)

WHITE HOUSE

George H. W. Bush—Director of Central Intelligence (1976–1977); President of the United States (1989–1993)

George W. Bush—President of the United States (2001–2009)

Richard B. Cheney—Vice President of the United States (2001–2009)

Bill Clinton—President of the United States (1993–2001)

Bill Daley—White House Chief of Staff (2011–2012)

Tom Donilon—Deputy National Security Adviser (2009–2010); National Security Adviser (2010–2013)

Rahm Emanuel—White House Chief of Staff (2009–2010)

Lt. Gen. Mike Flynn, USA, Ret.—Director of the Defense Intelligence Agency (2012–2014); National Security Adviser (Jan.–Feb. 2017)

Al Gore—Vice President of the United States (1993–2001)

General Jim Jones, USMC, Ret.—National Security Adviser (2009–2010)

Anthony Lake—National Security Adviser (1993–1997), Director of Central Intelligence nominee (1997)

Denis McDonough—Deputy National Security Adviser (2010–2013); White House Chief of Staff (2013–2017)

Lisa Monaco—Assistant to the President for Homeland Security and Counterterrorism (2013–2017)

General Colin Powell, USA, Ret.—National Security Adviser (1987–1989); Chairman of the Joint Chiefs of Staff (1989–1993); Secretary of State (2001–2005)

Condoleezza Rice—National Security Adviser (2001–2005); Secretary of State (2005–2009)

Susan Rice—U.S. Ambassador to the United Nations (2009–2013); National Security Adviser (2013–2017)

Donald J. Trump—President of the United States (2017–2021)

Ken Wainstein—Homeland Security Adviser (2008–2009)

STATE DEPARTMENT

Madeleine Albright—Secretary of State (1997–2001)

FBI

James Comey—FBI Director (2013–2017)

Louis Freeh—FBI Director (1993–2001)

Andrew McCabe—Deputy FBI Director (2016–2018)

Robert Mueller—FBI Director (2001–2013); Special Counsel for the U.S. Department of Justice (2017–2019)

John Pistole—Deputy FBI Director (2004–2010)

DEPARTMENT OF DEFENSE

General James "Hoss" Cartwright—Vice Chairman of the Joint Chiefs of Staff (2007–2011)

General John F. Kelly—Senior Military Assistant to the Secretary of Defense (2010–2012); Secretary of Homeland Security (2017); White House Chief of Staff (2017–2019)

Admiral Bill McRaven, USN, Ret.—Commander, Joint Special Operations Command (2008–2011); Commander, U.S. Special Operations Command (2011–2014)

Donald Rumsfeld—Secretary of Defense (2001–2006)

Admiral James "Sandy" Winnefeld—Vice Chairman of the Joint Chiefs of Staff (2011–2015)

UNITED STATES CONGRESS

Senator Saxby Chambliss—U.S. Republican Senator from Georgia (2003–2015) who served as Chairman and Vice Chairman of SSCI and subsequently as a member of the CIA external advisory board

Senator Dianne Feinstein—U.S. Democratic Senator from California (1992–) who served as Chairman and Vice Chairman of SSCI

Representative Porter Goss—U.S. Republican Congressman from Florida (1989–2004) who served as Chairman of the House Permanent Select Committee on Intelligence

Senator Lindsey Graham—U.S. Senator from South Carolina (2003–)

Daniel J. Jones—Democratic staff member, Senate Select Committee on Intelligence (2007–2016)

Senator John S. McCain III—U.S. Republican Senator from Arizona (1987–2018) who was an ex officio member of SSCI

Senator Arlen Specter—U.S. Republican Senator from Pennsylvania (1981–2011) who served as Chairman of SSCI

AL-QA'IDA

Usama Bin Ladin—Founder of al-Qa'ida; killed in 2011

Ayman al-Zawahiri—Bin Ladin's deputy who assumed leadership of al-Qa'ida in 2011

Abu Zubaydah—Member of al-Qa'ida captured in Pakistan in 2002, waterboarded by the CIA, and currently detained in Guantánamo Bay, Cuba

Umar Farouk Abdulmutallab—Nigerian national who attempted to detonate a bomb hidden in his underwear aboard a flight arriving at Detroit International Airport in 2009

Anwar al-Awlaki—Yemeni-American member of AQAP; killed in Yemen by a U.S. drone strike in September 2011

MIDDLE EAST

Bashar al-Asad—President of Syria (2000–)

Abdrabbuh Mansur Hadi—Vice President of Yemen (1994–2012); President of Yemen (2012–)

Muhammad Morsi—President of Egypt (2012–2013)

Hosni Mubarak—Vice President of Egypt (1975–1981); President of Egypt (1981–2011)

Ali Abdullah Saleh—President of Yemen (1990–2012)

Abdel Fattah al-Sisi—President of Egypt (2014–)

SAUDI ARABIA

Abdullah Bin Abd al-Aziz—Crown Prince (1982–2005); King (2005–2015)

Fahd Bin Abd al-Aziz—Crown Prince (1975–1982); King (1982–2005)

Muhammad Bin Nayif (MBN)—Minister of Interior (2012–2017); Crown Prince (2015–2017)

Muhammad Bin Salman (MBS)—Minister of Defense (2015–); Crown Prince (2017–)

Salman Bin Abd al-Aziz—Crown Prince (2005–2015); King (2015–)

Turki al-Faisal—Director of General Intelligence (1979–2001); Ambassador to the United States (2005–2007)

RUSSIA

Alexander Bortnikov—Head of FSB (2008–)

Mikhail Fradkov—Prime Minister (2004–2007); Head of SVR (2007–2016)

Sergei Ivanov—Chief of Staff to Russian President Putin (2011–2016)

Dmitry Medvedev—President (2008–2012); Prime Minister (2012–2020)

Vladimir Putin—President of Russia (1999–2008; 2012–)

CUBA

Alejandro Castro—Colonel in Interior Ministry and Coordinator of Intelligence and Counterintelligence Services; son of former president Raúl Castro and nephew of former president Fidel Castro

INDEX

ABOUT THE AUTHOR

© Washington Speakers Bureau

John O. Brennan served as director of the Central Intelligence Agency from March 2013 until January 2017. As director, he was responsible for intelligence collection, analysis, covert action, counterintelligence, and liaison relationships with foreign intelligence services. From January 2009 to March 2013, Mr. Brennan was assistant to the president for homeland security and counterterrorism, shaping the U.S. government's counterterrorism strategy and coordinating Obama administration policies on homeland security, counterterrorism, cyberattacks, natural disasters, and pandemics.

Mr. Brennan began his government service at the CIA, where he worked from 1980 to 2005 and specialized in Middle Eastern affairs and counterterrorism. He served as the CIA's intelligence briefer to President Clinton, chief of staff to then-director of central intelligence George Tenet, and deputy executive director. In 2003, he led a multiagency effort to establish what would become the National Counterterrorism Center, serving as the Center's first director in 2004. He retired from the CIA in 2005 and worked in the private sector for three years.

Mr. Brennan graduated from Fordham University in 1977 with a bachelor's degree in political science. He studied at the American University in Cairo from 1975 to 1976. He attended the University of Texas at Austin, earning a master's degree in government with a concentration in Middle Eastern studies in 1980.

Mr. Brennan currently is a distinguished fellow at the Center on National Security at Fordham Law, a distinguished scholar at the University of Texas at Austin, a senior intelligence and national security analyst for NBC and MSNBC, and an adviser to a variety of private sector companies.

CELADON
BOOKS

Founded in 2017, Celadon Books, a division of
Macmillan Publishers, publishes a highly curated list
of twenty to twenty-five new titles a year. The list of
both fiction and nonfiction is eclectic and focuses
on publishing commercial and literary books and
discovering and nurturing talent.